TRAVELLERS SURVIVAL KIT

Oman &
the Arabian Gulf

Dan Boothby

Illustrations by Mick Siddens

Published by Vacation Work, 9 Park End Street, Oxford
www.vacationwork.co.uk

TRAVELLERS SURVIVAL KIT: OMAN AND THE ARABIAN GULF

by Dan Boothby

Editor: Ian Collier

First edition 2001

Copyright © Vacation Work 2001

ISBN 1-85458-254-2

Maps by Andrea Pullen

Cover photograph provided by The Government of Dubai, Department
of Tourism and Commerce Marketing

Cover Design by
Miller Craig & Cocking Design Partnership

Typeset by WorldView Publishing Services (01865-201562)

Printed by William Clowes Ltd., Beccles Suffolk, England

Contents

THE ARABIAN PENINSULA AND ITS PEOPLES

PRACTICAL INFORMATION

OMAN

Oman: Practical Information

Exploring Oman

Qatar: Practical Information

Exploring Qatar

UNITED ARAB EMIRATES

United Arab Emirates: Practical Information

Exploring the Emirates

MAPS

Preface

During the 1970s and 1980s the idea of the Arabian Gulf conjured up images of Bedouins galloping about on camels through vast tracts of desert and very rich 'oil sheikhs' – sporting the obligatory goatee beard and mirror sunglasses – thundering along six-lane desert highways in Cadillacs packed with kids and veiled wives. In the 1990s – after the Gulf War – these images had changed to oil fields shrouded in wreaths of black smoke, and of pinpoint accuracy bombing of Iraqi targets shown on the television. Today, at the beginning of the 21st century, the images are changing again – a broader picture is coming into focus of cosmopolitan countries with landscapes and societies as individual as their identities.

The four countries outlined in this book – Oman, the United Arab Emirates, Bahrain and Qatar – are not full of Islamic fundamentalists and terrorists, but are some of the most stable, relaxed and safe countries in the Middle East. Dubai has recently been busily promoting itself to the world as a prime winter-sun holiday destination with its pristine beaches, cut-price gold, superlative golf courses and tax-free shopping. Bahrain has long been a freethinking and friendly destination to those in the know, and Qatar is coming of age and getting ready to host the Asian Games in 2006. Oman, for long the hermit of the region, has cautiously opened its doors to the outside world and offers the adventurous visitor thousands of miles of remote mountain, desert and coastline to explore. Omanis happily hold on to the traditions and values of a time before oil brought untold wealth to the region and Muscat is one of the prettiest destinations in the whole of the Arab World. If you are a desert freak then go to the Gulf – it is home to the one of the largest sand deserts in the world, over 500,000 square miles of sand and *sabkha*, and the infamous *Rub' al-Khali*, the Empty Quarter. If you can, combine a trip to the United Arab Emirates with Oman. Seeing one and not the other will give you a much different impression of the region. If you have to choose one place to visit, make it Oman.

Travellers Survival Kit: Oman and the Arabian Gulf sets out to help the visitor to make sense of an often mysterious region and of those who inhabit it. This book should at the very least help you to find a place to spend the night while in the Gulf and provide an informative read as well.

Dan Boothby
July 2001

Acknowledgements

A number of people have assisted me during the researching and the writing of this book. In particular I would like to thank Paul Middleton and Samantha Harley-Fleming in Dubai, and John Oberman in Bahrain for their truly Arabian hospitality. In Oman I received help and guidance from M.M.K. Mohammed and Peter Ochs II of Mark Tours and Jennifer Butler. I would also like to thank Sylvia Scarlett, Peter Ingram, José Maria Sanchez de Muniain, Stephanie Reed, Jules Copson, Richard Lett, Julia King, Helen Wood, Olivia Wilkes, Mr and Mrs David Roberts & Daisy Mia, Mr and Mrs Russell Harris, Mr and Mrs Derek Khan-Walker and Miriam O'Connor. At the University of Durham I should like to acknowledge the kindness and assistance of Rachel Hardy and the scholars of the Bernard Gilpin Society, the staff of the Centre for Middle Eastern and Islamic Studies, Avril Shields of the Middle Eastern Documentation Unit, and St Cuthbert's Society. I'd also like to acknowledge the support of the staff at the British Academy of Film and Television Arts in London; and Charles James of Vacation Work Publications.

THE ARABIAN PENINSULA AND ITS PEOPLE

THE PEOPLE

Before the spread of Islam, the term Arab referred to any of the largely nomadic Semitic inhabitants of the Arabian Peninsula. Today it refers to any of the Arabic-speaking peoples of the 'Arab World'. Early Arabs were pastoralists (the Bedouin) who herded goats, sheep and camels. There were also settled Arabs who practised largely date and cereal agriculture in the fertile oases of the desert. These settlements were also used as trading centres for the caravans transporting spices, ivory and slaves along the trade routes of the region. With the coming of Islam in the 7th century the people of the oases and the Bedouin were unified, speaking the same language and following the same religion. Not all Arabs however are Muslim. About 5 per cent of the total population of Arabs are Christians. The Bedouin make up about 5 per cent of the modern Arab population though many have given up the traditional nomadic lifestyle to take up stockbreeding or to work on the fringes of the tourist industry.

The Bedouin traditionally migrate into the interior of the desert during the rainy winter season to find grazing for their livestock, returning to the cultivated land around the oases during the long dry summers. The continual feuding that was such a feature of Bedouin life had to stop during the years that followed World War I when national boundaries were drawn up and countries with guarded frontiers were created. Before this time the nomadic Bedouin had ranged across vast tracts of land; individual tribes controlling different areas and all either at war or in a state of truce with one another. Crossing into a tribal area was often fraught with danger unless you were at peace with the tribe whose area you were passing through, or were accompanied by a member of a tribe that was. As free, arms bearing people the Bedouin always dominated the other classes of Arab society, and had a great dislike of manual labour and the occupations of settled Arabs. The tribal nature of these people continues to this day, with the head of a family, and of the larger tribal groupings known as sheikh, meaning 'the patriarch'.

RELIGION

Because the Gulf was until relatively recently a region without the interference of other creeds, Islam is strongly adhered to by the nationals, perhaps more so than in other areas of the Muslim world such as Turkey or Syria where non-Muslims are allowed to visit mosques (something that they are not allowed to do in the Gulf) and where there are ancient places of worship for Christians and Jews. Although the old

Hollywood image of a goateed sheikh wielding a curved sabre high above his head and snarling, 'Die! Infidel dog!' as he bore down on some unfortunate western soldier never in truth existed, Christians were for a long time held with deep suspicion, especially in Oman. However, this is also hardly surprising considering the meddling ways of the Europeans and their past exploitation of the Arabs' natural resources and involvement in the politics of the Gulf.

In truth Islam has always been very tolerant of all other religions including Judaism. Before the creation of Israel and the mass exodus of Jews from all corners of the Globe there were many Jews living and working in the Middle East.

Islam

One fifth of the world's population is Muslim; over 1 billion people with only about 20 per cent of this number living in the Middle East. Islam is the fastest growing religion in the world and unfortunately, in the minds of many in the West it seems to have taken the place of Communism as the demon lurking to overthrow the land of the free. There is a perception that the Middle East has taken over from Russia as the dark and terrible place – full of religious fanatics and mad mobs baying for blood.

The Arabian Peninsula is the birthplace of Islam and the countries of the Gulf were the first to take up the new religion and carry the message further afield, creating an incredible empire in the process. Islam is the youngest of the three Semitic religions and has many things in common with the teachings of Christianity and Judaism but it is held by Muslims to be the true and perfect faith. Although politics and religion – and the law – have always been to a large extent hand in glove in the Middle East, for the majority of Muslims their faith is a way of life which affects everything that happens to them day by day. You will often hear exclamations of *Insh'Allah* (If God wills it) and *al-Hamdulillah* (Thanks be to God) during your stay in the Gulf. Arabs are great believers in the power of God and that their fate lies in the hands of that god. The riches that oil has brought them was no accident, they were given the oil by God.

Muhammed the Prophet and the Quran

Muhammed is believed to have been born in 570AD in Mecca into the merchant Quraysh tribe. When he was about 40 years old he began to receive messages – which are believed by Muslims to be revelations sent to him by God through the Angel Gabriel. He received the first message while sleeping alone on a mountain above Mecca and continued to receive revelations between 610 and 632AD in Mecca and Medina. These revelations were collected together by Muhammed's followers (Muhammed could not read or write) in a book, the Quran, the holy book of Muslims. The Quran is God's word as revealed to Muhammed by the Angel Gabriel and because the language of the Quran and therefore the language of God is Arabic, both the book and the language are considered sacred.

The Quran is divided into 114 chapters called *suras* which are in turn divided into verses (*ayats*). The first sura, the al-Fatiha, is commonly intoned by Muslims going about their daily business and you are likely to hear it often in the streets. The book, together with the actions of the Prophet during his lifetime, contains the basis for the way of life that all Muslims should lead.

The Five Pillars

The five pillars of Islam upon which the holy Quran rests are all public acts of religious duty that unite Muslims the world over:

The shahadah. This is the declaration of faith which states that 'There is no god but God and Muhammed is the messenger of God.' You will hear this incantation at the beginning of every call to prayer.

Salah, or prayer. Prayers are carried out five times a day: at dawn, at noon, mid-afternoon, sunset and nightfall. Ritual ablutions are performed before prayer, and the ritual movements and prayers are always carried out facing in the direction of the city of Mecca in Saudi Arabia. Children will begin to carry out the ritual of prayers from seven years old accompanying their parents. Muslims will pray in a mosque should there be one conveniently close but otherwise they can pray anywhere. During Ramadan when everyone feels much more devout than usual and the mosques are often full, you will see lines of worshippers on carpets laid outside. The sight of someone prostrating themselves out in the middle of the desert, or alone among the mountains is one of the most affecting sights you will see in your life. Friday is the most important day for a Muslim when sermons are held in mosques. For the foreigner these sermons can sound unnervingly like fire and brimstone from the pulpit; Arabs are more passionate about such things than say the Church of England.

Zakah, the giving of alms or charity. Traditionally a voluntary act of charity; giving to the needy or for the very rich the building of a mosque. Zakah has in many places developed into a tax levied by government.

Sawm, or fasting. Observed during Ramadan, the ninth month of the Islamic calendar, Muslims refrain from eating, drinking, smoking or sexual congress from dawn until sunset. Ramadan celebrates the month in which the Quran was first revealed to Muhammed and is a time for spiritual contemplation and purification of the self. Breakfast (*suhur*) has to be eaten before sunrise. Those Muslims who are travelling, or are ill and pregnant women are exempt from fasting during Ramadan as long as they observe the fast at some other time during the year. During Ramadan, sunrise and sunset are announced by cannon fire and the night becomes a time of intense socialising and the working day is shorter; people tend to sleep more during the day and stay awake well into the early hours of the morning. Because everything slows down during Ramadan it is best to do business in the region outside of this time. The end of Ramadan is marked by the *Eid al-Fitr*, a three-day holiday much like Christmas when everyone who can afford it buys new clothes and presents and eats a lot of food.

The Hajj, or pilgrimage to Mecca. Every Muslim who has the means to do so, is expected to make the pilgrimage to Mecca at least once in a lifetime. Entry to Mecca and Medina, the two holiest cities in the Islamic world, is forbidden to non-Muslims but every year during the 12th month of the Islamic calendar millions of Muslims converge at Mecca. Once in Mecca there follow ten days of ritual before the return home. The end of the Hajj season is marked by the other big feast of the year, the *Eid al-Adha*. This is the time when those families that can afford it sacrifice a sheep.

The Divisions of Islam in the Countries of the Arabian Gulf

Sunni. The majority of Muslims in the world (around 80 per cent) are Sunni orthodox Muslims. The word Sunni comes from the word *Sunna* – which refers to the sayings and practices of the Prophet. Sunni Muslims follow the orthodox schools of Islamic law (the Sharia).

Shia. After the death of Muhammed there was a split between those who accepted the leadership of Abu Bakr (the successor elected to lead Islam) and those who felt that the Prophet's son-in-law Ali should have become Caliph. Those that supported Ali, the shia' Ali or Party of Ali, became known as the Shias. The majority of Muslims in Iran are Shia, and there are also a number of them in Bahrain. Shia mosques are incredibly beautiful and ornate, typified by blue tile mosaic work.

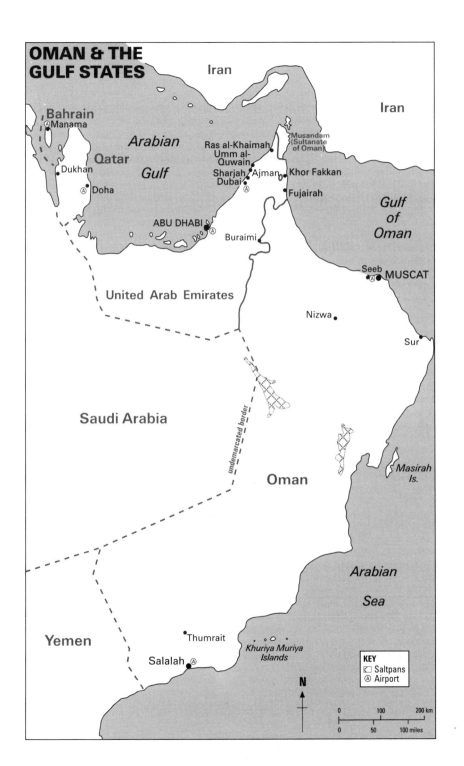

Ibadi. The Ibadis came about through the teachings of Abdallah ibn Ibad who formed a moderate branch of the more belligerent and anarchic Khawarij – a splinter group of the Shias. The Khawarij left the Shias after Ali agreed to arbitration over the question of who should become spiritual leader after the death of the Prophet. The Khawarij believed that the question of succession was in the hands of God alone and could not be brought about through talk or discussion. The Ibadis believe that a suitable spiritual leader (Imam) can be chosen on merit and that the position should not be a hereditary one. They also believe in living in harmony with other Muslims and have at various times gone into hiding when threatened. The majority of Omanis are of the Ibadi sect.

Wahhabi. Wahhabism is a movement of religious reform in Islam that was created in the 17th century by Muhammed ibn Adb al-Wahhab, based on the teachings of the theologians ibn Hanbal and ibn Taymiyah. Wahhabis aim at returning to the original teachings of Islam and at achieving the simplicity and austerity in public and private life as lived by the Prophet and the first Rightly-Guided Caliphs. In its most pure form Wahhabism prohibits imbibing alcohol, smoking, dancing, music and condemns all luxury in habitation, dress and food. The Saudi Arabians are the most famous followers of this doctrine and the majority of Qataris are also Wahhabis, though they are not as strict followers of the teachings as the Saudis.

The Sharia Law

The Sharia is the sacred law of Islam and applies to all aspects of daily life. Muslims view their religion as an integral part of their life – not just something to be thought about once a week when they go to Friday prayers in the local mosque. Through the revelations that the Prophet Muhammed received, the way of life for a Muslim to lead was laid down in the Quran. Aspects that weren't covered in the book were then derived from the Sunna (practices of the Prophet), from the consensus among Islamic scholars and through analogy. In this way a religious law was created which can be applied to everything from marriage, divorce and penal law to Islamic thinking on drugs, alcohol and debt. These days the Sharia is tempered with modern legal thinking.

Family Names

Islamic family names have a formal structure and show the paternal genealogy of a person. Forenames are often taken from the Quran which is why names such as Muhammed, Fatimah, Ahmed and Ali are so widespread in the Muslim World. Other common names are Aziz (meaning dear), Hassan (meaning good/kind) and Jameelah (meaning beautiful). Forenames are then followed by the name of the father, the grandfather and the name of the family or tribe.

The Arabic word *bint* means daughter or girl, and *ibn* and *bin* mean son. Parents are also known by the name of their first-born son so that a mother of four children (the eldest of them being called Ali) may very well be known locally as Umm Ali (the mother of Ali) and the father Abu Ali (father of Ali). The honorary term Sheikh (literally old man) refers to a tribal leader or his sons, while the feminine Sheikha refers to a sheikh's wife or daughters. As an example, Sheikh Ali bin Muhammed al-Fayed would tell us that Ali is the (very important) son of Muhammed of the al-Fayed family or tribe. When a woman marries she keeps her father's name rather than taking that of her husband.

WOMEN IN ISLAM

The traditional view of the Muslim woman in the West is of a down-trodden beast of burden, born to get married young (perhaps becoming one of a number of wives to a burly husband), to stay in the home and cook and look after the kids and, when she is allowed out of the house, to walk five paces behind the husband. This is, of course, mostly rubbish. Women in the Gulf – with the exception of Saudi Arabia – have the run of the place. They attend the universities in vast numbers and are a large force in the job market. But unlike in the West where the institution is falling apart, the family unit is considered the most important part of life. Therefore the traditional roles in a family remain – the husband brings in the money and the wife looks after him and the children, who will when grown-up look after the parents into old age and death. It is true that Muslim women do have less freedom than men and the strong traditions of Islam and tribal society continue to enforce this state of affairs but with exposure to the influences of the globe boundaries are changing.

Western Women in Arab Society

Islamic countries are conservative countries. The social mores are stricter and the family is far more central to daily life than it has been in the West for decades. In the countries of the Arabian Gulf these strictures are still far more ingrained than they are in the slightly more liberal countries of the northern Middle East where Christianity has played a larger part in the history of these societies.

Up until the 1950s the Gulf was still a place of few settlements and large expanses of desert populated by nomadic tribes. The pace of change outwardly has been incredibly swift and dramatic. For the native populations this change has been disorientating but traditions still remain strong.

Arab men have had a bad press with regards to their idea of western women. Tales are told by women returning to Europe of the bad treatment they have received from Arab men during their adventures abroad. But any Arab man is bound by the laws of the land in which he lives, and sex before marriage with a Muslim woman is both frowned upon and deeply difficult to achieve. If a women has sex before marriage and it is discovered that this has happened she may be cast out of the family and shunned by those she knew. In many cases the only way she can make a living thereafter is through prostitution. For a Muslim man, on the other hand, as for any man, sex is something that can be hoped for and his family will never know whether it has occurred or not. For sexually frustrated males the arrival on the shore of, in their eyes, scantily clad and flirtatious women from abroad – who are here today and gone tomorrow, is an opportunity to relieve some of that masculine frustration.

Arab men can be and often are charming, knowledgeable and free with what money they have. For a western woman travelling in the Middle East the idea of having a relationship with a man from a different culture can be both appealing and interesting. Many Western women have relationships with and marry Arab men, raising their kids and living a very interesting life compared to settling down with a man from their own culture. But the hangover from these relationships has been the idea that all western women are 'loose' and will fall into bed with a man at the drop of a hat.

AVOIDING OFFENCE

The Handshake. Arab society tends to be very polite and a sense of etiquette is still deeply ingrained. Shaking hands on meeting and leaving is big in the Gulf and the expats have picked up on this. You will find that hands are held out to you much more often than in Europe or the US, and even if you are only leaving someone's company for several hours a handshake of goodbye is often expected. You should also stand up when greeting someone. Arabs tend to put their right hand to their heart after shaking hands to show that they are sincerely pleased to make your acquaintance. A limp handshake means nothing more than that the person isn't used to the macho western vice-like grip.

Dressing Up. Even if you have a hankering to dress up and look like Lawrence of Arabia such things are best left for fancy dress parties back home. The embroidered *kumma* caps worn by Omanis are really quite stylish, and the *thobes* worn by men in the region are ideally suited to the climate. However, traditional dress (which has its own variations and styles depending on tribal and geographical reasons) is worn by nationals of the Gulf to give them a sense of belonging and to show that they are different to the mishmash of expats who inhabit their countries in vast numbers. For a foreigner to wear Gulf traditional dress is seen as a sign of disrespect; a slighting of the national pride. Western women are unlikely to feel the desire to wear an *abbaya* (the cover-everything black cloak). The wearing of shorts in the Middle East is still considered something of an eccentricity and especially in the more rural areas you may get funny stares if you decide to wander about wearing them. To avoid the gawping of men unused to seeing the outlines of a woman's body in the street, women should refrain from wearing tight fitting clothes. Any semi-nakedness in public places is frowned upon in Muslim society and beachwear should be worn only at the beach or swimming pool.

The Left Hand Law. Though you may be left-handed it is important to remember than in many other societies, including the Islamic, the right hand is dominant; the left hand considered unclean. You should also try not to show an Arab the soles of your feet or the underside of your shoe if you are sitting down.

Temperance. Losing your temper is seen as losing face in the Arab world and will not get anything done quicker or endear you to the person upon whom you have loosed your temper. When dealing with officialdom be extra polite, calm but firm. Things take longer to get done in the Middle East. It is a fact of life and you will need to come to terms with it.

Coffeetime. It is considered a slight to decline an offer of coffee in a business or even a social occasion but you should not feel pressurised into the prolonged company of a shopkeeper or someone you are unsure of. If you are invited to an Arab's house for a meal it is polite to take a present of food or sweets of some kind.

Shhh. Everybody knows that the three unmentionable subjects at a dinner table are sex, religion and politics. Although these may possibly be the three topics that are almost guaranteed to get conversation flowing it should be noted that they are also pretty much taboo in the Gulf. In the Arab world the family is sacrosanct, and though it may be polite to ask after another's family in general ('al-Hamdullilah' is likely to be the response), for a man to ask about another man's wife is invasive, and rude. Politics in the Middle East is always a dodgy subject to get on to and you should also be very respectful if drawn into a conversation about Islam.

A Question of Faith. The countries of the Arabian Gulf are far more focused on their religion than other Muslim countries further north that have been the home of Christians as well as Muslims for thousands of years. Gulf Arabs tolerate the practices of Christians and non-practising Christians in their countries, but they expect them to have respect for Islam. It would be extremely disrespectful to interrupt someone at prayer or to step on their prayer mat in shoes. During the month of Ramadan you will be expected to refrain from eating and drinking in public places during daylight hours.

NATURAL HISTORY

The Arabian Peninsula wasn't always the seemingly barren land with a terribly harsh climate that it is today. It was once the meeting place of three major zoological regions: the oriental, the afrotropical and the Palaearctic, which made it a place with a hybrid mix of fauna from all three regions. Twenty to thirty million years ago the region was attached to the surrounding landmasses of present day Asia, Africa and Europe. Some time later large areas of Arabia were covered by seas, evidenced today by the abundance of marine fossils dating back to the Jurassic period that have been uncovered in the region. Later still, about seventy million years ago there were large areas of forest (the petrified remains of which are still being unearthed today). Rivers ran through the Peninsula and flowed into the Gulf Basin. This was the time of the giant reptiles. Later, mammals crossed into the Peninsula along the land bridges that connected Arabia to the neighbouring landmasses.

Although one immediately assumes that Arabia is a landscape of desert this is not the case and the varied terrain; the wadi beds with their rock pools, the fertile plains and oases, the *sabkha* salt plains and the mountain ranges provide differing habitats for differing species of flora and fauna all of which have adapted in order to survive. The countries described in this book all have their own characteristic climate and terrain; Bahrain consisting of low lying islands with little elevation above sea level, Qatar a flat scrub desert with mangrove in the north and dunes in the south east, the United Arab Emirates with its great variety of geographical features from mountain to *sabkha* and Oman with its huge mountain ranges and wadis, the Wahiba Sands and the desert of the Empty Quarter. These features have led to a variety of wildlife that, though scarce, can survive if left alone from the invasion of man.

At one time wild oxen and ostriches used to live in the plains of the region as shown in rock carvings that were drawn at the time. Ibex and gazelles were once common in the Peninsula until hunting techniques using the gun and the internal combustion engine improved to such an extent that there are now very small numbers of the grazing herds which were once prevalent. Thankfully today the rulers of the region are committed to conservation and there are quite a number of projects throughout the Gulf preserving and breeding the indigenous wildlife of the region including the *al-Areen* Wildlife Park in Bahrain, the Oryx farm in Qatar, the *Tahr Project* in Oman and the *Breeding Centre for Endangered Species* in Sharjah.

Like humans, animals are pretty good at adapting to harsh and adverse conditions and climates. For the mammals of the Arabian Peninsula this has been a necessity. The **Arabian Oryx** has long been a symbol of Arabia but it could easily have become as symbolic as the Dodo. Hunted to the verge of extinction by the 1960s and with its natural habitat destroyed, zoologists captured several of the remaining Oryx and began a breeding programme first of all in Kenya and later in the Arizona Desert of the United States. By the 1980s enough had bred in captivity for them to be re-introduced back into the wild and the first batch were released into the Wahiba Sands in Oman. There are now Oryx breeding programmes in Bahrain and in Qatar. The Oryx is the largest of the cloven-hoofed animals of Arabia and measures about a metre in height.

The largest of the gazelles, those beautiful-eyed creatures of Arab fable and poetry, is the **Rheem** which remains in small herds on the edge of the Empty Quarter feeding on the desert succulents. **Wild goats** and the **Ibex** are found in the mountains of Oman and the **Arabian Tahr**, related to a small mountain goat found in India, survives due to its habitat of remote areas that are practically inaccessible to man. Of the predators, the **Arabian Leopard** and the **Cheetah** are the most famous. The Leopard still lives up in the harsh mountainous Musandam Peninsula of Oman and the Hajar mountains but is now extremely rare (ten times rarer than the Giant Panda) while the Cheetah, an animal of the plains, hasn't been seen in the region for several decades (the last specimen was found in Oman in 1977). Other smaller members of the cat family that are still indigenous to the region are the **Sand Cat** (with its pads covered by tufts of hair to give a better grip and to protect them from the heat of the desert sands), the **Caracal Lynx** with its long black and white ear tufts and **wild cats**, relations of the domestic cat. All these are primarily nocturnal and sightings remain rare.

Predators of the dog family generally exist out on the open plains and include the **Arabian Wolf** – smaller than the European Wolf and about the size of an Alsatian. The wolves are an endangered species today and are protected by law. The **Asiatic Jackal** roams in packs and their howls may be heard at night if you are camping out in the desert far from civilization. There are also several species of **fox** (the **Common Red**, **Rüppell's Sand** and the **Fennec**) and **mongooses** are quite a common sight in Bahrain.

Of the smaller vertebrates there are a number of **Indian House Shrews** which are tiny and probably originally came over the seas with traders from Asia. The **Ethiopian Hedgehog** is the most common of the three types of hedgehog found in the region along with **Brandt's** or the **Black Hedgehog** which originates from Iran and Southern Russia. There are nine known species of bat in the Gulf (happily all non-blood sucking) including the **Muscat Mouse-Tailed Bat**, the **Naked-Bellied Tomb Bat** and **Kuhl's Pipistrelle**, though there are thought to be more. Both Rattus norvegicus (the Brown Rat) and Rattus ratus (the Black Rat) are intelligent, agile creatures and these great survivors are common in seaports. The **Cape** or **Desert Hare** is still going strong in the region with several sub-species living in different parts of the Peninsula. A clever beast, the hare is also a survivor and its young, unlike rabbits, are born with their eyes open, fully furred and ready to run. Of the smaller rodents, most of which are burrowers and spend their days underground only coming out to feed in the cool of the night, **Gerbils**, **Jerboas**, **Jirds** and the **House Mouse** are the most common.

One animal that you are likely to see a lot of, funnily enough, is the **Arabian One-Humped Camel**. It is said that many words in Arabic describe something, its reverse meaning, and a camel. And although this is not even close to the truth it does reflect the importance than camels have had in the Arabian Peninsula. The camel has provided the people of the desert with transport, food, milk, fuel, materials from which to make bags and clothes, rugs and tents; and today camel racing is a big spectator sport as well as a way of proving the worth of a beast, and they sell for large sums of money. Like the gypsies with their horses, camels to the Bedouin are a symbol of status as well as of pride in their heritage. You will often come across camels roaming around the land and sauntering onto roads to get at a choice stretch of grazing. They are probably the animals that you will see the most of during your time in the Gulf. They are imperious, aloof and smell rather bad but are pretty in their own way, and rather beautiful to watch as they amble gently through the desert.

Birdlife

Over 500 species of bird have been recorded in the Gulf, both migrant and breeding. The area with its varied terrain of desert, oases, mountain and seashore attracts plenty of bird life and also lies on migration routes; birds flying from Eurasia to Africa or India in August to October and making the return journey in February to April to breed in the more temperate climates of the world. The most common birds that you will see if you are travelling in the winter will be **Sparrows**, **Crested Larks**, **Ring-Tailed Parakeets** and **Mynah Birds** (escaped from captivity and now breeding wild), and the **Hoopoe**. The Hoopoe is a delight to see with its black and white plumage, orange head and its raised black and white crest. You are likely to see Hoopoes strutting about on the newly sprinkled lawns around the UAE sticking their long bills into the turf looking for grubs and insects. In the Quran these birds are mentioned as the messengers of Solomon (or Sulayman).

Some of the resident bird life such as the **Arabian Babbler**, the **Black Bush Chat** and the **Arabian See-See Partridge** make local migrations in search of food and water supplies at various times of the year. The rather sinister looking **Black Socotra Cormorants** are often spotted perched on the edges of fish traps wings akimbo, and **flamingos** are a feature of many of the shallow waters of the Gulf. The Ostrich used to be common in the region earlier last century but due to the large amount of meat that could be had from the carcass of the bird and the omelettes that could be made with just the one egg these birds were hunted to extinction. There are several good books available locally and at home about ornithology in the Gulf.

Falconry

Falconry is still pursued as a sport in the Arabian Gulf though not generally as a means of catching food to eat. Mostly enjoyed by the rich and the ruling families these days due to the high cost of training a hawk or falcon (these are often imported from abroad and will inevitably travel first class!), the sport is practiced through the cooler winter months and you may be lucky to see a man and his bird training out on flat empty wasteland in any of the countries of the Arabian Gulf.

In the past both falconry and coursing with the fast Saluki dogs were ways for the Bedouin to supplement their often monotonous diet by getting hold of hares, bustards and stone curlews. The traditional bird of choice for falconers is the Peregrine Falcon which hunts by flying above the prey and then dive bombing it, sometimes reaching speeds of over 200km/h. With the arrival of fast transport between countries several other species of bird of prey are now imported into the Arabian Gulf; the Saker, the Gyrfalcon and the Lanner.

Peregrines migrate south across Arabia in the autumn and are trapped using snares, or fishing nets using pigeons as bait. Females are considered better birds than males due to their larger size. Once a falcon has been trapped the process of training it – which takes between 10 days and a fortnight – begins. This requires patience and a careful handling of the bird, trying to get it to equate the offer of food with being picked up and handled. Its wings may be bound at first to protect it from going into a bate and flailing its wings and it will be hooded and tied to a block shaped like a huge drawing pin to stop it from fretting at any alarming movements around it. Once a bird has become accustomed to being handled and associates being picked up with an offer of food, lines (*creances*) are attached to its *jesses* and it is persuaded to fly to the wrist from a distance, where it will be rewarded with food. A lure, made of a bundle of bustard feathers, is used to 'lure' the falcon to the *manqalah* (a cylindrical muff worn over the left wrist made of canvas or carpet) and it then begins to recognise that the lure means food. Once a falcon comes obediently to the *manqalah* from a distance it can be taken out on a hunt. A falcon has a very tempestuous and irritable nature and to get it to work for you requires a great deal of skill; feed it too much and it will sit about ignoring the lure and any prey that should fly by, underfeed it and it will lack the will to fly far.

The main quarry of the falconers is the Houbara Bustard which grows to about the size of a Heron, and the Desert Hare. Both have been in danger of becoming extinct through hunting and the encroachment of man on their natural habitat but through recent conservation programmes their numbers are increasing. Captured prey must be killed according to Islamic custom. In the spring when the falcons are migrating north the captured birds are released to follow the migration and breed.

LANGUAGE

Arabic is a fascinating and incredibly rich language and there are several different types of Arabic: Classical, Modern Standard, and the colloquial. Classical Arabic is the language of the Quran – ancient and considered to be the language of God. Modern Standard Arabic is learnt by all Arabs who have been to school and is the language of the press, radio and television. By using Modern Standard all Arabs, wherever they come from in the Arab World, can communicate. Each country throughout the Arab world has its own brand of Arabic, its own vernacular. These are often fairly similar in style but still distinct with country-specific words and accents. Broadly speaking the countries of the Levant (Syria, Jordan, Lebanon, Palestine and to some extent Iraq) all share a similar colloquial Arabic while the countries of the Arabian Gulf (Saudi Arabia, Kuwait, Yemen, U.A.E, Oman, Bahrain and Qatar) all speak from roughly the same dictionary. Egypt has its own guttural dialect, as do the Muslim countries further south in Africa like Sudan. The countries of North Africa (Morocco, Tunisia, Algeria, Libya) speak a colloquial Arabic that would be practically incomprehensible to an Arab from Oman, and vice versa. Because the Prophet Muhammed came from out of the Arabian Peninsula, today Gulf Arabic is the closest spoken colloquial dialect to that of Classical Arabic.

Due to the structure of Arabic (no short vowels are written in the script) transliteration is always an inexact science and the road signs that you see on the highways around the Gulf will be in English and Arabic though often the English spelling of a place name will create a word that sounds very different to what the locals themselves call the place. For example there is no 'e' in the Arabic alphabet but the word 'Emirates' begins with an 'e' not an 'i', and they are ruled by 'Emirs' not 'Amirs'.

The *lingua franca* of Oman and the countries of the Arabian Gulf is Arabic, though often wandering about the souk areas of these countries you would be forgiven for thinking that it was Hindi, Urdu or even English. Most business is conducted in English as this is pretty much a second language for a large proportion of the working population. This is good news for the tourists whose first language is English as any need to speak Arabic is minimal. Unless you are out in the wilds of Oman it is unlikely that not speaking Arabic will be of any hindrance. The things that you will miss out on though are the little asides that Arabs may make to each other and the meanings of all the road and shop signs (although a lot of these are also written in English and Philippino and one of the languages of the Subcontinent). The word *Sharia'* means both street and road in Arabic and you will find that these two English words are used indiscriminately throughout the region.

Below are some of the more useful words and phrases you may need or like to try out on your travels. Just make sure that you are actually talking to an Arab when you use them rather than a shopkeeper from Pakistan. The Arabic is written phonetically – pronounce the words as you see them on the page.

Numbers

One	*wahid*
Two	*ithnayn*
Three	*thalaatha*
Four	*arrbaah*
Five	*hamsa*
Six	*sitta*
Seven	*saba*
Eight	*thamaaniya*
Nine	*tissa*
Ten	*ashara*
Fifteen	*hamstash*
Twenty	*ashreen*
Thirty	*thalatheen*
Fifty	*hamseen*
Hundred	*miya*
Thousand	*alf*

Greetings and farewells

Hello	*marhaba*
Good morning	*sabaah al hayer*
Good morning (response)	*sabaah al norr*
Good afternoon	*masa al hayer*
Good afternoon (response)	*masa al norr*
Peace be upon you	*asalaam alaykoom*
Peace be upon you (reponse)	*walaykoom asalaam*
How are you? (to a man)	*kayf harlak?*
How are you? (to a woman)	*kayf harlik?*
Fine, thanks	*zayn al hamdulilla*
Goodbye	*ma salaama*

Words and Phrases

Yes	*eywa/naam*
No	*laa*
Please (to a woman)	*min fadlik*
Please (to a man)	*min fadlak*
Thank you	*shookran*
Good/Okay	*zayn*
Who?	*meen?*
Why?	*laysh?*
When?	*matta?*
Where?	*wayn?*
What?	*shoo?*
How?	*kayf?*
Don't worry/No problem	*ma fee mooshkilla/maalesh*
A little/Slowly	*shwiya shwiya*
Enough!	*bas!*
Forbidden	*mamnuwa*
Open	*maftuwa*
Closed	*mussaker*
I am British	*anna britaani*
Restaurant	*mataam*
Hotel	*foondooq/al hotel*
Hospital	*mustashfa*
Pharmacy	*sayyidaliyya*
Police	*shurta*
Mountain	*jebal*
Beach	*sharti*
Water	*my*
Left	*ala yasaar*
Right	*ala yameen*
Straight on	*alatool*
Stop	*qiff*

Literature

Writers, with their parables and craftily constructed critiques of their mother country, have often been treated with more suspicion than praise in the Middle East. There are few writers of fiction from the Gulf countries whose works have been translated into English but if you want a taster of Arab literature you could do worse than getting hold of a copy of *The Literature of Modern Arabia*, edited by Salma Khadra Jayyusi.

The book is a collection of prose and poems by prominent writers from all over the Arab world and is well worth a look.

Language Courses

If you are interested in taking a crash course in Arabic before you go out to the Gulf some local night schools do have Arabic classes but often these run for three terms and can be difficult to attend if you are also working. A couple of good teach yourself courses such as *Colloquial Arabic of the Gulf and Saudi Arabia* by Clive Holes and *Teach Yourself Arabic* by Jack Smart and Frances Altorfer come with cassettes and can be quite useful. Arabic, like Cantonese, is one of the hard languages and takes years to perfect and unless you are going to be travelling throughout the Middle East often, or into the remoter parts of Arabia, you can comfortably get by in all the countries outlined in this book by speaking English.

PRACTICAL INFORMATION

GETTING THERE

Independent Travel

If you are managing the itinerary of your trip alone then one thing you have is the freedom to go where you want when you want. The drawback to this is the expense of the initial flight out to the Gulf, and the ensuing intra-Gulf flights. If you are only going to be visiting the region for a couple of weeks for a sun and sea holiday then it may be more convenient and cheaper to look into a package holiday and letting a holiday company look after all flight and accommodation arrangements. They may even throw in some tours (which can be expensive to organise alone) as part of the deal.

BY AIR

As a rule of thumb, flying to the Gulf is going to be cheaper if you avoid the national airlines of the individual countries (*Emirates Airlines*, *Oman Air*, *Qatar Airways* and *Gulf Air*). The cheapest way to get to the Gulf will be to fly into Dubai or Abu Dhabi where a return fare from London can be as low as £230/$320. Dubai is a major transport hub in the region and there are many flights in and out daily. Getting to Bahrain or Qatar might be cheaper if you fly via Dubai, although Bahrain is the centre for all Gulf Air flights in the region and there are often deals offered by that airline. Flying to Oman is going to be quite expensive (expect to pay around £400/$560 return from London) as for the moment at least it isn't a busy destination. The cheapest way to get to Oman would be to fly to Dubai and then go overland.

When searching for flights a couple of places worth checking first are *USIT Campus Travel* (tel 0870-830 8124; www.usitcampus.co.uk) and *STA Travel* (tel 020-7361 6149; www.statravel.co.uk) both of which are pretty good, reliable and their prices compete with many of the other flight booking agencies. There are a number of websites devoted to flight only deals that are meant to be cheaper than booking through a travel agency but in fact seem to charge about the same, and sometimes more than other places. They are worth checking out though. Try www.deckchair.com, www.cheapflights.com and www.expedia.com.

OVERLAND TRAVEL

Providing that you have the necessary documentation it is perfectly feasible to drive between all the countries outlined in this book. The island of Bahrain has for a number of years been linked to Saudi Arabia by the King Fahad Causeway and Qatar also has a border with Saudi. Saudi Arabia is linked to Europe by the Trans-Arabia Highway via Jordan, Syria and Turkey which would make for a fascinating, and gruelling, trip. Practically speaking though, getting the necessary transit visas for such a drive may also be a gruelling experience and is likely to be a far from fascinating one. Additionally, distances between the countries of the region are large and desert driving is often monotonous to the extreme. There are also international bus services that operate throughout the region but for a non-resident foreigner it is going to be difficult to get transit visas for Saudi Arabia.

By Sea. Sea links between the countries of the Arabian Gulf, although a great idea, do not seem to have been set up yet. Some cruise ships do pass along the Oman coast and up to Dubai but not too often.

Onward Travel

Quite a number of visitors to the Gulf are on stopovers coming or going between America and Europe and the countries of the Far East and Australia. They may spend a couple of days shopping for gold in Dubai, take a week's wadi bashing and desert trekking in Oman or just spend a few hours holed up in the duty free area of Bahrain Airport. If you are on a long haul flight it is worth taking a few days to acclimatise slightly to the time differences and seeing another culture before continuing on your way. You may also make some good contacts.

Schedules

Things do move noticeably slower in a Muslim country and although the countries of the Gulf are very modern and most things run on time, there are as yet not the powerful communication networks which we run by in the West. Aircraft may be delayed, and perhaps even taken out of service, with no explanation being given. Such things happen and can't be helped. Muslims are firm believers in *kismet* or fate, and everything that happens happens for a purpose. The plane will run when the time is right, the bus will leave on time if God wills it.

GETTING BACK

It is unlikely that you will go out to the Gulf on a one-way ticket. Visa regulations often state that you must have a return ticket to enter a country and apart from the United Arab Emirates (where you may stay on a tourist visa for up to 60 days) most of the other Gulf States only allow you a month at most to visit their country. If time and money are quantities that you possess a lot of you may wish to buy a clutch of tickets that will take you throughout the Gulf and then fly you on to somewhere either in Europe or over towards the Indian subcontinent. From there you can continue overland. If you do travel on a one-way ticket you are probably best flying into Dubai and arranging onward visas and flights from there. Dubai is the commercial heart of the Arabian Gulf and although it sounds a bit of a cliché, you *can* get anything there.

BAGGAGE

Your choice of baggage should be chosen depending on whether you will be moving about a lot or staying in a hotel in one country for a fixed amount of time. Unless you are actually going to be doing a lot of hiking and camping (which is unlikely given the harsh terrain and climate of the Gulf States) it is better to take a strong suitcase or kit bag rather than a rucksack. You will generally only be moving your baggage from an airport to a hotel in a taxi and rucksacks with their flimsy material tend to leave your clothes all creased and mixed up with your other belongings. A much better bet, if you can fit all of your belongings in, is to take a cabin case (one of those small suitcases with wheels on the bottom and a handle that you pull up to pull it by). You will be able to stow this in the overhead locker of the aircraft cabin which will mean that you can swan through customs without having to hang around the baggage reclaim area waiting for a bag that looks as though it has just been dropped from a great height (which often it will have been). You can pick up cabin bags very cheaply in the Gulf as they are *de rigueur* at the moment, though quality varies. A good tip if you are planning on bringing home a number of souvenirs is to take two suitcases – putting all your belongings into the smaller of the two and then putting this inside the larger case. In this way you will have an extra empty suitcase to fill up on your travels.

TOUR OPERATORS AND TRAVEL AGENCIES

The average high street travel agency will be able to help you with booking flights or all-inclusive holidays to the more popular destinations of the Arabian Gulf – especially Dubai and Oman. Package holidays to these destinations are very popular and are also likely to be cheaper in the long run than independent travel. All the travel sections of the newspapers and the back pages of free magazines such as *TNT* and *Southern Cross* carry adverts for flight booking companies and adventure holiday specialists.

In Britain

Arabian Odyssey (tel 01242-224482; www.arabianodyssey.co.uk): arrange trips to Oman and Dubai.

British Airways Holidays (Worldwide Department, Astral Towers, Betts Way, London Road, Crawley, West Sussex RH10 2XA; tel 01293-723202; fax 01293-722640): offer all-inclusive short breaks to Dubai.

Somak Holidays (tel 020-8423 3000; www.somak.co.uk): offers three nights B+B plus all flights in the super exclusive Burj al-Arab Hotel in Dubai for £1,241.

Travel Dubai (tel 0870-748 7474; www.traveldubai.co.uk): offers five and six night breaks to Dubai for around £500.

Tailor-Made Tours

For a more expensive holiday you can contact:

Abercrombie and Kent: Sloane Square House, Holbein Place, London SW1 8NS (tel 020-7730 9600, fax 020-7730 9376; e-mail info@abercrombiekent.co.uk).

Abercrombie Kent International, Inc.: 1520 Kensington Road, Oak Brook, IL 60523, USA (tel +1-630-954 2944).

Cox & Kings Travel Limited: Gordon House, 10 Greencoat Place, London, SW1P 1PH (Brochure Requests: tel 01233-211401; e-mail coxandkings@bptts.co.uk. Reservations: tel: 020-7873 5000; e-mail cox.kings@coxandkings.co.uk).

Exodus Holidays (www.exodus.co.uk): offers all-inclusive trips for large parties to Oman and the Emirates for around £1,000 per person for trips through the desert and wadis of Oman.

World Exhibitions (tel 020-8870 2600; www.worldexhibitions.co.uk): a 14-day 'Journey Through Oman' costs from £1,495.

EMIRATES AIRLINE OFFICES AND SALES AGENTS AROUND THE WORLD

In the Gulf States

Bahrain: 1F13-1F19, 1F68-1F70, al-Al'ali Shopping Complex, Block 428, Road 2827, Building 2210, Al-Seef Street, P.O. Box 21354, Manama (tel (toll free) 801900/588700).

Oman: Universal Travel and Tourism Agencies LLC, P.O. Box 2802, Ruwi, Muscat 112 (tel 968-786 600).

Qatar: Abdulla Bin Jassem Street, P.O. Box 22488, Doha (tel 974-438 4477).

United Arab Emirates: *Abu Dhabi:* Bin Hamal Travel and Tourism, P.O. Box 45450, Abu Dhabi (tel 971-2-631 5888).

Ajman: Travel Centre, P.O. Box 3838, Ajman (tel 971-6-744 8444).

Dubai: Ticket Office, Sheikh Zayed Road, Dubai (tel 971-4-343 4204).
  Ticket Office, Souq Naif Road, Deira, Dubai (tel 971-4-226 0003).

Fujairah: DNATA, Bank Saderat Iran Building, P.O. Box 445, Fujairah (tel 971-9-222 2985).

Ras al-Khaimah: Omest Travels, P.O. Box 103, Ras al-Khaimah (tel 971-7-222 9413).

Sharjah: Sharjah Tower (al-Soor Building), Ground Floor, Al-Arooba Street, Sharjah (tel 971-6-572 4759).

Umm al-Quwain: UAQ National Travel Agency, P.O. Box 601, UAQ (tel 971-6-766 6684).

Around the World

Australia: *Melbourne:* Level 2, 257 Collins Street, Melbourne, Victoria 3000 (tel 1300-303777).

Sydney: Level 4, 36 Clarence Street, Sydney, N.S.W. 2000 (tel 61-2-929 09700).

Canada: 40 Shepperd Avenue West, 7th Floor, Suite 707, North York, Ontario, Canada M2N 6K9 (tel 1-800-777 3999 (toll free)).

New Zealand: Level 5, KPMG Legal Building, 22 Fanshawe Street, Auckland (tel 64-9-377 6004).

South Africa: Sandton Office Tower, 5th Floor, Sandton City, c/o 5th Avenue and Rivonia Road, Johannesburg (tel 27-11-303 1900).

United Kingdom: First Floor, Gloucester Park, 95 Cromwell Road, London SW7 4DL (tel 0870 243 2222).

USA: *Chicago:* 150 North Martingale Road, Suite 840, Schaumburg, Chicago, IL 60173 (tel 1-847-592 3470).

Houston: 5718 Westheimer Road, Suite 1090, Houston, Texas 77057 (tel 1-713-266 5491).

Los Angeles: 880 Apollo Street, Suite 302, El Segundo, Los Angeles, California 90245 (tel 1-310-414-3250).

New York: 55 East 59th Street, 5th Floor, New York, NY 10022 (tel 212-758 3944).

TRAVEL SAFELY

Both the UK Foreign Office and the US State Department have travel information offices which provide regularly updated free advice on countries around the world (see also *Health and Hygiene* for information on the health situation).

Travel Advice Unit: Consular Division, Foreign & Commonwealth Office, 1 Palace Street, London, SW1E 5HE (tel 020-7238 4503/4504 Website www.fco.gov.uk/travel).

US State Department: 2201 C Street, Washington DC 20520, USA (tel 202-647 4000 Website http://travel.state.gov).

RED TAPE

PASSPORTS

For all travel around the Arabian Gulf you will need a full ten-year passport. Application forms can be obtained from post offices and cost £28 for an adult passport (£38 for a 48 page passport) and £14.80 for a child passport. Since October 1998 the passport office has not been able to add or include children on British passports which means that if you wish to travel with your child, that child will need its own passport and a passport size photo, even if a baby (which seems rather ridiculous seeing how fast a toddler's face changes!). It should take about two weeks from date of receipt to receive your passport but should you need it sooner you can apply in person to one of the regional offices. If you do apply in person at a passport office although you will get your passport quicker, there is an additional handling charge of £12 which does not guarantee a same-day service.

If you already have a passport make sure that it has at least six months left to run and that there are enough blank pages (reckon on two pages for entry/exit stamps and visa) for immigration purposes in all the countries that you intend to visit. You should also be aware that though some of the Gulf States may recognise and have relations with Israel, an Israeli stamp in you passport might cause problems at immigration. If in doubt about this you are best to apply for a new passport. Should you lose your passport contact the police and then the Consulate/Embassy. Getting a replacement passport is always going to be easier and quicker if you have kept a record of the passport number and the place and date of issue.

Additional Passport Information

Australia: Apply at the nearest post office or passport office.

Canada: Apply at the nearest post office, passport office or contact the Canadian Passport Office direct (*Department of Foreign Affairs and International Trade*, Ottawa, Ontario K1A 0G3).

Ireland: Apply at nearest post office or contact the *Department of Foreign Affairs*, Passport Office, Molesworth Street, Dublin 2.

New Zealand: Contact the *Passport Office*, Department of International Affairs, P.O. Box 10526, Wellington.

USA: Information on passports can be obtained by calling 202-647 0518 or through the internet at www.travel.state.gov.

Identification

Student and youth cards are pretty worthless in the countries of the Gulf but if you are on a tight budget then an International Youth Hostel card (available from the Youth Hostel Association, Trevalyan House, 8 St Stephens Hill, St Albans, Herts AL1 2DY; tel 0870-870 8808; www.yha.org.uk) is a good investment as hotel accommodation around the Gulf is expensive. A YHA card will cost you £12.50 and will allow you to make use of over 4,500 youth hostels, including those in the Gulf.

An International Driving Licence can be obtained from some of the larger Post Offices for a few pounds and is a useful document to have (and obligatory if you want to drive in Bahrain). You should keep a copy of all important travel documents (passport, airline booking reference, your bank and credit card details, travellers cheque numbers, driving licence, address book etc.) somewhere in your luggage and it is a good idea to keep another copy at home.

VISAS

Unless you are a national of the country you intent to visit or a national of one of the member states of the Gulf Co-operation Council (Bahrain, Kuwait, Oman, Qatar, Saudi Arabia and the United Arab Emirates) you will need to apply for a visa. The countries included in this book are the easiest of all the Gulf States to visit and getting a visa will often entail no more than filling out a form, supplying a passport size photograph of yourself and handing over the visa fee. But this depends upon where you are from and which passport you hold. For the majority of prospective visitors from an affluent western nation this presents no problem. Unfortunately, if you are a passport holder from one of the Asian subcontinent countries, from one of the Middle Eastern countries that don't have particularly good relations with the Gulf country you wish to visit, or from one of the poorer Far Eastern countries you may encounter delays and difficulties getting a visa. This is because the countries of the Gulf are rich and are paranoid about individuals from poorer nations coming to their country and then disappearing into an underground work force. Don't take any delays in the processing of your visa personally, provide any documentation that is asked for as quickly as possible and keep a calm mind. It is just the way things are done in the Middle East.

All the countries outlined in this book are looking to diversify their economies and to expand their tourist industries. Previously insular countries like Oman and Qatar are relaxing their visa restrictions and welcoming foreign visitors. So visa requirements are changing and whereas a year ago you may have had to present evidence of having enough money in a bank account to fund your trip, or where you needed to be sponsored by a hotel, you now need none of these things. For a British passport holder you do not even need to sort out a visa to Bahrain or the United Arab Emirates before you travel but can collect them on arrival at the airport. If you are unlucky you may be asked for details of a sponsor to vouch for your good behaviour within a country. The middle to upmarket range of hotels will be able to provide this once you make a booking with them. Check under the accommodation section of each country chapter for hotel details.

WORK

Unless you already have contacts out in the Gulf it is difficult to pick up casual work while visiting the area, and it is also illegal. Every non-national employee in the Gulf needs a sponsor which involves paperwork, legal practicalities etc. You are also likely to need to leave the country before being issued with your residence/work visa. There is an ongoing programme in all the countries of the Arabian Gulf of creating incentives for nationals to start taking a more active role in businesses, however, this has yet to draw nationals to jobs that they believe are beneath them. Business is booming in the Gulf and there will be a need for expat workers in all sectors for many more years to come. The Gulf can find employment for anyone, from professionals working in manufacturing, oil, accountancy and the law etc., to waiters and waitresses, and semi-skilled clerical workers. Unfortunately there is no demand for casual labourers as the construction firms import cheap labour from Asia to work on the building sites.

If you are keen to work in the Gulf, and the benefits are very good, you could contact the recruitment companies already based in the Gulf such as *Ingram Executive Search* in Dubai (tel +971 4 3344 225; www.ingram-search.com) and those in Britain such as Arabian Careers (tel 020-7495 3285; www.arabiancareers.com). *Overseas Jobs Express*, a magazine devoted to positions available abroad, is quite useful and is available from Premier House, Shoreham Airport, West Sussex BN43 5FF; tel 01273-440220; www.overseasjobs.com. Another good source of job vacancies for teachers is the *Times Educational Supplement*. If you have access to the Internet you could also do a search for jobs in the Gulf or access the website devoted to work in the Gulf www.gulfjobs.com. Vacation Work also publish many books providing detailed information about finding work abroad including the very useful *Live and Work in Saudi and the Gulf* by Louise Whetter. A list of other publications can be found at the back of this book.

EMBASSIES OF THE COUNTRIES OF THE ARABIAN GULF

Embassy of the State of Bahrain: 98 Gloucester Road, London SW7 4AU; tel 020-7370 5132/3; fax 020-7370 7773; e-mail information@bahrainembasssy.org.uk.
3502 International Drive NW, Washington DC 20008, USA; tel 202-342 0741/2; fax 202-362 2192.
Embassy of the Sultanate of Oman: 167 Queen's Gate, London SW7 5HE; tel 020-7225 001; fax 020-7589 2505.
2535 Belmont Road NW, Washington DC 20008, USA; tel 202-387 1980/2; fax 202-745 4933.
Embassy of the State of Qatar: 1 South Audley Street, London W1Y 5DQ; tel 020-7493 2200; fax 020-7493 2819.
4200 Wisconsin Avenue NW, Suite 200, Washington DC 20016, USA; tel 202-274 1600; fax 202-237 0061.
Embassy of the United Arab Emirates: 30 Prince's Gate, London SW7 1PT; tel 020-7581 1281; fax 020-7581 9616.
1255 22nd Street, Suite 700, NW, Washington, DC 20037, USA; tel 202-955 7999; fax 202-337 7029.

MONEY

One of the ongoing mysteries of arriving in a foreign country is that for the first few days money will flow from your pockets like water, you will forget the real cost of things back home and for some bizarre reason believe that everything in this new country is an absolute bargain. If you are on a budget what this means is that your budget will have to be worked out anew after the first week away. In the Gulf nothing is really a bargain. The cost of living is quite high and if you want to eat western style food, drink alcohol and stay in reasonable hotels you will need to take a sizeable amount of money with you. Public transport when you can find it and can work out the routes is a bargain, intra-Gulf flights aren't too dear, and if you always eat in the cheaper Asian restaurants food won't break your bank. But hotels are priced according to what people can pay and in the oil rich countries of the Gulf most people can often afford to pay quite a bit. A hotel room that might cost you £5 in Syria or Egypt is likely to cost you more that five times that in the Gulf. There is a preponderance of five-star hotels in every major city, a number of hotels that seem to vary from two-star to four-star but all charge about the same, and a very few noticeably cheaper but often pokey hostelries. Outside of the main cities the options are much more limited, and you will often only have the choice of a couple of five-star hotels or a government owned Tourist Hotel or its clone. The only countries with Youth Hostels at the moment are the United Arab Emirates and Bahrain and these are often located quite far from the centre of town.

It is very likely that you will hire a car to get about more conveniently while you are away and to really see the country you will need to either hire a 4WD or go as part of a tour. All these extras will eat into your wad of travellers' cheques, wallet or credit. It is a good idea to travel with a group of friends as this will keep costs down through shared expenditure, to stay with friends or colleagues if possible and to check out possible bargain break all-inclusive holiday packages through travel agents. If you intend to travel alone expect to live on about £30-£40/$40-70 per day not including additional flights and visas.

TRAVELLERS' CHEQUES

Travellers cheques are in many ways an unnecessary waste of money while travelling in the Gulf and are often more hassle than they are worth when it comes to finding a bank that is a) open and b) willing to cash them at a reasonable rate of exchange. When you buy travellers' cheques the bank will usually charge you a one per cent commission and you will then have to pay another commission when you decide to cash them, unless you do so at a branch of the issuing company. Having said that, travellers' cheques are one of the safest ways of carrying money about in foreign countries and if they are lost or stolen will be replaced free of charge. The rate of exchange for travellers' cheques is often better than for cash and you can keep hold of unused cheques to use on subsequent trips abroad. The most recognised brands of cheque are Thomas Cook and American Express and you are advised to stick with these. Because the currency of all the Gulf States is tied in with the US dollar it is a good idea to take currency either in dollars or UK sterling as these currencies fluctuate less than some others.

ATM CARDS

The rise of the Automatic Teller Machine (ATM) throughout the region means that you need never worry about what day of the week it is or what time of the day it is to gain access to your money. ATMs never close and are conveniently located at airports, hotels and suburban supermarkets as well as major banks around city centres.

Using ATMs means than your money is safely tucked up in a bank back home and needn't be hoarded away in an unsightly bulging money belt or a bag slung round your neck (both of which show a rather unflatteringly untrusting attitude to the locals among whom you are moving). It does away with the need for travellers' cheques and a piece of plastic in your wallet weighs practically nothing. You are also likely to get a better rate of exchange this way than through using moneychangers and local banks. Most issuing banks offer an insurance cover should you lose your credit or debit cards or they get stolen and it is a good idea to pay for this service whether you are abroad or at home. ATMs in the Gulf are linked into most of the global access systems such as Plus and Cirrus but you should check with your bank or building society about the compatibility of your cards before leaving home. Most of the major cards such as Visa, Access, MasterCard and American Express will give you access to your money whilst abroad. Almost all banks will charge you a commission for withdrawing foreign currency using your cards so it is a good idea to take out large sums in one go rather than making a lot of withdrawals for smaller amounts. Make sure before you leave that you have set up a standing order to debit the monthly amount payable on any credit card, keep tabs on your spending limit and a record of your credit card numbers and the emergency telephone number of the credit card company.

Emergency Cash

It is a good idea before you leave to get hold of a small amount of the currency (in low denominations) of the country that you will be visiting. You can often order quantities of currency from a bank in advance or buy it at a branch of Thomas Cook or as a last resort from the exchange booths at the airport. Although the rate of exchange will not be as good as what you would get abroad it is better to arrive in a strange new place with enough money to pay for a taxi and a hotel etc., without having to worry about exchange rates.

Should you run out of money altogether, or fall foul of some heinous robber, it is possible to get money transferred through a bank back home to a bank overseas. HSBC has branches worldwide and is a big player in the banking sector of the Gulf. They have offices in all of the capital cities and it may be easiest should you need to get money transferred to arrange it through them.

WHAT TO TAKE

Maps

The most up to date maps of all the countries covered in this book are available in the individual countries themselves from bookshops. You may also be able to get hold of free maps from tourist information centres in the country that you are in though these are few and far between in the Gulf (see individual country chapters for tourist office addresses). Your local bookshop should be able to tell you what is available in Britain and if you are passing through London on your way out take a trip into Covent Garden to *Stanfords Bookshop* (12-14 Long Acre, London WC2E 9LP; tel 020-7836 1321; www.stanfords.co.uk) or the *Travel Bookshop* (13-15 Blenheim Crescent, London W11 2EE; tel 020-7229 5260; www.thetravelbookshop.co.uk). The Internet also has some fairly good websites relating to all things map; try *www.atlapedia.com* or *www.maps.com*. One of the most up to date maps covering the whole region is published by Hildebrand and costs £7.99.

Electrical Items

You can pick up discounted and tax-free goods at the airports on arrival in the Gulf and if you are in need of a good camera, DVD player or stereo this may well be the place to get hold of one slightly cheaper than back home. However, the choice of products on offer in the Gulf is considerably less than in Britain. Dubai has the best range of products in the Gulf.

All electrical sockets in the countries described in this book are the same as the British three-pin sockets. Electricity supply in the Gulf ranges from 220-240V and you should check whether any electrical appliance that you are planning to take needs an adaptor or transformer to run properly and safely.

Other Necessities

You can obtain most things that you may need on your travels, or their near equivalents, in any of the countries outlined in this book but if you are going out to visit friends who are living and working in the Gulf who drink, it is a good idea to take your quota of duty-free alcohol as a gift. Most expats are given a liquor licence which allows them to buy a certain amount of alcohol each month depending on their salary. It is best not to turn up empty-handed and help them drink their quickly diminishing quota. Most well-known brands of British food and drink and even pork products are available in the supermarkets and bars of the Gulf so expats do not generally suffer from cravings for a pint of Guinness and a pork pie for instance. Newspapers from home are usually on sale in the newsagents of the Gulf a day or so later but the bookshops of the region are not too well stocked so if you or your friends are voracious readers it is a good idea to stock up before you leave.

What Not to Take

It is always a bad idea to try and import firearms and ammunition, drugs and pornography into any country. Because of the conservative nature of the regimes of the Gulf countries you might find that books and any videos or DVDs that you take into the country may be taken away by customs to be vetted. You will get these back if they are deemed harmless to the morality and spiritual well being of the country you are visiting. Importing animals, live or dead, may also cause headaches at customs; as well as anything obviously originating from Israel.

HEALTH & HYGIENE

MEDICAL ADVICE

In the UK the Medical Advisory Services for Travellers Abroad (MASTA) is a good source of information and advice. It was set up in 1984 at the London School of Hygiene and Tropical Medicine to raise the awareness of health issues associated with travel. Services range from the supply of vaccines and travel medicines, to research on important travel issues, as well as the development of products for travellers. As part of their brief MASTA operates a Travellers Health Line (0906-822 4100, calls charged at £0.60 per minute) and a very informative website on the illnesses travellers face and precautions that can be taken. By telephoning them you can obtain a briefing tailored to your journey that covers up to six countries, which is then posted to you (to any country except the USA and Canada).

If your home base is the UK or South Africa, a visit to a British Airways Travel Clinic (BATC) should be on your must-do list. BATC has 28 clinics in the UK and 3 in South Africa and services include personal consultations, with advice tailored to your specific trip. With instant access to an on-line database BATC can call up the very latest information on 84 different health hazards in more than 250 countries worldwide. All information provided by MASTA or BATC is approved by the London School of Hygiene and Tropical Medicine, so you can rest assured you'll benefit from accurate advice on all appropriate vaccinations and any other recommended precautions. Such reliable advice is invaluable.

A range of healthcare products is available from MASTA or BATC, from simple but effective single and double-bed mosquito nets to a comprehensive sterile medical equipment pack, including sun protection lotion in both adult and child formulations; Trekker Travel Well pump-action purifier, which removes bacteria, viruses and parasitic cysts from water; an emergency dental pack to provide temporary replacement for dislodged crowns, bridges, fillings and the like; and a malaria wheel, which is a simple device for ensuring that you take anti-malaria tablets at the right time.

The Travel Clinic Helpline is a 24-hour service run from the Hospital for Tropical Diseases on 0839-337733 (calls charged at £0.50 per minute). You can also get a Travellers Guide to Health by calling the Department of Health's 'Health Literature Line' on 0800-555777.

Jet-lag

Getting into physical trim for a week or two before you travel helps to increase your stamina and reduces the fatigue known as jet-lag. Drink plenty of water before, during, and after the flight as dehydration is a distinct problem due to the dry air in pressurised cabins. Drink water even if you don't feel thirsty. Don't drink large amounts of alcohol; do try to sleep during long flights. On-board exercise – stretching and walking around – is a good idea. Limit activities on the day after your arrival until you feel rested and acclimatised and you'll enjoy your holiday that much more.

Inoculations

Check with your local medical centre a month or so before you depart about which inoculations if any are advisable for a trip to the Gulf. The countries are clean and modern and the high standard of hygiene means that you would be unlucky to be hit with Typhoid or Diphtheria for example. And if you are, the medical services are very modern, efficient and relatively cheap. Outbreaks of Cholera are rare but Malaria is still about in certain parts of Oman and the northern Emirates and it might be sensible to take anti-malaria pills if you will be travelling in the wilds for several weeks at a time.

Depending on how long you will be travelling for it is a good idea to have a dental check-up before you go and take a copy of your prescription if you wear spectacles. If you are on medication you should take a large enough supply to see you through the course or your time abroad and take the doctor's prescription with you. Customs can get picky about what is in your bag. If you have had inoculations in the past it is a good idea to take a record of these with you when you travel.

Useful Adresses

British Airways Travel Clinics: (Head Office) 29 Harley St, London, W1 (tel 020-7323 5862; www.british-airways.com/travelqa/fyi/health/health.shtml). For contact details of all 31 clinics telephone 01276-685040.
MASTA: Keppel Street, London, WC1E 7HT (www.masta.org).

Toilets

The standards are the same in all of the four countries: few public lavatories are provided and it is best to go into the five star hotels and use theirs as these are spruce and provide toilet paper. Elsewhere loos can be found outside mosques (but non-Muslims will not be welcome to use these) and in the restaurants and roadside cafés. The toilets outside roadside cafés are pretty rough holes in the ground and will provide a tap and little else, while the standard and plushness of loos in restaurants will increase with the richness of the ambience and expense of your meal. A western style eating establishment will provide western toilets with paper as well as a hose; the smaller cheap Subcontinental type eating places will provide a western style toilet and a hose, paper perhaps.

NATURAL HAZARDS

The main health problem that you may encounter will be to do with eating or drinking something a bit unhygienic or staying out in the sun for too long. The other main hazard is driving but you will be unlucky indeed to experience any serious problems during your stay.

The Sun

The biggest threat to your health that you will encounter while in the United Arab Emirates is the ever-present sun. Sunburn can get you very quickly and will be very painful and likely to ruin part of your holiday, so make sure that you cover up. Buy and use suntan lotion; don't forget to rub it into the tops of your feet, on your nose and forehead. One of those wide-brimmed floppy hats is going to be more effective than a baseball cap because it allows shade for the back of your neck as well as for the face. Sunglasses are also a pretty good idea unless you want to cultivate crows' feet and a squint. Protect your eyes from ultra-violet radiation by wearing quality sunglasses which block more than 90% of visible light and have protective side-shields. Cream to protect your lips from exposure is also recommended.

Prevention protect your skin by using a sunscreen that filters out damaging UV rays. SPF stands for Sun Protection Factor, and the number indicates the degree of protection a product offers. The higher the number, the better the protection. Children and those with sensitive skins or pale complexions need higher protection than adults with darker or less sensitive skins. Apply the stuff regularly, especially after you have been swimming or exercising. The back of your neck, upper arms and upper legs need special attention. Protection is necessary even on cloudy or hazy days, and especially at altitude. Apart from burning, you can also get sunstroke (heatstroke) or suffer from heat exhaustion from over-exposure to the sun.

Symptoms of sunstroke are chills, fever, nausea and delirium. Itching and peeling may follow any degree of sunburn and normally begin four to seven days after exposure. Severe sunburn or sunstroke should always be treated by a doctor.

Heatstroke and **heat exhaustion** are different conditions and are treated differently. The first is a medical emergency. If in doubt, treat for heatstroke, which occurs when high temperatures overwhelm the body's heat-control system. Immediate medical help is necessary. Heat exhaustion is caused by loss of salts and fluid during heavy sweating and can be rectified by drinking fresh fruit juice, which contains the right combination of water and electrolytes to fix you up. Avoid strenuous activity during the hottest hours and make sure you drink plenty of non-alcoholic, caffeine-free liquids to make up for the loss of body fluid through sweating.

Prickly Heat is an irritating rash caused by trapped sweat under the skin. If you get prickly heat bathe often and keep the skin as cool as possible. You can also buy zinc based prickly heat powder which is effective in getting rid of the affliction and against other fungal infections (which occur more frequently in hot weather).

WHEN TO GO

The countries of the Arabian Gulf are hot, desert countries. Muscat in the summertime is one of the hottest places on earth. Fortunately, these countries do have seasons (albeit with the delineating seasons of spring and autumn lasting a matter of days before summer/winter kicks in); the winter months lasting typically from November to February are considered the best time to visit the region when the weather is pleasant and humidity is quite low. It may even get a little chilly during the evening. As the climate around these parts is a desert climate, with little cloud cover to trap the heat, if you are camping it can get incredibly cold during the early hours around dawn. During the holy month of Ramadan things generally slow down business-wise and opening hours of museums and shops become rather erratic. Non-Muslims are expected to respect the culture they are travelling through and this will mean that you will not be able to eat, smoke or drink in any area where you might be seen doing so between the hours of sunrise and sunset. This can make wandering about and sightseeing a rather thirsty and hungry experience, though it can be interesting to 'do as the Romans do' and fast too if you are travelling in the Gulf during Ramadan. Joining in with the fast will certainly give you an insight into the life of a Muslim. Until 2006 Ramadan falls during the tourist season.

The Gulf is often touted as a winter sun destination with the weather forecast in all these countries almost an irrelevance when you know that warm blue-skied cloudless days follow day after day. The sea is warm and the beaches clean and the destination exotic. However, during the summer months the Gulf is unpleasantly hot and is best avoided; walking around on foot is no fun and many of the expats take their leave during these months. Having said that, the summer is the tourist low season and very cheap all-inclusive holiday packages can be had at this time of year if you are looking for a few weeks of tax-free shopping, a change of scenery, and staying in a beachside five-star hotel.

INSURANCE

Being covered by an insurance policy while travelling abroad is not a necessity and is often an extra expense that benefits nobody but the insurance company. Muslim countries are relatively crime free (penalties being rather harsh) and, unless you hand a prospective robber the opportunity on a plate, luggage is likely to remain untouched even if left in an unlocked hotel room. You would be most unlucky to come across any sneak thieves, pick pockets or muggers in the region. That said, driving in the Gulf is erratic and often downright dangerous and due to the paucity of public transport it is likely that you will be hiring a car while travelling around the countries. Car insurance is included in the cost of any car hire but personal accident insurance isn't. If you are unlucky enough to suffer personal injury abroad the medical expenses can often be quite high, and sometimes astronomical, depending on the damage done. The hospitals and medical care services in the Gulf are very modern and very good and in the event of an emergency operation being needed repatriation would not be necessary except in extreme circumstances.

For peace of mind insure yourself, but shop around for the best rates first. Insurers typically provide cover against cancellation, emergency medical expenses (including repatriation), personal accident, baggage loss or delay, hijack, scheduled airline failure, acts of God and many other unlikely occurrences. The *Post Office* (leaflets and information available from Post Office branches, the Internet at www.postoffice.co.uk or by calling 0800-387858) has various policies covering individuals, couples, and family groups with different rates depending whether you are buying a single-trip or a multi-trip policy. A month's individual cover worldwide will set you back about £66 with a £15 additional charge for every extra week that you are away. If you are over 65 years old theses rates are often higher. The Post Office also has bureaux de change where you can get commission free American Express travellers cheques if you take out an insurance policy with them. However, see the *Money* section relating to travellers cheques. *Endsleigh Insurance* (head office 97-107 Southampton Row, London WC1; tel 020-7436 4451; www.endsleigh.co.uk) has offices in most British towns and cities and offers several different policies depending on your age, and how long you are travelling for. Endsleigh's rates are pretty reasonable, and cheaper than those of the Post Office.

Driving Insurance

The necessity for hiring a car when in Oman and the Arabian Gulf (or to borrow one if you are lucky enough to know someone out there) is something that you will soon realise and appreciate. Many of the capital cities of the smaller states are compact enough to spend leisurely days walking around if you are visiting in the winter months. Unfortunately in the summer the region becomes unbearably hot and taking a stroll under even the early morning sun can hurt. An air-conditioned car, although not your only option for getting about, is a recommended one. Almost all prices quoted for car hire included the cost of comprehensive insurance and public liability cover. If you are planning to drive between the United Arab Emirates and Oman (the UAE has an enclave of Omani territory within it) you will need to check that your insurance covers driving between the two countries.

GETTING AROUND

BY CAR

It is very likely that you will want to hire a vehicle to get around the country or countries that you intend to visit. Bahrain is a small country and it is unlikely that you will be going anywhere within it where you would need a four-wheel drive (4WD). The country is mostly flat and the roads are good. Qatar's terrain is pretty much the same as Bahrain's, though slightly wilder in places and it may be a good idea to get hold of a 4WD for a day or so to visit the area of sand dunes in the south-east, or to explore the north-west corner of the peninsula around Zubarah. The United Arab Emirates, and especially Oman, are a different scene altogether. It is quite feasible to drive about the Emirates in a small saloon car as the network of tarmac roads is widespread and good. But if you want to explore the beautiful vastnesses of the Empty Quarter or try a bit of wadi-bashing you will need to either hire a 4WD or go as part of a tour group to these places. Both options are likely to be expensive. In Oman the road network is improving all the time but there still aren't that many miles of tarmac roads and due to the mountainous terrain of the country all of the more interesting and beautiful areas are hidden away from the main roads. It can be very frustrating to have to stick to the highways when all around you are places begging to be explored.

A word of caution. The standard of driving in the countries of the Arabian Gulf is pretty bad – scary at times, downright frightening at others. You will be overtaken and undertaken on busy highways, the hard shoulder is often used as an extra lane for bypassing any slow traffic ahead, and should you dawdle in the fast lane and get in the way of a speeding Landcruiser or sports car you are liable to at best a blast of horn and headlights, at worst aggressive intimidation tactics.

The speed limits of all these countries are fairly standard and the roads are in a generally good state but there are miles of open desert roads and speeding gets you through them quicker. Drive carefully and pay regular attention to what is going on behind as well as ahead of you, and for that matter to the left and right of you as well. Another danger to be aware of is camels wandering into the road. Often if there are camels, cows, goats or sheep grazing beside the road ahead of you the drivers of oncoming cars will hoot at you or flash their lights to warn you. If you hit a camel, because of its height it is liable to come crashing in on top of you from the roof of your car. You will be lucky to survive this and if you do, you will be expected to pay for the replacement of a dead camel – and they can be worth a great deal of money. Driving in the Arabian Gulf does take some getting used to, but at least the petrol is very cheap.

One of the amazing things that you are likely to see whilst driving are mirages, especially along the black-top tarmac roads. Ahead of you by perhaps a couple of juggernaut lengths the road will look as though there is a massive puddle covering it, then as you approach it looks as if the water in it is evaporating. Driving through the flat *sabkha* desert you may see a variation on this if there are outcrops or hills. Then these protrusions look as if they are floating above the desert.

Border Crossings

The main land border crossing that you are likely to experience is between the United Arab Emirates and Oman. There are several places where you can cross between the countries and all have slight problems with them such as being unmanned or only one side having border post facilities. See the relevant country chapters for details.

By Bus

Because there are no trains in the region buses are the main form of transport to carry people *en masse*, though more people travel by car than by bus. Distances in most of the countries described in this book are not too great and trips between towns are often covered by small Toyota minibuses which can seat about 15 people and leave the bus stations when they are full. Service taxis (often Peugeot 7-seaters) work on the same principle and may charge slightly more than the minibuses. In Oman distances are appreciatively larger and there are regular coach services between Muscat and the South. Coaches also travel between the United Arab Emirates and Oman.

CRIME AND SAFETY

The Gulf is a safe area. Relatively speaking. Unless you are foolish and decide to follow in the steps of the great explorers and wander into the desert alone you are unlikely to die of heat stroke. Jet lag is a pain but is soon over with, food is pretty good and the standard of hygiene high. Violent crime, mugging and theft are a very uncommon occurrence. The internal security services of all the Gulf countries are vigilant and unless you are very unlucky you are unlikely to be a victim of hijacking, a bomb attack or arson. The disharmony between Palestine and Israel, and the Iraqi question have little effect on day-to-day life in the Gulf States. Be extra vigilant when driving, treat the desert with as much respect as you would the sea, keep away from any animal that looks even slightly unfriendly and don't get involved in political, especially anti-government debates. It is also a bad idea to wander too near military installations and border areas, especially with a camera slung around your neck. Telling a suspicious and bored border guard that you are lost (which, in the desert, is not an uncommon occurrence) may not be believed without a bit of fact checking and detaining. Respect the laws of the land in which you are travelling. The governments of the countries in this book are actively seeking to encourage tourism and do not want to see this growing industry jeopardised. Also, in the great tradition of Arab hospitality any visitor to their country is a guest. And guests are looked after.

If you do find yourself in trouble abroad you should contact your embassy in the first instance. Embassy contact details are included in the individual country chapters.

HELP AND INFORMATION

International Dialling Codes:

When telephoning from any of the countries listed in this book include the following codes before dialling the number you require, please note that often an area code will have its initial number dropped when dialling from abroad.
United Kingdom: 00 44
USA and Canada: 00 1
Australia: 00 61
New Zealand: 00 64
South Africa: 00 27

Tourist Offices
Dubai and Bahrain are the only places in the region to have dedicated tourist offices. The country chapters of this book have details of Websites which are useful for more information about the individual countries.

Babies and Young Children
The institution of the family is sacrosanct in the Arab world and people love children in the region. If you are travelling with small children you should encounter no problems with finding anything that you may require. Many hotels offer a childminding service and the kids will be spoilt for choice of toys in the souks. The Gulf is a great place to bring up kids because of the warm weather and seas and the general outdoor life that can be led.

Gay Travellers
Homosexuality is officially illegal in the countries of the Arabian Gulf and is not condoned in Islam. Obviously homosexuality does exist in these countries as it exists everywhere else in the world. For anyone seeking others of the same persuasion Dubai is probably the best place to head for as it has the most relaxed views on drinking and dancing etc.

Disabled Travellers
Provision for disabled travellers in the Gulf is something that has yet to be tackled by the authorities in charge of access to public buildings and transport. Escalators and lifts are common but loos for the disabled and ramps are still very uncommon. Some of the top-end hotels make provision for disabled visitors by they will obviously charge you for the privilege of staying with them.

The Internet and Useful Websites
The Internet is a great invention and is a good friend to the traveller. If you want to find out about a country that you intend to visit you will find a wealth of information and propaganda on the Net. You will be able to find out news breaking in the region and read the local papers, book accommodation, buy your flight tickets, hire a car, etc. Once you are abroad you can move money around between your bank accounts back home through Internet banking and keep in touch with friends and family through e-mail. And if you begin to feel homesick you can read the news from back home. The Internet is also a vast virtual library so you never need be starved of intellectual stimuli or research material.

Not too many years ago when you went abroad you were on your own. Keeping in touch required standing in queues to make long distance telephone calls or trying to get people to understand that you wanted to buy a stamp not a box of matches. Getting letters or parcels from home meant getting hold of the address of some central post office Poste Restante in a city that you would be travelling through and hoping that the letters and missives from home would be waiting for you when you finally arrived there, tired, hot, hungry and expectant. Too often you would find that there was nothing waiting for you because it had been returned to sender. The Internet can help do away with all the uncertainly and *out-thereness* of travel. It may stop you having to really make an effort to understand the workings of the postal systems of a culture different to your own, but it is a great tool.

Luckily all the countries covered in this book have Internet cafés of varying degrees of sophistication and number and in the next year or so they will inevitably proliferate. At the time of writing the cost everywhere was around £2/$3 for an hour's Internet access, extra for a print out from the web or your own floppy disc or to use the Internet as a cheap telephone option.

If you do not have an e-mail address then get one before you go. Two of the most convenient and reliable e-mail account providers are Yahoo (which has national varieties: .com, .co.uk. etc.) and Microsoft's www.hotmail.com. If you go to their websites you can get a free e-mail account by following the simple signing up process. You will then have a means of keeping in touch with other e-mail account holders throughout the world, and have a permanent address where people can get hold of you in an emergency or to send you information, or just to say hello.

Time

Although all four countries outlined in this book look near neighbours there is a time zone between Bahrain & Qatar and the United Arab Emirates & Oman. Bahrain and Qatar are three hours ahead and Oman and the UAE are four hours ahead of Greenwich Mean Time (or Universal Co-ordinated Time – UCT – as it is now known).

USEFUL CONVERSIONS

The metric system is used throughout the countries of the Arabian Gulf. For those of you who are unsure of how imperial and metric weights and measures compare here is a guide.

Weight

To convert:
Ounces to grams multiply by 28.35
Pounds to kilograms multiply by 0.45
1 stone is equal to 6.35 kilograms
I imperial pound is equal to 0.453 kilograms

Distance

To convert:
Kilometres to miles multiply by 0.62
Miles to kilometres multiply by 1.61
Inches to centimetres multiply by 2.54
Centimetres to inches multiply by 0.39
Metres to feet multiply by 3.28
Feet to metres multiply by 0.91
Metres to yards multiply by 1.09
Yards to metres multiply by 0.91

Volume

To convert:
Litres to imperial gallons multiply by 0.22
Imperial gallons to litres multiply by 4.55
An imperial pint is 585 millilitres (just over half a litre)

Temperature

To convert:
Fahrenheit to Celsius subtract 32 then multiply by 0.55
Celsius to Fahrenheit multiply by 1.8 then add 32.

FURTHER READING

There are plenty of general books in and out of print that give an insight into the Arabia of today and yesterday. Below is a selection of books that are fairly easy to obtain and that should help make up the mind of anyone toying with the idea of visiting the Arabian Gulf. The individual country chapters also have a suggested reading section of more specific titles.

A History of the Arabs, Philip K. Hitti, Palgrave, 1960.
Arabia Through the Looking Glass, Jonathan Raban, Collins, 1979.
Beachcombers Guide to the Gulf, Tony Woodward, Motivate Publishing, 1994.
Behind the Veil in Arabia, Unni Wikan, John Hopkins University Press, 1982.
Birds of Oman, M. Gallagher & M. Woodcock, Quartet Books, 1980.
The Closed Circle, David Pryce-Jones, Weidenfeld and Nicolson, 1989.
Culture Shock! United Arab Emirates, Gina L. Crocetti, Kuperard, 1998.
Desert Driver's Manual, Jim Stabler, Stacey International, 1998.
Don't They Know it's Friday, Jeremy Williams, Motivate Publishing, 1999.
The Drinkers Guide to the Middle East, Will Lawson, Rebel Inc. 1997.
Flora of the Arabian Peninsula and Socotra Vol.1, (Ed.) A.G. Miller & T.A. Cope, Edinburgh University Press, 1996.
The Green Guide to the Emirates, Marycke Jongbloed, Motivate Publishing, 1999.
Live and Work in Saudi and the Gulf, Louise Whetter, Vacation Work, 2000.
Mammals of the Arabian Gulf, David Harrison, Allen and Unwin, 1981.
Mammals of the Southern Gulf, Christian Gross, Motivate Publishing, 1992.
The New Arabians, Peter Mansfield, J.G. Ferguson Pub. Co., 1981.
Sandstorms – Days and Nights in Arabia, Peter Theroux, W.W. Norton, 1992.
The Shell Birdwatching Guide to the United Arab Emirates, C. Richardson & S. Aspinall, Hobby Publications, 1998.

PUBLIC HOLIDAYS AND CELEBRATIONS

Most of the holidays in the Arabian Gulf are set according to the Islamic calendar rather than the Gregorian calendar that is in use throughout the West. The Islamic or Hijri calendar is based on twelve lunar months of between 29 and 30 days, and a 354 day year. The beginning of each Islamic calendar month depends on the first sighting of a new moon which means that the exact date of official holidays often shifts back between 10 and 12 days each year and the precise dates of a holiday cannot be announced until the new moon of the month has been sighted. The Islamic calendar began in 622AD, the year that the Prophet Muhammed made the migration (hejira) from Mecca to Medina. Dates in the Islamic calendar are denoted by having AH (anno hegirae) rather than AD or BC after them.

The countries of the Arabian Gulf all share the same Islamic holidays - which are calculated by the Hijri calendar - as well as secular holidays to celebrate New Year's Day and individual National and Accession Days which are calculated by the Gregorian calendar. The main Islamic holidays are:

Ras as-Sana. This is the New Year according to the Islamic calendar which celebrates the migration of the Prophet and his followers to the town of Medina from Mecca. The Islamic calendar takes its start date from the date of their arrival at Medina.

Ashura. Ashura is a day of commemoration for Shia Muslims and marks the death (martydom) of Husayn, the grandson of the Prophet and the son of Ali the spiritual leader of the Shias, at the battle of Karbala. During *Ashura* there are often processions of men in black chanting and banging drums in the streets, while the more devout of them carry out acts of self mutilation.

Mawlid an-Nabi. The Prophet's birthday. This day is generally given over to prayers and gatherings discussing religious matters.

Lailat al-Mi'raj. This is the date commemorating the night that the Prophet ascended to heaven.

Lailat al-Qadr. Occuring during Ramadan this date marks the night when Muhammed received the first revelations from the Angel Gabriel. The night is one of Quran recitations and acts of charity.

Ramadan. The month of fasting and religious contemplation begins.

Eid al-Fitr. The end of Ramadan and the start of a three-day holiday. In tone a bit like the Christian Christmas.

Eid al-Adha. The festival of the sacrifice and the culmination of the Hajj season. The celebration lasts for three days and those who can afford it sacrifice a sheep or goat.

Dates of Main Holidays and Festivals until 2005

	2001	2002	2003	2004	2005
Ras as-Sana	26 Mar	15 Mar	5 Mar	22 Feb	10 Feb
Ashura	4 Apr	24 Mar	14 Mar	2 Mar	19 Feb
Mawlid an-Nabi	4 Jun	24 May	14 May	2 May	21 April
Lailat al-Qadr	24 Dec	13 Dec	2 Dec	22 Nov	10 Nov
Ramadan begins	17 Nov	6 Nov	27 Oct	15 Oct	4 Oct
Eid al-Fitr	28 Dec	17 Dec	6 Dec	27 Nov	14 Nov
Eid al-Adha	6 Mar	23 Feb	12 Feb	2 Feb	21 Jan

Oman

Ruins of Bibi Mariyam's
Tomb, Qalhat

You can only behold beauty; never possess it. Oman is like that. It is one of the most beautiful, traditional and relaxed places in the Middle East. The country, for long considered a backwater, has been slowing coming out of its time warp to become a well-adjusted nation with its own buoyant economy and a very strong identity. Rather than rushing for wealth and worldly prestige Oman seems quite content to be itself. Visitors are welcome to come and partake in the beauty of the surroundings and the natives are very friendly, but you are expected to keep a certain distance and not to interfere too much. Tourism is a relatively new thing in Oman and although the country has been open to Arab tourists from the surrounding GCC countries for many years, foreigners from the West have only just begun to make inroads into Oman. It can be expensive to get to Oman, and the country is certainly not a cheap place to visit, but if you have the money and the time to really explore the place the memories will stick in your mind like few other destinations can. Hopefully Oman's practically untouched beauty will remain for many years to come, though somehow I doubt it. Get there soon.

GEOGRAPHY

Oman covers an area of approximately 309,500 square kilometres and has over 1,700km (about 1000 miles) of coastline, most of it pristine. The sultanate includes the Musandam Peninsula, which is separated from the rest of the country by the United Arab Emirates, and Madha – an enclave of Omani territory in the mountains of the UAE. The mainland is separated from Iran by the Gulf of Oman which, at its closest point across the Strait of Hormuz, is a mere 55km away.

To the north of the country the Batinah coast stretches from Muscat in the south to the town of Sohar, and on northwards to the border with the United Arab Emirates. This fertile plain is the breadbasket of the country and home to the majority of the population. The Batinah is separated from the interior of the country by the high, rugged – but not completely barren – Western Hajar mountain range, behind which lies al-Dhahirah, a sandy plain leading into the *Rub' al-Khali*, the Empty Quarter. A natural break in the Hajar mountain range, the Sumail Gap, links the capital city of Muscat with an inland area of mountains and wadis – the al-Dakhiliya region which, until the last decades of the 20th century, was traditionally isolated from the bustle and boom of the coastal area.

Typical Terrain, Oman

The Eastern Hajar mountains run southeast of Muscat through the ash-Sharqiya region. South of this range lies the Wahiba Sands, an isolated inland sea of orange sand dunes that run like waves north to south over an area covering 10,000 square kilometres. The coast is the home of large fishing communities, and the breeding ground of the green turtle.

The al-Wusta region, the interior of the country southwest of the Wahiba Sands, is a vast tract of rather desolate land where a lot of the oil fields are located out

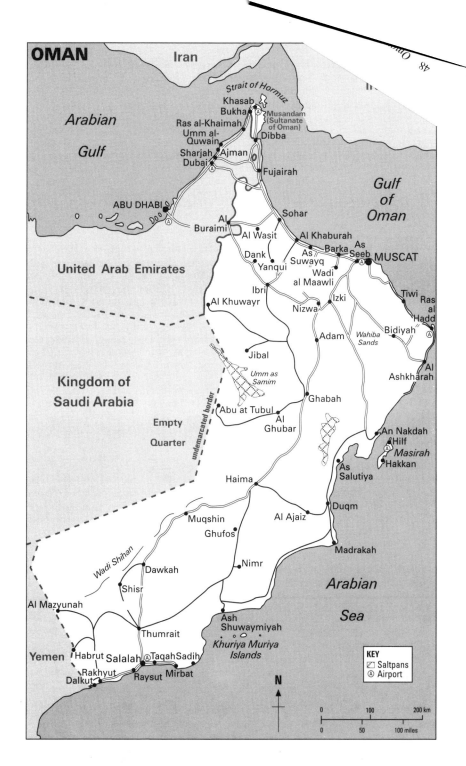

amidst blinding salt flats and featureless desert. This is one of the least touristy areas of Oman, with small fishing villages dotted along the coast and populated by more birds and animals than humans. There are very few tarmac roads in the region, and off the main highway linking Muscat and Salalah there no hotels.

Oman's secret, a place almost untouched by the West and its tourist hoards, is the area around Salalah – the Dhofar Region. Lying on the Arabian Sea, and next door to that anomaly of the Arabian Peninsula – the idiosyncratic Yemen, it is a beautifully 'big' landscape of tropical beaches backed by the Salalah plain and the three green and brown verdant mountain ranges of over 1,400 metres that rise above it.

The topography of Oman is varied and because of the way the country has developed over the last century, and the formidable terrain, much of the country remains inaccessible to the casual visitor without the use of a four-wheel drive vehicle.

CLIMATE

Because Oman is such a vast country with such differing landscapes – from the fertile Batinah coast in the north, the arid Wahiba Sands in the northeast through to tropical Dhofar in the south – climatic conditions throughout the country vary. In the north the region suffers much the same conditions as the neighbouring United Arab Emirates: hot and humid during the summer months of April to October (though the interior remains less so) and pleasantly warm and fine during the winter months of November to March. By comparison, in the south of the country around Salalah temperatures remain pleasant throughout the year. When the north is getting the worst of the midsummer heat the south is getting hit by the monsoon rains, the Khareef, which keeps the area shrouded in mist and pleasantly cool for much of the time. What rain does fall comes in January and February, quickly filling the wadis and the aflaj – the age-old system of interconnected channels that supply water to the villages and the plantations.

HISTORY

Ancient History

Man has inhabited Oman from the third millennium BC, establishing routes through the interior up into the present day United Arab Emirates and the coastal settlements of Abu Dhabi. Oman is believed to be the land of Magan, a civilisation that grew wealthy through the mining and exporting of copper, with its base at the port of Sohar on the Batinah coast.

The founder of the Persian empire, Cyrus the Great, conquered Oman in the 4th century BC and brought the invention of the falaj – the system of water channels that have irrigated the land and watered the inhabitants ever since. In the south of the country the Dhofar region produced vast quantities of incense that were used in religious ceremonies and shipped from the port of Sumhuram, close to Salalah to the lands in the north. In the 2nd century AD the great dam of Marib in Yemen collapsed and as the surrounding cultivated land was destroyed by flooding many of the inhabitants moved eastwards into Oman. From the north came Arabs from the Nejd and Nizamis from Iraq.

Islam came to Oman in about 630AD, when the Prophet Muhammed sent Amr Ibn al-As to convert the ruling family. Oman was one of the first places in the world to embrace Islam. After the death of the Prophet in 632AD Omanis moved towards the Ibadi doctrine of Islam rather than the Sunni. Ibadis stress the importance in the community electing the most suitable spiritual leader (Imam) rather than having to give the job to a descendant of the Prophet. The sect arose out of the split that formed in Islam after the death of the Phophet. Sunnis accepted a dynastic leadership of the Muslim community while the Shias (followers of Ali, the Prophet's cousin) believe that the Iman should be elected from within the tribe should he possess the right qualities. When Ali agreed to peace talks with the leaders of the Sunnis a further split occurred among the Shias and the Khawarij (the dissenters) broke from the party and based themselves in Iraq. Further splits occurred within this sect and the moderate Ibadis eventually ended up in Oman, occasionally having to go underground to protect themselves from persecution.

Colonisation

During the 10th century Sohar was one of the most important cities in the Arab world – it was from here that Sindbad is meant to have lived and begun his adventures.

The Portuguese arrived in the area in 1507 when a fleet commanded by Albuquerque sailed around the Strait of Hormuz and realised what a great boon it would be to control the region and protect their supply lines to all areas east. They established bases in Sohar, Qalhat and Muscat, building the two great forts Mirani and Jalali, that remain on either side of today's al-Alam Palace. But Portuguese influence never extended into the interior where the Imams held power. Nasir Murshid al-Yaarubi was appointed Imam in 1624 and he set out to expel the Portuguese, which he managed to do. By the time of his death in 1649 the Portuguese presence was limited to Mutrah and Muscat and during the rule of his cousin Sultan bin Saif the Portuguese were not only driven out of Oman but were on the run – followed by the fleet of Imam Sultan who took control of Portuguese territories in East Africa, most notably Mombassa and Zanzibar.

Renaissance

This period of Oman's history is often considered a time of renaissance. It was certainly a time of great wealth. The great fort at Nizwa was built during the time of the Yaarubi dynasty along with Jabreen Fort. It was a time of trade involving gold, slaves and ivory from Africa; rice and spices from India; cloth from Surat, dates and coconuts from Dhofar. The Omanis already had trading links as far as China. But by the early 18th century the Yaarubi dynasty's power was waning and a period of economic decline led to a civil war breaking out in 1718 between the two major tribes – the Hinawi and the Ghafiri. To stop the war the Shah of Persia was invited into the country by the then Imam Sultan bin Saif II. Persian troops helped to quell the war, and then began a policy of occupation imposing taxes on the towns they occupied and demanding tributes to the Shah. Sultan bin Saif II's rule was short lived and when the last of the Yaarubi dynasty was dead and the Persian's were still occupying parts of Oman, it was a descendant of the present Sultan who managed to unite the Omanis and drive the Persians out for the last time.

The al-Bu Said Dynasty

Ahmed bin Said al-Bu Said was Governor of Sohar during the time of the Persian occupation but after defending the town from the Persian advance he continued to liberate the country, driving the last Persians from the country in 1747. He was elected Imam and built up the Omani navy and also helped expel the Persians from Basra in what is now Iraq.

Ahmed was succeeded by his son Said who, though interested in the religious aspects of the Imamate, was not too concerned about the political nature of the post. Said continued to live in the town of Rustaq in the interior but appointed his son Hamid as 'Wali' (governor). It was Hamid who moved the capital city to Muscat, so beginning the Muscat and Oman divide and the split between the rule of the spiritual Imam and that of the political Sultan. Hamid died in 1792 and his uncle Sayyid

Sultan bin Ahmed ruled until 1802 when he was killed at sea fighting the Qawasim of Ras al-Khaimah.

Sultan was succeeded by his son Said, who was to rule from 1804-1856. It was during Said's reign that an Omani envoy sailed to New York in 1840, establishing the first diplomatic links of any Arab country with the United States. Said was popular and strong, developing the country's economy and establishing diplomatic links with the Netherlands, France, Britain and America. He took a renewed interest in the African possessions and during the latter part of his reign spent an increasing amount of time there. He built a modern capital in Zanzibar and introduced the hugely successful cash crop of cloves. In 1838 he sent a mission to Queen Victoria's coronation in Britain. During Said's reign the Omani dominions reached their zenith with Dhofar being incorporated into the territory in 1829. In 1845 Said signed an agreement with the British effectively banning the trade of slavery in any of his dominions.

A Period of Uncertainty

At the end of Said's 52-year reign his two sons split the Sultanship with the eldest – Thuwaini – governing Muscat and Oman while his brother Majid took control of Zanzibar. In 1866 Thuwaini was killed while attacking the Saudi Wahhabis at Buraimi and a period of political uncertainty followed during the reign of his successor Sayyid Turki who died in 1888. Turki was succeeded by his second son Faisal, whose rule was characterised by continuing inter-tribal fighting in the interior.

When Faisal's son Taimur was proclaimed Sultan in Muscat on the death of his father in 1913 a new Imam was elected in the interior in defiance of the Sultan. In 1915 the Imam's forces expelled the Sultan's army from Nizwa, Izki and Sumail and approached the gates of Muscat before being eventually driven back by a British force of Baluchi soldiers. Finally the Imam was persuaded to reach a settlement with the Sultan in 1920 with the signing of the Treaty of Seeb, which allowed free movement between the interior and the coast and non-interference of the Sultan in the internal affairs of the tribes of the interior. An uneasy peace ensued. Taimur, always a reluctant Sultan, abdicated in 1932 and was succeeded by his son Said.

Sultan Said inherited a country divided and deeply in debt. Though his rule has always been associated with a time in Oman's history of harsh petty rules and financial hardship, a time when Oman was considered the hermit of the Arabian Peninsula, Said did get the country out of debt.

Modern Oman

Following World War II oil exploration in Oman began in earnest. Meanwhile the Saudis were occupying the area around Buraimi and the Imamate was trying to establish an independent state based around Nizwa in the Interior. Negotiations with Saudi Arabia broke down but under pressure from the Sultan's forces and the Trucial Oman Scouts the Saudis eventually withdrew from Buraimi in 1955. The Sultan gained a foothold in the interior but the Imamate continued their rebellion until they were eventually defeated in 1959.

With the power of the Imamate broken the Sultan had control of the entire country but instead of consolidating his rule he withdrew to his palace in Salalah. From there he continued his autocratic style of rule, disallowing anything that smacked of the western world and forbidding government expenditure. The gates of Old Muscat were locked daily at sunset and even when oil came on stream in 1967 the Sultan remained unchangeable. All of this helped to bring about the Dhofar rebellion.

In July 1970 Sultan Said's son, Qaboos, staged a palace coup and took over the reins of power. Said had been pursuing an almost medieval and isolationist mode of rule for too many years and with the British decision to pull out of the Gulf, and the increasing revenues from oil, it was felt by many that it was time for Oman to enter the present. Sultan Qaboos immediately set about a policy of change following the example of the neighbouring sheikdoms. Using oil revenues he built educational, health and welfare services, programmes of economic expansion and modernised the justice system. The country for long known as Oman and Muscat became the Sultanate of Oman, joining the Arab League and the United Nations in 1971.

The Dhofar Rebellion

Many of the inhabitants of Dhofar region are not Arabs but members of the *Jebali* tribes who originated from Yemen. A dissatisfaction at the lack of any progressive development in the region sanctioned by Sultan Said bin Taimir led the *Jebali* tribesmen to form the Dhofar Liberation Front (DLF) in about 1962. Many of the *Jebalis* had already been employed in the new oil-rich Gulf States and had come into contact with Arab Nationalism and Marxist theories. In June 1965 the DLF ambushed and attacked lorries belonging to an oil company and the rebellion began.

The DLF had grown out of the Dhofar Charitable Association which had been set up to provide help for the poor of the area and to build mosques – though members were generally anti-Sultan and anti-British. The DLF has previously attacked oil company vehicles in 1963 and training was carried out in Iraq. There was backing for the rebellion by President Nasser of Egypt, the South Yemen National Liberation Front and later the communist countries of China and Russia.

From June 1965 the Sultan's forces were permanently deployed in Dhofar maintaining control of the only road over Jebal Qara linking Salalah with the rest of Oman. In April 1966 the British became involved in the conflict when DFL members of the Sultan's bodyguard staged an assassination attempt. By 1967 the two sides were at stalemate. Britain pressed the Sultan to make political concessions but without success.

With the withdrawal of British troops from Aden in South Yemen in 1967 the DLF now had a secure base in pro-Marxist South Yemen from which to operate, with arms being supplied by Russia and China through the port of Aden. The original tribal force fighting for a better living and infrastructure were now more of a Marxist-Leninist movement and adopted the name of the Popular Front for the Liberation of the Occupied Arab Gulf (PFLOAG) with a core force of about 2,000 men and another 4,000 armed supporters. They also had the support of the vast majority of the *Jebali* people who saw the Sultan's forces as an army of occupation. By 1969 the rebels controlled the whole of Dhofar region except for a heavily guarded Salalah (where the Sultan had a palace). In June 1970 a second rebellion was attempted in the Nizwa area by a group calling themselves the National Democratic Front. The group was quickly quashed.

In July 1970 the Sultan was deposed by his son – the present Sultan – who set about radically reforming the country. Sultan Qaboos built schools and hospitals, released prisoners and offered an amnesty for rebels who would give up their arms. Aid from Britain was increased and a force of SAS troops was sent to Dhofar to help deal with the rebels. In September 1970 the rebel leader Musalam bin Nufl surrendered, with many of the remaining rebels following his lead. These men were formed into *Firqah* units of about 100 men from individual tribes. They were well armed and well paid, trained by the SAS to seek out their former comrades.

In the same year the first of a series of guarded compounds was set up providing aid and services such as schools and clinics to *Jebalis* throughout the region in a bid to end the conflict through providing the services that had sparked off the original rebellion. However, skirmishes between the two sides continued, culminating in the attack on government forces in the coastal village of Mirbat in July 1972. Then, with help and support from Jordan and Iran, the Sultan managed to establish control of the region, driving the rebels back into South Yemen. Finally in December 1975 the Sultan was able to declare the rebellion crushed. Later he offered amnesty to most of the former rebels.

POLITICS

There are only two sultanates in the world and one of them is Oman (the other is Brunei). Oman is an absolute monarchy which means that the Sultan has the final say on what happens in his country. He rules by royal decree and is the minister of defence, foreign affairs and finance. He also appoints and dismisses members of his Diwan (somewhat similar to the Cabinet). There are eight governorates, or distinct regions, in Oman within which are a number of *wilayats* looked after by a *wali* or governor. Prominent citizens from each *wilayah* are elected to sit on a consultative council – the *Majlis ash-Shura* – which, though it has no legislative power, does advise on local economic and development issues. Every January the Sultan tours the country to meet with the inhabitants of the different governorates to listen to problems and situations. Political reform has been slow but the system so far has worked admirably.

The Constitution, which outlines the obligations of the state such as providing healthcare, education, security and the rights of its citizens, was promulgated in November 1996. The law in Oman is a mixture of the Muslim Sharia law and modern legal thought.

THE ECONOMY

Agriculture

Agriculture has always been an important aspect of the economy of Oman, employing a large number of nationals. It has allowed a certain amount of self-sufficiency in the production of foodstuffs and fuel. However, water is scarce and whereas the ancient falaj system regulated water usage and tempered production, with the advent of machinery and water pumping systems consumption has increased to a point where the water table along the coast is increasingly saline. Omani dates and limes are world-renowned.

Fishing. Fishing, that other stalwart of the economy, continues as it has done for millennia though most of it is localised and fishermen rarely roam too far offshore.

Oil

Oil has accounted for 30 per cent of GDP since 1980 but reserves are limited and expected to run out in the next 17 years if extracted at the present rate. However, natural gas has been found in large quantities and further exploration of the country is likely to turn up further oil reserves. As in most of the Gulf countries, diversification is on the lips of the strategists and Oman has set up a number of industrial areas and is keen to develop other ways to bring money into the country. The new port at Raysut, 10km outside Salalah and soon to be one of the largest transhipment container terminals in the world, will take advantage of the fact that it is on a major trade route. The government also wants to build a free-trade zone by the port to attract foreign businesses to invest in and to use Oman as a base for their Asia, Middle East and Africa operations.

Tourism

Oman received 503,000 tourists in 1999, most of them coming from the GCC countries. The government is keen to promote the country as a tourist destination but it is also keen to attract only those that it considers to be the right kind of tourist – the affluent rather than impecunious backpackers. The government is also wary of a flood of tourists tearing up the countryside and invading the privacy of the traditionally conservative tribes of the interior.

THE PEOPLE

The majority of Omanis are Ibadi Muslims – including the ruling family – and most others are Sunni Muslims. In Muscat especially, there are small populations of Shia Muslims originally from Iran and it is estimated that about a quarter of the population are Hindus. Unlike the other Gulf States an Omani national does not necessarily have to be a Muslim and there are several prominent Hindu families and descendants of Zanzibarian slaves who live and work in Oman enjoying all the benefits that being a national of the country entitles one to.

The character of Oman, the relaxed and friendly nature of the place, is affected by the topography of the country, the racial and tribal mix of the population with Zanzibarians, descendents of freed slaves, Persians and Indian merchants and the huge numbers of expats who have come to work in the country since the early days of Sultan Qaboos' reign. The population of Oman is estimated at around 2.33 million. Of this figure about 1.7 million are Omani nationals and 600,000 are non-nationals brought into the country to work. A staggering 50 per cent of Omanis are under 20 years old.

Guest Workers. As elsewhere in the Gulf the guest workers and expats are made up of populations from the English-speaking countries of the West as well as those from the Indian Subcontinent, Iran and South East Asia.

Making Friends

Oman is a large country with a small laidback population. Of all the countries in the Arabian Gulf Oman is one of the friendliest. The tourism trade is still in its infancy in Oman and you will be a seen as something of a novelty. Literacy rate is high and many Omanis speak English and a trip into the souks is never going to be the somewhat harrowing experience with hustlers that it can be in the poorer countries of the Middle East. If you can get an introduction to an Omani family before you leave then this can be a fascinating and privileged experience and you will see things that not even those long serving expats get to see.

FURTHER READING

Arabian Sands, Wilfred Thesiger, Longmans 1959.
Maverick Guide to Oman, Peter Ochs II, Pelican, 1998.
Muscat and Oman, Ian Skeet, Faber, 1974.
Oman: A Comprehensive Guide, Hatim al-Taie (Ed.), al-Roya Publishing, 1999.
Oman: A MEED Practical Guide, John Whelan (Ed.), MEED, 1984.
Oman and the United Arab Emirates, Lou Callan and Gordon Robison, Lonely Planet Publications, 2000.
Oman and the UAE: Insight Guide, Dorothy Stannard (Ed.), APA Publications, 1999.
Sultan in Oman, James Morris, Faber, 1957.
The Sindbad Voyage, Tim Severin, Hutchinson, 1982.
Travels in Oman, Philip Ward, Oleander Press, 1986.
Where Soldiers Fear to Tread, Ranulph Feinnes, Hodder and Stoughton, 1975.

PRACTICAL INFORMATION

Red Tape

Passports

You will need a full ten-year passport to enter Oman. Make sure that your passport has enough space left in it for immigration purposes (expect the officials to use a couple of pages for your visa and entry/exit stamps). A passport holder with evidence of a visit to Israel in their passport is likely to incur problems while travelling in the Arab world and is advised to get a new, clean passport before leaving home. Although Oman is one of the few countries of the Middle East that does not forbid you from entering the country if you have visited Israel it is always best to err on the side of caution when dealing with Middle Eastern bureaucrats.

VISAS

Apart from nationals of the other Gulf Co-operation States (Saudi Arabia, Bahrain, Qatar, the United Arab Emirates and Kuwait) all visitors need to acquire a visa to enter the Sultanate of Oman.

For UK passport holders a single entry visa allowing a stay of 21 days with a three month validity costs £40, a multiple entry visa with a six month validity costs £54, while a multiple entry visa with a year's validity costs £60. In exceptional cases a multiple entry visa with a two year validity can be obtained for £80. British visitors can apply for visas in person 9.30am-12.30pm, Monday to Friday at the embassy in London, or by completing a visa application form by post. The application form asks that you provide evidence of sufficient funds for your trip, either a letter from your employer or a recent bank or building society statement. If you intend visiting Dubai before heading to Oman you can apply for a visa at the Embassy of Oman there where this evidence is not a requirement. You will also be required to give details of which border you will be entering the country by. This is easy if you are simply flying in and out of the country through Seeb International Airport (the main airport located close to Muscat) but if you are going to be arriving overland there are several different border points between Oman and the UAE, the main one taken by travellers between Dubai and Oman being at Hatta, while if you are driving from Abu Dhabi the entry point is several kilometres past al-Ain and Buraimi at Hafit.

It is a good idea to type out the details asked for on the application form because if the officials can't read your writing they may very well delay your application. If you are a British citizen and are going to be travelling around the Gulf for several months before heading to Oman it is probably a good idea to get your Omani visa in Dubai.

For nationals of Austria, Belgium, France, Germany, Greece, Italy, Luxembourg, the Netherlands, Portugal and Spain a single entry visa allowing a stay of 21 days and valid for one month costs £14; a multiple entry visa valid for 6 months costs £24.

US citizens can apply for a single entry visa with a stay of 21 days which is valid for one month and costs £24. A multiple entry visa with two years' validity costs £40.

All other nationalities not listed above are eligible for a single entry visa with one month's validity allowing a stay of 21 days at a cost of £14. All will need to show either a letter from an employer confirming employment, or evidence of funds available for the trip (last bank or building society statement).

A joint UAE and Oman visa is available but only to groups. You should apply to the nearest Omani embassy for details.

Visa Extensions
Visa extensions are possible depending on your reasons for wanting to stay on in the country. As with all things in the Middle East there are no hard and fast rules as to any decision made on such an application. To extend your visa present yourself at the *Immigration and Passports Directorate* (tel 699 785) located in the al-Khuwair district of Muscat with your passport.

Immigration
Omani immigration officials are some of the most gentlemanly officials in the Arab world. They are efficient but thorough and your luggage will be searched for contraband whether you are entering the country by air or by land.

Customs
If you are arriving by air you are allowed to bring into the country the usual litre of spirits and 300 cigarettes but narcotics, weapons and all things pornographic are forbidden. However, you are not allowed to import liquor if you are coming into the country overland. Videos and DVDs may be taken by customs officers to be censored and will be returned after about a week. The same applies to any literature though to be of a seditious or salacious nature.

ONWARD TRAVEL
If you are flying in and out of Oman through Seeb International Airport you should find no difficulty getting in or out of the country although there is a departure tax of OR3. Going overland between Oman and the United Arab Emirates you may have difficulty if you enter by one frontier and leave by another. There is also a border post with Yemen but the erratic political climate of this area means that you can never be sure whether the post is open or closed. Also, there is no public transport between the two countries and hitchhiking though the tribal areas of Yemen is not advisable. Most of the major international airlines have offices in Muscat so onward travel from Oman should not be a problem.

OMANI EMBASSIES AND CONSULATES ABROAD
Britain: Embassy of the Sultanate of Oman, 167 Queen's Gate, London SW7 5HE (tel 0891-600 567).
South Africa: Export House 3rd Floor, corner Maude and West Streets, Johannesburg 2196 (tel 11-8840 999; fax 11-883 6569).
USA: Oman Embassy (deals with visitors from the USA or Canada), 2535 Belmont Road, NW, Washington, DC 20008 (tel 202-387 1980; fax 202-745 4933).
There are no Omani Embassies in Australia, New Zealand or Canada. Contact details for Omani embassies in the other Gulf states are listed in the individual country chapters.

Money The history of a country's currency can be a fascinating one and Oman is no exception. Through the ages it has used several different forms of currency including the Austrian Maria Theresa Dollar, the Venetian Ducat, the Larin, the Indian Rupee, the Anna and until the minting of the Omani Riyal in 1974 the Sa'idi Riyal, named after the ruling Sa'idi family, was the official currency. The Omani Riyal is linked to the US Dollar and the official rate is £1=OR0.53 ie 535 baizas and $1=OR0.38, 384 baizas. There is no restriction on the amount of currency you bring in to or take out of the country.

Notes and Coins

The Omani Riyal (OR), which is divided into 1000 baizas. Notes come in OR$^{1}/_{2}$, 1, 5, 10, 20 and OR50. You may also find a few OR$^{1}/_{4}$ notes knocking about though these are now no longer minted. There are baiza notes in denominations of 100 and 200. You will probably deal more in notes than coins during your stay but the baiza coins come in denominations of 5, 10, 25, and 50. Keep hold of the lower denomination bills for paying for rides around town in the minibuses and taxis, and for snacks.

Exchange

If you have decided to bring large quantities of cash or travellers cheques to spend during your time in Oman you will generally get a better rate of exchange from moneychangers than from the banks. Even between moneychangers rates do vary but not by a great deal and although they are open longer hours than banks, unless you are a student of economics it is going to be a waste of time to wander about checking rates of exchange.

Travellers' Cheques

Travellers' cheques are a safe way to carry money but with the lack of crime in Oman you could stick to bringing in cash or better still rely on credit and cash cards. If you do decide to take travellers cheques it is better to use *American Express* or *Thomas Cook* brands as the issuers of these brands have offices throughout the Gulf and they are recognised worldwide.

Banks

Banks are open from 8am-noon Saturday to Wednesday and from 8-11.30am on Thursdays. They are closed on Fridays. If you need to change money on a Friday the larger hotels and the moneychangers will be able to help you.

Credit and Charge Cards

Visa, MasterCard, Diners Club, American Express and many other credit cards are accepted all over the country, in the larger shops (and even some of the smaller ones) and the main hotels. Though outside Muscat cash will be far more useful than a card.

ATMs

HSBC, the *National Bank of Oman* and *Bank Muscat* are all linked to the Global Access network. ATMs are common around Muscat and there is almost always at least a National Bank of Oman ATM in all towns outside Muscat. That said, you should always keep enough cash on you in case of emergencies.

Tipping and Taxes

An annoying extra charge added on to all restaurant and hotel bills is the assorted taxes that are levied both on you and the establishment that is issuing the bill. You will be charged an extra eight per cent service tax, a four per cent tourism tax and a five per cent municipality tax on top of the stated price. That said, the person who serves you in the restaurant or hotel will not be getting any of this and so should you want to tip then do so.

COSTS

Oman isn't a cheap place to visit, and the government is looking to actively promote the country as a five star holiday destination. The cheapest way to get about the country would be to hitchhike and camp and doing so is perfectly feasible in the winter months. You would get to see the country from a ground up point of view and you would meet far more locals than anyone travelling as part of a tour group or in a hire car would do. If you can speak Arabic as well, so much the better. However, a tourist visa to Oman only allows you to stay in the country for three weeks at a time and unless you are a phenomenally proficient hitchhiker it is unlikely that you would get to see all that there is to see in Oman. You would also have to stick to the main roads of which there are relatively few.

Because a lot of the real sights – the dramatic landscapes – of Oman demand something a little more robust than a Toyota Tercel saloon car or its equivalent to get to them this necessitates the costly hire of either a four-wheel drive vehicle (4WD) or joining a tour. Both of these options don't come cheap and will account for a large proportion of your budget. There is a certain amount of cheap public transport available between the main towns but using it always limits the places that you can get to.

If you drink alcohol a pint of beer in a hotel bar often costs nearly twice the price of an English pint. The good news is that you can eat pretty cheaply and the food in Oman is very varied and a bargain.

Communications TELEPHONES

The national telecommunications network is run by *Omantel* which runs an efficient service throughout the Sultanate. You will find phone card telephone booths all over the country and you can buy cards which come in denominations of OR1, 3 and 5 from kiosks, cold stores (small grocery stores) and supermarkets throughout Oman. There is also a public telephone office with fax, telex and telegram services at the *Central Telegraph Office* on Ruwi High Street in Muscat and another in Salalah.

Charges. Cheap rates on phone calls apply from 10pm-7am daily and all day on Friday and public holidays.

Mobiles. You will need a roving facility on your mobile for it to be able to pick up signals in Oman. Contact your network provider before you leave for the Gulf.

Numbers

The country code for Oman is +968 followed by the six-digit number. If you are dialling a local number you do not need to use the country code. There are no area or city codes in Oman. To dial direct to the UK from Oman dial 00 44 followed by the area code leaving out the initial 0 of that code. To dial direct to the USA from Oman dial 00 1 followed by the area code.

Directories

If you are staying in a hotel the reception desk will be able to provide you with a telephone directory. Directories are in English and Arabic but only give telephone numbers and PO Box numbers of businesses rather than the actual address of a place.

Operator Services

For **emergency services dial 999.** For local directory enquiries call 198 and for international directory enquiries call 143. There is also a local news service which can be contacted by dialling 1106.

Calls from Hotels

If you use the telephone in your hotel room do not be surprised if your final bill comes to a lot more than you reckoned. Added extras in hotels will always bump up the cost of a room and using the telephone is a great way to incur extra charges.

Dial a Service

Home deliveries aren't such a big feature of life in Oman yet as they are in Bahrain or the United Arab Emirates. Some restaurants do also offer a home delivery service and your hotel is likely to have the telephone numbers of several that do.

POST

The postal system in Oman is pretty dependable but rather slow. You should allow two weeks for delivery both into and out of the country. If you want to send something urgently then either fax documents or use one of the courier companies. If you are sent a package while in Oman it is likely that it will be opened by customs to check its contents to make sure that it doesn't contain any material that is deemed to be against the laws of the state.

Post Offices

The main post offices are open from 8am-1pm and again from 4-7pm Monday to Wednesday with early closing at 11am on Thursdays. It is advisable to post mail from the main post office mail boxes as it will get dealt with quicker than if you drop post into one of the yellow post boxes dotted around the towns and villages.

Mail Collection

Mail gets delivered to private post office boxes. If you need a postal address during your stay use that of your hotel or get stuff sent to you c/o Poste Restante, Ruwi Central Post Office, Muscat, 112, Oman.

Courier Companies

There are several courier firms operating in Muscat. Try the *DHL* office (Rumaila 106, Sultan Qaboos Street; tel 563 599), or *Federal Express* (Sinau House, Ruwi, Muscat; tel 793 311).

E-Mail and the Internet

The Internet is catching on in Oman but isn't as widely available throughout the country yet as it is elsewhere in the Gulf. There are several Internet cafés in Muscat and a couple in Salalah. Elsewhere the upmarket hotels are likely to have business centres where you should be able to access the web.

THE MEDIA

Television

Oman's single television station broadcasts mainly in Arabic though there is a news programme in English broadcast nightly at 8pm. Occasionally it will also show English-language films. Most hotel rooms have satellite television showing the usual mixture of multinational films, Egyptian, Syrian and Lebanese Soaps, 24-hour news channels and Asian MTV.

Video

Videos and increasingly DVDs can be bought and hired in Oman though the content will have been censored. Prices are cheaper than back home but the film you get may be shorter than its normal length due to the snipping of the censors' scissors.

Radio Frequencies

Radio Sultanate of Oman transmits a regular diet of international music, news and cultural programmes in English from 7am-10pm daily on 90.4FM. You may also be able to pick up radio stations from Dubai which offer rather more up to date music and the *BBC World Service* can be picked up at certain times of the day on AM or on short wave. Frequencies for BBC World Service and programme schedules can be found at www.bbc.co.uk/worldservice.

Newspapers and Magazines

The two English-language newspapers in Oman are the *Times of Oman* and the *Oman Daily Observer*, both of which report pretty much the same news. You will also find newspapers published elsewhere in the Gulf such as *Gulf News* and the *Khaleej Times* from the UAE. English language newspapers and magazines are easily found in Muscat but are less abundant in Oman's second city, Salalah. Outside of these two centres you will have difficulty getting hold of anything written in English. Newspapers and magazines from Europe, America etc., can be found in Muscat but they will be several days old and pricey.

There are a couple of good magazines which are produced locally and are well worth buying in order to get a feel for what is going on in Oman. The bi-monthly magazine *Oman Today* costs OR1 and includes listings, forthcoming events, features and articles about places to visit in Oman and abroad. *Adventure Oman* is a quarterly costing OR1.5 and has articles written by local expats about the country and their adventurous sporting activities within it. It also has articles on serious conservation issues and a listings section. Another magazine worth buying if you can find it is *What's On*, a glossy monthly magazine produced by Motivate Publishing in Dubai which covers the Emirates as well as Oman and costs OR1.2.

Maps

The most detailed maps of Oman are those produced by the *National Survey Authority* which at present cover Oman, Salalah and greater Muscat. Their only drawback is that they are large and bulky. The *Apex Map* of Oman is available in bookshops in Muscat but is more of a gazetteer than a map and pricey. The maps that you will find in Britain such as the *Geoprojects* map of Oman (published in 1983) are quite old. However, there are several tourist maps produced by the local publishing house *Al Roya*, which cover Oman, greater Muscat, Dhofar and Salalah which are relatively cheap and useful though not to scale.

Place Names

Because of the perils of transliteration of Arabic into English you will find that in Oman, as in all Arab countries, that names of places, and people, may be spelt several different ways. Unless you read Arabic it is difficult to tell which English spelling sounds closest to the original Arabic word. Names on maps may be spelt differently to how they are pronounced by locals, and often the official name of a street will have been subsumed over the years by that used by the locals.

Arrival and Departure

If you are flying to Oman you will arrive at Seeb International Airport, which is about 40km outside Muscat. There are several land borders between Oman and the

United Arab Emirates and you should enter and exit the country through the border that you put on your original visa application form. The main border crossings between the two countries are at Hatta and Hafit in the UAE. There are coach services running between Muscat and Dubai/Abu Dhabi.

There are no frontiers between Oman and Saudi Arabia and Oman and Yemen that are feasible for the foreign visitor to cross without formidable bureaucracy.

Moving around Oman is easy enough as the roads are in a good state and there are coach, minibus and service taxis to practically all the main towns. However, you will need to explore off road to really appreciate the isolation and vast interior of the country. There are no railways in Oman, which is a great shame considering the distance between Muscat and Salalah.

BY AIR

Oman Air has domestic flights travelling daily between Muscat and Salalah. The flight takes about 90 minutes. There are also several flights a week between Muscat and Sur (30 minutes), Muscat and Khasab in the Musandam peninsula (1 hour) and between Sur and Masirah Island (1 hour). Flights can be booked through the Oman Air office which can be telephoned while in Oman on 707 222 or through travel agents.

Reservations

You should reconfirm any flight that you have booked about 72 hours before the flight is due to depart. Overbooking seems to be a common feature among the airlines operating locally and for *Gulf Air* flights reconfirmation is essential.

Airports

Seeb International Airport is the main gateway into Oman for international visitors. Though small it handles flights daily from all over the world and houses a bank, a restaurant and a duty free shop (though if you are visiting Dubai you should get your duty free purchases there as there is more choice).

BY ROAD

BUS

The *Oman National Transport Company* (tel 590 046) run coaches between the major towns in the country. In Muscat the bus terminal is on al-Jaame Street in Ruwi, which is also the ONTC hub. ONTC bus stops are recognizable by the red and green signs with a gazelle motif. A coach between Muscat and Salalah costs OR7 (£13/$18) one way, takes about 12 hours and stops three times in Adam, Haima and Thumrait all of which are in the middle of the flat desert and have small tea shops and restaurants but little else. It is worth taking the coach on this occasion rather than flying just to experience the monotonous vastness of the middle of Oman; and the stars seen in the desert shine the most bright.

ONTC also run coaches between Muscat and Dubai/Abu Dhabi at a cost of OR6. The journey takes five hours.

If the ONTC buses are full you needn't be stranded. *Gulf Transport Company* (tel 790 823) also run buses between the major destinations in Oman. They have offices in Ruwi near the main bus terminal and in Salalah and Nizwa and charge the same as ONTC.

Bus Types

There are small buses and larger coaches running between the main towns of Oman operated by the Oman National Transport Company. The other type of communal bus service is the 15-seater microbuses that run throughout the country screeching to a halt by the side of the road to pick up anyone who flags them down. You need to tell the driver your proposed destination and if he is going your way he'll let you know. Microbuses are cheap and an excellent way to mingle with locals.

TAXI
The orange and white taxis that cruise the streets and gather at taxi ranks can either be hired on an individual basis or as shared long-distance taxis. Depending on your destination a driver may offer to take you there as a single passenger or drive around looking for other passengers wanting to go in the same direction. You will need to negotiate what kind of a ride you are taking and unless the driver speaks English this can be a depressingly confusing conversation to embark upon.

Taxi Fares
The orange and white taxis are numerous in Muscat and Salalah though less so in other towns. They will often hoot at you in the hope that you need a ride. At present it is not mandatory for taxis to use meters and so you will need to either agree the price to your destination before you get in the cab or be ready to argue over the fare asked once you arrive. Muscat is not really small enough to walk around and if you are staying in the suburbs of Qurum, al-Khuwair or Madinat as-Sultan Qaboos you will need to take taxis or minibuses into the centre of town. A taxi between Qurum and Ruwi will cost you around OR2 (£3.70/$5.20) which isn't cheap. A cheaper and more exciting way of doing the same journey is to take the minibuses that speed up and down the highway connecting Ruwi to Seeb Airport and beyond to Sohar. The main minibus terminals are at the Seeb Roundabout and on either side of the roundabout at the top of al-Jaame Street in Ruwi. Most trips between Ruwi and Qurum, or Ruwi and Mutrah will cost you 200 baiza. You can also use radio taxis. *Bid Bid Taxis* are available 24 hours a day by calling 693 377, another such service is *ad-Dar Taxis* (tel 700 555).

HITCHHIKING
A good way to get out and see things that you might normally miss when passing through in the cocoon-like sphere of your hire car is to do a spot of hitchhiking. You will be forced into interaction with the locals and due to the hospitality of the Arabs may very well be invited to stay with a family and get a real insight into the traditional way of life in Oman. If you are driving a hire car you will see quite a number of hitchhikers – often Asians who are moving around the country, locals and out in the desert Bedouin on short trips to market. Give them a lift.

JOINING A TOUR
Tour companies do good business in Oman and they are a necessity for tourists due to the harsh terrain of the country. Most are based out of Muscat though there are a couple of local companies running in Salalah and Sur and they all offer the same kind of experience: historical tours, dhow cruises, city tours, desert camping and wadi-bashing. Tour companies can also help arrange tours to suit the individual and all are relatively expensive if you are on your own or travelling in a small group. The tour leaders are a mix of local guides and foreigners who have lived in the country for some time, fallen in love with the landscape and have found a way to continue to explore and share their knowledge of the place.

Two locally produced magazines *Adventure Oman* and *Oman Today* have details of a number of other tour operators with their contact details and what they offer. All the operators below have offices in Muscat.

Tour Companies:

Mark Tours (tel 562 444; fax 565 434; e-mail marktour@omantel.net.om) offer tailor made trips out to the interior led by an American, Peter Ochs II, the author of the Maverick Guide to Oman, who has been running tours in Oman for years.

Oman Travel and Tourism Bureau (tel 701 085) offer day trips and may have special deals on full packages at certain times of the year.

Orient Holidays (tel 567 785) offer different excursions every day of the week.

Oriental Oryx Tours (tel 771 1619; fax 771 1620; www.omanoryxtours.net) offer several tours including trips to Nizwa, Rustaq, the Wahiba Sands and wadi bashing. Typically, a full day's trip around the interior in a saloon car will cost OR40 (£75/$104) while a day's wadi or dune bashing is going to cost about OR80. These prices are per vehicle which can seat four people. Additionally they can organise a ten-seater launch for a dolphin watching cruise for OR120 (£224/$312). Check their website for the latest costs.

Zubair Tours (tel 708 081) offer tours to all points in Oman and have offices in Ruwi and the al-Bustan Hotel.

DRIVING

CAR HIRE

There are no two ways about it – in Oman you will need to hire a car; at the very least a saloon car and if you can possibly afford it a 4WD. Oman's beauty is in its inaccessibility; it is this that has helped the people to hang on to their traditional way of life for so long and the villages are still there, hidden away on the mountainsides and down beside the wadi beds. You can't get to see the pearls of Oman without diving into the hinterland and to do that you need a four-wheel drive. There are plenty of places to rent cars in Muscat and in Salalah and though it might not be a bargain to do so thankfully fuel is cheap.

Unfortunately, unlike the other countries of the Gulf Omani car hire firms add on an excess kilometre charge which means that in a country so large you are very likely to end up paying extra on top of the hire charge. Typically, you will be allowed 100-150km per day free after which you will be charged between 50-100 baiza (£0.09/$0.13) per additional kilometre. Some firms include insurance in the figure charged, some don't and count it as an extra. To hire a vehicle you will need either a licence from your home country or an international driving licence, and a credit card.

Thrifty (tel 604 248; e-mail haditha@omantel.net.om) has several offices around Muscat and at the airports in Seeb and Salalah. *Mark Car Rentals* (tel 562 444; fax 565 434; www.markrentacar.com) has the largest fleet of vehicles for hire in Muscat with both saloon cars and 4WDs available. They have an office in Hattat House in Ruwi as well as a 24-hour service at Seeb Airport. *Avis* (9310 481) has an office in the al-Bustan Hotel and charges from OR14 per day for the smallest saloon car (OR88 (£164/$228) per week) to OR40 per day for a Toyota Landcruiser or similar 4WD vehicle (OR270 per week). There are a number of car hire firms and it may be worth comparing prices. The more 'local' the firm, the cheaper their prices are likely to be. You may also be able to negotiate the mileage restriction depending on whether you are visiting in the high or low season.

Motorcycling
It is still quite rare to see motorcycles in Oman and it is also unlikely that you will find a place to hire a bike should you wish to do so. Desert riding is an expat hobby and small off-roading expeditions are organised occasionally.

Rules of the Road
The speed limit for cars on roads through towns and villages is 60km/h, 100km/h on the smaller roads increasing to 120km/h on dual carriageways. The traffic police in Oman are pretty thorough at carrying out speed checks and anyone in the front seat of a vehicle must wear a seat belt. As in the other countries of the Gulf, if you are unlucky enough to be involved in an accident on the road or out in the wadis or desert you must not move your vehicle before the police have arrived to make a report. Drive on the right hand side of the road.

Road Systems
Up until the 1970s Oman only had about 30 miles of tarmac road. Since the present Sultan has been in power there has been a transformation of the communication system (and pretty much everything else in the country) and today the roads are very good in Oman with quite a number of fast dual carriageways throughout the country. One sight that you will come to appreciate in Oman is the manicured roundabout. The highways department seems to have a penchant for beautifying roundabouts and the verges of the roads, especially around Muscat, which is nice.

Parking
You will find that apart from some areas of Muscat you can park pretty much anywhere you like for free. In the banking district and by some of the malls in the suburbs of Muscat you will find parking meters so make sure that you keep hold of coins if driving about in these areas.

Fuel

Apart from out in the country among the wadis, deserts and mountains (remember that a large amount of Oman is 'off road') there are a lot of petrol stations in Oman but you should fill up where you can as soon as the petrol indicator hits a quarter full. Petrol is much cheaper than in Europe and comes in two types: Regular and Super.

Breakdowns and Accidents

Should you be unlucky enough to have an accident you must remember not to move the vehicle from the scene of the accident until the police have arrived to make a report. You will need this report to be able to claim insurance. Although vast tracks of land in Oman are roadless, the Omanis often own 4WD vehicles and in every settlement there is likely to be at least one mechanic should you break down.

HAZARDS

Drivers in Oman are generally much more considerate than in the United Arab Emirates and the insanely fast driver dogging your tail lights is less likely to confront you than the plodder pootling along in the middle of the road in front of you. Roads are very well engineered though relatively limited in where they can take you. The usual Gulf country hazards apply with regards to camels on the road, mad drivers and unsigned or faded speed bumps that come at you unexpectedly. Another hazard that seems limited to Oman is the often disconcerting road markings which cause you to veer suddenly to the right around an unknown obstacle. Another regional road feature are wadi crossings. In the mountains the roads pass through wadis and you will notice posts on either side painted red and white. Often the wadis are dry but should water reach the red line on the posts you should wait until the level has descended. Drive in a constant state of awareness.

Night Driving. If driving at night be especially on the lookout for camels on the road and speed bumps. Sodium lighting lights certain sections of the highways but more often than not you are surrounded by total darkness.

DESERT AND MOUNTAIN DRIVING

Off-road driving requires a very different approach to the business than speeding along a black-top asphalt highway. Unless there is a large group of you, the cost of hiring a 4WD vehicle may be prohibitive and you may want to join a tour to see the interior of Oman. If you do decide to get out there in a Landcruiser it is a good idea to travel in a convoy of at least two. That way you'll have moral support when you inevitably get bogged down in the sand and there will be another vehicle to pull you out.

Despite all the safety precautions off-roading is a great laugh; exhilarating, slightly scary but the only way to get to see the fascinating interior of Oman. There are two types of terrain you will come across: the desert, and the rocky interior where you'll be driving through dried up (or still running) wadis.

Before you take off into the wilderness you should bear a few things in mind:

• Those pristine dunes and beautiful mountains have been there for centuries. Where possible keep to well worn tracks so as not to damage existing eco-systems and keep out of running river beds if possible; the water may be used by villages downstream. If you are camping take your rubbish home.

• 4WDs have a very different way about them than a saloon car. They are heavier, higher off the ground with a different suspension system and most have power steering. They are great for careering around off-road but require a careful handling on the highways.

• There are no petrol stations in the desert or in the wadis – bring your own.

- There are no taps or grocery stores in the desert or in the wadis – bring your own water and food.
- A two-wheel drive car with suspension made for flat road driving isn't going to get you very far in the desert or in pitted, rocky terrain.
- Tracks in the sand can often disappear during a period of sandstorm or rain.
- Always carry at least one spare tyre, and a towrope.
- Carry a pressure gauge and a foot pump if possible.
- If you are going to be driving through sand it could be a life saving idea to take a tarpaulin, a shovel and sand boards.
- If you can, take a mobile phone and let people know where you are going and when you should be expected back.
- If you are going to be doing a lot of serious off-road driving it is a good idea to invest in a GPS.

Desert Driving

If you have never sped through a trackless sand desert and revved up and over mountainous sand dunes under a broiling sun while dodging a herd of grazing camels here and there, then Oman is the place to experience that thrill. The Wahiba Sands south of Muscat cover an area of 10,000 square kilometres and are the place to head for.

First though, it may be an idea to test out your driving skills on a sort of beginners' slope a few miles outside Muscat where if you do get into trouble you'll not be far from rescue. If you head out on the highway from Muscat towards Seeb, turn left at the Bausher Roundabout and you'll see the Bausher dune chain ahead of you on the right by the Gala Wentworth Golf Club. There are several well-worn tracks up into the dunes and then you are on your own.

Several things to bear in mind when desert driving:
- You'll never be as skilful a driver on sand as the Bedouin. If you get well and truly stuck and can find an Arab to help you, then they'll get you out however bogged down you've become.
- Reduce the tyre pressure before you get onto soft sand. This will give you more traction. Back on asphalt take it easy speed wise until you reach a garage to re-inflate the tyres.
- You need to keep your foot on the accelerator and off the brake pedal; momentum will get you through the sticky patches but slamming on the brakes will bury the wheels.
- Before bombing up a blind crest get out of your vehicle and check that you're not going to end up in a head on collision with another vehicle hammering up the other side of the dune.
- Get in the right gear. You need momentum and speed to breach the crest of a dune and a low gear to slowly descend a dune without the need for braking.
- Ascend a dune at a right angle. If you attempt to ride over it diagonally then you will get less of a grip on the sand. A cavalier diagonal run up the side of a dune can easily lead to a vehicle rolling.
- Do not slow down too much, or stop, at the crest of a dune – doing so is liable to ground your vehicle; the wheels lifted free on either side of the dune, the chassis resting on the sand and you'll have to dig your car out. This is especially likely if you are driving a long wheel base vehicle.
- If you don't manage to get over the dune the first time, reverse for a longer run-up and put your foot down – but not too much.

- If you don't manage to get over the dune the first time, reverse for a longer run-up and put your foot down – but not too much.
- If you do get stuck – and you inevitably will – don't rev the engine furiously trying to extricate yourself because you'll only spin the wheels, overheat the engine and sink further into the sand. Either get a tow out, or dig out the wheels and make sure there is clearance between the chassis and axles and the ground. Use sand boards or a tarpaulin, or planks of wood under the wheels to get traction.
- Finally, don't panic.

Mountain Driving

The ride will be a bumpier one but the exhilaration comparable:
- Over-inflate the tyres slightly when driving over rocky terrain.
- If driving through water keep in a low gear and keep a steady speed until you are clear. Stalling could be the beginning of disaster.
- It is safer to drive through a running watercourse than through a still, murky pond. Still waters run deep and there may be several feet of silt at the bottom just waiting to suck your vehicle into its inky depths.
- Driving on graded roads (un-asphalted but levelled tracks) often throws up a dust cloud behind the vehicle. If stuck in such a cloud caused by a car ahead, slow down or stop till you have visibility once more.

Accommodation

Camping

Camping is a great way to experience the night in Oman. Many of the expats drive out into the desert or up into the mountains to camp for the weekend and the climate is ideal for it. You will often see locals sitting round fires by the roadsides at night, especially if they are long distance lorry drivers or commercial travellers. There are a couple of private campsites at present at the Ras al-Junayz reserve near Sur and at the Oman Dive Centre outside Muscat. Apart from these two places you will be camping wild which means bringing all your own gear with you and clearing up when you leave. Don't camp too close to wadis because if it rains somewhere upstream you may find yourself washed out a few hours later. You should also not camp too near villages as the Omanis are quite a reserved race and you should respect their privacy. At the time of writing there are no Youth Hostels in Oman.

HOTELS

There are hotels of all categories in Oman although they are few in number. Muscat has the monopoly on the hotel scene and choice. Outside Muscat there are fewer hotels catering for tourists and although more are being built to cater for the increased numbers of tourists visiting Oman each winter, hotels are not cheap. Most, and even the lowlier ones, offer rooms with en suite facilities, a fridge, air-conditioning or at the very least a fan and satellite television. Expect to pay at least OR7 (£13/$18) for a single room in the cheapest establishments, but reckon on budgeting at least £25/$34 per night for accommodation. There are practically no bottom end hotels outside Muscat and a glut of mid range hotels elsewhere in the country. There are also a lot of five star hotels in Muscat, a couple in Salalah and more being built in the interior. The top end hotels add on an eight per cent service charge, four per cent Tourism tax and a five per cent Municipality tax on top of the room rate.

Booking Accommodation

With the increasing numbers of tourists visiting Oman it is a good idea to book accommodation before you arrive, especially when travelling to areas of the country where towns may only have one or two hotels. Telephone, fax numbers and, where available, e-mail addresses are provided in the regional sections of the chapter.

Other Staying Options

If you have contacts who work in Oman it is a good idea to get in touch with them to see whether they can put you up for part of your stay. They may also have colleagues on annual leave who have an empty house needing to be looked after. Saving on hotel bills will cut down the cost of a trip to Oman considerably.

Renting

If you intend on remaining in one location for a week or more it is possible to rent furnished flats and these can be a pleasanter option if you are visiting with a family or want to find somewhere without the impersonality of a hotel. See individual regional sections for more details.

Eating and Drinking

RESTAURANTS

Unlike other areas of the Gulf where the menu of regional cuisine doesn't generally stretch past rice, fish, mutton and dates, the Omanis have a stronger tradition of varied cuisine. However, unless you are invited for a meal at someone's house you will be lucky to find it. There are few restaurants serving Omani dishes and although hotels may occasionally have Omani theme nights they are more likely to offer dishes from the Far East and Asia. Unless you eat in the fast food restaurants (of which there are an increasing number), hotel restaurants or the small number of privately owned themed establishments you will be faced mainly with the numerous hole-in-the-wall Indian and Pakistani eateries. Depending on your palate, be adventurous and try everything.

Opening Hours. Restaurants generally stay open until 10pm or 11pm but Omanis aren't known for burning the midnight oil, going to bed and getting up early.

Restaurant Behaviour

Because of the conservative nature of the Omanis almost every restaurant will have sections where only families are allowed to sit and may well have areas set aside in the unlikely event that an unaccompanied woman should come to dine.

You will find that the majority of diners in the cheaper restaurants will eat with the right hand, scooping and mopping food up with flat bread. You can join in this practice but more often than not a waiter will obligingly bring cutlery to any western-looking foreigner.

Cheap Eats

There are cheap eateries all over Oman and unless you eat out in the hotel restaurants expenditure on food needn't be a worry. A *shawarma* costs about 200 baiza (about £0.40/$0.50) while a filling meal of rice and dhal, or a biryani, or kima and flat bread will cost around 600 baiza (£1.20/$1.50).

Street Stalls. These are perfectly hygienic and often sell whole chickens roasting on a spit which are ideal for taking on picnics when off out to do some off-roading.

FOOD GLOSSARY

Though nowhere near exhaustive, here are a few of the kinds of dishes that you are likely to come across; mixture of Omani, Middle Eastern, Pakistani and Indian:

Al-Maleh Khambasa: Salt-fish in onions with rice.

Biryani: Pieces of chicken, mutton and occasionally fish mixed in a mild spiced rice.

Bilaleet: Cold sweetened vermicelli noodles, served with an omelette.

Dhal: Stewed lentils.

Falafel: Deep-fried balls of mashed chickpeas and herbs. Can be placed in pitta bread with salad etc. to create a falafel sandwich.

Fuul: Warm stewed fava beans served in a bowl and eaten with flatbread, often for breakfast.

Halwa: A sweet made from brown sugar, flour, milk, eggs, rosewater and various spices. Served with coffee on special occasions.

Harees: A mix of meat and wheat cooked slowly to form a thick paste eaten as a staple during Ramadan.

Homous: Chickpea paste with a dash of olive oil and lemon juice and eaten with flat bread.

Kibbe: Deep fried balls of finely chopped and spiced meat.

Kima: Minced meat (generally mutton) stewed with tomato and peas. Often served with bread, and occasionally in a rolled flatbread sandwich.

Samosa: Chopped vegetables, curried, wrapped in pastry triangles and fried.

Shawarma: Strips of braised lamb or chicken shaved from a kebab-like spit in warmed pitta bread with salad, tahina and garlic sauce, with pickles and chilli optional extras.

Shish Tawouk: Pieces of chicken grilled on the skewer served with chips and salad.

Shuwa: Slow cooked meat in an underground pit or clay oven. Usually served at feasts.

Tabouleh: Lebanese salad made from couscous, onions, tomatoes, parsley with lemon juice and olive oil.

Foreign Cuisine

There are a number of hotel restaurants in Muscat serving Italian, Mexican, Chinese and other food from all over the world. Elsewhere you are likely to find menus offering a combination of Indian and local cuisine with the addition of chips, eggs and burgers. For listings of restaurants and cafeterias throughout the country look in the pages of *Oman Today* or *Adventure Oman*.

Vegetarians

The good news for vegetarians is that because of the number of Indian eateries in the country there is often a good choice of vegetarian food available. Most of the higher end hotel restaurants will also offer vegetarian dishes. On the whole however, the omnivorous Arabs aren't too cognisant of the needs of vegetarians. Many dishes will have been prepared with meat stock and asking for a dish to be served without meat will merely mean that any meat will be lifted from the plate before being given you. However, because many of the chefs in Oman are from India or the Indian Subcontinent they understand the concept of vegetarianism and will be able to offer what you need.

Hygiene

Standards of hygiene in the Gulf are higher than in other areas of the Middle East. Although Oman is slightly less developed in some ways than the other countries of the Gulf, standards of hygiene are equivalent. It is an immaculate country and though there are fewer restaurants to choose from health inspectors are still rigorous in their inspections of eating establishments. Also, because a lot of the ingredients used in the restaurants are imported, including a lot of the meat, you will find that you will be served a higher standard of produce than in the less richer countries of the northern Middle East.

DRINKING

Alcohol is not illegal in Oman but its sale is restricted to bars in hotels and some of the posher restaurants. There is also no locally produced alcohol like *arak* such as you find in other parts of the Middle East, so all alcohol is imported and therefore expensive. Outside of the bars you will only be able to buy alcohol (and then only from one or two outlets) if you are a resident and hold a liquor licence.

Bars

The bars are all part of hotels and generally themed, often with a live Philippino band playing a few sets during the late evenings. The clientele tend to be a mix of expats and the wealthier Omanis. The bar staff in these establishments will be Christian Indians, Sri Lankans or Philippinos. There are a number of British 'pubs' around Muscat and a couple of bars in the five star hotels in Salalah. Elsewhere in Oman you will have trouble finding a drink.

   Happy Hours. Most of the upmarket hotels in Muscat, and in Salalah have happy hours where drinks are a little, though not a lot, less pricey than usual.

Beer and Wine

The range of beers available is pretty wide, with draught Amstel Light, Fosters and Heineken offered pretty much everywhere. There are usually a few draught bitters and cider available and most spirits are available. Wine is not so readily available and where it is available it is expensive, especially if served in restaurants.

Soft Drinks

Fresh fruit juices are one of the great treats on the streets of Oman. A freshly squeezed orange juice should set you back about 400 baiza; a fruit cocktail about 500 baiza (£0.93/$1.30). Most of the usual western type fizzy drinks, and cartons of fruit juice are available – the Coca Cola and Pepsi corporations made it down to Oman years ago and have headquarters in Saudi Arabia. A drink that can be quite refreshing, and very healthy once the taste for it is acquired, is *laban* – a yoghurt-like drink often served plain but sometimes flavoured with chocolate or lime.

Coffee

Many books about the region describe how important the ritual of taking coffee is among the Gulf Arabs. As a tourist you are unlikely to encounter the ritualistic coffee ceremony where strong coffee is drunk from tiny handleless cups and after three measures the guest is to refuse a fourth by shaking the cup from side to side. However, you may be offered coffee if doing business or during a bargaining session in a souk. In many of the tea shops run by Indians you will be served Nescafe with a splash of condensed milk, although a few may serve Turkish coffee which is served strong and black in small cups. If you are served Turkish coffee let it settle for a short while before drinking it as there are often quite a lot of coffee grounds lurking in even the smallest cup.

Tea

Tea shops will serve you a glass of tea for 100 baiza (£0.18/$0.25). This may be poured from a huge teapot ready milked and sugared Indian style, or served individually with a Lipton's teabag slowly brewing in the glass. If you are offered Arab tea this will be black and well sugared. You may also be able to get a refreshing mint tea, which is essentially black sugared tea with a sprig of mint dunked in it.

Exploring

THE GREAT OUTDOORS

Oman is the place for the outdoor fanatic, or even for those who aren't fanatical but like to drive through and explore a bit of dramatic scenery. The landscape of Oman is the major tourist attraction of the country rather than the museums or the buildings. Hire a car, preferably a 4WD and get out into the mountains, wadis and deserts.

The Desert

Oman has large stretches of desert, the most impressive being the gold and copper-coloured **Wahiba Sands** in the north east of the country. Elsewhere the desert landscape is of grey featureless salt flats running away from the eye for hundreds of miles. If you haven't seen a proper desert before arriving in Oman make sure that you visit the Wahiba Sands at least. They are home to the colourful al-Wahiba Bedouin tribe who still live a more or less traditional way of life while taking advantage of 4WDs, government water provision and the money to be made from tourism.

Beaches

With a coastline of approximately 1,000 miles, if beach holidays are your thing then you will be in your element in Oman. With a difference. Because of the terrain, getting to these beaches can involve some serious off-roading which can make the whole experience far more interesting than just taking the local bus to the local beach. Apart from those beaches near towns and villages you will need to pack a tent, and enough water, food and fuel to see you over the few days that it may entail getting to and returning from your destination.

Mountains

Oman is a mountainous country and to really be able to explore the country fully it will be necessary to hire a four-wheel drive vehicle, or join a tour group. Both options are likely to be expensive and although you can see much of the country by road it is the tracks that lead out into the interior that are the most interesting to follow and which will take you into the real heart of Oman. There are several good reads about the business of off-roading, *APEX Explorer's Guide to Oman*, which gives a good introduction to the country and the sport, and the *Maverick Guide to Oman* which is a useful general guide to the country as well as an in-depth guide to exploring the region in 4WD vehicles.

OMAN'S HERITAGE

Museums

Admission is now charged to all museums and most of the tourist sites in Oman. All forts and museums that aren't private enterprises are run by the *Ministry of National Heritage and Culture* which charges a standard 500 baiza (£0.93/$1.30) admission for anyone over six years old.

Mosques

The mosques in Oman are markedly different to those throughout the rest of the countries outlined in this book, often topped by domes painted blue or green and gold. The country's largest mosque, the Sultan Qaboos Mosque is being constructed near Athaiba on the highway out to Seeb Airport. When it is completed it will be the largest mosque in the Arabian Gulf.

Crafts

Although the government is keen to preserve the nation's heritage, traditions are being lost in Oman as the modern lifestyles mean that much that was once produced at home is imported. Oman has always been renowned for its boat building industry and luckily the knowledge is yet to be lost. The traditional dhows are still built by hand without blueprints or plans in the coastal town of Sur. The art of silver-smithing is unfortunately dying as Bedouin jewellery becomes looked upon as old fashioned and the raw material for it (the Maria Theresa silver dollars that were melted down to create new designs) has disappeared. Khanjars, the curved daggers that were once worn by all Omani men, are still produced – though often by guest workers from other countries who are taught the practice by the old silversmiths. Rugs are still woven up in the mountains but the need for woven camel and donkey straps have receded as the car has taken over from the camel as the main form of transport.

THE FALAJ

All over Oman you will come across the irrigation channels that have been used for millennia to move water across country, often for many miles at a time, by using underground channels, ditches, canals, aqueducts, wells, pools and siphon systems.

It is believed that the Persians introduced the *Falaj* to Oman during their occupancy of the country almost 2000 years ago. They taught the populace how to make a kind of cement by firing a mixture of palm wood and limestone in a kiln over several days. The ashes were then mixed with water to produce the cement to create and repair the channels.

Falaj (the plural is *aflaj*) originate from a mother well, which was traditionally found by a water diviner known as a *bashir*. Once water is discovered a shaft, sometimes over 60 metres in depth, is then sunk and from this a series of vertical shafts are sunk every 30 metres along the route that the falaj takes. Men from the *Awama* tribe are famed for their prowess in building aflaj and crawling though the airless passages to keep the channels clear of debris. Once the water reaches a village from the source there is a strict rotation of water usage and a committee is created to look after the maintenance and usage of the falaj. Before the advent of clocks water usage in a village was distributed between families in strict rotation and for a set time by means of a sundial during the day and by observing the movement of the sky at night. As the falaj enters the village the water is reserved first of all for drinking and household uses before it flows on to segregated bathing areas (often near the mosque) before flowing out of the village. The water is then used for washing clothes before being run out into the individual gardens and plantations.

WILDLIFE

Because of the fierce summer temperatures many of the mammals of Oman are nocturnal or are incredibly shy animals such as the **Arabian Tahr** which inhabits the Musandam peninsula and the as-Sarin Nature Reserve to the south west of Muscat. The **Arabian White Oryx**, which had been almost hunted to extinction by the beginning of the 1960s, have been saved through captive breeding programmes and there is now a sanctuary for them in the Jiddat al-Harisis region in central Oman.

The warm waters of the Gulf of Oman and the Arabian Sea in the south of the country mean that there are numerous species of fish and marine life around the coast of Oman and in 1996 a **Blue Whale** was spotted off the coast, the first sighting in over a century.

The country also lies on an important bird migration route, situated as it is between the landmasses of Europe, Africa and Asia. There are over 430 species of bird recorded on the Oman Bird List and Oman is a great place to go bird watching during the winter months of November to March. Falconry is not the popular sport that it is elsewhere in the Gulf though a few tribes in the interior do occasionally practice the sport.

PERMITS

If you are intending to visit **conservation areas** in Oman you will need to get a permit. Such areas include the nesting grounds of the **Green Turtle** at Ras al-Hadd, Masirah Island and the Damaaniyat islands off the Batinah coast. Permits should be applied for several days in advance of your planned visit from the *Ministry of Regional Municipalities and Environment* (tel 696 456) in the al-Khuwair district of Muscat.

Theatre

Acting and the theatre don't have a big following in Oman. Some touring shows occasionally visit to perform in the big hotels or are invited by the cultural institutes in Muscat. For those who may be staying in Oman for a while and would like to get involved in some acting the *Muscat Amateur Theatre* can be contacted by telephone on 562 511.

Music

Some of the large five star hotels often have traditional Omani music and dance sessions which will be advertised in the local press, and during the Muscat Festival in November there are a lot of traditional bands playing in venues throughout Muscat.

Nightclubs

Oman goes to bed early and nightlife is pretty much restricted to quiet drinking in the hotel bars or a late supper in a restaurant. These are the main late night activities. What nightclubs there are in Oman are attached to the big hotels in Muscat and Salalah.

SPORT

If you need to get your fix of contact sport be it football, cricket, rugby or tennis there are places in Muscat where these can be found. The listings section of *Oman Today* provides contact numbers. If you fancy a run in company of the local expat community you can contact the *Muscat Hash House Harriers* (tel 316 127).

Water Sports

Most water sports are available through the facilities of five star hotels in and around Muscat. Outside Muscat such sports are uncommon among the locals and unless you have your own gear it will be difficult to have a go at jet skiing, sailing, windsurfing etc. Diving and snorkelling in the warm waters of Oman are a popular pastime and there are several dive schools in Muscat such as *BluZone Watersports* (tel 737 293) and the *Oman Dive Centre* (tel 950 261) which offer PADI Open Water courses from around OR120 (£224/$312). In Salalah, *Samharam Divers* (tel 9481 265), based out of the Holiday Inn, offer dives, snorkelling and dhow trips. The *Khasab Dive Centre* (tel 830 464) in the Musandam Peninsula offers diving packages in one of the most beautiful, unspoilt and unvisited regions of the world.

Equestrianism

Horseracing and camel racing are not practised on a grand scale as, unlike the UAE, Qatar and Bahrain horseracing hasn't been taken up by the ruling family. However, horse riding is quite popular and there are several studs in Muscat. Camel racing takes place during the cooler winter months from October to March. Races are around a circular track of between six and ten kilometres. The jockeys are extremely lightweight, and are usually small boys who are attached to the saddles by Velcro. There is a good racetrack at Manah, about 180 km from Muscat near Nizwa. For more information about where to catch a race contact the *Horse and Camel Association* (tel 622 777).

Golf

There are no grass golf courses in Oman though there is a desert course out near Bausher on the outskirts of Muscat. Contact the *Ghala Wentworth Golf Course* (tel 591 248) for opening times and green fees.

FESTIVALS

During October and November the **Muscat Festival** is held which is a kind of national pride event to celebrate the culture and tradition of Oman and its people. Special events take place in the hotels, on the beaches and in the parks all over Muscat, and during the evenings the roads are packed with cars and traffic jams as families get out to the various locations. It's a great time for the kids of Muscat with circuses and children's shows by the sea and there are more serious displays of traditional crafts and folklore, poetry readings, music and dancing and theatre. During the festival many of the hotels offer discounted rooms and some of the airlines that fly to Oman, including *Oman Air* and *Kuwait Airways*, offer special discount rates.

The **al-Khareef Festival** is held in July and August around Salalah during the monsoon season when the countryside in Dhofar is hit by the rains.

 Of all the countries of the Arabian Gulf, Oman is the place to find the best souvenirs and traditional Arabian artefacts. Conversely, it isn't the best place to try to pick up the latest electrical equipment. You will be able to find most things that you might need in the way of electrical goods in the malls and shopping centres around Muscat but they are unlikely to be as state of the art as what you could pick up in Dubai.

Haggling

Everything in the malls and shopping centres will have a fixed price but this doesn't necessarily mean that there is no room for bargaining. However, the markets and souks will be the places to haggle if you become addicted to this way of doing things. Always ask the shopkeeper for their last price before bringing out your money.

Shopping Centres and Supermarkets

Muscat is the main shopping centre in Oman. There is more choice and more malls there than elsewhere in the country. Oman's second city, Salalah, is on a much smaller scale than Muscat and correspondingly has less to offer the shopper.

As in other countries in the Gulf you will find large supermarkets such as *Spinney's* wherever expats congregate. In Oman this means Muscat and Salalah. Outside of these population centres your food shopping will be limited to small grocers that will have a sign outside declaring 'Foodstuffs and Luxuries'. These shops offer the basics of life with no frills. There are also the fruit, vegetable, meat and fish souks where you can buy all your necessities cheaply.

Souks. The main souks that you should visit are in Muscat and the **Wednesday Women's Market** in Ibra (that is if you are a woman – men are prohibited from shopping in this one).

Shopping Hours. Most shops are open daily from 8.30am-1pm and again from 4.30-9pm. They are closed on Fridays although some may open on Friday evenings. Shopping malls generally stay open all day without the usual mid-afternoon break.

GIFTS AND SOUVENIRS

Antique silver khanjars, old rifles, silver and gold jewellery all make great gifts but are expensive. Frankincense is relatively cheap and can be found all over Oman and is the quintessential Omani souvenir. Make sure you buy a clay incense burner to put the incense in.

Carpets. Although there isn't the range of carpets for sale that can be found in neighbouring Dubai, there are carpet shops in Muscat but you will need to be prepared to bargain hard to get the price you want.

Gold. Oman is one of the cheapest places in the world in which to buy gold. Mutrah souk and the malls in Muscat have a lot of gold shops worth exploring.

Daggers

Khanjars, the traditional curved daggers that were once worn by all Omani men, make beautiful decorative gifts but can be rather expensive. They are still being made to the traditional designs and can be found all over Oman though the best places to look for a bargain are in Nizwa, Salalah and Muscat. Some of the galleries in Muscat sell beautiful examples of khanjars in frames which put the price up considerably.

Incense and Perfumes

Oman is famous for its Frankincense, which is considered by many to be the best available. The resin is collected from Frankincense trees in Dhofar and the hardened crystals are burnt in special clay burners. *Amouage*, one of the most expensive scents in the world, was commissioned by the Omani royal family and designed by a French *perfumier*.

Jewellery

Oman is the best place in the Gulf to buy genuine examples of Bedouin jewellery. Pieces are sold by weight rather than design or craftsmanship but are unlikely to be more than a couple of generations old. Pieces are becoming increasingly rare and you should beware of imitations.

Books

The widest choice of any reading material in Oman is in Muscat. Outside of Muscat you will find very little access to anything in the English-language except the two Omani newspapers. In Muscat the *al-Marifa* bookshop on Mutrah corniche has a good selection of local guidebooks and the bookshop at the *al-Bustan Hotel* has a very good and wide selection of books about the Arabian Gulf and Oman. *Al-Batra Bookshop* in the al-Wadi Commercial Centre in Qurum claims to be the largest in Oman and is well worth a look. A good second-hand bookshop, also in the al-Wadi Centre is the *House of Prose*.

Health and Hygiene

Medical Treatment

Oman is a very clean country and the improvement of the nation's health has been one of the main priorities of the Sultan since he took over the reins of power from his father in 1970. Today every region of Oman has health centres and hospitals, normally located in the main town but often in some of the other outlying towns as well. Both hospitals and health centres are clearly marked with a red crescent over the main entrance. Ambulances are only used for inter-hospital transferrals which means that should you fall seriously ill you will need to get yourself to the nearest hospital in a taxi or rely on your friends to get you there.

Pharmacies

Pharmacies are widespread and contain most things that you may require in the way of prescriptions, medicines, hygiene, contraception, baby requirements etc. They are also very good places for getting a first opinion on any minor ailment you may get while on holiday and staff will all speak English. Pharmacies are open from 9am-1pm and 4-9pm daily except on Friday when they are open in the evening only. There is always a duty pharmacy open 24-hours in Muscat. Check the newspapers for the address and telephone number.

Emergency Procedures

Should you fall ill and need the services of a doctor or dentist your hotel should be able to give you the telephone number of the nearest place where you can get help and will more than likely help get you to see a specialist. However, in a dire emergency you should call the police on 999, state your name, location and nature of your distress.

HEALTH HAZARDS

Oman is a hot country and you should always take care to keep up your liquid intake. If you are visiting in the summer months drinking five litres of water per day is about right. Although you ingest a fair amount of water through food you should try to stick to drinking mineral water whenever possible rather than soft drinks that usually have a great deal of sugar in them. Isotonic drinks which replace lost fluids more efficiently than straight water are also available in Oman.

Tap water in Oman is safe to drink but because the vast majority of it is desalinated it doesn't taste too pleasant. Bottled mineral water is cheap and plentiful.

Heat Disorders

A bit of a sun tan makes you feel great and look better but remember that skin cancer is linked to too much time under the sun or ultra violet rays. Wandering about anywhere in Oman is going to get you a tan; so lying out on a beach is not a necessity. It's wise to get hold of a broad brimmed hat and apply suntan lotion liberally and frequently. Keeping the arms covered may be part of the Islamic mode of dress (especially for women) but it also makes sense when the heat from the sun can be so strong.

Toilets

Public lavatories are few and far between in Oman. You will find a rough outhouse round the back of most roadside restaurants and petrol stations. There are washing facilities outside every mosque in the country and in restaurants, hotels and some cafés.

Creatures to Avoid

Because of the harsh climate many of the creatures of Oman are nocturnal which means that you won't come into contact with too many of them. Dogs, not as popular in the Middle East as in Europe, are few and far between although they are used as vocal guard dogs in the more out of the way places. There have been a few isolated cases of rabies and it is best to stay clear of most animals except those in wildlife parks. When swimming in the sea beware of **jellyfish** (which abound in the waters during the summer), **sharp coral** and **sea urchins** which look harmless enough underwater but whose spines can penetrate far into a bare foot. Broken shards of coral lie along and under the shoreline and can give a nasty cut. Cuts and grazes take far longer to dry and heal under the sun and humidity and forward thinking is a good idea. Sandals which are specially designed to wear in the sea are widely available in the water sport stores in Oman and at home and are fairly cheap.

Crime and Safety

SECURITY

Oman is a safe place to travel in and if you take the usual precautions that you would when travelling anywhere you should have a hassle free trip. The troubles in the northern countries of the Middle East are a long way from Oman and Omanis are a distinct group racially and spiritually from the Palestinians and the fundamentalists of the north. The Royal Oman Police keep a high profile and look so stern and efficient that their presence alone is often enough to deter any thought of wrongdoing.

Pickpockets, bag snatchers, hotel theft, violence, conmen; you will be very unlucky indeed to come into any contact with these phenomena while in Oman. Oman, like the other Gulf States is very safe and stable politically and socially. The Royal Omani Police look after all aspects of security within the country and are very efficient at their job. Outside Muscat there are few other truly urban areas and with a total population of only 1.7 million Omani nationals (of whom 50 per cent are under 20 years old) and a strong tradition of tribal relationships where justice is dealt swiftly and by consent of the whole tribe, crime rates are exceedingly low.

Arrest and Summons

If, for whatever reason, you are arrested you should immediately contact your Embassy who will send an official to help you get a lawyer and to inform your family back home. However, if you are involved in crime, drugs etc., don't expect any sympathy from your compatriots in the Embassy, or from the Omani judicial system.

Photography

The diverse terrain and wildlife of Oman is a landscape and nature-photographers dream. The country is exceedingly photogenic. The people too are very striking but taking photographs of them is a sensitive issue and you should ask permission before clicking away. It is forbidden to photograph politically or militarily sensitive areas, the interiors of mosques (where non-Muslims are forbidden entry in any case) and airports. Camera equipment is readily available in Muscat but can be quite difficult to find elsewhere. Film and photo-processing labs can be found all over the country.

Tourist Information

The official website of Oman's *Directorate of Tourism* can be found at www.tourismoman.com though there are no offices serving the needs of the itinerant tourist in Oman. The tour companies mentioned earlier should also be able to help with any specific enquiries that you may have. Several other useful websites that provide general information on Oman can be found at www.oman.org, www.omanonline.com, www.arabnet/oman and www.cityshow.com.

EMBASSIES & CONSULATES

Embassies & Consulates - The majority of embassies are located in the Muscat suburb of al-Khuwair and open from 8am-1pm Saturday to Wednesday.
Bahrain: tel 605 075; fax 605 072.
Kuwait: tel 699 626; fax 600 972.
Qatar: tel 701 802 fax: 794 588.
Saudi Arabia: tel 601 744; fax 603 540.
United Arab Emirates: tel 600 302; fax 602 584.
United Kingdom: tel 693 077; fax 693 087.
United States of America: tel 698 989; fax 699 778.
Yemen: tel 600 815; fax 609 172.

USEFUL INFORMATION

Business Hours

Government offices are open from 7am-2.30pm Saturday to Wednesday. Most other private businesses work from 8am-1pm and then again from 4-7pm after a long lunch break Saturday to Thursday. The official weekend is Friday, though quite a number of private businesses close early on Thursday and Western companies may give their employees a weekend of Friday and Saturday. Very few companies will work to the Western timetable.
Time. Oman local time is GMT + 4 hours.

Electricity

The electric current in Oman is 220AC. The British style three-pin plug and sockets are used. Adaptors can be bought while in Oman though these may not be as good as those available in the UK.

PUBLIC HOLIDAYS AND CELEBRATIONS

Islamic holidays are dependent on the Islamic calendar rather than the Gregorian and so fall on different days each year. Oman observes the five feasts and festivals common all over the Muslim world. Details of these can be found in the main *Practical Information* chapter. Oman's **National Day** is celebrated on 18 November every year and Omanis also take a holiday on 1 January. Ramadan, the month of fasting during daylight hours, will fall in the cooler months of October, November and December for the next five years. Because the Islamic calendar is dependant on the sighting of the new moon exact dates are not known until a few days in advance and therefore holidays are only announced in the daily press several days before they occur.

EXPLORING OMAN

MUSCAT

The Omani navigator Ahmed bin Majid, writing in 1490AD, described what is now the capital city of Oman thus,

> *Muscat is a port, the like of which cannot be found in the whole world, where there are businesses and good things which cannot be found elsewhere. Muscat is the port of Oman where year by year the ships load up with fruit and horses and they sell in it cloth, vegetables, oils and grain, and all ships aim for it. It is a cape between two different routes, safe in every wind and possesses fresh water and a hospitable and sociable people who love strangers.*

Today, more than 500 years later, Muscat still holds a considerable charm over the visitor, whether they arrive by sea, land or air.

Muscat has been occupied since about the 1st century AD and became increasingly important as an entrepôt, as a place for ships to stop and take on water and supplies on the routes between the East and the West. The natural harbour at Mutrah has always been both a haven and a refuge which must have attracted the Portuguese to use it as their base in the 16th century until they were ousted from the region in 1650.

Muscat became the capital of Oman in 1793 and remained a small peaceful spot well into the 20th century. Up until the present Sultan took over from his father in 1970 most of the inhabitants of Muscat lived in small wooden houses outside the city walls, while the wealthier merchants lived along the Corniche. The city gates were locked each night at sunset and there was only one tarmac road linking the old city to an airport at Bait al-Falaj.

Muscat is still beautifully preserved and though much has changed with the boom of the 1970s, new buildings have been kept low and adhere to strict rules governing their architecture. The city is remarkably clean and although there isn't the degree of choice of entertainment found in other cities in the Gulf the charm and gentleness of the place makes up for it in spades.

Getting Around

Arrival and Departure

Seeb International Airport is likely to be your arrival point unless you are coming overland from Dubai. The airport is about 40km and about 20 minutes from Muscat in a taxi. There are several car hire firms operating booths in the Airport. Taxis and microbuses crowd around Seeb roundabout outside the gates of the airport. You should haggle rigorously for a taxi into town because the drivers, being aware that you are new in town, will endeavour to overcharge you. Expect to pay around OR8 (£15/$21) for the trip into town by taxi, 500 baiza (£0.93/$1.30) if you take one of the shared microbuses. If you are entering Oman overland the main highway, once over the border, runs along the Batinah coast and you will drive past the Airport on your way towards Muscat. This highway, as-Sultan Qaboos Street, passes Seeb Airport on the way towards the major Muscat settlements of al-Khuwair, Madinat as-Sultan Qaboos and al-Qurum before reaching Ruwi, the transport hub of Muscat. From Ruwi the main road leads to Mutrah (the corniche) where many of the cheaper hotels are located, and on to old Muscat.

CITY LAYOUT

Muscat's setting is dramatic. The city is really made up of several towns lying in the wadis surrounded by the mountains; bald, wrinkled, brown and purple with red and white painted pylons and the ubiquitous watch towers standing on top of them. Low level buildings, practically all of them painted white or beige, are huddled under the craggy mountains and travelling between the districts of Muscat, whether in a hire car or in a packed minibus, you'll catch many glimpses of the sea only ever a mile or so away. There are three central districts of Muscat and several suburbs:

Muscat or **Old Muscat**, is a small area dominated by the two cliff-side forts of **Mirani** and **Jalali**, the **al-Alam Palace** and the city walls. It has something of the air of the British Mediterranean garrison town Gibraltar. There are a couple of important museums in old Muscat but no hotels and only a few small grocery stores. You can enter old Muscat by road along the Corniche where you will pass through the New Gate, a stone entrance that seems reminiscent of Windsor Castle. The main road winds through the town and on towards the eastern fishing villages, the marinas and the al-Bustan Palace Hotel.

Mutrah, a few kilometres to the north-west of old Muscat has retained much of its Arabian style and feel, with a small harbour and port and old 18th century Portuguese-style merchant houses facing it across the Corniche. Above the houses the 16th century **Mutrah Fort**, still used by the police today, looks out over the port, and watchtowers are scattered along the rugged peaks of the mountains that range throughout the area. Behind the merchants' houses on the Corniche lie a labyrinthine network of streets and the beautiful **Mutrah Souk** – the most picturesque souk in the Arabian Peninsula. Mutrah has many of the cheaper hotels and is the most atmospheric place in Muscat.

Ruwi, southwest of Mutrah, is the commercial heart of Muscat and home to the banking district, some of the middle to top end hotels and the central bus station and taxi ranks. A wide dry wadi runs through the middle of Ruwi and in it you will find the Ruwi Driving School and its red and white striped cars that look like sweets.

Wide highways run out west from the three settlements in Muscat proper towards the newer residential areas of **Qurum**, **Madinat as-Sultan Qaboos** and **al-Khuwair**. These districts are full of large villas and the diplomatic and government ministry areas as well as the large shopping malls and top-end hotels. The beaches along this stretch of coastline are far wider and more populated than those along the rugged east coast and not as beautiful.

CITY TRANSPORT

Distances between the different areas of Muscat are quite large – especially between Ruwi and the next major settlement at Qurum – and if you do not have your own vehicle taxi fares can become very expensive.

Taxi

Taxi drivers are likely to want to overcharge any tourist they can persuade to get into their cabs. And until you know the correct prices you will always be overcharged. There are a number of dial-a-cab companies who use meters and one of the best and most efficient is the 24-hour *Hello Taxis* (tel 607 011/2) which has an office in the al-Fair Centre on Qurum Beach.

Microbus

Toyota and Nissan microbuses bomb about the various districts of Muscat picking up and dropping off passengers. There are several microbus stations, two of which are beside the Ruwi roundabout: one serving all destinations west towards the suburbs and Seeb, and the other, on the opposite side of the roundabout for Mutrah harbour. From Mutrah you can pick up a minibus to old Muscat or walk there along the corniche. The bigger microbus station opposite the main bus station in Ruwi is for long distance destinations. When you want to get out of a microbus tap a couple of times on the roof of the bus. Microbuses charge a fixed rate so Ruwi-Qurum costs 200 baiza (£0.38/$0.52); trips between Ruwi and Matruh, and Matruh and Muscat will cost 100 baiza.

Bus

In addition to the taxis and microbuses there are local government run bus services that run every 20-30 minutes between 6.30am and 10pm daily with reduced services during the mid-afternoons and late evenings.

HOTELS

Muscat has a large choice of hotels suitable for all budgets. Around Shatti al-Qurum (Qurum Beach) there are a number of mid to top-end hotels and most are either on the beach or a short distance away from it. However, for atmosphere and real beauty (the place not necessarily the hotel) you should stay in one of the hotels that line the corniche and face the harbour in Mutrah. If you have come to Muscat on business then the *Sheraton Hotel* in Ruwi is ideally located a few minutes away from the banking district while nearer the airport in the modern districts of al-Khuwair and Madinat as-Sultan Qaboos there are a number of five star hotels. For opulence you will be hard pressed to beat the *al-Bustan Hotel* which year after year is voted one of the best hotels in the world. Bear in mind that hotel prices fluctuate depending on the time of year and the season. Many hotels offer a discount on the quoted price without being asked and especially during the Muscat Festival most hotels enter into the spirit of the occasion by dropping prices and holding special events.

If money is not a problem to you then there is only one place to stay in Muscat – the *al-Bustan Hotel* (tel 799 666; fax 799 600; albustan@interconti.com). The hotel is immaculate with a good bookshop, a private beach, an *Avis* rentacar desk and *Zubair Tour Company* in the foyer. There are several restaurants to choose from with a daily themed buffet. The place is opulent, no other word describes it – apart from luxurious perhaps. Prices start from OR129 (£241/$335) + taxes for a double room.

Mutrah

Just off Mutrah High Street is the *Al-Howda Hotel*. The management charges OR7/10/13 (£13-24/$18-34) for single/double/triple rooms which are basic and somewhat down at heel overlooking a busy back yard. However, the al-Howda is the cheapest option in town and fairly centrally located.

Just off the corniche, opposite the fish market, is the *Marina Hotel* (tel 711 711; fax 711 313), the newest hotel in Mutrah with a fish restaurant on the top floor. Rooms cost from OR14.400/29.250 (£27-55/$37-76) per night. Twin beds cost slightly less. If these two hotels are full up there are several other medium priced hotels along the corniche.

If you find the normal sea views rather drab then the *Naseem Hotel* (tel 712 418; fax 711 728) on Mutrah Corniche has the best views in town, especially from its double rooms, which look out over the corniche to the port and harbour beyond. Pleasantly appointed rooms cost from OR10.900 (£20/$28) including taxes for a single, OR15.400 (£29/$40) for a double.

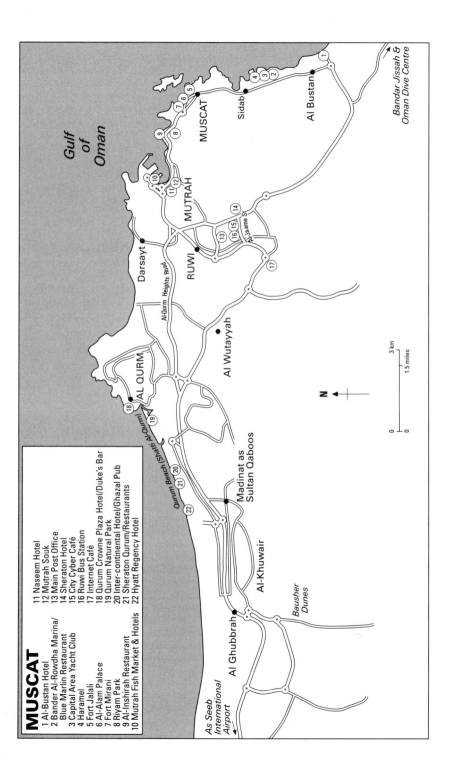

MUSCAT

1 Al-Bustan Hotel
2 Bander Al-Rowdha Marina/
  Blue Marlin Restaurant
3 Capital Area Yacht Club
4 Haramel
5 Fort Jalali
6 Al-Alam Palace
7 Fort Mirani
8 Riyam Park
9 Al-Inshirah Restaurant
10 Mutrah Fish Market & Hotels
11 Naseem Hotel
12 Mutrah Souk
13 Main Post Office
14 Sheraton Hotel
15 City Cyber Café
16 Ruwi Bus Station
17 Internet Café
18 Qurum Crowne Plaza Hotel/Duke's Bar
19 Qurum Natural Park
20 Inter-continental Hotel/Ghazal Pub
21 Sheraton Qurum/Restaurants
22 Hyatt Regency Hotel

Gulf
of
Oman

MUSCAT

Sidab

Al Bustan

Bandar Jissah &
Oman Dive Centre

MUTRAH

Darsayt

RUWI

Al-Jaame St

Al-Qurm Heights Road

AL QURM

Al Wutayyah

Qurum Beach (Shatti Al-Qurm)

Madinat as
Sultan Qaboos

Al-Khuwair

Bausher
Dunes

Al Ghubbrah

As Seeb
International
Airport

N

0   3 km
0   1.5 miles

Ruwi

The *Sheraton Oman Hotel* (tel 799 899; fax 795 791; e-mail sheraton@omantel.net.om) is located at the top of al-Jaame Street in Ruwi and has an excellent view over the hills surrounding Muscat as well as being ideally placed for the business traveller with the financial district a few minutes distance from the hotel. Double rooms start at OR69 (£127/$175) + 17% taxes.

Qurum

The *Muscat Inter-Continental Hotel* (tel 600 500; fax 600 012) is located on Qurum Beach about 15 minutes drive from the airport. It offers the five star trappings that you would expect, has its own beachfront and is quite a key meeting place for the local expat community (that is until the next new place is built). It has quite a few good restaurants and an olde English pub serving pub grub as well as the Polynesian Islands theme cocktail bar and restaurant, *Trader Vic's*. Rooms start at OR70 (£131/$182) + 17% taxes for a double room. Rooms with a sea view cost extra.

The *Qurum Crowne Plaza*, formerly the *Gulf Forum Hotel* (tel 560 100; fax 560 650; e-mail mcthc@interconti.com) has a lofty location on a cliff top looking out over the Gulf of Oman and a good bar and terrace. It also has a gym should you be a fitness fanatic and want to run on a machine rather than along the beach below. Prices, for Oman, are pretty reasonable with a double room starting at OR58 (£108/$151) + taxes. Rooms with a sea view – better than the view from the pricier Inter-Continental – cost extra.

Another hotel in Qurum is the *Beach Hotel* (tel 696 601; fax 696 609; e-mail beachhtl@omantel.net.om) which is located a few yards away from Qurum Beach but is far more oriental in ambience and charges considerably less than the other hotels nearby. It has a swimming pool and a Lebanese restaurant and charges from OR27 + taxes for a double room.

The *Sheraton Qurum* (tel 605 945; fax 605 968) is an annex and beach club of the Sheraton in Ruwi and is located on Qurum Beach. It has seven rooms overlooking the Gulf of Oman, a swimming pool and gym and also lays on theme nights in its restaurants. Double rooms here are slightly cheaper than at the sister hotel at OR50 excluding taxes.

Others

There are also a lot of mid- to top-range hotels in the Muscat suburb of al-Khuwair. The *Hyatt Regency* (tel 602 888; fax 605 282; e-mail reservations@hytmuscat.com) is the best of these with a good bar and good views. Expect to pay around OR90 (£168/$234) excluding tax for a double room.

The cheapest option around Muscat, and the best location if you are after isolation with comfort, is the *Oman Dive Centre* (tel 950 261; fax 799 600) in Bander Jissah. The Dive Centre is situated in its own small bay some way out of Muscat to the south, past al-Bustan. To reach the Centre you turn right just before reaching the beach at Bander Jissah and follow a single lane road up and around a headland dropping down into the private bay. The Dive Centre has a rather pricey restaurant, showers and offers PADI diving courses. An Open Water Diver course will cost you around OR120 (£224/$312) but you do not have to be diving to stay here. If you have a tent you can camp on the beach for OR4 (£7/$10) per tent per night or stay in the homely portacabins for OR10/15.

Self-catering

If you are intending to stay for an extended time in Muscat and want to self cater there are furnished apartments available. One of the biggest operators of apartments

DISCOVER OMAN

Standing powerfully amid the
hustle and bustle of capital city life,
the Sheraton Oman Hotel
is a welcome resting place for visitors
from all over the world.

Offering 217 well appointed rooms,
swimming pool, tennis courts,
healthclub, bowling alley,
discotheque and much much more!

As an extra treat, we have scheduled
complimentary transfers to our
exclusive beach club, it's the
perfect 'rest nest'.

Why not *discover* Oman and *discover*
what the Sheraton Oman hotel can
do for you!

FOR RESERVATIONS CALL THE
FOLLOWING TOLL FREE NUMBERS
UK, IRELAND, FRANCE & GERMANY
TEL: 800 325 35353

Sheraton Oman Reservations
Direct Tel: 968 799844
Direct Fax: 968 762526

فندق شيراتــون عُمان
Sheraton Oman
H O T E L

P.O. BOX 3260 RUWI,
POST CODE 112, SULTANATE OF OMAN
TEL: 799 899 FAX: 795 791
E-mail: sheraton@omantel.net.om
http://www.sheraton.com

is *Safeer Tourism and Hotels* (tel 691 200; fax 692 227; e-mail safer@omantel.net.om) who have a number of properties in different locations around Muscat.

Eating and Drinking

Although the choice of places to eat and drink in Muscat is not as cosmopolitan as some of the other more developed countries of the Arabian Gulf, the city still has a lot to offer. Many of the better restaurants and almost all of the bars are located in the top hotels but there are also a number of traditional family run places that are worth a visit as well as a number of fast food joints and street stalls selling Middle Eastern staples such as shawarma and felafel.

RESTAURANTS

The *Blue Marlin Restaurant* (tel 737 940) is a Mediterranean seafood restaurant set in beautiful and quiet surroundings and worth a trip out from the centre of Muscat. The *Blue Marlin*, located in the Bander al-Rowdha Marina, is on the road from old Muscat to al-Bustan. The restaurant is licensed to serve alcohol and is in one of the most romantic settings in Muscat.

For those who like their meals swift and ordinary there are a lot of fast food places around the complex of shopping centres and malls by Qurum roundabout on the road west from Ruwi. Aside from the usual burger and pizza chains one place that serves good food at a reasonable price is *Fuddruckers* (tel 568 618) in the CCC Complex in Qurum.

If you are staying near Qurum Beach there are several eateries nearby that are worth a visit. By the al-Fair shopping centre there is *D'Arcy's Kitchen* (tel 600 234) which serves light meals at some very reasonable prices and next door to it is the licensed Italian restaurant *O Sole Mio* (tel 601 343) which is open until midnight and has a regular live singer to serenade diners. The *Oasis by the Sea Restaurant* (tel 602 757), facing the beach on Shatti al-Qurum serves dishes from all over the world, has live entertainment six nights a week and has a couple of terraces where you can watch the beach life while indulging in a shisha and a drink.

Unfortunately Mutrah Corniche has a dearth of restaurants which is a great shame considering the view. The *Marina Hotel*, opposite the fish market does however have the *al-Boom* rooftop restaurant. The *Mina Hotel* (tel 711 828) also has Indian restaurants on the premises with views out over the port. Opposite the incense landmark towards the Muscat end of the corniche is the licensed *al-Inshirah Restaurant* (tel 711 292) which serves international cuisine and also organises two-hour Dhow cruises twice a day if there are enough customers. Ruwi doesn't have that many great eating places. *KFC* and *al-Tajaz*, next door to each other both serve meals based around chicken which cost from around OR1.500.

For a night of Omani culture and cuisine you could try the *Seblat al-Bustan* (tel 799 666). Organised by the al-Bustan Hotel every Wednesday, diners are bussed out to a mock-up Bedouin village among palm groves where traditional Omani food is served, accompanied by musicians and dancers. It is one place where you will get to savour authentic Omani cuisine and pretend that you are experiencing Arabia as it once was. You are advised to book ahead as demand for this experience is often great.

Drinking

The *Ghazal Pub* at the Qurum Inter-Continental has pool tables, a live Philippino house band and special events throughout the year. A pint of draught beer will cost around OR2.100 (£3.92/$5.45), spirits about OR2.200. The Ghazal is an English theme pub and is very popular with the expat crowd in Muscat. *Trader Vic's* cocktail lounge is next door and part of the hotel. Another popular place to drink, with great views, is *Duke's Bar* in the Crowne Plaza Hotel which offers pretty much the same as the Ghazal with pub grub and a terrace. Also in the Crowne Plaza are a couple of upmarket Italian and Iranian restaurants. In Ruwi the Sheraton has a small pub, *Oliver's*, and an Italian Restaurant, *La Mamma*. If you make it out to the *Regency Hyatt Hotel* in al-Khuwair there is the *John Barry* piano bar and the *Copacabana* nightclub to follow.

ENTERTAINMENT

Life can be slow in Oman and the capital city is no exception to this rule. Explore the surrounding countryside, take a wander in the souks and eat well. Aside from this if you have time to spare you may want to look into taking a diving course in some of the most enchanting waters of the Gulf. *BluZone Watersports* (tel 737 293) organise scuba diving excursions and PADI recognised courses for around OR120. *Z-Tours* (tel 737 613) specialise in Aqua Tourism charters taking people game fishing, dolphin watching, and organise cruises around the surrounding bays.

Sport. Many of the expats indulge in sports and there are listings of local clubs in *Oman Today* magazine which is available locally.

Cinema

There are several cinemas in the suburbs which show English-language films. The main movie theatre in central Muscat is the *Star Cinema* in Ruwi which has a big screen and several mini-screens and shows films in English and Hindi. Tickets cost OR1.500.

SHOPPING

The main malls and shopping centres are to be found in al-Khuwair and Qurum. If you are interested in buying some very high quality artefacts and antiques you should visit the **Bait Muzna Gallery** (tel 739 204) opposite Bait al-Zubair in old Muscat which has some very beautiful but expensive fine art paintings, prints and antiques including khanjars (expect to pay about OR245 (£457/$636)), coffee tables made from old carved doors (OR600) and calligraphy. The Gallery is open from 9.30am-1.30pm and again from 4.30-8pm Saturday to Thursday.

The **Oman Heritage Gallery** (tel 696 974) in the Shatti al-Qurum complex of shops near the Hotel Inter-Continental sells genuine handmade articles from Omani craftsmen and although the prices may seem high these are the real McCoy, rather than some of the objects you will find elsewhere that have been made abroad. When you buy here you are also putting money and hope back into local communities that are increasingly losing their traditional skills.

HELP AND INFORMATION

Internet Cafés

City Cyber Café near the Sheraton in the banking district has fast Internet access and snacks and charges OR1 per hour.

First Internet Café is on the ground floor of the CCC Complex in Qurum.

There is also an Internet office in Muscat behind the flyover and roundabout that leads into Ruwi near the hospital. Look for a blue sign with Ali Abdulla al-Rawali Trading Internet Services in white lettering. It is open from 9am-midnight Saturday to Thursday, 4pm-midnight on Friday. The charge for access is OR1 per hour.

Post Office. The main branch is in Ruwi at the northern end of Markaz Matruh at-Tijari Street opposite the Star Cinema. There is another branch in Mutrah near the port buildings.

Telephone Office. The main telephone office is on Souk Ruwi Street, south of the main bus stations in Ruwi. You can also send faxes from there.

Medical Services. The main hospital is *al-Nahda Hospital* (tel 701 255) on the outskirts of Ruwi in Muscat. There are also a number of pharmacies and medical centres around Muscat.

Useful Organisations

British Council: tel 600 548.
Caledonian Society: tel 503 239.
Catholic Church of St Peter and St Paul: tel 701 893.
Historical Association of Oman: tel 708 494.
Oman Bird Group: tel 695 598.
The Protestant Church in Oman: tel 702 372.
Whale and Dolphin Watch: tel 700 894.

Mutrah Corniche

The corniche is the *piéce de résistance* of Muscat, and arguably of Oman. A stroll along here, at any time of the day or the night, is something to be savoured for life. The area still feels untouched and unfazed by the rush and turmoil of the western world and you will end up trying to think of some way that you could actually acquire one of the beautiful **merchants houses** that line the corniche in order to look out at such a view for the rest of your life. There is a renovated **watchtower** beside the al-Inshirah restaurant which is worth the climb up to it for the great views that it gives over the harbour and across to old Muscat.

Mutrah Souk

Mutrah Souk is one of the best, one of the most traditional souks in Arabia. The main entrance is by a pelican crossing on Mutrah Corniche. With its restored palm frond roof and its maze of alleyways lit by lanterns, the souk gives you a real feel of what the place must have been like before the coming of oil in the region.

The Fish Market

In front of the hotels at the northern end of Mutrah Corniche, the colourful market is not only for fish vendors, as there are also stalls selling fruit, vegetables and spices. Traders rush around finding out the prices from their competitors and the odd trader sells produce from mats on the ground – splattering the fish or fruit with water to make it look fresher. The market is a very colourful slice of Omani life and a great place to wander around for a morning.

The area of housing known as the al-Liwatiya quarter, guarded behind a large ornate gate to the right of the entrance to the souk, is the home of a Shia sect originally from Hyderabad. The quarter is unfortunately off-limits to outsiders.

OLD MUSCAT

The Sultan's Palace, **Qasr al-Alam**, is set between the two fortresses of Jalali and Mirani which guard Muscat Harbour and its entrance. The gaudy front of the palace, built in 1972, makes a strange contrast to the often conservative architecture of the

Arabian Gulf. On the cliffs on either side of the natural harbour in front of the palace are the names of visiting ships scrawled in huge letters. Elsewhere within the walls of old Muscat, a photogenic town reminiscent of a summer's day in an English garrison town, are stretches of well-tended lawns, 18th century buildings and mosques.

Mutrah Fort, Muscat

The Twin Forts

Fort Mirani to the west and **Fort Jalali** to the east of Muscat Harbour were built in the 1580s by the then occupying force of Muscat, the Portuguese. Mirani was one of the first Omani forts to house cannon and has round towers rather than the traditional square design in order to deflect attack by cannon better. It is still used today by the armed forces and is unfortunately closed to the public. Across the harbour is Fort Jalali (meaning 'the momentous') which up until the 1970s served as a prison. Today it is used by the Omani army and has a small museum which is open to tour groups though not individual visitors.

Omani French Museum

Near the al-Alam Palace is the Omani French Museum (tel 736 613) which houses artefacts commemorating the historical links between France and Oman. The museum is open from 9am-1pm Saturday to Thursday and again from 4-6pm Saturday to Friday.

Bait al-Zubair

Bait al-Zubair (tel 736 688) in old Muscat charges OR1 entrance fee and is well worth a visit. It is open from 9.30am-1pm and from 4-7pm Saturday to Thursday. The museum, in the former home of a noble family, shows photographs of Muscat from the early to middle years of the 20th century and exhibits outlining the lives and livelihoods of the Omanis with detailed accompanying descriptions in Arabic and English. There is an hour-long video well worth watching that describes the traditional Omani way of life out in the villages and mountains and deserts. There is also a separate space in a large room upstairs for travelling exhibitions and a small gift and coffee shop. In the grounds of the museum there are recreations of several traditional Omani dwellings.

EXCURSIONS

If you can find a fisherman to take you (try at the small fishing villages out towards al-Bustan) there are several Christian cemeteries in a cove below Muscat Harbour.

The area south of old Muscat is worth exploring and has some of the most dramatic coastline in the area. **Haramel**, on the road past the village of **Sidab**, is an absolutely knockout pretty fishing village set in its own secluded cove. There is a small mosque by the sea wall, fishing boats drawn up, people mending nets that the wandering goats seem intent on eating, and kids playing among the accoutrements of fishing. A length of low housing fronts the beach and if this was anywhere but the Gulf where foreigners are prohibited from owning land there would now be a small tourist café with a guesthouse attached.

Further along the road is the rather posh **Marina Bander al-Rowdha** that has a few rather glitzy yachts tied up on the pontoons, and a chandlery. There are also sea tour companies operating from here and the *Blue Marlin Fish Restaurant*. On an outcrop of rock overlooking the Gulf of Oman near the Marina sits the spectacular location of the British Ambassador's residence.

Down the road from here is the **Capital Area Yacht Club** which has a very quiet and fine white sandy beach. There is a small bar and restaurant here and you can get day membership to use the beach and facilities for OR1.

Al-Bustan village, along the beach heading south from old Muscat, is a small, quiet fishing village with boats pulled up on the beach. The **beach** between the village and the hotel is usually quite empty and a beautiful place for a picnic. The beachfront of the nearby hotel has a plantation of palm trees between it and the hotel. It will cost to use the hotel facilities but you can hire windsurfing equipment, sailing dinghies etc., here. The sand here is whiter than the brown rather muddy stuff at Qurum Beach and the scenery far more rugged. Nearby, on al-Bustan roundabout, is the British explorer Tim Severin's dhow 'the Sohar' which was made in Sur and sailed to China in 1980. The reconstruction of an 18th century voyage between Oman and Canton took Severin and his crew eight months to complete.

MODERN MUSCAT

Natural History Museum

The modern suburbs to the west of Muscat hold less of historical interest for the visitor though the **Natural History Museum** (tel 605 406) in al-Khuwair is worth a visit. It costs 500 baiza to enter and is open from 9am-1pm Saturday to Thursday and again in the afternoons from 4-6pm Saturday to Friday. It is very useful for information on the geology and natural history of Oman and there is a separate new gallery devoted to whales and dolphins found in the Arabian Sea and Indian Ocean.

Oman Museum

In Medinat as-Sultan Qaboos, also to the west of Muscat is the Oman Museum (tel 600 946) which charges the same entrance fee as the Natural History Museum and has the same opening hours. Unfortunately, it is quite difficult to find and Bait al-Zubair in old Muscat covers much the same ground and is better presented, though lacks the Oman Museum's coverage of history. The Museum covers Omani arts and crafts, traditional weapons, architecture, manuscripts and documents, the land and its people, early history, agriculture and the mineral wealth of the country. All this is housed on two levels and because the lights in the rooms are on a timed sensor the lights quite often cut out when you are particularly engrossed in reading a description or explanation.

PARKS

Qurum Natural Park
Both a kind of funfair and a nature reserve, Qurum Natural Park is located between the Inter-Continental Hotel on the beach and the Crowne Plaza Hotel on the cliff above Qurum. Apart from the funfair and a huge man-made waterfall there is a boating lake. In line with the Sultan's conservation ethic a large part of the park is given over to a rare black mangrove forest.

Riyam Park
Riyam Park, by the southern end of Mutrah Corniche and home to the incense burner landmark on the mountain above it has cafés, landscaped lawns, a funfair and is very popular with families at the weekend. The view from the incense burner is pretty impressive.

BEACHES
Jissah Beach, south of old Muscat is one of the best public beaches around Muscat and motor boats can be hired from the local lads hanging about who can take you to find deserted beaches further along the coast. There is a car park, a small canteen and shop and a few sunshades on the beach. The nearby **Oman Dive Centre** also allows day membership to use its beach and restaurant.

Another beach worth visiting is **Qurum Beach** where you can hire **jet skis**. It is a popular picnic spot with the locals and has a number of shops, cafes and restaurants.

THE BATINAH COAST

The Batinah region stretches along the length of the coastal plain running from Muscat in the south to the border with the United Arab Emirates in the north. It is the agricultural area of Oman, the second most populous region of Oman and has the ancient port of Sohar as its capital. The coastline runs for about 270km, and the towns along its length are connected by a fast highway. The forts, mountain ranges and wadis inland are also part of the Batinah region and are easy to visit from Muscat.

SOHAR

Sohar is an ancient town 180km from Muscat. It could be a day trip from Muscat but quite a long one and it may be better to base yourself here for a few days to explore the surrounding countryside.

Sohar was mentioned in the 1st century AD as 'Omana' and was the centre of the copper mining industry, an important port linking Oman to India and the Far East. The richess of Sohar dates from the 3rd millennium BC when it was the capital of the Magan Empire that was based on the supply of copper from the surrounding copper mines – some of which are now being reworked at nearby Wadi Jizzi. Copper from the mines was transported from Sohar up the coast to Dilmun (present day Bahrain) and from there to Sumer. Sohar is also believed to be the home of the fictional

Sindbad the sailor, hero of many tales in the *1001 Nights*. With the decline in the frankincense trade in the south of the peninsula Sohar became the most important trading centre in the region. When the Portuguese had bases in Oman, Sohar was incorporated into its territory and it was also occupied by the Persians, who were finally driven out of the town and Oman by Sultan Ahmed bin Said, a descendent of the present Sultan.

Today Sohar is smaller than it was in its heyday with a population of around 90,000. Its main sights are the fort and the souks. The **Fort** (8am-2pm Saturday to Wednesday, 8am-noon and 4-6pm Thursday and Friday) is located in the old part of town (there is a modern commercial centre several kilometres inland) which stands well restored, whitewashed with a high square tower rising behind its walls. The fort has a small museum and houses the tomb of a past ruler of Oman, Sayyid Thuwaini bin Said who was murdered in the fort by his son in 1866.

Accommodation

If you visit Sohar from Muscat you are likely to want to spend the night there because of the distance. There are a couple of hotels to choose from and unfortunately neither are located in town. The *al-Wadi Hotel* (tel 840 058) is the cheaper of the two at around OR30 (£56/$77) for a double room. The other option is the *Sohar Beach Hotel* (tel 843 701) which charges more for a room but overlooks the beach. The only other staying options on the coast are much closer to Muscat and probably not worth it when Muscat has the most to offer at night.

BARKA – Bull Butting

The small seaside town of Barka is home to an impressive **fort** (open daily 7am-5pm), a **fruit and vegetable souk** on the beach (daily a.m.) and **Bait Nu'aman**, a splendid example of a fortified house with escape tunnels and a falaj built by the Imam Bil'arab bin Sultan and his brother in the 17th century. However, the main reason most visitors stop off at Barka is to watch the strange spectator sport of **Bull butting**. The only other place on the Arabian Peninsula where you will encounter this odd but useful sport is south of Fujairah on the east coast of the United Arab Emirates. The bullring in Barka is a few kilometres north of the town centre along the beach road. It is a circular, low amphitheatre and you will know that you've come to the right place by the crowds of locals who sit around the bullring and the farmers bringing their brahmin bulls along the roads leading to it. Bull butting tournaments take place in Barka every second Friday in the late afternoons of winter. Pairs of bulls are led into the centre of the ring where they scuffle for a bit until one manages to force the other out of the inner circle. In this way the farmers get to see who has the best bulls and prices can be fixed accordingly. The bulls huff and puff a bit but the only wounds that occur are to their pride.

Ras As-Sawadi

Twelve kilometres from the main Muscat to Sohar highway, and about 18km further west from Barka is a stretch of broad white **beach** with small rocky islands offshore. Ras as-Sawadi is a popular Friday destination with locals but during the week you are likely to have the area much to yourself. It is possible to haggle with the local fishermen to take you out to the islands and collect you later or you could just potter about the shoreline. The area is particularly good for shell seekers.

Damaaniyat Islands

These nine islands lie about 16 kilometres off the Batinah coast between Seeb and Barka and are known for the large variety of wildlife that have made these islands

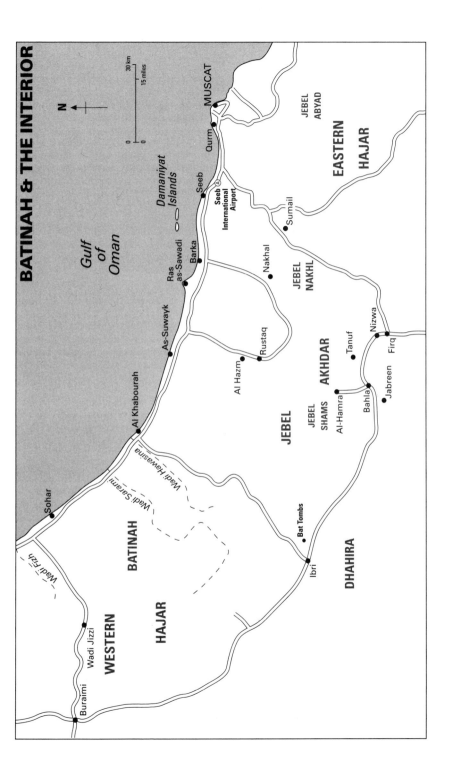

their home and breeding grounds. Two of the islands are also sites of religious significance for Omanis. The islands are closed at certain times of the year to protect breeding species. If you would like to visit the islands for bird watching, diving etc., you will need to contact the *Ministry of Regional Municipalities and Environment* (tel 696 456) in Ministries Street in the al-Khuwair district of Muscat.

Nakhal

About 35km south of Barka, on the edge of the Batinah plain, with its back to the mountains behind, rises the impressive **Nakhal fort**. Once the base of the Yaarubi tribe the fort is 30 metres high and commands the surrounding landscape. The original structure, probably a watchtower, is believed to have been added to in the 9th and 16th centuries and was fully restored in 1990. The fort is open from 7am-5pm daily.

Nearby are the **ath-Thowarah hot springs**, a few kilometres outside the village of Nakhal and sign posted from the road. The water isn't boiling but pleasantly warm and the spot is a favourite with locals who come here to picnic and bathe.

RUSTAQ

Rustaq is the administrative capital of the interior region of Batinah and was for a time in the 17th century the capital of Oman. The town gained a fair amount of infamy in the 1950s by being the stronghold of the Jebal leader Talib bin Ali. There are several reasons for taking a trip to Rustaq: the fort, an old **souk** near the entrance of the fort, and the nearby **al-Kasfar hot springs**. The springs have been channelled into a series of bathing areas for people seeking a cure but the water is very hot and you'll need to take your time immersing yourself.

The Fort at Rustaq

The old souk, one of the last bastions of craftsmanship in the area, was once a great place to look for antiques but it has now been almost superseded by the new souk in town. **Rustaq fort**, though not as beautiful as Jabreen fort, is the largest fort in Oman apart from Bahla (which is undergoing extensive renovation and closed to the public). Rustaq is about 170km from Muscat and taken in conjunction with a visit to Nakhal makes for a good day's journey out of the capital.

Wadi Bashing

There are several trips into the interior of the Batinah region that are well worth taking if you can get hold of a 4WD. Many of them are also on tour company itineraries and you may find it easier to sign up with one of these rather than attempting to do the intrepid alone. It is also likely to be safer. There are several good books about off-roading in Oman that give detailed descriptions of routes through the mountains from odometer settings: *Off-Road in Oman* by Klein, Heiner and Brickson, and the *Maverick Guide to Oman* by Peter Ochs II. You may also find the *Apex Explorer's Guide to Oman* useful if you can find a copy locally.

THE INTERIOR

SUMAIL

The Sumail Gap is a pass through the two mountain ranges of the Eastern and Western Hajars, and the main route connecting the interior with the coastal regions. The area is one of small villages, wadis and plantations. **Sumail village** is worth a visit for its **fort** – the most important of the fifteen that were built to guard the Sumail Gap. Today the fort remains unrestored and closed to the public but looks impressive nonetheless, perched on its hilltop with a few watchtowers on the surrounding peaks. The other reason for stopping at Sumail is to see the **Mazin bin Ghadouba mosque**, the first mosque to be built in Oman. The mosque was constructed by the first Omani to go on the pilgrimage to Mecca in the sixth year of the Hijra. Mazin bin Ghadouba met the Prophet Muhammed in Medina and upon his return constructed the mosque, now a place of pilgrimage. The mosque, known locally as Masjid al-Midmar, is in the heart of the village past the old souk. It is a simple building made of stone, distinguishable by its small domed roof and unlike most other mosques has no minaret.

NIZWA

The busiest town in the interior, especially for tourist traffic, is probably Nizwa. It is a pretty oasis town about 165km from Muscat and was the capital of Oman during the 16th and 17th centuries when it was the home of the Imamate. It has traditionally been the conservative heartland of the country, cut off from the cosmopolitan way of life on the coast. Arriving at the town after the long drive through the mountain scenery brings with it a sense of relief. Nizwa is peaceful, sleepy and safe these days – though less than sixty years ago a Christian entering the town may not have got out of it alive. Today Nizwa is a long established stop on the route that the tour companies take and coach loads of tourists arrive throughout the day to spend an hour or so meandering through the alleyways of the souk and climbing the stairs of the 17th century fort before getting back into the bus to see somewhere else. Nizwa is a good place to be based for a few days to explore the surrounding region and makes a pleasant change from the highways and general bustle of Muscat.

Accommodation

There are a couple of places to stay and though they are not in the town itself they are nearby. The *Majan Guest House* (tel 431 910; fax 431 911) charges OR17 (£32/$44) a night for a double room and is about 10km from Nizwa and 1km from the village of Firq, in a pretty location next to an old fort. Next to the guesthouse is the *Tanuf Restaurant* which serves decent international fare.

Another nearby and pricier hotel is the *Falaj Daris Hotel* (tel 410 500), which is about 4km from Nizwa on the Muscat road. It has a swimming pool and charges OR27 (£50/$70) per night. The other staying option is the rather posh *Nizwa Hotel* (tel 431 616), about 18km outside Nizwa. It charges OR35 (£65/$91) per night and has a licensed restaurant but is rather far away from anywhere else.

Nizwa isn't blessed with a great choice of restaurants and you may find that the best food is served in the hotels. There is however a much-praised Omani restaurant, *Bin Atique*, down by the wadi that runs through the town, close to the car park and opposite the fort.

TANUF

From Nizwa take the road to Bahla heading towards the impressive Jebel Akhdar. The name means green mountains and the range contains the highest peak in Oman. After about 20km you will see a signpost for Tanuf and a track off to the right. Tanuf is a ruined mud-brick village that was destroyed in the 1950s during the Jebali clashes. One of the only buildings with four walls left intact is the old mosque. Behind the old village lies a riverbed that flows into a deep high-sided **gorge** and on to a reservoir, which is unfortunately often empty. The wadi runs past smallholdings into the mountains behind but you will need a 4WD to explore the area further. Arriving in late afternoon the place is very atmospheric with chickens and dogs and the echoes of children playing in and exploring the falaj systems nearby. There is also one of the **beehive-shaped tombs** here (similar to those to be seen near **Bat** 60km to the northwest), and the gorge is so big and eerie that it all feels a bit like *Picnic at Hanging Rock*. During your time in Oman it is likely that you will at some point drink a bottle of Tanuf mineral water and it is from the plant near here that the water is bottled.

Back on the road heading west from Nizwa you will come to the town of **Bahla**. Before reaching the town you will pass the turning for several places that are well worth a visit but you will need a 4WD to reach them.

Wadi Ghul

This is the riverbed and village out of which rises the highest peak in Oman at nearly 10,000 feet, **Jebal Shams**. To get there, take the turn off from the road leading to al-Hamra signposted for Wadi Ghul. Follow the graded road to the village of Ghul and then follow the track up the side of the mountain. Although the top of Jebal Shams is a restricted military area you will reach a plateau where it is possible to camp. And from here you can look over the almost sheer drop of about a mile – straight down. Further on is the village of **al-Khateem** where you can follow a track that leads halfway down the gorge along the rim of the gorge. The villagers around here weave very **beautiful rugs** and **blankets** and you are likely to be approached by hawkers. Haggle fiercely.

Bahla

Back on the main road from Nizwa you will arrive at Bahla, about 40km further on. The main sight here is the massive **fort**, a UNESCO World Heritage site, though unfortunately (at the time of writing) it is closed for renovation and is likely to be for several years. It is reminiscent of European castles with old mud-brick houses around it that are still inhabited, and a surrounding wall of 12km pierced by seven gates. Bahla is one of the oldest settlements in Oman and you get a feeling that it has been lost in time out among the mountains. Bahla was also the home of Oman's pottery industry though like many traditional crafts the old ways are fast dying out. **Potters** can still be visited in a village behind the busy souk. *Bahla Motel* (tel 420 211), on the road back towards Nizwa is the only place to stay nearby.

JABREEN

It is often said, quite rightly, that if you only get to see one fort in Oman (and there are so many throughout the country that fort fatigue is a real possibility) make it **Jabreen Fort**. Jabreen is an incredible labyrinthine place. A massive fort with a 360° view of the surrounding plains and mountains, it is off the main road about 11km from Bahla heading west.

The fort was designed as the residence for the Imam Bil'arab bin Sultan al-Yaarubi in 1671 and became a seat of learning as well as a retreat for the Imam. The interior of the fort has been restored in all its glory and houses the **tomb of the Imam**, ornately painted ceilings in the *majlises*, gypsum carved arches and walls inscribed with verses of the Quran. It has been refurnished with utensils and pottery, saddlery, even manacles and rifles, books and furniture. Some rooms are labelled, others not. Some of the rooms are still used as a meeting place for the local *majlis*. The fort's layout is like something out of an Escher drawing and would be a great place for an international game of hide and seek. To see everything it is a good idea to hire a guide. Jabreen Fort is open daily from 8am-5pm and admission costs 500 baiza.

THE BAT TOMBS

If you continue on the road that runs through Bahla towards the modern administrative town of Ibri the prehistoric Bat tombs are well worth a detour. These tombs date from around BC3000 and are linked to both the Umm an-Nar and the Hafit civilisations, both of which have been excavated in the United Arab Emirates.

Bat Tombs

The tombs can be reached along an ungraded track from Kubarah on the main Bahla to Ibri road. Head for the village of al-Ain (pronounced al-eye with an n on the end) and ask there for directions to the tombs. Approaching them you will see about twenty of the distinctive beehive-shaped tombs in a line on top of a ridge against the backdrop of the 2,500 metre high Jebal Misht.

Buraimi

Due to its strategic location on the trade route between the Arabian Peninsula and the coastal ports of Oman, Buraimi has long been the scene of tribal disputes over claims to the region. Saudi Arabia only gave up claims to the region in 1975. The town lies next to and is practically conjoined with the Abu Dhabi emirate town of al-Ain. To reach Buraimi from the Oman side you will need a road pass and a visa for the United Arab Emirates as the town lies the other side of 30km of UAE territory and you will pass through the Hafit border post. Buraimi is a place where day-trippers from the Emirates come to soak up a little of Oman's charms while the Omanis enjoy the range of goods for sale in the shops of al-Ain. Omani Riyals and Emirate Dirhams are interchangeable in the shops.

SUR AND THE NORTH EAST

The region that lies between the Wahiba Sands, the eastern Hajar mountains and the northeast coast of Oman is called ash-Sharqiya and is one of the most impressive regions in Oman with the light tanned sands of the coast, the miles of ragged café-crème mountains and the ochre sand dunes of the Wahiba Desert. South of the main coastal town of Sur lie the breeding grounds of the **Green Turtle**.

SUR and the Dhow-Yards

Depending on how you are travelling, Sur is at least a four-hour drive by saloon car from Muscat at a distance of about 350km, or a 200km bumpy ride in a 4WD along the coastal tracks. Either way it is a very long drive to make the return journey in a day and you would do well to stay the night either in Sur or at the campsite further down the coast at Ras al-Junayz.

Sur has been on seafarers' maps for centuries and was an important port and ship building centre well into the 19th century. It had strong links with the Omani dominions in East Africa with goods being imported and re-exported through Sur. Today Sur is a quiet but picturesque town with a beautiful shoreline and a peaceful countenance. The countryside around the town is stunning with hilltop watchtowers, a lagoon that runs wide and far inland, the famed dhow builders yards, and fishermen landing tuna and swordfish on the beach.

Sur is above all famous for its **boatyards** where **dhows** are still made by hand and by eye from imported teak using basic hand tools. They are all built without the aid of a drawn blueprint or plan. Demand is down for the dhows and only a handful are now made each year. The yards are located beside the lagoon, off the corniche on the way to the neighbouring settlement of al-Aija.

Past the dhow builders yards is a huge restored ocean-going type of dhow called a *ghanjah* standing on crutches on land in the dramatic setting of beached dhows, the lagoon and watchtowers high above. The landed dhow, the *Fatah al-Khair*, is thought to be the last passenger-cargo vessel built in Sur about 80 years ago. Nearby in an exhibit case is a small selection of nautical implements and instruments.

A **ferry** takes you across the mouth of the lagoon to the neighbouring village of **al-Aija**, a very pretty village of low, whitewashed villas and ornate merchants houses. There is also a road that leads around the lagoon to al-Aija.

Accommodation

There are several places to stay in Sur. The *Sur Beach Resort Hotel* (tel 442 031) is expensive and several kilometres outside the town centre but is located on the beach. Also on the outskirts is the *Mercure Hotel* (tel 443 777) which is the newest of the hotels and charges OR30 for a double room. An alternative to the hotels is to rent furnished accommodation where a room comes to about OR6 per night. Call *Abu Faiz Trading Establishment* (tel 440 784; mobile 946 2619) and ask about the *Musa Sur Furnished Flats*.

Eating and Drinking

The best place to eat in Sur is the *Beach Restaurant* (tel 441 396) opposite the *Arabian Fish* restaurant which has the usual menu of Indian/Pakistani grub, omelettes, and a couple of local dishes on offer. The restaurant is run by Mohammed who is a good contact regarding local car hire, trips to the surrounding area and finding accommodation.

Green Turtles at RAS AL-HADD and RAS AL-JUNAYZ

The headland and beaches around Ras al-Hadd are noted for the fact that between September and December **Green Turtles** come ashore in large numbers under cover of darkness to lay their eggs in deep pits up on the beaches. Ras al-Junayz is also the easternmost point of the Arabian Peninsula.

To visit the **campsite** and **turtle nesting areas** in Ras al-Junayz you will need to apply for a permit from the *Ministry of Regional Municipalities and Environment* in the Ministries area of al-Khuwair in Muscat (tel 696 456). You should apply for this at least several days before making the trip out to see the turtles. Permits from the ministry cost OR1 per person. A 4WD trip to Ras al-Hadd with an overnight stay at the breeding grounds can be arranged through any of the tour companies mentioned earlier. *Zubair Tours* for example charges from OR225 (£417/$584) per vehicle of four people. Park wardens lead visitors down to the egg laying grounds around midnight and because the turtles are wary of light and movement no torches or cameras are allowed. Turtles can lay around 100 eggs at a time in the large pits that they dig and then cover with their flippers. The eggs take about 50 days to hatch and then the tiny baby turtles (measuring about 5cm in length at birth) dig their way out of the sand before sprinting down to the sea dodging peckish seagulls.

Qalhat

Those globe trotters of the ancient world Marco Polo and Ibn Battuta both passed through the ancient city of Qalhat and wrote of it as a thriving port. Pliny, writing in 70AD also mentions Qalhat. However, the city was decimated by an earthquake and then again in 1508 by the Portuguese who sacked the place and today very little remains except the last vestiges of the city wall and a sad lonely ruin overlooking the sea known as **Bibi Mariyam's Tomb**. This is believed to be the mosque described in such glowing terms by Ibn Battuta in 1338.

QURIYAT

If you head out on the tarmac road southwest from Muscat, after about 90km you will reach the town of Quriyat where the tarmac ends and the tracks begin. This is as far as you will be able to get in a saloon car – after this, if you want to head along the coast to Sur and Ras al-Hadd you will need a 4WD. Quriyat was once a thriving port before the Portuguese sacked the city during their occupation of the seaports in the

16th century. The surrounding plains were used for rearing horses which were exported by sea.

About 20 kilometres inland from Quriyat is the **Wadi as-Sarin nature reserve**, home to the shy and exceedingly rare **Arabian Tahr**, a species of wild goat that until a few years ago was close to extinction and is found only in Oman. The Tahr live high up in the mountains and should you get a permit to visit the nature reserve a sighting of these creatures is not guaranteed. You may be able to get permission to visit the reserve by enquiring at the *Ministry of Municipalities and Environment* (tel 696 456) in Muscat.

Bimah Sinkhole

If you continue on the track running along the coast from Quriyat you will reach the Bimah Sinkhole after about 50km. The area around here is a great place to camp and the sinkhole, 40 metres wide and 20 metres deep is just the place for a swim. The water in the hole is a mix of freshwater and saltwater and the place is very popular with locals and tourists alike. You are more likely to have the place to yourself if you visit during the week.

WAHIBA SANDS

After about three hours, driving on the Muscat to Sur road you will start to see the Wahida Sands, the phenomenal 180km by 80km area of rolling sand dunes, away to the right. There is a falaj (now disused) that runs for 190 kilometres under the Sands and you may see the maintenance shafts if you explore.

The best place to access the desert is through the village of **Minitrib**, about 190km from Muscat. Drive through the village, turn right at the circular **fort** and continue until the tarmac ends and the Sands begin. The al-Wahiba tribe, the local Bedouin, have settlements along the edge of the desert and are far less nomadic than they used to be – giving up the hardships of the old way of life for the comforts of modern living. Unless you have a 4WD you should not attempt to head out along the tracks through the sand past the end of the tarmac road, however solid they look.

Tour companies in Muscat can arrange guided tours through the Sands or you can tour around the area camping at night or based at the *al-Qabil Resthouse* (tel 481 243), 10km away from Minitrib back towards Muscat. Closer to the Sands there is the *al-Raha Tourism Camp* just outside Minitrib (tel 934 3851/483 130), owned by al-Raha Travel and Tourism. If you are looking to buy Bedouin artefacts the towns that surround the Sands such as **Sanaw** and **al-Mudayrib** have souks which are worth taking a look at.

IBRA – The Women's Souk

There is not a lot for the visitor in Ibra, a mainly agricultural town surrounded by low hills topped by watchtowers. However, at 150km from Muscat on the Sur road it is a convenient place to stop, eat and rest before continuing on your way. If you happen to be driving through the town on a Wednesday morning and are a woman then you will be able to take a wander round a souk that is a women only affair. The souk, which was set up about ten year's ago, is run by women and all men are prohibited from shopping in it. It has become justifiably famous as a place where women can go to shop and to socialise without the impatient accompaniment of the men folk. If you arrive on a Tuesday and wish to stay the night in Ibra to see the souk, the *Ibra Motel* is a clean and friendly place to stop and charges OR9 (£17/$23) for a single and OR10.500 a double room.

DHOFAR AND SALALAH

DHOFAR

The southern region of Oman, known as Dhofar, is famous for several things – the **frankincense trees** that proliferate in the region, the fiercely independent **Jebali tribes** who live there and the **monsoon** (the *Khareef*) which hits the region and leaves the countryside in bloom. Salalah is also the place where Sultan Qaboos was born and has a palace and where his father spent much of his time during the last years of his reign. The high season here is during the Khareef when many tourists, especially from neighbouring GCC countries, come here to experience the cooler climate and see the rains. The Khareef lasts from June until September and so comes as the summer heat in the north kicks in. This is why Salalah is such a pleasant retreat for those nationals who perhaps can't afford to fly to Europe or America for part of the summer. Coming here during the winter the mountainsides are not covered in green but look like a British national park after a long dry summer.

Because of the guaranteed annual rains the agriculture and local produce is very different to the northern regions. You can buy mangoes, papaya, and other tropical fruits here. Salalah is on the Arabian Sea which is noticeably warmer than the northern seas. The best place to see the frankincense trees (*Boswellia sacra*) are on the northern slopes of Jebel Qara behind the monsoon zone. Considered to be the finest in the world, frankincense is made from the dried resin of the trees which is collected between March and May, stowed and then sold in September. The frankinsence tree is only found in Dhofar, the Hadhramaut and Somalia.

SALALAH

Salalah is Oman's second city and is a rather new town with a strong resemblance to Goa in India with its roadside stalls selling coconuts and bananas, and groves of palm trees. The **beaches** here are magnificent with miles of pure white sand and empty warm sea where the occasional school of **dolphins** break the surface near the shore. If you ever wondered about where to find the clichéd miles upon miles of unspoilt seashore you will find it here.

There isn't a great deal to do in Salalah and four days is adequate to see the main sights unless you are after a beach holiday and stay in one of the five star hotels or resort complexes. Unless you are in a group it may be cheaper in the long run to hire a car from the local firms to explore the area than hiring taxis. You can get around pretty much all of the sites in a saloon car.

Arrival and Departure

There are three ways to arrive in Salalah: under your own steam and preferably in a 4WD, by coach or by aeroplane from Muscat. Salalah is 1,040km by good tarmac road from Muscat; the journey (a monotonous one through flat *sabkha* desert) takes about twelve hours and there are several resthouses and restaurants along the way. By air the trip takes about 90 minutes.

Oman Air flies between Muscat and Salalah twice daily and tickets cost OR50 (£93/$130) return. Salalah airport (tel 204 311) is located a few kilometres to the north of the city. There isn't a bus service between the airport and the centre of town so you will need to take a taxi and haggle over the fare. If you arrive by ONTC coach you will be dropped opposite the *Salalah Tourist Hotel* at the ONTC station. There are several other coach companies with offices near the new souk (next to the ONTC station). There are usually two daily services each way between Muscat and Salalah and the fare, whoever you travel with, is OR7 (£13/$18) one way.

City Layout

Salalah is spread out over several kilometres and walking from the centre of town to the beach can take about an hour. The central area of town is around the intersection of an-Nahda Street (which runs north-south) and as-Salaam Street (which runs east-west and parallel to 23 July Street). Many of the shops and banks that will be useful to you are along as-Salaam Street. Walking south on an-Nahdah Street will take you to **Sultan Qaboos' Palace** and the Arabian Sea.

City Transport

Behind HSBC on as-Salaam Street is a small taxi and minibus rank. The minibuses wait until they are full before heading out in the direction of Mirbat. There is often a much longer wait for a minibus out to Mughsail beach as there isn't a great demand. Best to get there early in the morning if you intend travelling to Mughsail. The taxi drivers are pretty honest around Salalah and are less likely to charge you over the odds than in the more touristy areas of Oman or in Muscat. Taxis out to the two five star hotels (the only places where you will be able to drink alcohol and dance) cost between OR1.500-OR2 (£3/$4).

There are a number of small offices around Salalah which hire out cars. One of the cheaper places to rent a car is from *ash-Shiya Rent-a-Car* (tel 297 366) whose office is on 23 July Street near the Amer al-Mashani Centre. A day's car hire, all in, costs OR9 (£17/$23). Another is *al-Miyasa Rent-a-Car* (tel 296 521) next to the *Redan Hotel*. If one office doesn't have a car available they will often ring round until they manage to get you one. There are also car rental firms in Salalah Airport.

Accommodation

The *Holiday Inn* (tel 253 333; fax 235 137) is the oldest of the tourist hotels here and lies on the beach about 5km east of Salalah town. It has a swimming pool and a couple of bars with a full length snooker table. Rates vary depending on the season. At the time of writing the hotel was being refurbished with rooms from OR18/20 (£33-37/$47-52) + 17% taxes. The Holiday Inn was for a long time the centre of all expat activity and can arrange tours out to the nearby sights.

The other five-star hotel, the *Hilton* (tel 211 234; fax 210 084; e-mail sllbc@omantel.net.com), is the newest hotel in town and it about 6km to the west of Salalah near the port. The hotel has a better bar than the Holiday Inn with restaurants, and rooms cost from OR58/60 (£108/$151) + 17% taxes. Rooms with a view and suites cost proportionally more. A local tour company and *Europcar* have an office here and for those looking to dance there is the *Mayfair Bar* and *Whispers* nightclub.

Salalah Tourist Hotel (tel 295 485; fax 292 145) has friendly staff and good rooms with satellite TV and a fridge. It is a fairly new building with balconies in some of the rooms at the back of the hotel but due to its position on the edge of a large patch of waste ground the wind tends to howl around it. Apart from the gusting wind the location is good, opposite the ONTC bus station and the central meat, fish and vegetable souk is very close by. Rooms cost a bargain OR10/15 (£19-28/$26-39) per night with a light breakfast of toast and tea/coffee included in the price.

The *Dhofar Hotel* (tel 292 272; fax 294 358) has rooms for OR10/14 + taxes in the low season and OR18/23 + taxes in the high. Rooms come with air-conditioning and satellite TV. It is some way away from the centre of town but is quite clean and has a good restaurant though as a government owned hotel it does not serve alcohol. It also has furnished apartments for let by the week.

The *Hana Hotel* on 23 July Street near the Dhofar Hotel charges the same as the *Salalah Tourist Hotel* but isn't as conveniently located.

There are plenty of signs around town offering furnished apartments should you

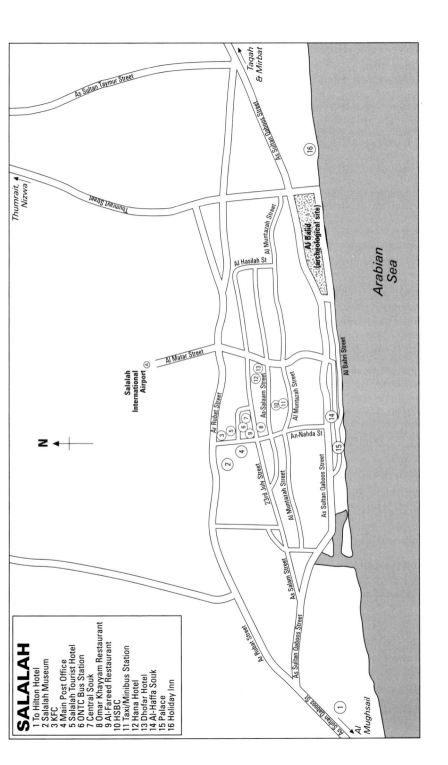

SALALAH

1 To Hilton Hotel
2 Salalah Museum
3 KFC
4 Main Post Office
5 Salalah Tourist Hotel
6 ONTC Bus Station
7 Central Souk
8 Omar Khayyam Restaurant
9 Al-Fareed Restaurant
10 HSBC
11 Taxi/Minibus Station
12 Hana Hotel
13 Dhofar Hotel
14 Al-Haffa Souk
15 Palace
16 Holiday Inn

N

Thumrait,
Nizwa

As Sultan Taymur Street

Thumayt Street

Al Matar Street

Salalah
International
Airport

Al Hasilah St

Al Muntazah Street

Ar Rubat Street

As-Salaam Street

Al Muntazah Street

An-Nahda St

23rd July Street

Al Muntazah Street

As Sultan Qaboos Street

As Salaam Street

Al Bahri Street

As Sultan Qaboos Street

Al Balid
(archeological site)

Taqah
& Mirbat

As Sultan Qaboos Street

Arabian
Sea

Ar Rubat Street

As Sultan Qaboos St

As Sultan Qaboos Street

Al
Mughsail

decide to stay longer than a few days. Salalah is small and if one office cannot help you the owner is likely to put you on to someone who can.

Eating and Drinking

Apart from the restaurants in the hotels there are a couple of good eateries on 23 July Street. *Omar Khayyam* is an ostensibly Indian restaurant which also serves Chinese and international dishes. They also serve a deliciously refreshing lime soda.

Across the street from the Omar Khayyam and set back a little is the *al-Fareed Restaurant* which offers mainly Omani food with main courses of mutton or chicken for OR2. Grilled lobster will set you back about OR5 (£9/$13). It is a traditional place with private rooms where you sit on bolsters on the floor eating a meal served on mats spread out in front of you. If you don't want to talk to your companion there are televisions in each room though they are operated centrally by the receptionist so don't be surprised if the television keeps channel hopping.

Entertainment. There are two cinemas in Salalah: one next to the HSBC on as-Salaam Street and one in al-Haffa opposite the taxi rank on Sultan Qaboos street. Both show films in Hindi and English most days.

Shopping

The **central souk** is by the ONTC bus station and is a great place to wander about to watch the old ways of life still continuing. *Jebali* men sit on the ground beside chunks of meat with their rifles by their sides, women with pierced noses in from the surrounding countryside sit behind their fruit, vegetable and incense stalls swapping stories with the neighbours and customers. The **fish market** is always full of fish and people. *Al-Mashoor* supermarket is a large department store open all day which sells pretty much anything you might need. If it doesn't the *Lulu* department store near the Dhofar Hotel will.

Lying in the shade of the Sultan's Palace is the *al-Haffa Souk* which is an area of small kiosks and shops selling all kinds of incense, brand new khanjars and ornamental swords as well as anything else you might be after in the way of trinkets, clothes and bags. It is also the home of the tailors whose little shops line both sides of the street making you wonder how they pull in customers when there is so much competition about.

Useful Information

Tourist Offices. *Dhofar Tourism* has an office opposite the Lulu Centre and can help with tours and accommodation.

Medical Services. The *Sultan Qaboos Hospital* can be reached on 211 555.

Internet Cafés

There is an Internet café on 23 July Street near al-Khareef supermarket near the Police Station lights. It is open from 9am-1pm and 4pm-2am daily and charges RO 1.200 per hour. If you can't find it telephone 297 686 and they will be able to give you directions. Another can be found on as-Sala Street near the Dhofar Hotel.

Post Office

The main post office can be located on an-Nahda Street north of the Salalah Tourist Hotel. The telephone office is also on an-Nahda Street but south of the post office, at the cross roads with al-Montazah Street.

Exploring

If you don't want to explore on your own you can always ask tour companies if they are taking a group out. *United Tours* (tel 787 448) is based in the *Europcar* office in the Salalah Hilton. They offer a four-hour tour of Salalah, 'the Frankincense Trail', and 'Archaeological Adventure'. The tours are quite expensive at around OR35 (£65/$91) per car of three persons but might be worthwhile as a guide will be able to tell you a lot about the local history.

Most of the sights are located outside Salalah but the **Museum** (open 8am-2pm Saturday to Wednesday) is worth taking a look at for the photographs by Wilfred Thesiger and the exhibits explaining the history of the region. The museum is part of the **Cultural Centre** (al-Markaz ath-Thaqaafi) on ar-Rubat Street to the northwest of the ONTC station in the Ministries district.

Not much remains of old Salalah now that modern buildings have been constructed and the area has boomed. There are some of the old, low buildings left derelict throughout the area to the south of the modern town as you walk towards the Sultan's Palace and the very beautiful Salalah Beach. From the palace end of the beach you can walk along it east to the Holiday Inn about 6km away. During the week the beach is pretty much deserted during the day and you'll have it to yourself. It is usual to see **dolphins** off the coast here, but swimming can be dangerous due to the **rip tides**. Walking eastwards from the palace you will pass the ancient city of **Dhufar** which flourished through the frankincense trade between the 12th and 16th centuries. It was visited by Marco Polo and Ibn Battuta but today all that remains are the ruins of a mosque and some tombs all but submerged in undergrowth.

Further Afield

MUGHSAIL

Heading west out of Salalah the road to Mughsail beach passes through ranges of mountains that look as though they have been created from huge mounds of instant coffee, and where there are scores cut into these mountains the underside is the colour of powdered milk. Mughsail is a long stretch of beach washed by the Arabian Sea with nobody on it except you during the week, and a few fishermen. There is a beach resort situated on the western end which has a few **beach huts** for rent costing OR15 (£28/$39) a night and a **restaurant**, with a covered upstairs terrace, where you will want to while away several hours just sipping tea and staring out to the blue ocean and the mountains behind. It is a truly beautiful spot. The beach is long and set back from it across the mostly deserted road is a small, newly constructed row of housing for the local fishermen.

Past the Beach Resort are the **Mughsail blowholes**. These are funnels in the sharp-edged volcanic rock through which water on an incoming tide shoots up with the surge of the sea. There are about four blowholes of different sizes, some of them covered with rusting grates to stop people falling down them. The sound of the sea rushing into the confined space and bits of debris being blown up into the air is rather unnerving. On a high tide the spume shoots many metres into the air.

The Furious Road

If you carry on past Mughsail beach the road climbs steeply and after about 10 minutes you will come to the so-called Furious Road. This is an amazing piece of engineering. Divided by a wadi at the bottom the road becomes a sharp series of zigzags down one side of a mountain before ascending through another series cut into the face of the opposite mountain. There is a parking area at the top where you can look over the ocean toward Yemen and back down over the mountain range you have just driven through. The area around here is great for camping out and is a better alternative than the hotels in Salalah. A track from the parking area leads back to a point overlooking the pass with a large flat circle of cement, possibly as a base for a tank to command the area. Camels and cattle are free to graze anywhere they like up in the *Jebali* regions with the occasional herder in *dishdasha* and camouflage jacket tending them. The hillsides are scored with the tracks of years of wandering livestock, stumpy trees, greens and browns and the occasional low buildings of the *Jebali* smallholdings.

Job's Tomb

The road to the tomb of Job (*Nabi Ayoub* in Arabic) leads north across Salalah plain towards Jebal Qara. As you approach the ascent of this 1,800 metre escarpment you will pass mounds that look like the burial mounds in Bahrain. Carry on up the mountainside for about 18km until you see the sign pointing left for 'an-Nabi Ayoub'. The tomb is about a mile after this turning, and it is open 24-hours a day. There is a car park nearby and close to this a restaurant with great views out towards Salalah. Non-Muslims are allowed to enter the tomb but make sure that you are dressed modestly.

East of Salalah

Travelling east out of Salalah you will reach the seaside town of **Mirbat** after about 75km. Mirbat was once the capital of Dhofar and the main port of the region where it grew rich from exporting horses and frankincense. There is a **restored fort** here and Mirbat was the scene of one of the fiercest battles during the Dhofar war. The beaches here are reminiscent of those in the highlands of Scotland with craggy bays intermingled with sandy white beach. There are several shops in the town and minibuses make the trip between here and Salalah.

Beach near Mirbat, Dhofar

Khor Rawri

If you have your own transport, heading out to Mirbat from Salalah along the coast take the turning off to the right about 7km after the town of Taqah. This track leads down to Khor Rawri, a long inlet that is now the home of many species of migrant and indigenous **birds** but was once an important port named Sumhuram. A fenced

ruin is all that remains of a pre-Islamic settlement and the site of what is thought to be a palace of the Queen of Sheba. It was from this natural harbour that frankincense from the Nejd inland was loaded and shipped to the Hadramaut (Yemen) where it was then transported overland to the markets in the north. The area is now a protected archaeological site but you may be able to get a guided tour by enquiring at the local tour companies.

UBAR

The village of **Shisr** is thought to be the site of Ubar – the fabled Atlantis of the Sands. The remains of Ubar date back to around BC2000 and it was an important meeting and trading place on the edge of the Empty Quarter. Archaeologists had been searching for this city, at the crossroads of several caravan trade routes and a place where the important commodity of sweetwater could be obtained, for many years. Then, in the early 1990s LandSat and aerial photographs pinpointed a convergence of routes at the present day village of Shisr where ongoing excavations are unearthing the remains of what looks likely to be the site Ubar. To date, artefacts including a chess-set dating from 1000AD, a frankincense burner from around 300AD and the remains of towers, walls and gates have been unearthed. It hasn't been proved conclusively that Shisr is the site of Ubar – a city mentioned in the Quran as doomed for its excesses and corrupt citizens – and there is little of the city left to see today. Shisr is about 140km northwest of Salalah and signposted from **Thumrait**.

THE MUSANDAM PENINSULA

The Musandam Peninsula is the most dramatic of all the mountainous locations in the Gulf and although difficult to get to it is well worth the effort. Located outside the main landmass of Oman, you will have to either fly there from Muscat or go overland through the UAE. It you go by land from Muscat you will need a multi-entry visa for Oman. The Peninsula covers approximately 3,000 square kilometres and has 600km of dramatic coastline. It is about 70km from the rest of the country, situated at the northernmost tip of the United Arab Emirates. The area is full of fjords, cliffs that drop vertically into the sea with occasional stretches of beach and is an expensive place to visit due to its remoteness.

Strategically situated on the Strait of Hormuz – one of the busiest shipping lanes in the world – until relatively recently the only way to reach the Peninsula was by sea, which meant that the inhabitants were cut off from the rest of the world and lived mainly by fishing, the cultivation of dates and a little trading. Rather than the khanjar traditionally worn by men in the rest of Oman, the inhabitants of the Musandam Peninsula carry a *jerz* – a long thin piece of wood about a metre in length and a few centimetres in diameter which has a small steel axe-head on one end. Although *jerz* are still made locally, many that you see on sale in the souk at Khasab will have been made in India or Pakistan, selling for around OR4 (£7/$10). You will be able to tell a locally produced *jerz* because the asking price will be about ten times that of a copy.

Because of the terrain, the best way to get to see the Musandam Peninsula is by boat. You can either organise half- or full-day trips through KT&T or do a deal with one of the local fishermen to take you out in one of their boats. Both options are, unfortunately, going to be expensive.

The main town in Musandam is Khasab.

Arrival and Departure

You do not need a special permit to visit the region and flights to Musandam cost OR40 (£75/$104) return from Seeb Airport in Muscat. The trip takes 90 minutes and there is one flight daily except at weekends (Thursday and Friday). Although the interior of the Peninsula is only accessible by 4WD there is a way into Musandam by road: by continuing northwards along the west coast from Ras al-Khaimah in the UAE. If you are entering the Peninsula via Dibba on the east coast road you will need a 4WD to continue. If you are driving to the Peninsula from Muscat you will need insurance and a visa for the UAE and permit from the Royal Oman Police in Muscat to see you through checkpoints. There is a departure tax of Dhs20 (£24/$33) payable when leaving UAE by road. The distance from Muscat to Dibba is about 350km and Khasab is another 110km further on.

Accommodation

The *Khasab Hotel* (tel 830 267; fax 830 989) is the only hotel in Musandam with basic rooms from OR20 (£37/$51) per person per night. It has a restaurant (licensed), a pub and an outdoor swimming pool. It is the centre of tourism in the region and can provide car hire, boat trips, and excursions. Be warned that because it is the only hotel in the region it is popular (especially during public and school holidays) and it is a good idea to either phone or fax for a reservation at least several days before arriving – if not before arriving in Oman – to reserve a room.

If you can't get a room at the Khasab Hotel there are also several self-catering apartments run by *Khasab Travel and Tours* (KT&T – tel 830 464; fax 830 364). KT&T have the monopoly on running trips out around the Peninsula and the price of excursions is expensive, but if you want to see the place you will need to employ their services. They can tailor trips to your individual wishes and they run regular boat tours out to the fjords and to the interior. The other accommodation alternative is camping wild in the mountains.

Eating and Drinking

The only restaurants in Musandam are in Khasab. The restaurant in the hotel serves Middle Eastern, Asian and European food, while the other restaurants such as the *Bukha* and the *Shark* serve the usual Indian/Pakistani fare. There are *shawarma* stalls in town and several grocers' shops.

EXPLORING

Khasab

Khasab is likely to be your base while exploring the area and this bustling port town has quite a bit going for it. Because of its proximity to Iran the Persian influence is palpable in the souks and around the port area. Khasab harbour is always alive with fishing boats, and dhows from Iran bringing in goods to trade. Due to its proximity Khasab does a roaring trade with Iranian 'traders' who nip across the Strait of Hormuz to Oman to buy cheap American cigarettes in the souk to take back home under cover of darkness to sell.

Khasab Fort, on the coast road, is thought to be around 250 years old. The fort is officially open from 7.30am-2.30pm on weekdays but the caretaker tends to keep his own hours. From the top of the fort's towers you'll get great views over the surrounding town and the sea.

Kumzar

If you only manage to take one trip out to sea, you should make it to Kumzar. Extremely isolated, the village is accessible only by boat from Khasab. The trip through a particularly treacherous stretch of water takes between one and two hours depending whether you are travelling in a speedboat or a dhow. The village, below a steep gorge, now has all mod cons including electricity, television and a desalination

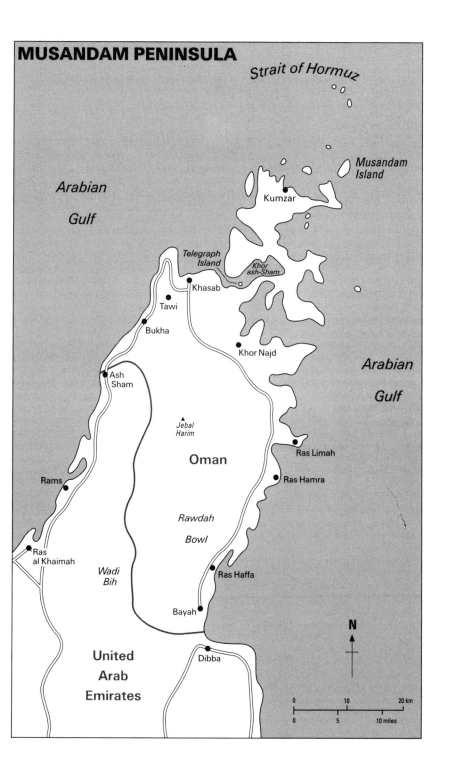

plant to supplement the water source of the village well. The inhabitants of Kumzar speak a unique dialect that has elements of Arabic, Farsi, Portuguese, Hindi and even English; they have been involved in trade with the main power mongers of the Gulf for centuries.

Telegraph Island

Telegraph Island or Jazirat al-Maqlab is a small island in Khor ash-Sham, a large inlet east of Khasab, where the British established a waystation for submarine telegraph lines that they laid to link London and Karachi. Little remains today of the base that was once the home of perhaps the most isolated employees of the British Empire except a few bricks and the remains of the cable on the sea floor.

Rawdah Bowl

If you are travelling up to Khasab through the interior of the Peninsula on the Dibba-Ras al-Khaimah route, once past the Omani border checkpoint you will be in the **Rawdah Bowl** – a fertile area surrounded by mountains and occupied and farmed by the local *Shihuh* tribe during the winter months (during the hot summers the farmers move down to the coasts and to Khasab to work on the date harvests). The Rawdah Bowl is also known for the remains of a large number of pre-Islamic cairn tombs and for the settlements that have existed here for hundreds of years. There are also a number of examples of the *bait al-Qufl* (**lock houses**) in the area. The rooms of these houses are dug about a metre into the ground and lined with stone. The semi-subterranean rooms are then covered with acacia timbering or stone slabs which in turn are covered with a mixture of earth and gravel. These houses have tiny entrances which, due to their seasonal occupation, are often kept shut up by a specially designed locking mechanisms (thus the name of the houses). Travelling from the Rawdah Bowl towards Khasab you will pass a radar station on the top of **Jebal Harim**, the highest peak in the Musandam at 2,087metres. From here the road winds down through the fertile Sayh plateau to the coast and Khasab.

The village of Tawi, off the eastern coast road about 10km from Khasab, has examples of **prehistoric rock drawings** of animals, warriors and boats on a series of boulders beside the wadi bed track that runs through the village.

Bahrain

Al-Khamis Mosque

Bahrain is promoted by its Tourism Board as the island of smiles and it is true – Bahrain is one of the friendliest countries in the Arabian Gulf. It has long been a cosmopolitan place and is thought to be the longest inhabited area of the Gulf region. Whereas the nationals of some of the other Gulf States have a bit of a reputation for haughtiness and arrogance nationals in Bahrain tend to mix freely with their expat neighbours and this has led to a pleasant hail-fellow-well-met attitude throughout the country.

GEOGRAPHY

Bahrain is the second smallest Gulf Co-operation Council state after Qatar with a total land area of about 700 square kilometres though this is increasing as more land is reclaimed from the surrounding sea, and is an archipelago made up of 33 islands. The name Bahrain means in Arabic 'two seas' and refers to the natural phenomenon of fresh water springs under the sea rising to the surface and mingling with salt water. It is also the name given to the largest island of the group which is where you are likely to be staying. This island is connected to Muharraq (the second largest island of the group and the location of Bahrain's International Airport), Sitra (a mainly industrial area) and Saudi Arabia by causeways. Outlying islands are mostly low-lying, uninhabited sandbanks. The majority of the land of Bahrain is barren limestone rock and saline sand. Jebal ad-Dukhan, Bahrain's highest point, is a mere 137 metres above sea level. Apart from a few small towns the interior of Bahrain is quite barren and although distances aren't great anywhere on the mainland it can still feel isolated driving about in a featureless desert.

If you are looking for Arabian sand dunes here you will be disappointed. The desert is mainly scrub with low-lying outcrops of rock. Bahrain is also the sovereign of the Hawar islands that are located a few miles off the coast of Qatar but are always drawn on any local map as lying off the coast of Bahrain. The Hawar Islands have been a continuing bone of contention between Qatar and Bahrain and have only just been finally ceded to the latter after a long battle in the International Court of Justice. Bahrain actively encourages excursions out to the resort it has built on the Hawar islands. The sea surrounding Bahrain is quite shallow with an average depth of 35 metres.

CLIMATE

The weather in Bahrain is characteristically very hot and humid in summer and mild and occasionally rainy in winter. The best time to visit is between November and April when the climate is not too hot with temperatures averaging around 15-24°C. There may be rain occasionally during these months and it can get cool between December and March due to prevailing northerly winds. However, the temperature is distinctly warmer than a northern winter and is the time for getting about and sightseeing on foot. Summer temperatures (from July-September) average 36°C with high humidity, hot winds and the occasional dust storm blowing over from Saudi Arabia. During these months everyone drives everywhere and remains as much as possible in air-conditioned environments. Average annual rainfall is 77mm. When the rains do come groundwater tends to remain on the streets of the capital until it is evaporated by the sun due to a lot of the infill of the reclaimed land around Manama being made up of clayey ex-seabed which doesn't drain the water away.

HISTORY

Beginnings

Bahrain was the home of one of the most ancient civilisations in the Arabian Gulf. It has been inhabited since at least the early Bronze Age and was known in the chronicles of pre-history as Dilmun. There has also been a continuing question mark over whether Bahrain was the original site of the Garden of Eden as mentioned in the Bible due to the abundance of greenery and sweetwater in the north of the island. Situated on the ancient trade routes between Mesopotamia and India the island, and the Dilmun Empire, flourished through trade and its religious sites. Dilmun was at its peak in about BC2000 when it cornered the market in the copper trade but subsequently went into decline due to the collapse of the trading routes into India and the absorbing of Dilmun into the nearby Babylonian Empire.

The first Muslims arriving in Bahrain found a country populated by a mix of Christians, Jews, Zoroastrians (from Persia) and pagans. The ruler of Bahrain

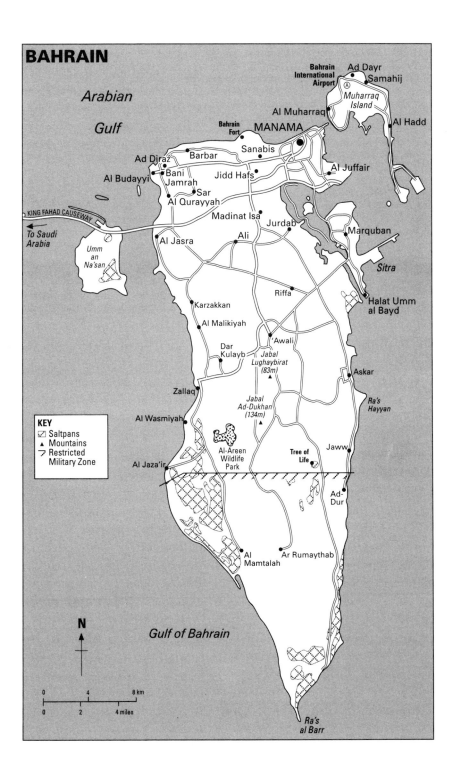

converted to Islam in about 640AD as did many of the inhabitants, though different religions continued to live side by side peacefully. During the Middle Ages the ownership of Bahrain changed hands fairly frequently due to the conflicts in the area at the time. It was a prize possession due to its strategic and independent location in the Gulf and its wealthy port. Oman occupied the island in the 1480s before being dislodged by the Portuguese, who established a base there. The Portuguese were in turn run off the island by the Persians in the 17th century. Control of Bahrain continued to shift from one great power to another until the coming of the al-Khalifa family from the east in 1782.

Conquerors from the East

The al-Khalifa family have ruled Bahrain since 1783; the first ruler being Sheikh Ahmed bin Mohammed al-Khalifa. As part of the *Bani Utbah* tribe, originally from the deserts of Iraq and the Nejd in Saudi Arabia, the al-Khalifa family gave up the nomadic life and decided to settle in Kuwait at the beginning of the 17th century. The family became wealthy through trading and moved to Zubarah in the northwest of Qatar where they established a fort and an increasingly important trading centre. The Persians, at this time the dominant power in the area, deciding that the al-Khalifas were a threat sent a force to attack Zubarah. An army led by Sheikh Ahmed (known as *al-Fatih*, the conqueror) defeated the Persians and then pushed on to take control of Bahrain.

In the early years of their rule the family's control of the islands was fairly shaky; in 1799 the Imam of Muscat attacked and defeated the al-Khalifas, forcing them back to Zubarah in Qatar, and built the 'Arad Fort in Muharraq. Then in 1809 the Omanis were driven out of Bahrain by the Wahhabis of Saudi Arabia, who in turn were ousted from power by a returning al-Khalifa force from Zubarah. In 1820 the British, who had begun to play an increasingly significant role in the Arabian Gulf, signed a general treaty of peace with the al-Khalifas in a bid to stop what it termed 'piracy' in the region. By this treaty the Sheikh of Bahrain agreed not to allow the sale of any goods obtained by 'piracy or plunder' in his dominion.

In 1825 the Sheikh, Sulman bin Ahmed, died and was succeeded by his son Khalifa who shared power with his elderly uncle, Sheikh Abdulla. Internecine conflicts between Sheikh Abdulla and Khalifa's son Mohammad arose after the death of Khalifa in 1834. Continuing rivalry between the two rulers eventually led to Mohammad occupying Muharraq Island and Abdulla claiming Manama town. In 1842 Mohammed, expelled from Bahrain by his great uncle, retreated to Zubarah where he gathered a force together and returned to Bahrain the following year to seize control and depose Abdulla. In 1856 Sheikh Mohammed signed an agreement with the British to reduce slavery and the docking of slave ships on the islands and in 1861 signed the *Treaty of Perpetual Peace and Friendship* with Britain which, in return for protection from outside aggression and allowing Britain to trade with Bahrain with minimal excise duty, Bahrain agreed to stop maritime warfare i.e., piracy.

However, further political infighting led Sheikh Mohammed to attack Qatar in 1867 and this act of aggression, a contravention of the 1861 treaty, and backed as it was by Persia and Turkey, led to intervention by the British. They sent a man-o-war to sink the Bahraini fleet and depose Mohammed, installed his brother Ali as ruler and forced him to pay 100,000 Maria Theresa dollars as a fine. The indomitable Mohammed fled to Qatar only to return in 1869, murder his brother Ali at Riffa' Fort and proclaim himself ruler once more. Shortly after his resumption of power however, he was himself deposed by one of his cousins.

Because the British viewed the stability of the Arabian Gulf as essential in order to protect their supply routes to and from the dominions in the East, once again they decided to intervene in the turbulent Bahraini politics of the day. They sent another man-o-war to Bahrain, deported both Mohammed and his cousin to Bombay and brought Isa, the son of the murdered Ali, out of exile in Qatar and installed him as ruler of Bahrain. Isa was 21 years old at the time and was to rule Bahrain for 54 years.

Sheikh Isa bin Ali al-Khalifa formed a close alliance with Britain, resisting the overtures of both Persia and Turkey who were rival powers in the region at the time. He signed treaties with Britain in 1880 and 1892 agreeing not to enter into any negotiations with foreign powers without British consent, and in effect handing over the responsibility for Bahraini defence and foreign policy to the British.

Dynastic feuding led to the abdication of Sheikh Isa in 1923 and the succession of his son Sheikh Hamad, who led the country as deputy ruler until the death of Sheikh Isa in 1936. A progressive ruler, Sheikh Hamad set about transforming Bahrain into a modern state; establishing health, education and social services, creating municipalities and communication networks. Sheikh Hamad's reign saw the decline of the pearling industry but the boom of the economy with the discovery of oil in 1932.

In 1942 Sheikh Hamad died and his son Sheikh Sulman succeeded him, ruling for twenty years and continuing the expansion of public and social services, particularly in the areas of health and education. In 1958 Sulman negotiated with Saudi Arabia to share the profits from oil reserves in a disputed territory lying between the two countries which was to improve the wealth of Bahrain considerably. But British interest in and involvement with Bahrain during this time was still very much a hands on affair. From 1926-1956 the Sheikhs of Bahrain were advised by an Englishman named Charles Belgrave in almost all policy matters. Belgrave is to be seen frequently in old Court photos of the time casting a patrician eye over the group. Eventually his and Britain's power over the rulers, together with the rise of Arab Nationalism in the 1950s, led to increased resentment and after Belgrave's forced retirement in 1956 Britain reduced its intervention in Bahraini affairs.

Sheikh Isa bin Sulman succeeded his father in 1961 and in the late 1960s Bahrain became for a time the centre of Britain's Middle East military command after its withdrawal from Aden in 1967. Then, a year later in 1968, the British Labour government declared its intention to pull out all its forces east of Suez by the end of 1971.

Independent Statehood

In January 1970 Sheikh Isa established a Council of State and halved the number of government departments and established a new set of ministries. Bahrain formally declared its independence on 15 August 1971, joining the United Nations and the Arab League shortly afterwards. Sheikh Isa's Council of State was then replaced with a Council of Ministers and in December 1972 elections were held for an Assembly to draw up a Constitution. This Constitution was promulgated in June 1973 and was genuinely democratic, dealing with women's rights and trade unions. It also stipulated that a National Assembly of thirty delegates be created which, together with the Council of Ministers would form the legislative body of Bahrain. The election of a National Assembly took place in December 1973 and although over 100 meetings of the elected assembly and council took place, the government became uneasy with the radical nature of the assembly and its activities. In 1975 Sheikh Isa dissolved the Assembly and banned all trade unions.

Following the death of Sheikh Isa bin Sulman, his son Sheikh Hamad bin Isa al-Khalifa succeeded as Emir of Bahrain on 6 March 1999.

POLITICS

Although all political parties are banned in Bahrain, the present ruler, Sheikh Hamad, is looking to introduce reform and liberalisation into Bahrain though his views on reform differ to a certain degree from those of the present Prime Minister, his uncle Sheikh Khalifa bin Sulman. To this effect, in late January 2001 the government released a prominent Shia opposition leader, Sheikh Abdul 'Amir al-Jamr from house arrest where he had been held since 1996, and a group of around 1,000 political dissidents were released from prison (the State Security Act allows the imprisonment without trial for up to three years of anyone suspected of being a threat to the government). The Emir has also invited human rights groups to visit Bahrain and in 1999 visited the Pope at the Vatican – again evidence of a more tolerant attitude towards people holding different views to his own.

However, dissidents and political prisoners still remain in jail. And the London-based Bahrain Freedom Movement continues to call for the restoration of an elected legislative assembly, the return of political exiles, the freeing of all political detainees, freedom of expression and free labour associations and an end to the State Security Act.

The appointed *shura* of September 2000, a consultative council with no legislative rights, included a Jew, a Christian, four women and an equal number of Shia and Sunni Muslims. For the politics of the Gulf this was quite a radical step to take and looks towards a more liberal system of government. Sheikh Hamad has also pledged to extend the *shura's* legislative role.

In November 2000 the Emir appointed a 56-member Supreme National Committee to draft a charter concerning the future of constitutional reform in Bahrain. In December of that year the National Action Charter was submitted to Sheikh Hamad by the Committee. It sought to turn the country into a constitutional monarchy with an elected parliament and an appointed council. However, it did not specify how much legislative power either body will have and this lack of clarity led four of the committee members to resign. In February 2001 a referendum with more than 218,000 eligible voters practically unanimously called for the formation of a constitutional monarchy. If Sheikh Hamad does become a king it will give him a broader power base at home and additionally it will raise his profile internationally. Changes in the constitution are likely to be gradual to avoid any rifts among the ruling family.

Bahrain joined the United Nations and the Arab League in 1971 and the Gulf Co-operation Council (GCC) – consisting of Saudi Arabia, Oman, Kuwait, Qatar and the United Arab Emirates – in 1981. In December 2000 Bahrain hosted a GCC summit which focussed on enhancing military co-operation between member states, enlarging the 'Peninsula Shield' defence force from its present 5,000 troops to a strength of 22,000, establishing an early warning system and linking the military headquarters of GCC nations. The creation of a customs union and introduction of a unified currency along the lines of the Euro has also been proposed.

On matters of most foreign policy issues Bahrain continues to follow the more powerful lead of its neighbour Saudi Arabia. With the resumption of the Israel-Palestine conflict in 2000 Bahrain has tended to refrain from making unilateral statements on the issue, generally content to do so in conjunction with the GCC or the Arab League. The United States 5th Fleet is based in Bahrain and there are more than 1,000 American troops stationed on the island. It is likely that the United States will move more troops to Bahrain from their bases in Saudi Arabia in the near future.

THE ECONOMY

Even before the discovery of oil in 1932 Bahrain was always one of the more affluent countries within the Gulf through its pearling, boat building, fishing and weaving industries. It was also an important regional trading centre acting as a conduit on the trade routes between Mesopotamia and the Indus Valley. Today its principle exports are mineral products including oil, base metals and textiles while its chief imports are also mineral products including oil, machinery, appliances and chemicals. Bahrain exports mainly to Saudi Arabia, the United States, India, Qatar and Taiwan; importing most of what it needs principally from Australia, the United States, Saudi Arabia, Britain and Japan.

Agriculture

Due to the low rainfall, what agriculture there is is mainly confined to the northern areas of Bahrain where freshwater springs are found. Today agriculture is mainly focused on the date palms though other local produce includes tomatoes, lettuces, okra, aubergines, garlic, pumpkins, figs, mangoes and bananas. However, a great deal of Bahrain's food is imported from abroad.

Fishing

Fishing has always been part of the Bahraini way of life providing food, fodder for the livestock and manure for the crops, as well as oil for fuel and the sealing of boats. Although most fishermen today use fibreglass dinghies with powerful outboard engines you will still see fish traps in use around the island. The *Garageer* trap works on the lobster pot design and look like semi-circular baskets made of wire and are often up to 8ft in diameter. Introduced in the 1950s you will often see these stacked up around quays and out in the bays at low tide where they are baited and left. Fish swim in through a narrow funnel in the side of the *garageer* where they become trapped.

The other type of trap, the *al-Hadr*, is far older and slightly more complicated in design. Looking like arrowheads sticking out of the water these traps were originally built using palm fronds but today are more likely to be constructed using steel stakes and wire netting. Stakes are planted in the seabed in the shape of an arrow with the sides of the diagonals covered in wire to create a funnel leading to a circular enclosure at the 'arrow' head. As the tide comes in the fish approach the shore; when it recedes they are funnelled into the jaws of the trap. These traps and the sites that they inhabit are privately owned and rented to fishermen on an annual basis.

Fishing dhows still head out to sea daily in convoy, setting off from Muharraq, Sitra and Manama. One of the best places to watch them depart, at around sunset, is beside the Ponderosa Steakhouse on the King Faisal Corniche in Manama.

Pearl Diving

A pearl develops when a foreign element, say a piece of sand or a tiny piece of shell, finds its way into the shell of one of the pearl oysters. Once inside, the oyster will try to isolate the foreign body by coating it with layers of its inner shell (*nacre* – or mother of pearl). Subsequent layers of *nacre* cover the original until after a time, after perhaps several years, a pearl is formed. The colour of a pearl can vary depending on the colour of the mother of pearl lining of the mollusc. The most precious pearls are white, rose, cream and black. Pearls are rarely perfectly round in shape and many of the oysters that were brought up from the seabed by the divers were without pearls (as much as 95 per cent of oysters lack pearls). Pearls are valued depending on their weight, lustre, colour and their shape (the most sought-after being the drop-like and spherical).

Before the discovery of oil in 1932, and its subsequent stranglehold on the economy of Bahrain, pearls were the basis of Bahrain's economy. It was often said that due to the fresh water springs that well up from the seabed around Bahrain the pearls found around the island were the purest and most lustrous in the world. Even in the literature of classical times Bahrain and pearls were often linked.

Up until the 1930s Bahrain was the king of pearldom. After this time, with the invention by the Japanese of cultured pearls, the worldwide economic depression, and the over-fishing of the pearl beds, the market for the real thing waned. Before the industry crashed, pearls provided a large proportion of the male population of Bahrain with a living wage. It is estimated that during the 19th century 30,000 people earned their living through pearling.

The fertile oyster beds around Bahrain are extensive and, although occasionally shifting, stretch along a 700-mile embankment from Ras al-Misha'ab south of Kuwait to Ras al-Khaimah, the northernmost of the United Arab Emirates. The traditional time for pearling was always June to October and boats would remain at sea throughout this period, with the occasional trip back to port in order to re-supply. Shorter trips were also made during the spring and autumn.

At the time of departure the fleets would be sent off with bands of drummers and singers bidding them farewell. A pearling boat would be made up of about 60 men; divers, rope pullers and oarsmen and the ship's crew, the divers wearing dark coloured cotton garments so as not to attract predators and to protect them from jelly fish. Each diver had two ropes: one was weighted with a rock on which the diver would descend; the other was attached to a rope basket in which were put the oyster shells that the diver collected. Divers wore a nose clip and had leather guards that they wore over their fingers and big toes to protect them from sharp coral and the edges of the shells that they pulled up from the seabed. A puller would let them down on the weighted rope and on being given the signal from below haul them up again. Divers often went to a depth of 20 metres and would stay under water for up to two minutes at a time.

Typically a diver might collect eight to twelve shells before pulling on the rope to be hauled to the surface. He would do about ten dives before climbing back on board to be replaced by another who would take his place in the water. The work was generally accompanied by a great deal of singing, clapping and foot stamping to keep the momentum and mood up. The collected shells would be left overnight and opened in the morning when the boat's captain (the *Nakuda*) collected such pearls as were discovered and awaited the pearl merchants' launches that would come out periodically on buying trips.

A pearling crew were paid a share of the profits on a trip; a puller being paid less than a diver and they were often given an advance at the beginning of the season and again during the off-season. This offer of as yet unearned money attracted many men to the industry but also meant that they were often compelled to work another season once they had accepted yet another advance from the *Nakuda*. It was a tough, physically demanding occupation and although it made some people very rich (the pearling industry was what first attracted the al-Khalifa family to Bahrain in the 18th century) most of the divers remained poor.

Pearling in Bahrain is now practically extinct though the government is seeking to rejuvenate the ancient industry. It has also banned the sale of cultured pearls – which are cheaper than natural pearls – so those that you see in Bahrain are real saltwater pearls.

Oil

The person responsible for the discovery of oil in Bahrain was an ex-British Army Major from New Zealand named Frank Holmes. He had begun prospecting for oil in

Bahrain in the 1920s, drilling artesian wells around the island to discover the composition of the land, on behalf of the British company Eastern and General Syndicate.

In 1925 this company was granted a two-year prospecting concession from the then ruler of Bahrain Sheikh Hamad. Major Holmes then set about trying to gain backing from British oil companies all of whom declined getting involved, remaining unconvinced that there was oil to be found in commercially viable quantities in Bahrain. Eventually Holmes started approaching American companies and in November 1927 the US Eastern Gulf Company acquired a two-year option which they then transferred to the Standard Oil Company of California (SOCal) in 1928.

In 1930, after lengthy negotiations with the British Foreign Office and the US State Department (Bahrain at that time being a British Protectorate) – and five years after the original concession had been granted – a fully owned subsidiary of SOCal, registered in the British Dominion of Canada, the Bahrain Petroleum Company Ltd (BAPCO) began drilling for oil on the island. The first oil well was spudded in on 16 October 1931 and oil was struck on 1 June 1932 at a depth of 2,000ft. The site of the first oil well can be visited today close to Jebal ad-Dukhan.

The first crude oil to be produced in Bahrain was sold and shipped in 1934. At this time there were only 16 wells producing. In 1936, with the decision to refine crude on the island, BAPCO started the construction of a small refinery in Sitra to process the 10,000 barrels per day that its wells were producing and extended shipping and tanking facilities on the east coast. At around this time the American marketing and distribution company Texaco Inc. acquired a half share in BAPCO and formed the jointly-owned marketing company Caltex.

In 1945, with the refinery at Sitra capable of processing more crude oil than Bahrain was producing, a 34 mile pipeline (17 miles of which was under the sea) was laid linking the Dammam oil field in Saudi Arabia to the refinery. At the time it was the longest commercial pipeline in the world.

In 1979 the state-owned Bahrain National Oil Company was established to develop oil exploration and drilling programmes but oil production in Bahrain has peaked and with only an estimated 10-15 year's worth of oil reserves left at present extraction rates Bahrain has had to look to other strategies for economic growth.

Tourism and Business

Tourism is felt to be one of the ways in which the economy of Bahrain can be diversified and to this end the government is calling for the setting up of a company to develop the country's tourism infrastructure.

Around 200,000 tourists visit Bahrain each year, with many more passing in transit flights through the International Airport. Recently it was decreed by the Emir that all foreign firms may now own property for the purpose of setting up businesses. This is likely to swell the number of firms from abroad looking to invest in the tax-free region of the Gulf and Bahrain's relatively free-wheeling lifestyle will continue to be an attractive place to work for serial expats.

THE PEOPLE

Bahrain has a population of around 617,000 with about 40 per cent of this figure being non-Bahraini nationals. As in all of the Gulf States the majority of expatriate workers are from the Indian Subcontinent, South East Asia and the English-speaking countries of the West.

Bahrain is a stable place but one of the continuing thorns in the side of the government is the division between the Sunni and Shia population of the country. The Shias account for between 50-70 per cent of the population depending on whose figures you take (there are no official figures). The majority of the Shias are descendents of the indigenous *Baharinah* and Persian immigrants who tend to be concentrated in the villages. Although the Shias have been given some political and administrative authority, Sunnis are still favoured in government, the private sector and commercial legal disputes. Overall the Shia population is much poorer than the Sunni and this has led to demonstrations and rioting throughout the years. Serious rioting occurred in 1979 (during the time of the overthrow of the Shah of Iran when the Shia cleric Ayatollah Khomeini became the leader of Iran) and again in the 1980s. There were further demonstrations in the 1990s which were again blamed by the government on Iran backed dissidents.

Health and Education

Up until 1925 when the first doctor was appointed by government most medical treatment was carried out at the American Mission Hospital. The first state hospital was opened in 1940 followed in 1957 by the Salmaniya Hospital. Education is compulsory from the age of six to eleven and free to nationals. The literacy rate is high at 85 per cent overall but among young people the rate approaches 100 per cent. State schools are single sex until age 12 though most private schools are co-educational. Education is the third largest expenditure for the government after security and defence.

FURTHER READING

The Islands of Bahrain, Angela Clarke, The Bahrain Historical and Archaeological
    Society, Bahrain, 1981.
Bahrain: Island Heritage, Shirley Kay, Motivate Publishing, 1993.
Welcome to Bahrain, James Belgrave, The Augustan Press, 1975.
Resident in Bahrain, Parween Abdul Rahman and Charles Walsham, North Star
    Publishing, 1998.
Bahrain, Kuwait & Qatar, Gordon Robison and Paul Greenway, Lonely Planet
    Publications, 2000.
Looking for Dilmun, Geoffrey Bibby, Stacey International, 1997.

PRACTICAL INFORMATION

Red Tape

Passports

Except for nationals of the GCC countries (who require only an identity card), all visitors to Bahrain require a valid passport with at least six months validity left to run. You should also ensure that your passport has enough blank pages left for visas and entry/exit stamps (generally a page is taken up by each). If you have an Israeli stamp in your passport you are very likely to encounter problems moving about the Gulf and may well be refused entry so it is best to apply for a new, clean, passport before travelling.

VISAS

Members of GCC countries do not need a visa to visit Bahrain. Tourist visas can be obtained upon arrival at Bahrain airport (or at the customs post on the King Fahad Causeway that links Saudi Arabia to Bahrain) for a duration of up to two weeks for nationals of the following countries: Britain, Germany, France, Belgium, Luxembourg, Holland, Eire, Spain, Italy, Sweden, Finland, Austria, Denmark, Switzerland, Norway, Japan, Australia, New Zealand, Canada and the USA. The visa must be paid for on arival in local currency and costs BD5 (£9.39/$13.26). It is easier to have the Dinars to hand over otherwise there will be the rigmarole of having to change money at the airport bank's prices. The visa is stamped directly into your passport and saves the time and hassle of applying for a visa before leaving.

Nationals from the USA, Canada, Britain and Eire can obtain a multiple entry visa valid for five years and which allows a stay of up to four weeks at a time for £40 ($56). Apart from those nationalities mentioned above all others must obtain a *No Objection Certificate* from either a sponsor or an agent from the Ministry of Interior and Passport Directorate, and then apply to the nearest Bahraini embassy for a visa. It is advisable to contact your nearest Bahraini Embassy some time before planned departure as regulations on visa requirements in the Gulf are changing all the time.

Visa Extensions

Anyone overstaying the two-week period stated on their visa is liable to a hefty fine upon departure from Bahrain. The island is a small place and a fortnight's stay is more than enough time for most people to see the sights and to get an idea of what makes the place tick. However, should you wish to extend the period of your stay you will need to visit the General Directorate of Immigration and Passports in Manama (tel 535 111) fill out the requisite forms and pay the fee. You will also need to find someone who will sponsor your stay. A sponsor can be a Bahraini resident, a business or a middle to top-end hotel who will vouch for your good behaviour for the duration of your stay. This isn't as serious as it sounds and some hotels will sort the whole process out for you but you are likely to be charged for this service.

Visas to other Middle Eastern Destinations

Unless you are planning to spend a few months in Bahrain you are better off sorting out visas to neighbouring countries before you leave home. Some countries are more difficult to visit than others and may ask for documentation which is far easier to get at back home. For example the visa application form for Oman asks for evidence of enough funds to cover your intended trip. The officials who process visa application forms may not actually ask to see this but such requests for documentation may arise and it is better to know that you can definitely visit a country than merely wait and hope for the best.

Immigration

If you are flying to Bahrain you are likely to be given a disembarkation card to fill out on board before landing. This will need to be handed in to the immigration officials on arrival. For most visitors immigration procedures are pretty swift and painless. If you are entering Bahrain by the causeway that links Bahrain and Saudi Arabia you should allow for delays through immigration due to traffic jams caused by commuters and freight travelling between the two countries. Friday evenings on the Causeway are always slow due to Saudis and foreigners driving over to Manama to take advantage of the nightlife and booze.

Customs

If you forgot to buy your duty free before arriving in Bahrain don't worry; there is a duty free shop in the baggage reclaim hall of the airport. The duty free allowance is limited to 200 cigarettes or 50 cigars and 250 grams of tobacco; a litre of spirits and six bottles of beer (non-Muslims only), 8 ounces of perfume; gifts up to the value of BD250 (£469/$663).

Prohibited Goods

Bahrain is one of the more lenient of the Gulf States when it comes to alcohol and the importation of pork, the consumption of which is against the tenets of Islam. You can bring both into the country but any video cassettes and literature may be taken away at customs to be viewed to make sure that they are not of a sensitive or seditious nature. If they are deemed to be harmless they will be returned in due course. Other prohibited items include firearms, ammunition, drugs and items originating in Israel. If you are on medication it is a good idea to keep a copy of the doctor's prescription to show any suspicious customs officials.

Onward Travel

The only way out of Bahrain, unless you are able to get hold of a visa for Saudi Arabia (unlikely unless you work there or are a Muslim) is by air. The departure lounge at Bahrain International Airport is like a small village and there is pretty much anything you might need within its portals: post office, telephone and fax centre, a bank, prayer rooms (segregated for men and women), a television room, business centre, several cafés and restaurants, a hotel and shower rooms. There is even an art gallery showing paintings and sculptures by local artists all of which are for sale. There is a departure tax of BD3 (£5.63/$7.95) to be paid at the airport. You will need to pay this once through security. There is a kiosk by the departure gates where you can pay.

BAHRAINI EMBASSIES AND CONSULATES ABROAD

Britain: Embassy of the State of Bahrain, 98 Gloucester Road, London SW7 4AU (tel 020-7370 5132; fax 020-7370 7773). Visa section open Monday to Friday, 9am-noon.
Canada: Consulate of the State of Bahrain, 1869 René Lévesque Boulevard West, Montréal, Québec H3H 1R4 (tel 514-931-7444; fax 514-931-5988).
USA: Embassy of the State of Bahrain, 3502 International Drive, NW, Washington, DC 20008, USA (tel 202-342 0741; fax 202-362 2192).
There are no Bahraini heads of mission in Australia, New Zealand, South Africa or Qatar.

The Bahraini Dinar (BD) is linked to the US Dollar and remains reasonably stable. The official rate of exchange at the time of writing is £1=BD0.53 (530 fils) and $1=BD0.37 (377 fils). There are no restrictions on the import or export of local or foreign currency. You may occasionally find that you receive change in Saudi Riyals (SR). This is quite common as the two currencies are interchangeable though the Bahraini Dinar is the stronger currency. The exchange rate between the two currencies is standard at BD1=SR10.

Notes and Coins

The dinar is divided into 1,000 fils. Banknotes are available in denominations of 500 fils (brown), BD1 (red), BD5 (blue), BD10 (green) and BD20 (peach). There are 5,

10, 25, 50 and 100 fils coins. It is advisable to hoard the lower denomination notes, especially the BD1 and 500 fils notes for taxi fares.

Exchange

Money can be changed at the banks, hotels or with the moneychangers in the souk who are completely trustworthy. The airport and hotels will give a poorer rate than the moneychangers and commission charges are equally variable. You will find the latest exchange rates reported daily in the local newspapers.

Travellers' Cheques

With the wide availability of ATMs in Bahrain, and the Gulf States in general, travellers' cheques may very well soon be a thing of the past. However, for now they are cashable with varying degrees of complication at banks throughout Manama but may be harder to use in the outlying towns. When cashing travellers' cheques you will need to present your passport and occasionally the original purchase receipt. Thomas Cook and American Express travellers' cheques are recognised the world over and you would be wise to travel with these in your pocket rather than your bank's own brand.

Banks

HSBC has a large presence and numerous branches in the Middle East and ATMs all over the Gulf. The main office in Manama is on al-Khalifa Avenue opposite the elaborate back door of the Pearl Diving Museum. Many of the other main banks operating in Bahrain including the *Bank of Bahrain and Kuwait* have branches and ATMs along Government Avenue near Bab al-Bahrain. Banking hours are 7am-noon, Saturday to Wednesday and 7.30-11am on Thursday. Some banks may open again from 3.30-5.30pm Saturday to Wednesday but this varies from branch to branch. Moneychangers keep longer and more varied hours. Banks are closed on Friday although you will always be able to change money at the top-end hotels and use the ATMs. Throughout Ramadan timings of all businesses vary but everything tends to open later in the morning and stay open later in the evening.

ATMs

ATMs (Automated Teller Machines) which are linked to the global access network are dotted throughout Bahrain. These machines are a godsend and save a lot of time and money wasted through trips to banks to exchange travellers' cheques or get an advance through a local bank affiliated to your own back home. And because the exchange rate that you are quoted is the interbank rate it also often means that you getting a better rate of exchange than you would do through a moneychanger. You will however be charged a fee for using the service but this is generally a lot less than you would have paid in commission if changing travellers' cheques or cash.

Most ATMs in Bahrain accept cards linked to Visa, MasterCard, Cirrus, Maestro, Electron, Plus and American Express. Check with your bank where you plastic is accepted before leaving home. The Bank of Bahrain and Kuwait operates a number of ATMs around Manama. *HSBC* operate ATMs on al-Khalifa Avenue, outside Jasanmall by Seef Mall among others. There are also several ATMs on Government Avenue down from Bab al-Bahrain.

Credit Cards. The major credit cards such as Visa, MasterCard and American Express are accepted by most businesses throughout Bahrain. However, don't trust to plastic and often it is far simpler to pay with cash.

Tipping

Most employees in service industry jobs are not paid particularly well and a tip is always appreciated if not automatically expected. As a rule of thumb ten per cent of the total bill is a good starting point. Be aware that in many of the more upmarket hotels and restaurants a 15 per cent service charge is automatically added to all bills. Of this 12 per cent is a government tax with the remaining three per cent going to management. If you decide to use the services of a porter at the airport a tip of 200 fils per item of baggage is quite usual.

COSTS

Bahrain is a bit cheaper than some of the other Gulf States but as with elsewhere in the region accommodation is where most of your budget will be spent. Supermarket prices are about the same as in Britain though if you intend to buy imported brands from home you will spend more. Restaurants are slightly cheaper than in Britain but if you want to drink alcohol with your meal you will see your bill skyrocket. Taxi fares are reasonable and comparable with the price of taxis in the Emirates and Oman, though not as cheap as in Qatar. Sample costs: canned soft drinks 200 fils (£0.37/$0.53), pastries 200-300 fils, Heinz tinned soup 450 fils (£0.85/$1.19), Chinese takeaway for 2 people BD3.5 (£6.50/$9.28), tea or coffee in a café 500 fils (£0.93/$1.32).

TELEPHONES

The national operating system is run by the government monopoly, *Bahrain Telecommunications Company (Batelco)*. The system is efficient and excellent and most of the world can be dialled or faxed directly.

Telephone Offices

Batelco has offices all over Bahrain where you can go to send faxes or make local and international calls. You can also rent mobile phones from here. The larger offices are located at Bahrain Airport and the Batelco building in the Diplomatic Area of Manama,

Fax. You will find fax machines in most hotels, in the Batelco offices, in some of the Internet cafés and often in stationery shops. The cost of sending a fax will depend on how long it takes to send and where it is being sent to.

Mobiles. You will need a roving facility on your mobile for it to be able to pick up signals in the Gulf. Contact your network provider before you leave home. You can hire mobile phones while in Bahrain from the Batelco offices in Manama.

Operator Services. An English-speaking local directory enquiries service is available by dialling 181. For international directory assistance call 191. Dial **999** for ambulance, fire and police and 140 for the speaking clock.

Calls from Hotels. Making calls from your hotel will always incur very high charges. Unless you have an unlimited budget or are being put up in the hotel by your company you are best off using a public phone booth.

Directories. If you are staying in a reasonable hotel you are likely to find English-language telephone directories in your room. If not the hotel will have a directory in reception.

Numbers

The country code for Bahrain is +973 followed by the six-digit number. If you are dialling a local number you do not need to use the country code. There are no area or city codes in Bahrain. To dial direct to the UK from Bahrain dial 00 44 followed by the area code leaving out the initial 0 of that code. To dial direct to the USA from Bahrain dial 00 1 followed by the area code.

Dial a Service

Home delivery is a big industry in Bahrain. For a small additional fee, and often for free, most things can be delivered straight to your door. Fast food outlets can nearly always offer home delivery. A couple of useful telephone numbers should you be in need of a taxi or a bite to eat are *Speedy Taxis* (tel 682 999), a radio taxi service and *Gourmet Taxi* (tel 712 713) which can deliver food to your door from a number of restaurants including Chinese, Lebanese, Italian, Indian, Thai and American. They will also deliver cigarettes.

Coin Operated and Card Phones

You will find public phones located throughout Bahrain on the streets, in shopping malls, hotels and outside some of the small kiosks. There are a number of blue payphones outside kiosks which take 100 fils coins (100 fils will last for six minutes calling anywhere in Bahrain) but booths requiring phone cards are now more numerous than coin operated phones. To use these you will need to buy Batelco phone cards from one of the outlets dotted around which display signs showing phone cards. Cards are available in denominations of between BD1 and BD15 (£28/$39). You can make international calls from these booths. There is a reduced call charge rate from 7pm-7am everyday and all day on Friday and public holidays.

POST

The postal service is generally efficient and anything posted from Bahrain is likely to turn up at its destination within a week. If you want extra security you can send mail by one of the express courier services that have offices in Manama, or use the registered mail service at the post office. A postcard or aerogramme sent from Bahrain to Britain or continental Europe will cost 160 fils (£0.30/$0.42) while the same sent to the United States costs 210 fils (£0.40/$0.55).

Post Offices

The main post office in Bahrain is located opposite Bab al-Bahrain on Government Avenue in Manama. It is open from 7am-7.30pm, Saturday to Thursday. There are other offices located throughout Bahrain but the centrality of this office makes it the most convenient. Anything posted here is also likely to reach its destination quicker than from the outlying branches and freestanding post boxes located around Bahrain.

P.O. Box Numbers

Most people if they are living and working in Bahrain get mail sent to the P.O. Box address rented by their office, but personal post office boxes can be rented for around BD15 (£28/$39) for a year. You will need to contact the central post office on Government Avenue in Manama about this. Frustratingly the addresses of almost all businesses in Bahrain are listed in the telephone directories as P.O. Box numbers which means that you never know where anything is located and so have to telephone to find out, which can then be doubly frustrating if you are new in town and don't know your way around.

Poste Restante

Most central post offices around the world have a section to receive and keep letters for a limited period for travellers. This is especially useful in the Gulf States where there is often no postal delivery service, everyone being expected to rent a P.O Box. For the traveller who isn't sure about where he or she may be staying on arrival in a new city poste restante can be invaluable. In Bahrain, letters should be addressed to you c/o Poste Restante, Manama Post Office, Government Avenue, Manama, Bahrain.

Parcels

Parcels arriving in Bahrain are sent to a sorting office in Muharraq and the addressee is then informed by card. Packages will need to be collected in person and depending on the contents duty may need to be paid. There are several international express parcel delivery companies operating in Manama.

E-MAIL AND THE INTERNET

With the ease of using the Internet to keep in contact and to send and receive documents while travelling abroad the need for poste restante facilities is becoming a thing of the past. One of the quickest ways to get an e-mail address is to log on to the Internet and go to one of the web portals that provide web-based e-mail accounts such as Yahoo (www.yahoo.com, www.yahoo.co.uk), Hotmail (www.hotmail.com) or Netscape (http://home.netscape.com/webmail). You will need to fill in a simple form and choose an identifying name or 'address' and password. Once you have this you can access your personal mailbox anywhere in the world from a computer terminal connected to the web.

In Bahrain Batelco is the sole service provider for the Internet. There are increasing amounts of Internet cafés opening up in Manama which typically charge around BD1 (£1.87/$2.65) for an hour's surfing with a half-hour minimum time limit. The most central of these is *Comtech Internet Café* situated opposite Pizza Hut, a little to the west of Municipality Avenue behind Gold City. Another, *Internet Plus Café* is at 214 Exhibition Avenue opposite the *Dairy Queen* fast food outlet. *Capital Internet Café* along the Gold Souk Road (Sheikh Abdalla Avenue) charges 800 fils (£1.48/$2.10)per hour. Another cyber café is the *Euro Internet Café* (tel 280 973) on Palace Avenue.

THE MEDIA

Because of the cosmopolitan nature of Bahrain there are plenty of newspapers, radio programmes and television stations to choose from for the English-speaking visitor.

Television

Bahrain has five TV channels broadcasting in English and Arabic at various times of the day. *BBC World* broadcasts 24 hours a day on Channel 57, the Arabic-language *Middle East Broadcasting Corporation* (MBC) transmits on Channel 46, while other channels feature a mixture of news, Egyptian and Syrian soap operas and films. Depending on how powerful your television antenna is you may also be able to pick up channels from the neighbouring Gulf States. Details of programmes are listed daily in the newspapers.

Cable & Satellite

Most homes and even more modest hotels in Bahrain have a satellite link with the usual mixture of international great to drab shows beamed in to your television set. Indian MTV is a pretty good source of entertainment with a mixture of Subcontinental pop, western rock and the ever-cynical *Beavis and Butthead*. All satellite channels seem to be highly repetitive but for news broadcasts Sky or CNN seem less so than BBC World.

Video

Videos and increasingly DVDs are available to buy and rent for rather less than in Britain and often the latest films are available to rent here before being released back home. Be warned however that anything you buy here will have been past the Saudi

Arabian censors, in consequence the running time may be a little shorter and the content a lot tamer than in the original version.

Radio

Radio Bahrain transmits in English 24 hours a day on 96.5 and 101FM broadcasting news bulletins, music and general interest programmes. Its Arabic service transmits on 801KHz and 1458KHz. The *BBC World Service* can be picked up on 15070KHz and *Voice of America* on 1260/1548KHz. There are other English-language stations operating which can often be picked up in Bahrain, especially those broadcasting to Gulf-based American forces. All programmes are listed in the newspapers.

Newspapers and Magazines

There are two English-language daily (except Friday) newspapers printed in Manama which both replicate national and world news and cost 200 fils. The *Gulf Daily News* is a popular tabloid deeming itself 'the voice of Bahrain' with good classified and entertainment sections while the dourer *Bahrain Tribune* is a broadsheet with more focus on business and politics. Both newspapers have sections dealing with news from Britain, the Subcontinent, the Philippines and the Middle East. Other English-language dailies produced elsewhere in the Gulf, especially the Dubai-based *Khaleej Times* and *Gulf News* are available on the day of publication. The two Arabic newspapers produced locally are *Al-Ayam* and *Akhbar Al-Khaleej*. English, American and international newspapers and magazines are available a day or so after their original publication date but at a much higher cost than the published price.

Bahrain Gateway is the glossy official magazine of Bahrain International Airport and is given away at the Airport. It features articles on Bahrain, other destinations and information about duty free and the airport. It is an interesting read, albeit slightly useless. *bahrain this month* (BD1) is a more gripping read with a good listings section and articles on what is going on in Bahrain throughout the month of publication. Another useful magazine cum brochure to pick up if you can find it is the annually produced *Visitor's Complete Guide to Bahrain* (BD1.5). All are available from hotels, bookshops and supermarkets. A pocket-sized brochure *What's on in Bahrain*, written in Arabic and English and published by the *Bahrain Promotions and Marketing Board*, gives a quick low down on what is coming up in the next two months in the music, art, theatre and sports arenas.

Maps

There are several maps available. The *Bahrain Map* (BD1) produced by the Ministry of Information is fairly detailed with a map of the island, and Manama on either side plus information on the various sights around the island. GeoProjects publishes *Bahrain – with City Map of Al-Manama*. A rather expensive new map costing BD3.5 (£6.57/$9.28) and a CD-ROM guide to Bahrain, *Discover Bahrain* (BD15) has recently been published by the Directorate of Tourism.

Place names

Many of the streets and roundabouts are known locally by different names to those that are printed in the official maps. Also, many of the smaller roads and streets are numbered rather than named (and even then in no discernible sequence) which can make directions slightly complicated. All this can be confusing to begin with and if given an address you should ask for a couple of nearby landmarks that will help to navigate by.

Arrival and Departure

Bahrain is one of the co-owners of *Gulf Air* and Bahrain International Airport acts as the hub of Gulf Air flights throughout the world. The airline has regular flights to all the major cities of the world. The Airport is located in Muharraq, the second largest of Bahrain's 33 islands, which is connected to Manama city by a 1 1/2 mile causeway.

BY ROAD

Cycling

There are some Indian made bicycles about but none to rent. You might be able to do a deal with one of the bicycle repair shops and get hold of a bike for a few days and it would be an interesting way to get around Manama if you were visiting in the winter. Cycling isn't a sport that the Bahrainis have taken to in any great numbers.

BUS

A national bus system runs with terminals in Manama and Muharraq and this can be okay for trips to and from the airport. However, working out the routes can take time and for a short stay in Bahrain buses are a poor option though if you do decide to take buses they are very cheap. There is a flat fee of 50 fils per trip. Number 122 travels between Muharraq and Manama and stops at the bus stop across the road from the airport terminal.

TAXI

Taxis are recognisable by their orange colour. There is a taxi rank outside Bab al-Bahrain in Manama, at the airport, and if you are staying at one of the top-end hotels there are usually queues of taxis waiting outside. There are plenty of taxis in Manama and finding one should present no problems. In fact, it is very likely that taxi drivers will seek you out and you will become heartily sick of taxis honking their horns at you. Should you wish to take trips to the outlying towns finding a taxi to take you back into Manama can present more of a problem.

Taxis are metered with flag fall at 800 fils for the first three kilometres and 100 fils per km thereafter. This charge goes up after 10pm. There is a surcharge of BD1 from the airport but strangely not to the airport. Drivers are generally very good at using the meter though especially outside the big hotels they may try for a higher hire charge. Better to walk on a bit past the hotel environs. You will also notice that often the meters are placed craftily in the drivers' footwell, almost out of sight of the passenger seat. If you intend to visit the sights outside Manama it can be more trouble and expense than it is worth to hire a taxi by the hour. You will be better off renting a car for a day or so. Tip as you see fit.

Shared Transport

Shared taxis are the Toyota pick-ups recognisable by a yellow circle on the door and an orange and white number plate which circumnavigate Manama. Shared taxis do not have to use meters and unless you are staying in Bahrain for quite a while or know Manama well, it is best to avoid them and the hassle over language and fares that taking these entails.

HITCHHIKING

Hitchhiking in the winter is an option if you have unlimited time and patience but is not as widely practiced here as in some of the other Gulf States. Also, Bahrain's drivers aren't the most diligent in the world and walking along a highway is somewhat risky. You may also be viewed with suspicion by security services out among the oil fields and military zones. Bahrain is a small country, and with most of the southern half a no go military zone you are better off hiring a car for a day or so to visit places outside Manama. If you do decide to do some hitching the accepted method is to stick your right arm out palm down. Bear in mind that you may be asked to pay for a lift and for safety (though it is unlikely that you will come to any harm) it is advisable to travel in pairs. A woman hitching alone could be asking for trouble.

JOINING A TOUR

One of the most hassle-free ways of getting out and about to see the sights in Bahrain is to join one of the excursions organised by tour companies. These allow you to take in the scenery while someone else is concentrating on the road ahead and a multilingual guide will often be able to tell you far more about a place than you could find out yourself. Prices vary and there is normally a minimum number of people required to make up a group before the excursion can go ahead. Look to pay around BD12 (£22/$32)) per person (children half price) for a half-day tour. *Oasis Travel and Tourism* (tel 587 720) offers several different themed tours based around Bahrain's heritage and culture, scenery, flora and fauna, history, sporting life and shopping.

Arab World Tours (tel 9637737), *Gulf Tours* (tel 211 025) and *al-Reem* (tel 710 868) all offers half- and full-day tours with different emphases on life in Bahrain. Gulf Tours (tel 294 446) run boats from the al-Fatih Highway Corniche on sightseeing tours twice a day. (9.30am-12.30pm for BD7 (£13/$18) and 3-6pm for BD8). They also run a daily dhow cruise around Manama Bay from 4-5pm (Adults BD3, children half price), boats to ad-Dar Island and they operate a floating restaurant. Most of the trips require a minimum of five people before they depart so check with the operators as to what is on offer at any given time.

DRIVING

If you are staying only a short time there is no problem driving on an international driving licence but if you are to become a resident you will need to apply for a Bahrain licence and take the local driving test. Driving in Bahrain is pretty hassle free and drivers tend to be a bit less fierce than in Qatar or the United Arab Emirates. However, you should remain vigilant.

CAR HIRE

There are a number of car hire agencies located throughout Manama. The international agencies charge around BD10 (£20) per 24 hours for a Toyota Tercel 1.3 saloon, BD45 for a four-wheel drive (4WD). Unlimited mileage and insurance are included in any hire price. The terrain in Bahrain is pretty flat and the roads well surfaced and it is unlikely that you would need to hire a 4WD. All the International agencies such as *Budget, Europcar, Thrifty* (tel 290 989) etc., have booths at the airport and in Manama. *Budget* (tel 534 100) has an office in al-Burj Mall by the Sheraton Hotel. *Hertz* has an office on Exhibition Road. You will need to show a driver's licence and leave a credit card imprint as a deposit. There are also local car hire firms that may charge less, depending on how long you intend to hire the car and the season. It is always worth asking for a discount. *Sara Rent a Car* (tel 210 260/297 600) and *Oscar Rent a Car* (tel 291 591/742 742) have offices next to each other in the Royal Gulf Centre beside the Saudi Bahrain bus station in the Hoora district and can usually give a discount.

Motorcycling. Motorcycles are still a rarity in Bahrain though you might see some very powerful beasts being driven at high speeds along the corniche roads by the locals. Some of the expat Asians have old Hondas that they potter about on.

Rules of the Road

Drive on the **right hand side** of the road. The wearing of a seat belt in the front seats of a vehicle is compulsory. Unlike in Britain, traffic lights at crossroads only allow one section of traffic to move on a green light. This allows for u-turns, of which you will make many while driving in Bahrain. To drive in Bahrain you will need either a full driving licence or an International Driving Licence.

Speed Limits. Driving in built up areas the speed limit for cars is 60km/h which increases to 80km/h on the outer limits of built up areas. You are allowed to drive at 100km/h on highways.

Parking. Parking meters operate in some parts of downtown Manama especially around the banking and diplomatic areas. Elsewhere there are plenty of empty lots to park in.

Fuel. Thankfully fuel is very cheap with a full tank in a petrol saloon car costing about BD5 (£9/$13). There are two types of petrol: Regular and Premium.

Road Systems

All road signs are in Arabic and English. The roads in Bahrain are in a very good state generally and outside of the city there are dual carriageways, and as in the other Gulf States a number of roundabouts. You can get around all the sights mentioned in this chapter without a 4WD. Traffic jams in Bahrain are rare. Bahrain authorities are as strict as anywhere else. If you are caught driving with alcohol in your veins you will be taken to a jail and only released on the payment of a large sum of money in cash. Speeding and illegal parking can lead to fines.

Breakdowns and Accidents

Should you be unfortunate enough to be involved in an accident the most important thing to remember is that you must not move your vehicle, even if it is blocking the road or a roundabout. Call the police (999) and wait for them to arrive. They will survey the scene and write an accident report. Without this report damaged vehicles cannot be repaired and insurance cannot be claimed. If you are hiring a car this is doubly important as in the event of an accident and no police report being made out the total cost of repair will be charged to the hirer.

HAZARDS

Drivers in Bahrain seem to drive slightly better and slower than in other Gulf States, but there are still quite a number of speed demons out there so beware. Another hazard that is common in Bahrain as well as other countries of the Arabian Gulf is speed bumps. These protrude much higher from the road surface than the sleeping policemen in Britain and there are often no warning signs. Because they are often covered in dirt they can be hard to see and if you hit one at high speed it will damage your car. Camels on the road are also common outside Manama and if you hit one of these you and the car will suffer severe damage.

Road Blocks. The southern part of Bahrain is a no go military zone and you are likely to encounter army checkpoints towards the south of the island. These will indicate that you have come too far south and should turn around and head back northwards.

Apart from the resort on the Hawar islands, and the *al-Bander* Resort in Sitra there are no accommodation options open to the casual visitor outside of Manama. This will mean staying in the city, which is not such a bad option considering the quietude of the rest of the island after dark, or camping wild.

Youth Hostels. Bahrain has one of the four youth hostels of the region (the other three being in the United Arab Emirates) which means that accommodation costs can be among the cheapest of any trip to the region.

Camping

There are no official campsites in Bahrain but desert camping goes on around Jebal ad-Dukhan and it is possible to camp wild anywhere on the island as long as you keep a sensible distance from any military and politically sensitive areas. There are several palaces in the south of the island and it is a good idea to keep a distance from these also. If you would like to spend a night out under the stars but do not have camping equipment there are several 'desert camps' set up in the interior of the island especially for tour groups. Contact the organisations listed above in *Joining a Tour* or ask at your hotel for details of companies.

HOTELS

Almost all hotels under the five-star category are not very good value for money. The price you pay for what you get in the way of accommodation in Bahrain really isn't a bargain. For the price of an average bed and breakfast establishment in Britain you are likely to get a pokey room that would cost perhaps a third of the price in the northern Middle Eastern countries such as Egypt, Syria etc. If, when you arrive, you haven't booked into any particular hotel, pay what you can afford the first night and then look around the following day for something to your taste and budget. Room rates are often raised at the weekends when Saudis rush over the causeway to let their hair down for the weekend. Prices are almost always negotiable and you are likely to be offered a discount before you have even mentioned the word.

Booking Accommodation

Having to find somewhere to suit your budget as soon as you arrive in a strange and unfamiliar country, loaded down with baggage, can be a bit of a hassle, especially if you arrive on your own and know nobody locally. Booking a hotel room in advance, before you leave home, saves you a lot of hassle and stress. Although Internet bookings are taken by the international hotels many of the smaller hotels have not got to grips with the technology. Hotels in the Manama accommodation section have fax numbers listed where available.

Other Options

If you have friends, or friends of friends you can stay with in Bahrain it will save a large chunk of your travelling money. If, on the other hand you have money to spend freely and without caution then the *al-Bander Hotel and Tourist Resort* (tel 701 201), located in Sitra, has one of the best locations on the island. It is a pretty place with good views out to sea and self-catering accommodation. Next door is the *Bahrain Yacht Club* with a marina and a lagoon. You can hire water sports equipment here and need never move from the spot for the duration of your holiday. Further afield is the *Hawar Islands Resort Hotel* (tel 290 377). As the name suggests it is a resort on one of the Hawar islands located off the west coast of Qatar. The islands have only recently been ceded to Bahrain after a long territorial dispute with Qatar. The islands are fairly isolated and you would do well not to use them as a base for exploring Bahrain.

Manama also has a number of furnished apartments that are often let by the week. Try *Elite Residences* on 740 760 who operate several of the residences. If they can't help you they will be able to pass on the name of other operators. As a last resort, should you find that your flight is delayed or that you have arrived at night and would rather tackle Bahrain in the broad light of day there is also a hotel in the Bahrain airport.

Eating and Drinking

Eating out in Manama is one of the most popular occupations of the locals. There are many restaurants catering to all tastes and because Bahrain is a cosmopolitan place you can find anything from Afghani to sushi. Although many individual restaurants are licensed to sell alcohol to accompany meals some establishments that are not attached to a hotel may not be licensed. Because dining out is so popular it is a good idea to book ahead and the serious gastronome could do worse than getting hold of a copy of the locally available *Bahrain Restaurant Guide*.

Restaurants

There are a great many restaurants in Manama, often attached to the big hotels but also privately run businesses. Many of the hotel restaurants have themed cuisine nights and it is worth checking in the local press and in the magazine *bahrain this month* about what is being offered where. Outside of Manama city your eating options are severely curtailed and the choice will be limited to cheap Asian eats in small eateries and roadside stalls.

Cheap Eats

In Manama souk, especially among the back streets, there are a number of Indian and Pakistani restaurants. They have the menu chalked up on boards and there are no frills to the service or the food. Throughout Manama there are a number of small stalls selling mainly sandwiches and freshly squeezed fruit juices which are very good value. Stalls selling the cheap and filling *shawarma* (pitta bread filled with spit-roasted slices of chicken or lamb, salad and sesame sauce) abound.

Vegetarians

The concept of vegetarianism is nothing new to many of the Indians and Asians who work in the kitchens of a number of the restaurants around Bahrain. Many of the restaurants offer vegetarian dishes as a standard option on their menu.

Hygiene

Restaurants and almost all eating-places have a very good standard of hygiene in Bahrain. You are unlikely to get ill unless you decided to change your diet so radically that your stomach finds it can't cope with the alien cuisine. Bahrain is an island and the fish will be fresh.

Regional Specialities

Middle Eastern food from the Gulf is often only available to the foreigner if he or she is invited into the home of a Bahraini. A restaurant that advertises itself as serving Middle Eastern dishes will rely heavily on the delicious Lebanese cuisine.

DRINKING

Because all alcohol has to be imported it costs about twice the price that it does in Europe. Bars are well stocked with a fine selection of keg and bottled lagers and ales, and the usual choice of spirits that can be found in Britain and Europe. However, the range of wines is a lot more limited than you will find back home with some novel labels from around the world. Expect to pay around BD1.8 (£3.50/$4.75) for a pint of draught lager such as Fosters in a mid-end bar, a lot more in one of the five-star hotels. Spirits cost around BD1.6 a shot, mixers around 300 fils (£0.55/$0.80).

Because of the restrictions on the consumption of alcohol (Bahrain is, after all, a Muslim state) all bars in Bahrain are attached to hotels. Many of them have separate entrances to the hotel that they are part of and there may be signs stating that they are members-only establishments. This is nearly always not the case but allows the management to turn away anyone they regard as undesirable.

Happy Hours and Free Drinks

Almost all bars have happy hours, generally between 5-8pm, when the prices of drinks drop substantially. Many of the more popular (and less seedy) bars have ladies nights aimed at the female expat population. These are a ruse to bring women into an otherwise rather male dominated environment. One or two nights a week women entering bars can pay BD2/3 and drink for free all night. Another offer may be for women entering at certain times of the night getting a number of free glasses of wine or spirits. On these nights there is generally an increase of men visiting the pubs and the same number of women as always.

Buying Alcohol

Alcohol can be bought in several outlets. *Gulf Cellar* has shops beside the Gulf Hotel, the Palace Inn Hotel and at the Central Market near al-Osra supermarket by the Pearl Roundabout in Manama and is open from 9am-9pm daily. It stocks almost anything you may desire except Absinthe. *Bahrain Marine and Mercantile International* (BMMI) has an outlet in Adliya in Manama and is open from 9am-9pm Saturday to Thursday and sells pretty much the same selection of booze.

Soft Drinks

Most of the canned drinks cost 200 fils (£0.37/$0.53), fresh fruit juices are delicious and usually cost around 700 fils for a large orange juice, fruit cocktail or milkshake.

Coffee and Tea

There are still quite a few traditional coffee shops serving Turkish coffee and shisha in the alleyways that run between the al-Khalifa and Government Avenues past Bab al-Bahrain on the way towards the bus station in Manama. Tea in the lobby of the *Meridien Hotel*, accompanied by the sound of a maestro at the piano, is a bit of a treat, and a snip at BD2.

Bahrain is very low-lying and there are no sand dunes on the island. This means that expats and visitors are deprived of the joys of wadi and dune bashing while in Bahrain. The highest peak in Bahrain is the flat-topped Jebal ad-Dukhan (Smokey Mountain) which is a mere 137 metres above sea level, and so Bahrain is hardly a mountaineer's dream destination. What Bahrain offers best is the surrounding seashore and all the water sports than can be thought of take place here. There are several **public beaches** in Bahrain the best of which is at **al-Jaza'ir** to the south-west of the island which is a long stretch of sandy beach with palm trees, shades and *barasti* huts along its length. **Ad-Dar Island** is a very small island a little way off the coast of Sitra with a pretty beach, watchtower and restaurant on it. Boat taxis for ad-Dar Island leave from the fishing port near the coast guard station and al-Bander Resort in Sitra. The island is a great place to chill out, looking back towards Manama and the water world going on all around.

Beach clubs

The majority of beaches in Bahrain tend to be private affairs the most exclusive of which is the Meridien Beach Club. It has a gym and tennis courts and private beach with water sport equipment for hire, waiter service etc., etc. However, if you are not staying at the hotel you will need to be a guest of a member and pay the rather extortionate fee of BD5 (£9/$13) to use the facilities. *Bapco* (Bahrain Petroleum Company) has a private beach at Zallaq on the west coast of Bahrain that allows day membership. Call 753 666 for details of opening times and prices.

Museums

Arriving in any country for the first time the first place that you should visit after finding a place to stay is the National Museum. Unless a curator is particularly clueless or exhibits badly labelled a National Museum will give you a clear insight into how a nation views itself and its history, and how it likes to present itself to the outsider. Bahrain has several very good museums in traditional and purpose-built buildings.

MOSQUES

Non-Muslims are not allowed to enter the majority of mosques in the Arabian Gulf but in Bahrain there is one active mosque where non-Muslims are welcomed. The **Grand**, or **al-Fatih Mosque** is located on the al-Fatih Highway that runs parallel to the sea. You can't miss it, it's the largest mosque on the island. You are allowed to explore the mosque at any time except prayer times. Make sure that you are modestly dressed before entering. There is also the **al-Khamis Mosque** which dates back to the early 8th century AD and is no longer used as a place of worship. After recent renovation work it is now open to visitors, see *Exploring: Bahrain Island* for details.

WILDLIFE

Although Bahrain's natural habitat is under threat from the industrialisation of much of the coast of the main island and the land reclamation schemes around Manama, the interior of Bahrain Island is still home to many different species of flora and fauna. Bahrain is home to 13 species of mammal including the **Ethiopian Hedgehog**, the **Indian Mongoose** and **Desert Hares** as well as **lizards**, **snakes** and an assorted array of spiders, beetles and butterflies. Around 25 species of bird including the **Barn Owl**, the **Bulbul** and **doves** breed on the islands and because they lie on the spring and autumn migration routes several hundreds of species have been sighted and recorded. If you are interested in bird-watching while in Bahrain you can contact the *Natural History Society* (tel 685 882) for more details on Bahrain's wildlife.

Because of the high salinity and high temperature of the waters around Bahrain due to the shallowness of the Gulf, marine life is quite limited. You may encounter the odd **sea snake** or **jellyfish** but shark attacks are practically unknown.

Theatre

Bahrain isn't big on theatre although some of the cultural institutes may sponsor troupes to perform in Bahrain from time to time. Check the local press or *bahrain this month* to see what it coming up. There is an amateur dramatics society (the *Manama Theatre Group* – tel 640 447) for serious thesps who want to get involved.

NIGHTCLUBS

For the visitor adamant not to stay cocooned in a hotel room, nightlife in Bahrain is likely to centre on the various drinking establishments, going for dinner in one of the restaurants, or visiting a coffee house in Manama. There are also the nightclubs.

Nightclubs in Manama range from rather seedy dives attached to some of the hotels in the souk area to flash modern clubs pumping out western dance music. The souk nightclubs should to be experienced to take a look at the underbelly of the place, especially on a Thursday or Friday evening. Although a bit dank these places are safe and can make for an interesting break from the kind of night out you may be used to at home. They are also cheaper than the clubs in the upmarket hotels. A lot of these places have Philippino bands (and increasingly bands from the former states of the Soviet Union) playing or miming western hits. Most hotels have a bar and stay open till late. Western bands and singers occasionally do one-off gigs around the Gulf States. Bryan Adams is a regular. One of the most popular nightclubs in Manama is *Barnaby Joe's* (known locally as BJ's), around the corner from *Murphy's Pub* in Adliya. It gets pretty packed with a mixed crowd most nights towards midnight.

PARKS

Kids Kingdom is a small amusement park on King Faisal Highway Corniche beside the dhow harbour and *Ponderosa Steakhouse*. It has fairground rides and a bouncy castle and is a great place to take bored kids. The park is open 8.30am-12.30pm and 4-11pm Saturday to Friday. Next to it is the *Pizza Haven* restaurant which has a special kids menu and indoor games to keep kids amused.

The King Faisal and al-Fatih Corniches are pleasant places to take a stroll but apart from these there are not too many open areas in Manama. There are plans to put some beauty back into the *al-Andalous* and *as-Salmaniya Public Gardens* in Adliya but for the present they remain in a sorry state – nothing more than patches of walled waste ground with a few palm trees and patchy grass.

Festivals

The **Bahrain Festival** is an annual countywide event that brings national and international performers together to take part in a month of celebrations. Check the *Bahrain Promotions and Marketing Board's* website www.bpmb.com or the Festival's dedicated website www.bahrainfestival.com for events taking place throughout the year.

SPORT

The climate of Bahrain is ideal for all sorts of **water sports** – scuba diving, jet skiing, water skiing, parasailing and windsurfing are all popular sports here. Contact the *Marina Club* (tel 291 527) or the *Bahrain Yacht Club* (tel 700 677) about hiring equipment. *Sitra Yacht Club*, next to al-Bander Resort, allows guests of members to pay BD2 (£3.75/$5.30) to use its private beach where you can hire dinghies and use the clubhouse. *Bahrain Sailing Club* (tel 310 252) on the al-Fatih Highway Corniche offers sailing courses for dinghies and catamarans and windsurfing lessons (BD40 for a 16-hour course). Dinghies can be hired out for about BD4.

Indoor sports are also popular and many of the five-star hotels have **tennis** and **squash courts**. Check *bahrain this month* for listings. It you enjoy **running** the *Bahrain Hash House Harriers* can be contacted on 694 684. *Bahrain Roadrunners* can be contacted on 756 568. There is an **ice rink** in the *Funland* complex (tel 292 313) on the al-Fatih Highway Corniche. For a safe speed kick **Go-karting** takes place at *Rally Town* (tel 612 992) in Manama.

Equestrianism

The *Equestrian and Horse Racing Club of Bahrain* holds races every Friday during the winter season of October to March at the Sakhir Racecourse near Awali. Out among the browns of the low-lying desert is the bright green racecourse and a huge stadium. Betting is against the teachings of Islam but a system called *dicaste* and *tricaste* is used whereby if you correctly guess the first two or three horses to finish you get a share of the total jackpot. Calling 440 330 can get you the race timings and schedules. There are also international show jumping events and gymkhanas organised during the winter months. Horses can be hired from the small stables on the al-Fatih Highway Corniche and the *Bahrain Riding School* (tel 690 448).

Football

Football is the favourite sport of the Bahraini masses. Major games are held at the National Stadium near A'ali and there are smaller stadiums in Riffa and Muharraq. Check the local press for details of fixtures.

Golf

Riffa Golf Club (tel 750 777; fax 750 756; info@golfbahrain.com) is an 18-hole, 6817 yard Par 72 championship PGA course set incongruously like all Gulf golf courses in the middle of the desert. There is a floodlit driving range, a golf shop and a bar and restaurant attached. Green fees for 18-holes cost from between BD23-BD27 (£43-50/$60-72) depending on the day and season. You can hire clubs, equipment and carts from the club. Telephone to confirm opening times.

Shopping You will find nearly everything you might need or want in the souks and shopping malls and supermarkets of Manama. Outside of the capital, apart from the craft villages there is little choice in the few shops that there are. Bahrain is famed for its **pearls** and these are available, along with the traditional Arabian staples of **gold**, **jewellery**, **spices** and **carpets**, all at a cheaper price than you would pay back home. Haggle in the souks to get the price right for you. Additionally, an annual island-wide sale is held in October when many shops drop the prices on stock.

Shopping Hours

The larger supermarkets, and many of the cold stores (the small grocery stores) are open all day and often late into the evenings. A working week in Bahrain is a moveable feast and it is best to telephone ahead to find out individual businesses times of opening.

Books

All the bookshops are in Manama. *Books Plus* has a good selection of modern novels and magazines and is located on Road 402 which runs past the *Qatar Airways* office near HSBC on al-Khalifa Avenue. Another good bookshop is *al-Hilal* in the *al-Burj Mall* next to the *Sheraton Hotel* on Palace Avenue. Close to *Woodlands Vegetarian Restaurant* in the souk there is a small stationers with a ragged selection of much used novels in English. There is also a branch of the Gulf-wide chain of *Family Bookshop* on Sheikh Isa al-Kabeer Avenue.

Gifts

Pottery, cloth and **palm weaving** are three of the traditional crafts that are still practised in certain villages in Bahrain. These items can make good gifts to take back home. Bahraini gold is mostly 21 or 22 carat which is a very yellow gold. The **Gold Souk** in Manama is the place to go if you want gold. You can get individual designs made up. The price of gold is quoted in the newspapers daily. Electronics are also a good buy in Bahrain but make sure you get an international guarantee with the product.

Health and Hygiene

Depending on when you travel you should dress appropriately. The summer months of June to September call for light cotton clothing, a hat and a pair of sunglasses while the winter can get quite cool so it wouldn't be a mistake to pack a sweater.

Medical Treatment

Should you fall ill while abroad your hotel will be able to provide you with the name of a doctor or medical centre. If the illness is not too serious it is often worthwhile talking to a pharmacist before going to find a doctor. They are often founts of knowledge on preventative medicine and their advice will cost you nothing – save the price of the medication that they may prescribe. Should you fall terribly ill then the main hospitals are Sulmaniya and the *American Mission Hospital. Sulmaniya Hospital* (tel 255 555) is Bahrain's largest hospital while the American Mission Hospital (tel 253 447) is the smallest. Both are of use.

Pharmacies

There are enough pharmacies in Bahrain to provide anything you may need in the way of drugs, contraceptives and medicines. Many of the products that are prescription only in Britain can be bought over the counter in Bahrain. *Jaffar Pharmacy* (tel 291 039) opposite McDonald's off Exhibition Avenue is open 24-hours and is one of the biggest pharmacies in Bahrain.

Crime and Safety

Security

Bahrain is a very safe country to visit, unaffected by any of the tensions that have arisen in the countries in the northern Middle East. Petty crime is virtually unknown and the police and security services are very efficient should you be unlucky enough to be involved in any crime, accident or misdemeanour.

The American 5th Fleet has a base on the island which means that the security of the island is guaranteed from any neighbouring dictator with an eye on occupying other parts of the Gulf. Apart from a few drunken expats, marines, and tourists staggering about at night trying to appear sober and upright in order not to offend Muslim sensibilities the island is a quiet, law-abiding place. The biggest danger that you will encounter is while driving a car on the roads but as long as you keep your wits about you are unlikely to come to any serious harm.

Drugs

You would be unwise to travel to Bahrain with any drugs of any class. Penalties for possession of cannabis, hashish or stronger are severe.

Restricted Areas

The southern tip of Bahrain Island is a restricted military area. This begins just south of a line drawn from al-Jaza'ir beach in the west to Jaww in the east. If you are driving around near the demarcation line you will see army checkpoints and unless you are driving off-road it is very unlikely that you will end up in the restricted area. Needless to say if you do end up there whatever you do don't take any photographs.

Help and Information

TOURIST INFORMATION

At present Bahrain doesn't operate any tourist offices abroad and Embassy staff are generally loath to act as unofficial tour guides. In Bahrain there is a tourist office in the Bab al-Bahrain building in Manama but the staff there are keener to sell souvenirs than to tell you where the best hotel or restaurant in town is. There is also a tourist information desk at the Airport. You will be able to get a fair amount of information from the Internet. Try a subject search through the particularly useful search engine www.google.com. The official website of the tourism section of the *Ministry of Cabinet Affairs and Information* is www.bahraintourism.com. Another useful website that has links to many other sites about Bahrain is www.arabnet/bahrain.

If you are involved in business and want to know about business opportunities in Bahrain you should contact the *Bahrain Promotions and Marketing Board* (tel +973-533 886; fax +973-531 117; www.bpmb.com) for relevant brochures and information pertaining to your trip.

For business travellers with little time on their hands the *al-Dana Meet and Assist Services* (tel 321 076; fax 321 995; danamna@batelco.com.bh) operates out of Bahrain International Airport and offers a very useful service. For a price they will meet you at the airport and assist with booking hotels, visa formalities, renting a car and planning excursions. They also operate a business centre in the departures lounge which has state of the art conference room facilities.

EMBASSIES & CONSULATES

The majority of embassies are located in the Diplomatic area of Manama and open from 8am-1pm Saturday to Wednesday. At present there is no Qatari embassy in Bahrain.

Kuwait: tel 534 040; fax 533 579.
Oman: tel 293 663; fax 293 540.
Saudi Arabia: tel 537 722; fax 533 261.
United Arab Emirates: tel 723 737; fax 727 343.
United Kingdom: tel 534 404; fax 531 273; e-mail britemb@batelco.com.bh.
United States of America: tel 237 300; fax 272 594; e-mail usismana@ batelco.com.bh.
Yemen: tel 277 072; fax 262 358.

USEFUL INFORMATION

Business Hours

Differing types of businesses operate different hours, and all tend to open later in the morning and stay open longer in the evenings during Ramadan, working shorter hours. This can be quite frustrating for anyone hoping to do serious business during Ramadan. Throughout the year almost all businesses close during the early part of the afternoon for several hours, this being imperative in the summer when the midday temperatures are akin to living in a furnace.

As a rule government offices open from 7am-2pm Saturday to Wednesday; private businesses and shops from 8am-1pm and 3-6pm Saturday to Wednesday and from 8am-1pm on Thursday. The official weekend is Thursday and Friday. Some of the international businesses work to a western timetable taking Saturday and Sunday off but many follow the Arabian Gulf timetable.

Time. Bahrain local time is GMT + 3 hours.

Electricity. The current used in Bahrain is 230 volts. British style three-pin electrical plugs and sockets are used.

USEFUL ORGANISATIONS

British Club: tel 728 245; www.arabian.net/british.
British Council: tel 261 555; www.britishcouncil.org/bahrain.
Caledonian Society: 692 370.
Welsh Society: tel 727 127; www.bahrainwelsh.com.
Sacred Heart Church: tel 253 598.
St Christopher's Cathedral: tel 253 866.

Emergency Services Numbers

All toll free: Police, Ambulance and Fire **999**.

PUBLIC HOLIDAYS AND CELEBRATIONS

Islamic holidays are dependent on the Islamic calendar rather than the Gregorian and so fall on different days each year. Bahrain observes the five feasts and festivals common all over the Muslim world. Details of these can be found in the first chapter of this book. Bahrain's **National Day** is celebrated on 16 December every year and Bahrainis also take a holiday on 1 January. Because of the large Shia population in Bahrain the anniversary of the death of the Prophet's grandson Husayn is also a public holiday. Again, this anniversary is dependent on the Islamic calendar and varies from year to year. Ramadan, the month of fasting during daylight hours, will fall in the cooler months of October, November and December for the next five years.

EXPLORING BAHRAIN

MANAMA

The English translation of Manama is 'sleeping place' which may have something to do with the number of burial mounds that lie on the outskirts of and probably underneath the city. Manama is an ancient place that has taken to the 21st century with élan. Situated on the northwest corner of Bahrain Island and connected to the smaller islands of Sitra and Muharraq by causeways, Manama is the throbbing heart of Bahrain which took over as the capital city from Muharraq in the 1930s.

Arrival and Departure

Arriving at Bahrain International Airport in Muharraq, once through customs, you can either hop in a cab into Manama for about BD2 (plus the BD1 surcharge that is placed on all taxi rides from the airport) or cross over the car park outside the airport and wait for a bus. Unless you are on a very tight budget or you know Bahrain well you will be better off paying the £6/$8 or so that it will cost to take you to the hotel of your choice.

CITY LAYOUT

Manama is growing. Every year more and more of the surrounding land is being developed and land reclamation schemes drive the sea further away. When it was built Bab al-Bahrain stood on the seafront. Today it is in the centre of town. Along the north of Manama runs the King Faisal Highway and Corniche which runs west towards the large shopping malls and the Meridien Hotel and on towards the causeway linking Saudi Arabia and Bahrain, and east towards Sheikh Hamad Causeway to Muharraq and the airport. The eastern area of Manama is bordered by the al-Fatih Highway and Corniche that runs past the National Museum and the al-Fatih Mosque, past Juffair towards the port, Mina Sulman, and on to the heavily industrialised Sitra Island and the southeast.

The main drags of Manama central are Government Avenue which runs from the diplomatic area in the northeast of the city where the main banks and offices are, past Bab al-Bahrain and the entrance to the souk, towards the central markets and the Pearl Roundabout in the northwest. Another important thoroughfare is Exhibition Avenue which runs parallel with al-Fatih Highway and has a number of useful places on it to eat, drink and shop.

City Transport

Manama is small enough to get around the central areas on foot but some hotels and a few of the better restaurants are located far enough away to necessitate a trip in a taxi. If you are visiting during the summer months the heat will also drive you into taking taxis as walking about under the burning sun is unbearable. Cars are pretty cheap in Bahrain and most people who can afford one drive their own car. Nearly all have air-conditioning fitted as standard.

ACCOMMODATION

The *Youth Hostel* (tel 727 170) in Juffair opposite the Bahrain School and signposted from the al-Fatih Highway charges BD2 per night (BD4 for non-International Youth Hostel Association members) which is an incredible bargain and the cheapest place

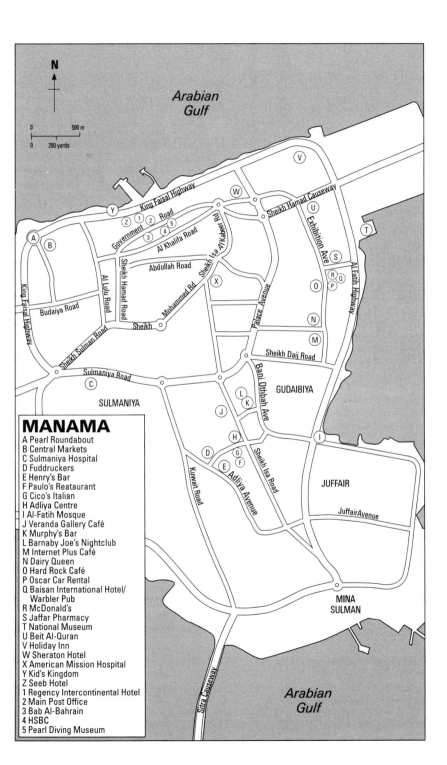

MANAMA

A Pearl Roundabout
B Central Markets
C Sulmaniya Hospital
D Fuddruckers
E Henry's Bar
F Paulo's Reataurant
G Cico's Italian
H Adliya Centre
I Al-Fatih Mosque
J Veranda Gallery Café
K Murphy's Bar
L Barnaby Joe's Nightclub
M Internet Plus Café
N Dairy Queen
O Hard Rock Café
P Oscar Car Rental
Q Baisan International Hotel/
  Warbler Pub
R McDonald's
S Jaffar Pharmacy
T National Museum
U Beit Al-Quran
V Holiday Inn
W Sheraton Hotel
X American Mission Hospital
Y Kid's Kingdom
Z Seeb Hotel
1 Regency Intercontinental Hotel
2 Main Post Office
3 Bab Al-Bahrain
4 HSBC
5 Pearl Diving Museum

in Bahrain by far. If you do not have an International Youth Hostel membership card you can buy a year's membership at the Hostel for BD8 (£15/$21). Juffair is about a BD2 taxi ride away from the centre of town and unless you are on a very tight budget you might well do better to stay at one of the hotels in downtown Manama.

Hotels

The *Seef Hotel* (tel 224 557; fax 593363) is pretty grotty at rates of BD8 (£15/$21) for a single or BD12 (£22/$31) for a double but in a good location near the Government Municipality and King Faisal Highway Corniche. Again, unless you are on a very tight budget you are best off choosing one of the mid range options.

The *Central Hotel* (tel 223 439) in the souk is pretty basic but in a great and atmospheric location. It charges BD8/12.

The *Bahrain Hotel* (tel 227 478; fax 213 509) on al-Khalifa Avenue down the road from Bab al-Bahrain has an old-fashioned wooden façade and a veranda. Once upon a time it was probably located on the sea front but today it is near the heart of Manama. Its rooms are not as great as the hotel's façade promises but they are cheap at BD8/12 with air-conditioning and a fridge.

Despite the romantic name the *Half Moon Hotel*, on Municipality Avenue, is centrally located in an interesting area of town but unfortunately rather grimy. Single rooms are BD12 and doubles BD30 (£56/$79).

The *Aradous Hotel* (tel 224 343; fax 210 535) just off Bab al-Bahrain Road is in a very central location with a rooftop swimming pool and bar, and charges BD18 (£33/$48) for a single, BD25 (£47/$66) for a double room including taxes.

The Aradous' sister hotel, the *Adhari* (tel 224 242 fax 214 707) is also centrally located on Municipality Avenue. It costs about the same as the Aradous for a room with a/c, fridge and satellite linked television and has a bar on the top floor.

The *Hotel Bab al-Bahrain* (tel 211 622; fax 213 661) is also very central, slap bang next to its namesake, however the place is a bit of a dive. It charges BD18/25 plus taxes but as ever these prices are negotiable.

There are many more upmarket hotels than mid range but the *Hotel Claridge* (tel 291 888) is somewhere in between the two. Fairly new and conveniently located near the al-Fatih Highway Corniche opposite the 24-hour *Jaffar Pharmacy* it charges BD20/30 (£47/£56, $53/$76).

The *Holiday Inn* (tel 531 122; fax 530 154) is in the diplomatic area downtown and charges BD45 (£85/$119) single and BD50 (£94/$132) double, plus 20% tax.

The *Sheraton* (tel 533 533; fax 534 069) is in the same area and offers the usual top-end hotel experience for BD60 plus taxes.

The *Regency Intercontinental* (tel 227 777; fax 229 929) is in the banking district with some of the top floor rooms having great views over the Gulf and charges BD60/68 plus taxes.

The best location of all the hotels is that of the *Meridien Hotel* (tel 580 000; fax 580 333) which is opulent and probably the best place to stay in Bahrain. It charges BD90 (£169/$238) plus 20% taxes.

All the top-end hotels offer differing rates depending on whether you are a corporate or a private guest. They also have deals running at various times of the year.

EATING AND DRINKING

There are branches of *Pizza Hut*, *Burger King*, *McDonald's* and various other home grown and imported fast food eateries all over Manama. There is also a *Hard Rock Café* on Exhibition Avenue opposite the Oscar Rent a Car office. *Schlotsky's Deli* (tel 717 797) in the Adliya Centre has a great menu of reasonably priced American-style open sandwiches, Pizzas and salads. They also deliver.

Ponderosa Steakhouse by the dhow harbour at the end of King Faisal Highway Corniche serves great steaks at generous prices with views over the sea. *Paulos* is an almost as good as genuine traditional Italian pizza/pasta restaurant in Adliya. It charges around BD3.5 (£6.50/$9.28) for a decent sized pizza and is licensed to sell alcohol. Above the restaurant is a bar with big screen playing MTV and a fast set crowd – a good place to go eating before going on. For a different burger restaurant experience try *Fuddruckers* burger place near Adliya Mosque. The staff are over attentive and over the top with a greeter at the door and someone else who can't wait to take your order. But the food is good value costing about BD3 for burger, fries, a large soft drink and as much salad as you can eat.

Cico's Italian restaurant in Adliya (tel 713 710) is one of the best in Bahrain with reasonable prices and a mixed clientele of expats and locals. It has a good wine list and serves meat, fish and pasta dishes. Expect to pay about BD10 per head for a 4-course meal with wine and aperitifs.

For a Chinese meal two of the best restaurants are the *Hong Kong* (tel 728 700) in Budaiya and *Umm al-Hassan* which has been serving up the best for twenty years.

Coffee Houses

Casa Blu (tel 717 797) is a coffeehouse that wouldn't look out of place in a film of an updated version of *1001 Nights*. A traditional coffeehouse recently opened above *Schlotzsky's Deli* in Adliya it has a rather plush but dark interior and serves flavoured coffees from BD1 and Shisha for BD2. Customers can idle away an afternoon or evening sitting on the banquettes people watching, listening to live music and integrating with Bahraini nationals, expats and tourists of both sexes. Casa Blu is open 10am-2am Saturday to Thursday and 2pm-2am on Fridays.

For a piece of the old Middle East, *Layali Zaman* (tel 293 097) next to the Ice Rink on al-Fatih Highway Corniche is a place where you can sit at tables beside Manama Bay smoking shisha and drinking mint tea. Borrow a backgammon set and while away the evenings here. If you get peckish there is a wide menu of staple Middle Eastern snacks and main meals such as shish tawouk, humous etc. The waiters are Indian but the clientele are a mix of Bahrainis, a few foreigners, students and professionals.

The *Yateem Shopping Centre*, next to the Batelco Commercial Centre, down the road from HSBC on al-Khalifa Avenue has a small café on the first floor with views over the banking district to the sea and dhows beyond. The *Veranda Gallery Café* (tel 715 868) on Sheikh Isa Road is a pretty little hideaway with a beautiful trellised terrace, set back a little from the road, and comes highly recommended.

ENTERTAINMENT

Cinema

The biggest and best cinemas showing films in the English-language are in the *Cineplex* at Seef Mall (tel 582 229) and the *Delmon Cinemas* (tel 296 090) in the GOSI Mall on Exhibition Avenue in Manama. Listings of films are better in the *Gulf Daily News* than the *Bahrain Tribune*.

Pubs and Bars

Taxi drivers are used to ferrying foreigners about Manama between the different bars and clubs. Even if you don't know which road a certain place is on the drivers will. Because of the banning of alcohol consumption in Islam the staff in bars and pubs are generally Christian Indians or Philippinos though punters are a mix of expats from all over the world, Bahraini nationals, men and women. You will often find that certain establishments are frequented by say, a mainly Philippino crowd, or mainly Europeans or Indians etc., because although Bahrain is the most non segregated country in the Gulf nationalities still tend to keep to their own kind.

The Warbler (tel 290 128), part of the Baisan Hotel off Exhibition Avenue, is one of the oldest 'pubs' in Bahrain and one of the most popular. It is a large sports pub with satellite TV screens, pool tables, a big screen and a good variety of draught beers and spirits. They also serve food with soups costing from BD1.2, burgers BD1.8, steaks BD3.5 and vegetarian meals from BD1.5. Live bands often play there, or a resident DJ and to add to the fun there are several ladies nights each week.

Henry's Bar (tel 713 971) is attached to Mansouri Hotel in Adliya, just down the road from *Paulo's* italian restaurant. It has table hockey and pool tables for the competitive and a good selection of beers. The *Sherlock Holmes* pub in the Gulf Hotel plays music loud and is often very busy with a mixed clientele of off-duty Gulf Air stewardesses, nationals and expats. The bars and restaurants of the Arabian Gulf seem to love the idea of being themed and the *Wrangler Bar* is a homesick American marine's dream. The building, part of the Elite Hotel in Juffair, is a rather cavernous place done out as a cowboy's retreat serving Budweiser beer among other tipples. It is, needless to say, pretty popular with the marines.

Trader Vic's in the Meridien is a newly opened branch of the south sea island-themed restaurant and cocktail chain. The cocktails are pricey but the ambience and beachside venue is worth it. Irish themed pubs have also arrived in the Gulf and are doing great business. *J.J. Murphy's Pub* is a very popular place serving the black stuff as well as very good food. It is located off Sheikh Isa Road, across from the Guest Palace and next door to *Barnaby Joe's* nightclub. *Fiddler's Green*, in the Diplomat Hotel, also has its wild nights.

SHOPPING

The souk area takes up a fair proportion of central Manama. Although it has long since ceased to look like an old-fashioned Middle Eastern souk with covered alleyways and interesting little nooks and crannies to explore, Manama Souk is still an atmospheric place. Some of the lanes off Municipality Avenue are home to small flea markets where the poorer inhabitants lay out their wares on the ground. The spice stalls still leave that aroma of the East lingering in the nostrils long after one has passed by and wandered into an area that is the territory of the shoe vendor, or the toy seller. You will also see traders squatting in their open fronted cubicles chopping up huge tobacco leaves with machetes or repairing sandals that look as though they have lived on long past their sell by date. The souk is one of the more interesting places in Manama and well worth many hours' wandering. Remember to bargain hard if you see something you like the look of, a shopkeeper is never going to sell something at a loss to himself.

For those after a more orderly shopping experience Manama is full of shopping centres and large malls selling everything you can get at home but generally at a cheaper price. The *Bahrain Commercial Shopping Complex* (also known as al-Burj) has a number of boutiques and shops selling upmarket products. The *Lulu Centre*, next to the Saudi-Bahrain bus terminal and close to the Pearl Monument Roundabout, has a post office and a *MegaMart* department store in its complex.

Behind this complex are the meat, fish, fruit and vegetable **markets**. These markets, collectively known as the *Central Market*, are a hive of activity and well worth a visit just to see how the Bahraini wholesalers conduct their business. A day's trading is a colourful business and you would do well to take a camera with you on a trip out there. It you do decide to take photographs of the traders, remember to ask their permission before doing so.

The biggest and newest mall in Bahrain is the *Seef Mall* on the way towards the Meridien Hotel, which houses big brand name stores such as *Marks and Spencer*, *Debenhams* etc. Taxis to the Seef Mall from Bab al-Bahrain should cost no more than BD1.5. The area around Adliya has a number of useful shops and services and the *Adliya Centre* on the corner of Sheikh Isa Avenue and Osama bin Zayed Road has a mass of useful shops around a small square including three Internet cafés, a delicatessen and an *al-Jazira supermarket*. Branches of the al-Jazira supermarket chain also have *Woolworths* on the premises and good notice boards.

Carpets
Bahrain is also a good place to buy that Persian rug you always promised yourself. Prices for handmade carpets and rugs from Iran, Pakistan, Turkey, Afghanistan etc., are much cheaper here than in Britain or the USA. Look for a shop with a wide selection and a proprietor who is happy to discuss carpets with you without necessarily pressurising you into buying.

Electronics
You will find all the international brands of electronics in and around Manama souk at prices equivalent to or slightly cheaper than back home. If you do buy make sure that the warranty covers you for use back home. The award winning duty-free at Bahrain Airport also has a good stock of electrical goods and the prices here will be slightly less than on Manama high streets.

Gold
The Gold Souk building and Gold City, both near Bab al-Bahrain, have the market pretty much covered and if you are interested in buying gold or pearls then these are the places to visit. There is also an area in the souk (ask anyone for directions to the gold souk) where smaller traders have shops.

Music
There are a number of shops selling Asian, Middle Eastern and Western cassettes at incredibly low prices in the streets behind Bab al-Bahrain. Although the selection is not great (every nation seems to have a different taste in pop) a cassette can be had for about BD2 (£4). Supermarkets and music shops in the malls sell CD-ROMs a little cheaper than can be bought back home but again the choice isn't great.

Textiles
Cloth and tailor fees are also much cheaper in Bahrain than back home and if you ever wanted to get a suit tailor-made but were always too broke to get one made at home then push the boat out in Bahrain. Tailors can work to any design that you provide and can copy designs from magazines and catalogues.

Exploring

There are several sights in Manama itself but many of the more interesting things to see are located outside the capital. Manama is small enough to wander about in at leisure, get lost and find a way back towards either the northern or eastern corniche without too much worry.

Bab al-Bahrain
'The Gateway of Bahrain' is likely to be the starting point for many of your peregrinations about town. The building was designed in 1945 by Sir Charles Belgrave, the then British Political Advisor, to house the government offices. At that time, before the land reclamation projects, it stood on the seafront facing the

Harbour. Refurbished in 1986, it now houses the tourist information office (open 8am-noon and 4.30-6pm Saturday to Thursday) and a local craft and souvenir shop. Bab al-Bahrain is also the starting point for a number of sightseeing tours and the archway serves as the entrance to the souk area behind. The taxi rank in front is a useful communications centre.

The National Museum
The National Museum (tel 292 977) is open 8am-2pm Saturday to Wednesday and 10am-5pm on Thursdays (admission 500 fils). Opened in 1988 at a cost of a cool BD13 million the museum is located at the northern end of the al-Fatih Highway Corniche towards the causeway that leads to Muharraq. There are nine exhibition halls covering the life and history of Bahrain including Customs and Traditions, Natural History, Contemporary Art, Documents and Manuscripts and the Dilmun Civilization. The Hall of Graves has a huge reconstructed burial mound. The museum is very well laid out, with clear and concise explanations in English and Arabic and is incredibly spic and span. There is also a small café, lecture room and a gift shop. The Bahrainis are justifiably proud of their heritage but you can't help but get the feeling that the place feels like a mausoleum on two floors. Photography is allowed in most of the rooms but not all.

Pearl Diving Museum
What was once the Heritage Museum has recently re-opened as the Pearl Diving Museum in the old law courts building in the banking district which dates from about 1937. The main entrance is on Government Avenue and the museum is open from 4-8pm daily and admission costs 500 fils. It doesn't overload the visitor with information but houses some very good exhibits on two floors. The ground floor has rooms around a central courtyard open to the sky. Above it and all around it the glass-faced tower blocks of the modern world loom over the museum walls. The various rooms off the courtyard house reconstructions of the High Court, a traditional pre-oil boom kitchen, a 1940s living room with old clock and wireless. A wonderful display of costumes includes an exhibit of 47 embroidery designs for gold and silver thread and a popular music reconstruction exhibits traditional Bahraini instruments including the weird but wonderful Bahraini bagpipe (*al-Jorbah*). A wedding room is highly decorative with swathes of red embroidered wall hangings and ceiling and walls covered in mirrors. Another room has reconstructions of the traditional Bahraini trade of fishing accompanied by evocative sound effects, and old black and white photographs of Pearl Diving. The upper floor has open terraces and a feeling of seclusion in the middle of the banking district. The rooms here exhibit popular children's games, traditional folk medicine together with a chart on the wall outlining details of herbal prescriptions for various ailments and a mock up of the guest room and *majlis* with gypsum carvings in the wall. Strangely, although the *majlis* feels as though it should overlook the sea, a village or the desert it actually looks out onto the parking lot below, a busy highway and the al-Ahly bank beyond.

A further three rooms house photographs of the ruling family from 1932-1982 with a room dedicated to each of the reigns of Isa bin Ali, Salman bin Hamad and Isa bin Salaman al-Khalifa. The photographs outline the rise of Bahrain from its small beginnings to the present day.

Al-Fatih Highway Corniche
On the al-Fatih Corniche past the Grand Mosque there is a **Dolphinarium** (adults BD4(£7/$10)/kids BD2) with shows three times a day and an aquarium and restaurant within its confines. The **Ice Rink** (tel 292 313) is also along this corniche and moored nearby are the boats that make trips out around the bay as well as further

afield to the Hawar Islands off the coast of Qatar. **Trips** to the island resort in Hawar take about an hour and a half and can be booked through the *Hawar Reservations Office* (tel 290 377) near the Baisan International Hotel off Exhibition Road. You can get to the office from the corniche by crossing over the footbridge opposite the boats. Day trips cost BD8 and an apartment for four people can be had for BD20 (£37/$53) per person, or BD24 for a double room.

Al-Fatih Mosque, Manama

Beit al-Quran

The Beit al-Quran, ('The House of the Quran') is located on the other side of the al-Fatih Highway from the National Museum and houses rare Islamic manuscripts. The walls of the building are inscribed with Arabic calligraphy and the place, devoted to the Quran, acts as a museum, a study centre and, with the modest al-Rahman Mosque incorporated into the structure, a place of worship. Unlike the majority of other mosques in the Gulf non-Muslims are permitted and encouraged to visit as long as they dress modestly and leave their shoes at the door. Beit al-Quran is open 9am-noon and 4-6pm Saturday to Thursday. Admission is free.

Craft Centre Gallery

The Gallery (tel 245 688) opposite the Police Fort on Sheikh Isa al-Kabeer Avenue is open from 8am-1.30pm daily and is a great place to go to see local craftsmen making things with local materials. Glass, paper and pottery and wood are all used to create objects for sale.

BAHRAIN ISLAND

Al-Jasra

Al-Jasra, a village on the northwest coast of Bahrain close to the beginning of King Fahad Causeway, is worth visiting for the **Handicraft Centre** and **Beit al-Jasra**, the birth place of the present ruler's father Sheikh Isa bin Sulman. The Handicraft Centre encourages the continuance of traditional Bahraini handicrafts such as weaving, pottery and woodwork and has a shop where tourists are encouraged to buy. Beit al-Jasra is very near to the Handicraft Centre and was built in the traditional style of the time in 1907 using coral and palm. The house was vacant from the 1930s and was restored and turned into a heritage museum in 1986. Sheikh Isa was born here in 1933. The house is open 8am-2pm Saturday to Wednesday, and 8am-5pm on Thursday.

Al-Khamis Mosque

Situated a few kilometres southwest of Manama on the Sheikh Isa bin Sulman Highway the al-Khamis Mosque, no longer used as a mosque, is the oldest in Bahrain. The original foundations date back to the early 8th century AD during the reign of the Ummayad Caliph Omar bin Abdul Aziz. The two minarets date back to the 11th century. The completion of restoration work on the mosque means that it is now open to visitors. It is open from 7am-2pm Saturday to Wednesday and 8am-noon on Thursday and Friday.

Bahrain Fort

About 5km west of Manama following the King Faisal Highway you will see the signs for Bahrain Fort (Qala'at al-Bahrain). The fort is undergoing extensive restoration but it is possible to walk in and around this impressive example of a complex fortress. The fort visible today was originally constructed in the 14th century but sits on top of the site of the remains of earlier fortresses. Half of the outer walls have been rebuilt and you can explore the runways and rooms built within the inner and outer walls. Nearby are the remains of the Dilmun civilisation dating back to between BC2800 and BC450.

Karbabad

Driving to or from Bahrain Fort you are likely to pass the wares of the **basket weavers** of Karbabad village who are famed for making mats etc., from palm fronds. Natural dyes have been replaced by chemicals to colour the fronds that are deftly woven into household objects but the tradition still continues. Objects are for sale and there are *barasti* huts beside the roads with displays laid out for tourists.

Sa'ar and the Barbar Temples

Bahrain is full of important archaeological sites, having been an important trading centre due to its position on trade routes and the supply of fresh water it offered. Lately a team of archaeologists from University College, London have been excavating a site in the village of **Sa'ar** uncovering an organised 4,000 year-old settlement complete with street and houses intact.

Nearby, the **Barbar Temples**, west of Bahrain Fort, are three temples built on top of each other, the earliest dating back to the third millennium BC. These temples are thought to have been dedicated to the God of Spring Waters, Enki, who was believed to live beneath the adjacent sacred well. Nearby is the **ad-Diraz Temple**, constructed some time after the Barbar Temples, and its purpose still something of a mystery.

There are also large fields of the famous **Bahraini burial mounds** around A'ali and Sa'ar. These drumlin-shaped mounds of stones (and there are thought to be more than 150,000 of them) cover prehistoric tombs, some of them dating back to BC3000. Bahrain was one of the biggest burial centres in the Gulf region and A'ali has the largest burial mounds of them all, known as the 'Royal Tombs', due to their vast size.

Riffa

Further away to the south of Manama in the interior lies the town of Riffa and **Riffa Fort**. It is not very well signposted from any of its approaches but you will see this impressive fort perched high up on an escarpment. Open 8am-2pm Sunday to Tuesday, 9am-6pm on Wednesday and Thursday and 3-6pm on Friday Riffa Fort is a traditional 19th century example of Islamic military architecture, built using desert stone, lime, gypsum and clay. The small mosque next door was built during the same period and is still used by locals today.

Originally there was also a mosque within the fort for the soldiers' use but today this has gone. The site was first built on in the 17th century during the reign of Sheikh al-Gabri to defend the villages of east and west Riffa but after the cessation of border disputes with the consolidation of the al-Khalifa reign the fort became a private residence, which it remained until the 1970s. It was here that Sheikh Ali al-Khalifa was killed in 1869 by his brother in an attempt to seize control of the islands.

Al-Areen Wildlife Park

Some way south of Riffa, about 20km south of Manama and off the Zallaq Beach Highway is the al-Areen Wildlife Park (tel 836 116). Created as a sanctuary for rare and endangered species of Arabian wildlife such as the **Arabian Oryx** and gazelle and covering eight square kilometres of desert, the park also has a number of non-indigenous species of birds and animals. Admission costs BD1 for adults, 500 fils for children and the park is open 11am-4.30pm Saturday to Wednesday, 8am-noon and 1-4.30pm on Thursday and 8-10.30am and 1-4.30pm on Friday.

The Oil Museum

For an insight into the recent history of Bahrain and the story of oil exploration the Oil Museum, under the shadow of Jebal ad-Dukhan, is worth a visit. Opened in 1992, the museum displays photographs and drilling equipment from Bahrain's oil producing days and is well signposted from Awali and Zallaq by brown UK-type heritage signs. Next to the museum is the site where oil was first discovered anywhere in the Gulf. A plaque reads 'Jebal ad-Dukhan No.1; spudded in Oct 16, 1931, struck oil June 1, 1932 Initial flow 400 BBLS/hr'.

The Tree of Life

Also down in the south of Bahrain is the Tree of Life. It is quite impressive that a mere tree should be writ large on the tourist map of the world. However, the Tree of Life continues to grow in a rather peaceful setting and some of the graffiti scrawled along its boughs are quite philosophical in tone. It stands in isolated splendour about 2km south of Jebal ad-Dukhan. To get there from the Oil Museum make sure that the museum is on your right and take the first left after it, following the road through the oil fields until you reach a T-junction with the main road. Turn right here and follow the brown heritage signs to the tree. It is easy to spot in the distance, a lone piece of greenery standing on a small hillock. The road past the Tree of Life leads south to the military zone – a no go area.

Jaww, 'Askar and Zallaq

Although they have no particular sights to see, Jaww and 'Askar are quiet fishing villages toward the end of the public access roads on the east coast, laid back and pretty. Zallaq, on the west coast is also quite an attractive fishing village. Nearby is the private beach for Bapco employees which may allow you day membership.

King Fahad Causeway

One of the great feats of engineering in the past twenty years has been, arguably, the construction of the 25km King Fahad Causeway which links Bahrain and Saudi Arabia. It is one of the longest bridge links in the world and was completed in 1986. Unless you are a GCC national you will need a visa to get across into Saudi Arabia but it is possible to drive along the length of the causeway to the customs point on an island within sight of Saudi. There is a tower here with an upstairs restaurant and superb views open daily from 9am-11pm.

MUHARRAQ ISLAND

Across the Sheikh Hamad Causeway from Manama is the island of Muharraq, home to Bahrain's airport. Once the home of the ruling family, Muharraq is much less developed than Manama, has several sights and is worth exploring. **Arad Fort**, originally built by the invading Portuguese in the 15th century, used by the Omani occupiers of the island in the 1800s and restored in 1980s, dominates the bay between the Arad Peninsula and south Muharraq and is well worth a visit. It is open 8am-2pm Sunday to Tuesday, 9am-6pm Wednesday and Thursday, 3-6pm Friday.

   Sheikh Isa bin Ali's House on Sheikh Abdulla Avenue in Muharraq is a traditional Bahraini house complete with wind towers. It was home to Sheikh Isa during his long reign of 1869-1932 and is open 8am-2pm Saturday to Thursday and 3.30-6.30pm Monday and Tuesday. Nearby is **Beit Siyadi**, a 19th century pearl merchant's house with fine examples of the architecture of that time - stained glass windows, carved screens and ornate ceilings. Next to the house is a small mosque with a detached minaret worth seeing. Beit Siyadi is only open on Thursdays from 4-6pm.

Qatar

Fort at Umm Salal Mohammed

Though small in stature Qatar has its eye on being a big shot in the Arabian Gulf. It regularly plays host to international sporting events and will be hosting the Asian Games in 2006. In the past Qatar has been known, somewhat meanly, as the land that God forgot, but as an independent oil and gas producing Gulf State with a tiny national population, she is fast becoming a force to be reckoned with. Though not known primarily as a tourist hot spot Qatar still has something to offer the casual visitor. The difficulty in finding a place that serves alcohol is not such a bad thing and though rather quiet (some might say sleepy) the place has more charm than some of her brasher neighbours, with souks that are still recognisable as Middle Eastern and the courtesy that you would expect from a very devout Muslim nation.

GEOGRAPHY

Qatar is a peninsula that juts thumb-like off the Arabian Peninsula, out into the shallow waters of the Arabian Gulf. Its only land border is with Saudi Arabia. With a total area of just over 11,400 square kilometres, barely 85km across at its widest point and 165km from northernmost to southernmost point, the country is a small one. Outside of the capital city Doha there is little to see or do unless you are involved in the hydrocarbon or cement industries. There is an area of sand dunes in the southeast around the inland sea of Khor al-Adaid but much of the coastal regions consist of flat *sabkha* plains (salt flats which are below sea level). The highest elevation on the peninsula is a diminutive 103 metres in the south. To put it fairly bluntly, Qatar's landscape is barren desert.

Little natural vegetation can grow in this stony and sandy terrain and although irrigated farms do exist out in the desert much of the underground water is unsuitable for agriculture or drinking due to its high mineral content. The vast majority of Qatar's water is supplied by desalination plants. Beautification of the country, especially of Doha, is an ongoing process due to the various summits, conferences and major international sporting events that take place there.

CLIMATE

Most tourists tend to visit Qatar during the winter months. Between November and February the temperature ranges from 7-30°C, which can be fairly pleasant and is vastly preferable to a European winter. The temperature rises between March and May with daily temperatures of around 42°C until July, accompanied by strong north-westerly winds which create an oven-like heat. August to October is the time of the largest increase in humidity. The average annual rainfall is about 74mm. Though this may sound like a harsh desert climate (it is!) if you visit Qatar during the winter months the climate is ideal for water-sports, sunbathing and walking about without becoming a blob of perspiration. In the summertime you will definitely need to drive about in an air-conditioned car: it gets very hot.

HISTORY

Ancient History

The majority of the archaeological sites of Qatar can be found on the coasts. The first investigations into the country's far distant past were carried out by Danish archaeologists between 1956 and 1964. Later, during the 1970s, British archaeologists also explored the region. Small encampments and settlements have been discovered dating the earliest inhabitants of the peninsula from 5,000 to 7,000 years ago. Ubaid pottery has also been found at sites dating from the sixth to the fourth millennium BC and a number of burial mounds have also been uncovered, particularly in the Ras Abruk Peninsula on the west coast. Man was wandering in Qatar from Stone Age times and some of the most remarkable archaeological remains are the pre-Islamic ancient designs carved on rock outcrops which can be seen along the east coast.

The Europeans Arrive

With the Portuguese explorer Vasco da Gama's voyage round Cape of Good Hope in 1498 came the opening up of the Arabian Gulf to Europeans. However, due to Qatar's particularly desolate climate and location the country was not thought of as being of much importance or bearing any threat to neighbouring territories. Bedouin from the Arabian mainland would enter Qatar during the winter months to graze

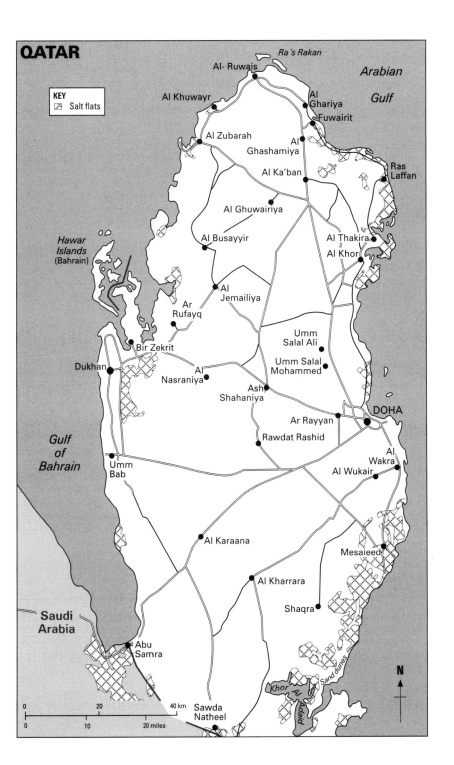

livestock on what scant vegetation grew during the winter rains while settled tribes inhabited the small number of towns and villages on the coast engaging in fishing, pearling and trading. Islam came to Qatar in 628AD with the prophet's envoy al-A'la bin Abdulla al-Hadhrami.

Self-rule and Subjugation

Dates are hazy but sometime in the 1760s members of the Bani Utbah tribe (including the al-Khalifa family, the future rulers of Bahrain) moved down the coast from Kuwait and settled in Zubarah on the northwest coast of Qatar. At this time the only settlements in the peninsula were a few fishing villages on the east coast, notably Huwaylah, Fuwairit and al-Bidda (the site of present day Doha). Zubarah quickly became a flourishing trading centre and the al-Khalifa family set out to conquer and become rulers of Bahrain. To begin with they also claimed sovereignty over Qatar, however this was disputed by the other members of the Bani Utbah tribe who were still living there. Bahrain's authority over Qatar at this time was administered from Doha by a member of the al-Khalifa family who acted as deputy or *wali*. Uprisings against him forced him to leave and in 1867 the ruler of Bahrain, Sheikh Muhammed bin Khalifa al-Khalifa formed an alliance with Sheikh Zayed bin Khalifa of Abu Dhabi and pillaged Wakrah and Doha in an attempt to subjugate the Qataris. In the following year the British political resident in the Gulf, Colonel Lewis Pelly (at that time Britain being a major player in the politics of the region) extracted from the ruler of Bahrain damages for breaking a treaty they had previously signed in 1861, promising to cease from any maritime warfare. The British then signed an agreement with the most powerful man in Doha at that time, Sheikh Muhammed bin Thani. The Sheikh agreed to refrain from maritime conflicts. The al-Thani had moved from Fuwairit to Doha in about 1847 but still had to pay an annual tribute to the ruler of Bahrain.

The Ottomans established a base in Qatar in 1871 (stationing troops at the al-Koot fort in Doha) after being permitted to do so against his wishes by Sheikh Muhammed's son Qasim. In 1879 the Ottomans made Qasim Governor of Doha but he wisely resisted their attempts to impose Ottoman rule upon Qatar. The Ottoman influence came to an end with the signing of the Anglo-Turkish Convention in 1913.

On 3 November 1916 Sheikh Abdulla bin Qasim al-Thani signed an agreement with Britain which brought Qatar into the Trucial system. By signing the document he agreed to abstain from piracy and the slave trade as well as agreeing to consult Britain before entering into any negotiations with foreign powers, in exchange for British protection from attack by land and sea.

Oil Strikes

Oil was discovered in Qatar in the 1930s which led to foreign powers taking a far keener interest in the Gulf, and it was the striking of oil in the region that led to the final demarcation of Qatar's borders.

In 1935 Sheikh Abdulla signed an oil concession with the Anglo-Persian Oil Company which granted exclusive rights to the production, refining, marketing and transportation of any oil discovered in Qatar over a period of 75 years. This concession was in turn transferred to Petroleum Development (Qatar) Ltd which struck oil in the Dukhan field in October 1939. However, oil wasn't exported until 1949 due to the shake up of the globe caused by World War II.

Power Politics and Economics

Although primogeniture had been decided upon as the best way to keep power in the family Sheikh Abdulla, already rather elderly, handed most of the reins of power over to his second more-favoured son Hamad in 1944. However, by the time Abdulla died in 1949 Hamad was already dead and therefore Abdulla's eldest son Ali became ruler due to the fact that Hamad's son and heir Sheikh Khalifa, was at the time far too young to rule.

Unfortunately for Qatar, Sheikh Ali was a fairly dissolute ruler and spent much of his time outside the country spending the vast revenues accrued from oil. And although it had been decided upon his succession that Sheikh Khalifa would be his heir apparent, Ali in fact abdicated in 1960 in favour of his own son, the equally dissolute Ahmed. Throughout the reign of Ali his nephew Khalifa, the rightful heir to Qatar, had been deeply immersed in the affairs of his country and was to a large extent running the place acting as prime minister and deputy ruler due to Ali's and Ahmed's disinterest in the affairs of state.

Economic progress in Qatar during the 1960s was slow, although during Sheikh Abdulla's reign the building of the first hospital and the modernisation of the education system had begun and oil revenues were increasing year on year. However, the majority of all the revenues produced by the sale of oil were going straight into the private coffers of the ruling family. In the 1960s Qatar's finances went something like this: A quarter of all revenues went to the ruling Sheikh, another quarter went to all other al-Thani sheikhs and a further quarter was confined to the family's reserve fund. The final quarter was divided amongst the rest of the population of Qatari nationals. The economics of this may seem strange but it should be noted that a large percentage of Qatar's tiny population of nationals are related in some way to the ruling al-Thani family.

In order to provide the labour force needed to work in the petrochemical industries and the booming construction industry a major programme of immigration was initiated. By 1969 the population of Qatar was approximately 80,000 of which 60 per cent were an immigrant labour force. Qatar joined the Organisation of Petroleum Exporting Countries (OPEC) in 1961.

POLITICS

When Britain announced it was going to pull all its forces out from east of Suez in 1968 Qatar, until then reliant for much of its strategic planning on British advisors, still had little sign of economic stability. All the countries of the Arabian Gulf that had been protectorates of Britain were now looking for a way to retain their independence but also provide some kind of protection against the threat of outside powers. Oil wealth was at stake as well as national pride.

At a summit meeting in Dubai attended by the leaders of the Trucial States (present day UAE), Bahrain and Qatar in February of the same year a proposal was put to those present of a federation of Arab Emirates consisting of a Higher Council (the rulers of the separate states) and a Federal Council of Administration. Initially this idea was agreed with Sheikh Khalifa bin Hamad of Qatar elected chairman of the Temporary Federal Council but then a continuing source of conflict between Bahrain and Qatar led to the dissolving of the council and both Qatar and Bahrain pulled out of the federation – eventually becoming independent states.

In 1970 Sheikh Khalifa bin Hamad took over as de facto ruler of Qatar from Sheikh Ahmed who up until this time had been ruler in name only and on 3 September 1971 Qatar became an independent sovereign state, joining the United Nations and the Arab League soon after. In February 1972 Sheikh Khalifa finally deposed his cousin Sheikh Ahmed and assumed supreme authority of Qatar. In accordance with the 1970 Constitution Sheikh Khalifa decreed the first advisory Council in 1972. This advisory council was to have the right to debate legislation drafted by his appointed council of ministers but no legislative power.

By the 1980s a social infrastructure was almost complete in Qatar providing education, health services and utilities free to all Qatari citizens. On 27 June 1995, in a bloodless coup, the heir apparent Sheikh Hamad deposed his father, claiming the support of both the royal family and Qatari citizens. Sheikh Hamad's rule was endorsed by the United States, Britain and Saudi Arabia and he set about reforming the country, relaxing censorship of the press and allowing greater transparency of Government procedures. Meanwhile the deposed Sheikh Khalifa took up residence in the United Arab Emirates vowing to return to power, and at one point gaining control of a large proportion of Qatar's finances. In February 1996 it was reported that an attempted coup had been thwarted by security forces though Sheikh Khalifa denied any involvement. Subsequently several members of Qatar's intelligence service and a former minister of Economy and Trade, among others, were arrested.

In March 1999 the first elections for a municipal council were held in Qatar.

The Gulf War

Qatar condemned the invasion of Kuwait by Iraq, though it had sided with Iraq in the Iran-Iraq war of 1980-1988. Qatar permitted foreign forces on its territory during the Gulf War and participated in the multinational task force. Qatar and Iraq resumed tentative relations in 1993.

THE ECONOMY

The traditional economy of Qatar up until the discovery of oil in the 1930s was fishing, pearling and the nomadic farming of livestock. Today the main industries are oil and gas, fertilisers, petrochemicals, steel and cement and most of Qatar's heavy industry is based in the south of the country around Mesaieed. Elsewhere the saline and stony terrain of the country has always made it unsuitable for arable farming but agriculture does go on on a small scale, but it is small (less than one per cent of the GNP) and the farms are government owned. Most food is imported although Qatar is pretty much self-sufficient in the production of poultry and eggs.

With the discovery of oil in 1939 and the subsequent growth of the gas industry (production of the North Field – the world's largest natural deposit of gas – began in 1999) and its small population, Qatar is one of the richest of the Gulf States.

In 1997 in a bid to bring Qatar nationals into the workforce and reduce the number of expatriate workers, the Government ordered that all private sector businesses should ensure that at least 20 per cent of their workforce be Qataris. However, so far this has had little effect.

Qatar's major trading partners for exports including petroleum products, steel and chemicals are Japan, South Korea, Brazil, UAE and Singapore. Machinery, consumer goods, food and chemicals are imported mainly from Japan, Britain, the United States, Germany and France. Today Qatar's oil reserves account for about 70 per cent of the government's revenues and should they begin to dry up, which they will do, its Liquified Natural Gas (LGN) exports will continue to see Qatar a rich country for a very long time to come.

Tourism

In 1998 a total of 451,000 tourists visited Qatar and the country is actively promoting tourism. Recently the government has outlined five new projects to improve tourism facilities: a hotel and spa at Doha Golf Club, a hotel and leisure resort beside the beach at al-Khor, an eco-tourism resort and heritage village at al-Ghariyeh, the extension and revamping of Aladdin's Kingdom and a festival bazaar at al-Bidda Park. The construction of four luxury hotels in the West Bay area of Doha is already well underway.

THE PEOPLE

The last census, taken in 1997, put the total population of Qatar – including expats – at 522,000. Of this figure more than half lived in Doha. The official estimate of March 1999 reckoned there to be around 566,000 people living and working in Qatar, of whom only about 20 per cent were Qatari nationals. So who make up the population of one of the smallest Arab countries?

Arabs

The indigenous population of Qatar is made up of tribal Arabs – the first settlers of the peninsula, descendants of Persians who arrived in the 1930s, and a fair number of the descendents of freed slaves who were bought over from East Africa in the 19th century.

You can spot Qatari nationals by the way they dress. Men traditionally wear long-sleeved white garments (*thobes*) over loose-fitting trousers, embroidered caps are worn under the headdress (*ghutra*). These can be plain white, black and white or red and white check held in place by the black, rope-like *agal*. Ceremonial cloaks, (*bisht*), and the very old-fashioned sheepskin or camel hair lined winter cloak are seldom seen these days.

Women generally wear a black *abbaya* over western clothing. This thin but all-enveloping garment covers the whole frame of a women and it is strange to see young women covered totally in black, the only visible feature being a pair of eyes at one end and a pair of brand new trainers at the other, power-walking along the Corniche in Doha. In the villages you may see women wearing the richly embroidered overdresses (*thobe al-Nashl*) and the long baggy trousers (*sirwal*) worn under them.

Expats

The rest of the population is made up of English-speaking Westerners, South East Asians (Philippinos, Malays), and Pakistanis, Indians and Bangladeshis. There are also quite a number of Arabs from the poorer Middle Eastern countries of Egypt, Palestine and Jordan and Syria. When Qatar boomed these workers, both skilled and unskilled were brought in to build the infrastructure of an – until then – quite unsophisticated society, and then to run it. The Qatari nationals, being such a small population, live a comfortable traditional lifestyle without needing to work.

While the average white westerner has a very good standard of living with a tax-free salary, a villa, an alcohol allowance etc., the majority of expats from the poorer countries of the world don't have it so good. Though everyone makes more money than they could back home you only need to walk along Wadi Musheireb Street in downtown Doha of an evening to get an idea of the privations that the Indians *et al* suffer. The place is crowded with workers, all of whom will be sending most of their earnings back to their family in their native land. Unless they are very lucky or well connected they will not be able to bring over their spouses or children to stay with them and so this is a society of homesick men.

Religion

The majority of Qatari Muslims follow the most puritanical sect of Islam – Wahhabism. Like the Saudis they are followers of the teachings of Muhammed ibn Abd al-Wahhab. However, the Qatari interpretation of his teachings is slightly less austere and unlike in Saudi Arabia, alcohol is not totally banned (though hard to find) and women are allowed to drive.

Making Friends

It can be extremely difficult to get to know a Qatari. The Gulf is a conservative place, Qatar especially, and cocooned from the rest of the populace by their culture, religion and wealth, the nationals tend not to socialise with non-Qataris. This segregation is pervasive throughout the Gulf with each nationality, not only the nationals but expats as well, keeping to their own kind.

See if you can get an introduction to a Qatari family from someone back home before you visit. Many Gulf Arabs study abroad and seeing how Qataris really live behind the high walls of their villas is a great education. You should remember that Qatar is a conservative country and both men and women should respect the culture they are passing through and dress modestly. Revealing wear, or even not so revealing (shorts worn by either a man or a women can lead to stares from locals be they looks of astonishment or contempt) should be worn only on private hotel beaches or at the swimming pool.

FURTHER READING

Arabian Time Machine, Helga Graham, Heinemann, 1978.
Bahrain, Kuwait & Qatar, Gordon Robison and Paul Greenway, Lonely Planet
    Publications, 2000.
Qatar: A MEED Practical Guide, Edmund O'Sullivan (Ed.), MEED, 1997.

PRACTICAL INFORMATION

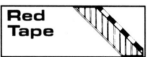

Red Tape

Passports

Except for nationals of the GCC countries (who require only an identity card), all visitors to Qatar require a valid passport with at least six months validity left to run. You should also ensure that your passport has enough blank pages left in it for visas and entry/exit stamps. Allow a page for each. If you have an Israeli stamp in your passport you are very likely to encounter problems moving about the Gulf and are advised to apply for a new, clean, passport before travelling.

VISAS

Visa fees for UK passport holders are £36 for a single entry visa valid for six months, £50 for a multiple entry visa valid for six months, £71 for a multiple entry visa valid for two years and £130 for a multiple entry visa with a validity of five years.

Irish passport holders must pay £20 for a single entry visa valid for one month which allows a one month stay. For £40 Irish citizens can obtain a multiple entry visa which is valid for two years and allows a one month stay each visit.

US passport holders need confirmation of a hotel booking hotel in Doha to be eligible for a visa. They can then apply for a multiple entry visa which costs £30 and is valid for ten years. Contact the Qatari embassy for latest visa requirements.

Passport holders of EU member nations, Japan and Brazil will need to present a letter of invitation from a company in Qatar or confirmation of a booking in a hotel in Doha. Prices can be obtained on application at the Qatari embassy.

All other nationalities must arrange a visa through a hotel in Doha or through a company or the Qatari family being visited. Proof of approval will be sent to the applicant by fax. On presentation of this fax at the airport a visa will be issued.

Visa Extensions

Qatar is a small place and unless you become embroiled in the country a visit of two weeks is more than enough to get a feel for the country and explore it pretty thoroughly. It is however possible to extend your tourist visa for a further two weeks. You will need to visit the *Department for Passports and Residence* (tel 882 882) in Doha, fill out the requisite forms and pay the fee.

Visas to other Destinations

If you wish to travel onwards from Qatar to other destinations in the Middle East and haven't picked up the required visas before leaving home you may be able to get them from the Embassies in Doha, most of which are located in the Diplomatic Area in West Bay, north of the Doha Sheraton Hotel. However, picking up visas along the way can sometimes be problematical depending on your nationality, especially in the paranoid Middle East, and there may be some countries that do not keep embassies in Qatar.

Immigration

Because Doha Airport is relatively small the immigration process is usually swift. Customs officials are pretty fierce but then that's their job and as long as you don't arrive smelling of alcohol or clutching a bottle of whisky and a packet of bacon you should pass though without any trouble.

Customs

The duty free allowance is 454 grams of tobacco and perfume up to the value of QR1000 (£197/$274). The importation and the sale of alcohol – except in a few of the top-end hotels – is illegal. If you are carrying books, video cassettes, DVDs or magazines they may be confiscated and checked by the Ministry of Information if it is suspected that they contain material of a salacious or politically seditious nature. If you are bringing prescribed medicines make sure that you have a doctor's prescription for them so that you can order more if you run out and also to show any suspicious customs official. You will need an import licence for guns and ammunition. Doha Airport has a small duty-free shop but it doesn't sell alcohol.

Onward Travel

It is unlikely that you will arrive in Qatar without a ticket for onward travel and you may not be allowed into the country without proof of such a ticket. If you do get stuck in Qatar the cheapest way out of the country is to get a flight to Bahrain or Dubai. Bahrain is the centre for all Gulf Air flights and you might pick up a cheap ticket from there. Dubai is an important transport hub of the region and it is possible to pick up cheap flights from there onwards to the East, Africa or back to Europe. Leaving Qatar there is a departure tax payable in cash to the *Doha International Airport Public Corporation* of QR20 (£3.94/$5.48).

QATARI EMBASSIES ABROAD

Britain: Qatar State Embassy, No. 1 South Audley Street, London W1Y 5DQ (tel 020-7370 6871). The visa section is open from 9.30am-13.30pm Monday to Friday.

USA: Embassy of the State of Qatar, 4200, Wisconsin Avenue, Suite 200, NW, Washington, DC 20016 (tel 202-274 1600; fax 202-237 0061). This embassy also deals with Canadian visa enquiries.

There are no Qatari Embassies in Australia, New Zealand, Canada, South Africa or Bahrain. Would-be visitors from Australia and New Zealand should contact the embassy in Japan.

 Up until 1966 the Indian Rupee was the legal tender in Qatar. Today it is the Qatari Riyal (QR) which is linked to the US Dollar and remains reasonably stable. The official rate is £1=QR5.07 and $1=QR3.64. There are no restrictions on the import or export of local or foreign currency. If you happen to have visited Saudi Arabia and have spare Saudi Riyals you will find that some shops accept them at an equal rate of exchange.

Notes and Coins

The Qatari riyal is divided into 100 dirhams. Banknotes are available in denominations of QR1, QR5, QR10, QR50, QR100 and QR500. It is advisable to hoard the lower denomination notes for taxi fares. Coins of 1, 5 and 10 dirhams are still legal tender but were last minted in the 1970s and are a rarity. You may occasionally be given the 25 dirham and 50 dirham coins as change but more often than not prices are rounded up or down to the closest riyal.

Exchange

You should have no problem finding places to exchange money or travellers cheques. Better rates of exchange will be given by the moneychangers rather than the banks. Hotels will give the worst rate and charge the most commission on each transaction. You will find the latest exchange rates reported daily in the local newspapers.

Travellers' Cheques

Travellers' cheques are a good safe way of keeping emergency funds but it is simpler and quicker to make sure that you leave home with a bankcard that allows you to withdraw funds from your current account using the ATMs. When cashing travellers' cheques you will need to present your passport and occasionally the original purchase receipt. Thomas Cook and American Express travellers' cheques are recognised the world over and you would be wise to travel with these in your pocket rather than your bank's own brand.

Banks

Banks are open from 7.30am-noon Saturday to Thursday, although outside Doha times may vary. There are several international banks in Doha. *HSBC* has its main office on the Doha Corniche opposite the Pearl Monument and another on as-Sadd Street. *Standard Chartered* and *Grindlays* also have branches in Doha.

Credit and Charge Cards

Nowadays many people rely on credit cards for doing business and while travelling they are very useful. In Qatar all major credit cards are accepted by businesses and handing over your credit card for an imprint is obligatory if you intend to hire a car.

ATMs

Automatic Teller Machines (ATMs) operated by the *Commercial Bank of Qatar*, *HSBC*, *Qatar National Bank* and several others take Visa, MasterCard, Cirrus, Maestro, Electron, Plus and American Express and are dotted about Doha; at the

Airport, in the five-star hotels, outside the *Doha Club* on the Corniche and in the malls. There are ATMs in the smaller towns of Doha but it is advisable to make sure that you leave the capital with enough cash in case of emergency.

Tipping. Most restaurants and hotels will add a service charge to a bill and tipping is at your discretion.

COSTS

Qatar isn't a particularly cheap place to visit. Because there is no Youth Hostel, accommodation is limited to hotels that charge from around QR160 (£31/$44) a double for a fairly basic room and this, as in all the Gulf States, is likely to be your biggest expense. Taxis in Qatar are the cheapest in the Gulf, which is a blessing as there is no public transport. Getting out and about you will need to either hire a car or hitch but because the country is so small you won't need to do either for very long. Food is quite cheap and as you will have trouble getting hold of alcohol you won't be able to blow any of your budget on overpriced booze. For the men, a trip to the barber's for a traditional wet shave with a cut-throat razor will set you back about QR5 (£0.98/$1.37), the same again for an accompanying head and upper torso massage.

TELEPHONES

The national telephone system is run by *Qatar Telecom* (Q-TEL) and allows International Direct Dialling to most countries around the world. There are now no coin-operated phones in Qatar which means than you will have to buy phone cards if you want to make a call to either a local or an international number. These are available in denominations of QR30, 50 and 100 from the main telecommunications centre on Wadi Musheireb Street and from cold stores and kiosks throughout Qatar.

Telephone Offices. The main Q-TEL centre is open round the clock and is on Wadi Musheireb Street in the central area of Doha. From here you can telephone and fax but as yet there is no Internet service.

Fax. Quite a number of the small stationery kiosks around town have fax machines though they may charge higher rates than the Telecommunications office in Doha (but not as much as the business centres in the top-end hotels).

Mobiles. Mobile phones can be rented through the *Doha Sheraton Hotel* and some of the bigger hotels also have information desks.

Operator Services. If your hotel room doesn't have a telephone directory you can get hold of the English language operator service by calling 180. If you can't get through when trying to dial home you can book an international call on 150.

Call Charges. There is a reduced charge rate every day between 8pm and 7am and all day on Friday and public holidays. Local calls from private landlines are free though if you phone locally from a hotel they will charge you the usual extortionate fee for the service.

Numbers

In June 2000 all landline telephone numbers in Qatar were increased to seven digits instead of six. If you find that a number you are trying to dial isn't connecting try adding a 4 as a prefix to the old number. The country code for Qatar is +974 followed by the seven digit number. There are no area codes within Qatar. To dial direct to the UK from Qatar dial 00 44 followed by the area code leaving out the initial 0 of that code. To dial direct to the USA from Qatar dial 00 1 followed by the area code.

POST

The main post office in Doha is on Majlis al-Tawoon Street which runs parallel to the Corniche. The interior of the building is pretty impressive; this is a super-post office built alongside a multi-storey car park. It is open daily from 7am-8pm, and Fridays from 8-10am only. There is an ATM inside the building and you can rent PO Boxes there. There is also a smaller post office next door to the Postal Museum on Abdulla bin Jasim Street with shorter opening hours but more conveniently located in the centre of town.

Stamps. Most of the more upmarket hotels, kiosks and of course the post offices sell stamps. Stamps for postcards to the UK cost QR1 (about £0.19/$0.27). Airmail between Qatar and Europe takes about a week.

Parcels. You can send parcels through the post office though for a speedier delivery you will be better off using Express mail services. Companies such as *DHL* (tel 4621 202) and *TNT* (tel 4622 262) and EMS (tel 4433 771) have offices in Doha.

E-MAIL AND THE INTERNET

There is only one Internet café in Doha but it is a very good one.The *Internet Café* in the Gulf Complex by the roundabout on al-Khaleej Street has lots of computers to use, a small fruit juice and coffee bar and charges QR10 (£1.97/$2.75) per hour. You can also telephone through the net here for the cost of a local call. The only other places with Internet access at the time of writing are the business centres in the five-star hotels.

THE MEDIA

Television

Qatar Television has two channels: QTV Channel One broadcasts in Arabic and QTV Channel Two broadcasts predominantly in English. With a good aerial other channels from around the Gulf can also be picked up. Most hotels will have a television with satellite links to *CNN*, *BBC World* and *MTV*, *Discovery Channel*, *Movie Channel* etc., which show the usual eclectic mix of news, films, travel documentaries and chat shows.

Radio Frequencies. *Qatar Broadcasting Service* transmits programmes in English on 102.6FM and 97.5FM. *BBC World Service* transmits on 15304/ Short Wave 177705.

Newspapers and Magazines

The two English-language dailies are *The Peninsula* and *The Gulf Times*. Both are broadsheets, cost QR2 (£0.39/$0.55), and report the same information from local news to reports from India, Asia, Europe and the rest of the world. They usually have a small section on the Gulf, a page on UK news, a couple of pages on India and the subcontinent, the Far East, the rest of the world and financial pages. You will find that most reports are taken from Reuters and Associated Press sources. *The Peninsula* is a bit more topical and popularist than the rather staid *Gulf Times*. The Arabic language newspapers are *al-Sharq*, *Arrayah* and *al-Watan* but unless you are fluent in Arabic you'll find these incomprehensible. They also have less pictures in them than the English-language dailies. Other newspapers published in the Gulf such as *The Khaleej Times* and *The Gulf News* can also be bought in Doha.

Magazines in Arabic and English are available at some of the bigger hotels and a few of the newsagents and bookshops around the city. International newspapers generally arrive in Qatar 24 hours after publication. Outside of Doha you will have difficulty finding any printed material in English.

A Qatar publication worth mentioning is *Marhaba* magazine. A free brochure cum guide to Qatar published three times a year by the *DANA PR* company, it is a good reference to what is on out and about in Qatar. The magazine is distributed free to many outlets and if there isn't a copy in your hotel room you can get hold of one by calling DANA on 4655 533.

Maps

There is a very limited choice of maps of Qatar but the maps in this book should be sufficient to guide you through the country. If you need a larger roadmap, Geoprojects publishes a map of Qatar at a cost of £7.50 though the newest edition is from 1993.

BY ROAD

Taxi

Finding one of the distinctive orange and white-coloured taxis is never much of a problem in Doha and often passing taxis will toot at you expecting that you need a ride when you are walking around town. If by some chance you cannot find a taxi a 24-hour radio taxi service is available by calling 4682 999. Many taxi drivers navigate by landmarks and may not know individual street names. If you have been given an address it is advisable to get the person to also give you a notable nearby landmark to navigate towards. Taxi flag fall is QR2.

Cycling

Cycling is a good way to travel about Qatar during the winter months though with the speed and cavalier handling of many of the vehicles driven in Doha you may find it a bit hairy. If you do decide to cycle there are quite a number of cycle repair shops that may hire you a bike for a negotiable fee.

HITCHHIKING

Hitchhiking in the winter is an option if you have unlimited time and patience but is not as widely practiced here as in some of the other Gulf States because distances are so much smaller. Qatar is a car hungry society and walking along a highway can be somewhat risky. You may also be viewed with suspicion by security services if you happen to be hitching out among the oil fields and military zones.

Qatar is a small country, and you are better off hiring a car for a day or so to visit places outside Doha. If you do decide to do some hitching the accepted method is to stick your right arm out palm down. Bear in mind that you may be asked to pay for a lift and for safety (though it is very unlikely that you will come to any harm) it is advisable to travel in pairs. A woman hitching alone in these parts could be asking for trouble. That said, hitchhiking often leads to offers of unexpected hospitality and is a great way of getting to meet locals.

JOINING A TOUR

Qatar is not yet a big tourist destination and in consequence tour operators are still limited to a select few. *Fahed Tours* (tel 4315 555) is one of the bigger tour companies organising trips out to the desert, the camel racetrack and dhow trips. *Arabian Adventures* (tel 4361 461) also offer tailor made trips to suit the individual visitor.

DRIVING

To drive in Qatar you will need a full driving licence which will allow you to drive about in the country for up to seven days. After that time you will need to apply for a temporary Qatari licence by taking a short driving, eye and road sign test. Car hire firms will be about to tell you how to go about obtaining this. International driving licences aren't recognised in Qatar.

Motorcycling. There are few motorbikes in Qatar though some expats are enthusiasts. Walking along the Corniche you will often see locals screaming along the highway beside you.

CAR HIRE

Most of the big car hire firms have a booth at the Airport. If you would rather wait and hire a car later there are also offices in Doha. The international firms such as *Europcar* (tel 4622 140), *Budget* (tel 4419 500), *Hertz* (tel 4416 891) and Avis (tel 4444 167) all have offices in Doha and there are also a number of smaller firms but the rates are pretty much standard wherever you decide to hire from. *Thrifty* (tel 4433 800) have an office behind the Sofitel Doha Palace.

Expect to pay around QR80 (about £16/$22) per day for a Toyota Tercel saloon car, decidedly more for a four-wheel drive (4WD) vehicle. Car hire firms are generally very trustworthy and reliable but make sure that the bodywork has been checked for any scratches, and especially dents, and that these have been noted by you and the car hire firm. Always carry the driving papers and rental documentation with you in the car.

Rules of the Road

Drive on the **right hand side** of the road. If you are used to driving in Britain this can take a little getting used to. However, more often than not you will be following in the wake of plenty of other cars going in the same direction so follow them. Anyone sitting in the front seat of a car must wear a seatbelt.

Speed limits

Speed limits for cars in Qatar are 50km/h in built-up areas, 80km/h on the outer limits of built-up areas and 120km/h on highways. Some areas are targeted with radar and driving over the limit, speed-wise or alcohol-wise could lead to a hefty fine of between QR300 (£59/$82) and QR1,000 (£197/$275) and/or even imprisonment.

Road Systems

The main roads in Qatar are generally very good. Most of the roads leading off the main Doha to al-Ruwais Highway in the north of the country, and those in the interior, are not black-topped tarmac roads and if you are interested in exploring the country thoroughly you will definitely need a 4WD.

Parking. Parking is generally unrestricted in Qatar as there is so much unused space but clamping does go on, especially in the central areas of Doha.

Fuel

Fuel is cheap in Qatar. A full tank for a saloon car comes to around QR30 (£6/$8). There are two grades of petrol: Regular and Super. You will also find unleaded petrol at some, but not all petrol stations. One of the great things about driving in the Gulf is that when pulling into a petrol station you do not need to get out of the car. An attendant will fill up the car and take care of the money while you remain seated. They often clean your windscreen while you wait too.

Breakdowns and Accidents

There are a number of garages throughout the country where you can get your vehicle fixed should you have a breakdown but for the most part hire cars have a very low mileage and are regularly serviced so are reliable.

If you are involved in an accident it is imperative that you do not move your vehicle from the crash scene until the police have arrived to investigate and write out a report. Do not contemplate moving the vehicle until they arrive, even if it is blocking a roundabout. Without a police report you or the car hire business will be unable to claim any insurance which means that, should you be found to have caused the accident, the bill for any repairs will be laid at your feet.

HAZARDS

Night Driving. You are unlikely to be doing much night driving out in the country side so the risk of a camel coming at you out of the darkness is not a major worry while in Qatar.

Desert Driving

The interior of Qatar is desert and you should venture out there taking the usual precautions. Take enough water, food and fuel to see you through any unexpected eventuality. If you have a mobile phone with you so much the better. The main traffic outside Doha's city limits consists of large trucks. Make room for them. The roads in the interior can get quite rough and you will often find that the surface of some of the roads near industrial areas look ribbed due to tarmac melting and shifting under the weight of loaded trucks in the summer heat.

Highway Hazards

All of the roads in Qatar, apart from the motorways leading to and from Doha, have speed bumps and sleeping policemen across them which are often difficult to see. These can often seem to come at you out of the blue and if hit at high speed will cause damage to both the car and your head.

Qatar's road builders, like road builders all over the Gulf, seem to have a penchant for breaking up the mundanity of the straight stretch of road with lots of roundabouts. Getting round these roundabouts, especially in Doha more than the other cities in this book, can be very scary for the first time driver because everyone comes at them at a terrific speed and is loathe to give way. It takes some getting used to but you will need to take the bit between your teeth and approach with confidence. Any hesitation will lead to a cacophony of honking as impatient drivers queue up behind you.

A hazard that you wouldn't expect is **mist**. If you are driving in the desert in the early morning this can come down very low across the road and makes visibility very difficult. Put the fog lights on and slow down. Once the day warms up the mist disappears. Also, beware of taxis that will often stop dead in the road to pick up a fare, often without using indicators. And out on the desert roads beware of camels ambling along or on the highways. They will always expect you to give way.

There are no hotels outside Doha, apart from the *Sealine Beach Resort Complex* in the south of the country at Mesaieed but this is no bad thing considering the paucity of activity going on outside the capital. Unfortunately the youth hostel in Doha is now closed which only leaves the budget traveller with the even cheaper option of camping. There are no official campsites in Qatar though desert camping is permissible, the best camping spot being among the sand dunes in the south of the country.

It is possible to rent fully furnished apartments by the week and some of these will be advertised in the press. A good place to start the search for an apartment is *al-Muftah Services* (tel 4328 100) who also operate a car hire service.

Hotels
Because Qatar has mainly attracted tourists from other Gulf States and business travellers, all of whom can afford a decent hotel room, there are very few bargain-priced hotels in Qatar. The cheapest hotel in Doha will set you back about £24/$36 for a very basic, shabby double room. There are a few other places that offer a bit more comfort at a slightly higher price but then the cost of hotel rooms rockets. There are plenty of three-, four- and five-star hotels in Doha and many more are being constructed as the push to attract tourists from all over the world continues.

Booking Accommodation
Because of visa requirements, as well as for peace of mind, it is always a good idea to book a hotel room in advance – at least for one night, after which you can look for a better, cheaper, plusher option. Internet booking is not yet widespread among Qatar's hotels but most can take bookings by fax.

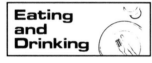

Eating and Drinking

Restaurants
Eating out is one of the pleasures of Qatar and there are plenty of restaurants to cater to all tastes in Doha. Outside of the city you will find very few. Restaurants open around 6pm but places don't start to fill up until around after about 8pm.

Fast Food. Fast food is big business in the Gulf, whether it be based on the American design or the home grown variety, and there are plenty of diners in Qatar to chose from.

Mealtimes
Because of the midday heat in the Gulf people generally rise early and eat breakfast early before the heat of the day sends them soporific. Then they may have a light lunch before taking a nap in the early afternoon. People eat much later in the evenings than they do in colder climates and because of the long siesta in the middle of the day people finish work later in the evening. This means that they may not sit down to eat the main meal of the day until nine or ten o'clock at night.

Vegetarians
Unlike the northern Middle Eastern countries where vegetarianism isn't quite understood, there are many vegetarian Indians who live in Qatar. Quite a number of chefs are from India (sometimes even a meal in a Chinese restaurant in Doha can have a suspiciously Indian tang to it) and the concept is well understood and catered for.

Foreign Cuisine
With 80 per cent of the population coming from overseas, Qatari restaurants are a mélange of cuisines from around the world. Whatever you want you should be able

to find. If it's not on the menu the chances are that the chef will know how to make it.

Regional Specialities

As elsewhere in the Gulf the cheapest eat is the *Shawarma*. Similar to the kebabs in Britain they cost around QR5 (£0.98/$1.37) and consist of warmed pitta bread stuffed with strips of either lamb (*lahma*) or chicken (*dajjaj*) with salad and sesame sauce and chillies. You will also see stand alone glass-fronted ovens roasting chickens which can be bought whole accompanied with flat bread and chillies. *Falafel* (deep fried pasted chick peas) and *fuul* (beans) are traditional Middle Eastern staples but more often these days the small food stalls will be selling dishes from India, Pakistan, Nepal, and South East Asia.

Soft Drinks

You will find anything you can buy back home, along with many others that you can't, on the supermarket shelves in Doha. Freshly prepared fruit juices are widely available and are good for that protein/vitamin rush. Expect to pay about QR3 for a large glass of orange juice, a fruit cocktail, mango juice etc.

Tea and Coffee

Unfortunately Turkish coffee, the real McCoy when it comes to a blast of caffeine to pick you up out of that sun-induced stupor, isn't as easy to get hold of in Qatar as it is in other countries in the Middle East. The Indian influence over the coffee shops has led to the demise of the coffee pot and the rise of ready sweetened, and milked instant coffee. But bastions of Arab drinking can still occasionally be found where you can get a nip of real coffee and partake in a blast of shisha. On the other hand the Indians know a thing or two about making a cup of tea. For 50 dirhams (£0.09/$0.13) you can get hold of a ready sugared Liptons tea with a splash of condensed milk. Very refreshing.

Museums. Apart from the small museum in al-Khor all the museums are located in Doha, the best of which is the *National Museum* on the Corniche.

The Desert

The desert in Qatar is pretty much featureless, rather flat and barren land. The only area of sand dunes is in the southeast of the country and you will need a 4WD to explore the area. If you do decide to head out into the dunes it may be a good idea to go with someone who knows the terrain. The area where the dunes are is quite close to the Saudi Arabian border and if you stray too far towards it you may incur the wrath of border guards. There are tour companies in Doha who can take you on desert safaris.

Beaches

The best beach is at **Fuwairit** in the northeast of the country. There are plenty of other beaches, either isolated because of the difficulty of reaching them, or the hotel beachfronts which are clean and have water sports equipment for hire but are expensive to use unless you are a guest of the hotel. Be aware that most beaches lack any kind of shade whatsoever due to the lack of vegetation in the country so take a big umbrella if you are tripping out to the wilder shores. **al-Wakra**, southeast of Doha has a good clean sandy beach but relatively little shade while **Dukhan**, on the west coast, has a large sandy beach with a sailing club (tel 4716 225) nearby. Again there is little shade here with no natural vegetation but the beach is clean and you feel a long way from the city.

Wildlife

Due to the shallowness of the seas around Qatar (the average depth is only 35 metres) the water is highly saline and this limits the species that can exist in these waters. However, the coastal regions are rich in shellfish such as whelks and limpets and further out to sea off the northeast coast **rays**, **sailfish** and **hammerhead sharks** can sometimes be found. Dhows still go out after fish such as **snappers**, **barracuda** and **tuna**.

Qatar is on many migration routes and bird life is varied and colourful. Spring and autumn are the best times to be here to catch sight of some rare and interesting species.

Theatre

Unless you are fluent in Arabic the theatre may leave you at a bit of a loss. The *Qatar National Theatre* on the Doha Corniche holds productions, mostly in Arabic. Some of the big hotels and foreign cultural centres occasionally host performances by visiting dance troupes and theatre companies.

Cinema

Because of the sparseness of wild, debauched or drunken nightlife in Qatar a visit here might be a good time to catch up on the movies that you may have missed back home when they were released the first time round. There are several cinemas in Doha that show English-language films. The *Gulf* and *Doha* Cinemas on C Ring Road have been slightly overshadowed by the *Mall Cineplex* (tel 4678 666) and *Landmark Mall* multiplex (tel 4875 222) but all are worth the QR15 (£2.90/$4.10) admission charge. Though violence and swearing are permitted in films any lewd behaviour is likely to be cut before screening. Listings can be found in the daily newspapers.

Nightlife

Bars and nightclubs that serve alcohol are limited to the larger international hotels. You must officially be a guest of the hotel or hold membership to be able to purchase a drink but may be able to sweet talk your way in depending on the leniency of the staff.

SPORT

Qataris are pretty keen on sports and keeping fit. Many of the more upmarket hotels have squash and tennis courts and gyms and/or beach clubs where equipment for various water sports can be hired. Even if you are not a guest of the hotel it is often possible to become a day member for around QR25 which will give you access to the facilities. There are clubs in Doha for practically every sport you can think of. The paving of the Corniche is pounded every day by hundreds of joggers and power walkers. Check the local press for telephone numbers of clubs and associations, or ask at your hotel. If you fancy a run while you are visiting, the *Qatar Hashers* meet every Monday approximately one hour before sunset. Telephone them on 4673 829 to find out where and when they are meeting.

Equestrianism

The horseracing season lasts from November to May at the *al-Rayyan Racing and Equestrian Centre* about 10km west of Doha city centre. Check the local press or ask at your hotel for race meeting timings. If you are already an accomplished rider horses can be hired at the al-Rayyan Racing and Equestrian Centre (tel 4805 901).

If horseracing is in your veins then the *al-Shaqab Stud* is well worth a visit. It is owned by the Emir, Sheikh Hamad bin Khalifa al-Thani and tours can be arranged through the *Arabian Adventures* tour company (tel 4361 461).

Football

Football is the favoured sport of the Qataris and the Sheikh Khalifa Stadium seats 50,000. Matches take place in the evenings during the season (November-June) and tickets cost QR10 (£1.95/$2.75) and are available at various outlets in Doha. Call 4316 532 for further information.

Camel Racing

The main racetrack for camel racing (big business in Qatar) is at Shahaniya about 30km west of Doha. Check with tour companies or your hotel for days and timing of the races, which take place in the cooler winter months. Shahaniya is a bit like Chantilly, Newmarket or Newbury out in the desert with the town given over to the training and breeding of camels. You will see groups of camels being taken out with their tiny jockeys for early morning training sessions. On race days locals follow the camels in their 4WD vehicles keeping up with them as they canter round the 18km racetrack. Make sure you don't get in the way of either the camels or the cars.

Golf

Qatar has taken to golf along with the other countries of the Arabian Gulf. The *Doha Golf Club* (tel 4832 338) has a 150-hectare, 18-hole championship course with a floodlit 9-hole academy course. It is open to visitors as well as its membership, and has a restaurant and bar (one of the few in Qatar). The Golf Club is located on the northern outskirts of town past the diplomatic area. The *Sheraton Doha Hotel and Resort* (tel 4836 363) has a practice range and a 5-hole pitch and putt.

 Shopping in Qatar means shopping in Doha. The fad these days is to construct huge malls and fill them with designer shops and the high street chains that we are familiar with back home. However, the traditional souk scene still lives on albeit less Middle Eastern in tone and often full of end of the line products that have long since disappeared from the shelves back in the West.

Haggling. Bargaining can be fun or a hassle and it is up to you whether you want to enter into it. It is usual to just ask for 'the last price' on an item and take it from there.

Shopping Hours. Shops are generally open from 9am-1.30pm and 4-9pm Saturday to Thursday. Opening times vary on Friday, shops are often closed in the morning then open in the late afternoon and stay open till late into the night.

Books

Books in English cost a lot more in Qatar than they do back home and the choice is limited. There is a branch of the *Family Bookshop* in al-Marqab al-Jadid in Doha that has a good selection of books about the Middle East though it is surprisingly deficient in books about Qatar. There is also a branch of the bookshop in the Doha Sheraton. The *Arabian Library* on Abdulla bin Thani Road up from the *Sofitel Hotel* is a stationers/newsagent/bookshop with a good selection of magazines, books and newspapers. They also stock the MEED Guides to the countries of the Arabian Gulf.

Gifts

Good buys, if you have space to carry them, are bolster cushions covered with heavy woven fabric of regional designs. Luggage is also cheap and, if you are planning to feed the 5,000 you can get hold of aluminium trays about 6 ft long and cooking pots that could contain enough stew to feed the hungry and homeless of London or New York. Watches, gold and cloth (mostly imported from India and Iran) are also good value. If you want to get hold of an old Phoenix bicycle (the ones with metal one-piece brake cables) you can buy these here too.

Traditional Qatari items to take home (depending on how much room you have in your bag) include brass coffee pots, incense burners and incense, rosewater sprinklers, camphor wood storage chests, model dhows and gypsum carvings. Gold is pretty good value in Qatar (though not as cheap as in Dubai) and you can get pendants made to your own design here.

Spices are also a good buy here and can make an interesting and cheap gift. Tailors in the Middle East are excellent and will make up a suit to your own design or copied from magazines. Material is also pretty inexpensive and to get a tailor-made suit here is well worth it. *Souk al-Waqif* in Doha has quite a number of perfume shops that sell dozens of scents and they can even make up a scent that is totally original to you. Qatari traditional dress is something you may also want to take home as a souvenir.

Health and Hygiene

Like all the other countries of the Arabian Gulf, Qatar is a prosperous, clean and hygienic country and you are unlikely to fall ill if you are already in good health before you arrive. Should you get ill the health system is very modern and there are a number of private clinics and pharmacies in Doha which will be able to advise on correct medical treatment. Outside of Doha services are scarce but the country is so small that you will only ever be a few hours' drive from the capital.

Depending on when you travel you should dress appropriately. The baking summer months of June to September call for light cotton clothing, a hat and a pair of sunglasses while the winter can get quite cool so it wouldn't be an oversight to pack a sweater.

Medical Treatment

Should you fall ill in Qatar it is a good idea to first seek advice from a pharmacy. For more serious ailments ask you hotel for advice on doctors. The main hospital in Qatar is the *Hamad Hospital* on al-Rayyan Road (tel 4392 222). There is also a private medial clinic *The Qatar Medical Centre* opposite *The Centre* hypermarket on Salwa Road.

Pharmacies

The vast majority of the pharmacies of Qatar are in Doha which will contain anything that you may need in the way of toiletries, contraceptives, medicines, baby food etc. There are quite a number scattered throughout the city. Try *al-Waha Pharmacy* on al-Mansoura Street (tel 4429 979) and *al-Yamama Pharmacy* on al-Salaam Street (tel 4811 525). Duty pharmacy names, addresses and telephone numbers are printed in the newspapers.

Crime and Safety

Qatar is one of the safest places in the world in which to travel and explore. Crime is practically unknown and you should feel safe walking about at any time of the day or night. Because the population are members of the conservative Wahhabi branch of Islam they are very devout Muslims and live a more structured existence compared to other parts of the Middle East where Islam is often not so strictly adhered to. Even the taxi drivers are less inclined to pull a fast one.

The Qataris are, however, more liberal in their attitudes than their Saudi Arabian Wahhabi neighbours; allowing women to drive cars and a certain amount of alcohol to be consumed in private delegated premises. What this means is that freedoms that we are used to in the West are controlled and you should refrain from flouting the law of the land. A very grim view is going to be taken by authorities of public drunkenness and as a foreigner and an outsider you have less recourse to the law than a Qatari national has should you transgress. Drive carefully and keep your wits about you when tackling those roundabouts in Doha.

Restricted Areas and Photography

Be careful of where you point your camera. It is polite to ask locals if they mind having a photograph taken (nobody wants to feel like a colourful exhibit in a zoo). Do not start swinging a camera around anywhere near military, important political buildings or industrial areas. Arabs are paranoid about spies.

Help and Information

TOURIST INFORMATION

Qatar does not have a tourist office as it is still a relatively new destination for western tourists. For general information about the country your best bet is to get on the internet and search out a few of the dedicated websites. A very useful website, with links to many sites relating to business, education, government ministries, news, hotels and tourism in Qatar can be found at www.qatar.net.qa. A couple of other useful sites are www.qatar-info.com and www.qatar-online.com.

If you are going to Qatar on business and want to be shepherded through customs as fast as possible the *Qatar National Hotels Company* (tel 4857 777; fax 4833 328; www.qnhc.com) operates a meet and greet service from its offices in Doha International Airport which can be handy for the rushed business traveller. Hostesses can take care of all immigration procedures for the traveller and they run lounges equipped with business facilities.

EMBASSIES & CONSULATES

The majority of embassies are located in the West Bay area of Doha and open from 8am-1pm Saturday to Wednesday. At present there is no Bahraini embassy in Qatar.

Kuwait: tel 4832 111; fax 4832 042.
Oman: tel 4670 744; fax 4670 474.
Saudi Arabia: tel 4832 030; fax 4832 720.
United Arab Emirates: tel 4885 111; fax 4882 837.
United Kingdom: tel 4421 991; fax 4438 692.
United States of America: tel 4864 701; fax 4861 669.
Yemen: tel 4432 555; fax 4429 400.

USEFUL INFORMATION

Business Hours

Anyone working for the government will be working 6am-2pm Saturday to Wednesday. Private businesses are likely to work 7.30am-noon and 3.30-7.30pm but timings vary and it is wise to telephone companies to find out their individual opening hours before traipsing over to do business. Shopping malls are often open 9am-9pm daily and most other shops tend to open 8.30am-noon and again from 4-9pm after a long lunch break.

Time. Qatar local time is GMT + 3 hours.

Electricity. The electrical mains in Qatar operates on 220-240 volts. The sockets and plugs are three-pin British style.

Useful Organisations

American Cultural Centre: tel 4884 101.
British Council: tel 4426 193.
Doha Club: tel 4327 965.
French Cultural Centre: tel 4671 037.
Natural History Group: tel 4402 253.

Emergency Services Numbers

All toll free: Police, Ambulance and Fire **999**.

PUBLIC HOLIDAYS AND CELEBRATIONS

Islamic holidays are dependent on the Islamic calendar rather than the Gregorian and so fall on different days each year. Qatar observes the five feasts and festivals common all over the Muslim world. Details of these can be found in the opening chapters of this book. Qatar's **National Day** is celebrated on 3 December every year and Qataris also take a holiday on 1 January. Ramadan, the month of fasting during daylight hours, will fall in the cooler months of October, November and December for the next five years.

EXPLORING QATAR

DOHA

Doha is okay. People who live and work in the Gulf tend to scoff if you say that you are going to Doha. They are likely to tell you that it is a dull backwater with little going for it. And of course it is in a country that bans the consumption of alcohol on religious grounds. However, Doha really is a charming place to visit.

It is one of the smaller cities of the Gulf and for all the sky scrapers, five-star hotels, luxury office blocks and highways that have sprung up over the past couple of decades through the vast wealth created by oil and gas, the place still retains a certain amount of charm. Perhaps what it has retained that other places in the Gulf have lost is a sense of innocence. The inhabitants of Doha, and Qatar, like to partake in the more innocent pleasures of life. The Corniche and the souks are the heart and lungs of the city and fitness and family life seem to be one of the main hobbies of the populace.

Downtown is always at its busiest in the cooler evenings when the souks and restaurants re-open and the streets are crowded with people shopping, eating or just hanging out. The city centre hasn't become as modernised and sanitised as Dubai or Abu Dhabi and perhaps because of this Doha still feels exotic and Eastern. But the infrastructure of the city is modern, and provides all the services that the business traveller or the get away from it all tourist might require.

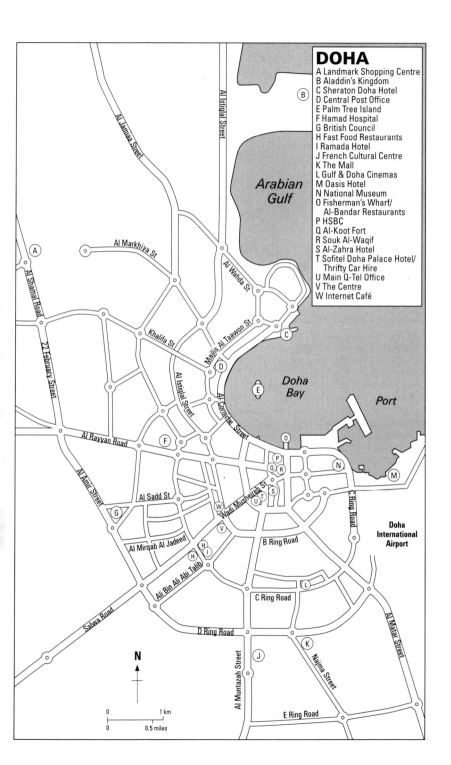

DOHA

A Landmark Shopping Centre
B Aladdin's Kingdom
C Sheraton Doha Hotel
D Central Post Office
E Palm Tree Island
F Hamad Hospital
G British Council
H Fast Food Restaurants
I Ramada Hotel
J French Cultural Centre
K The Mall
L Gulf & Doha Cinemas
M Oasis Hotel
N National Museum
O Fisherman's Wharf/
  Al-Bandar Restaurants
P HSBC
Q Al-Koot Fort
R Souk Al-Waqif
S Al-Zahra Hotel
T Sofitel Doha Palace Hotel/
  Thrifty Car Hire
U Main Q-Tel Office
V The Centre
W Internet Café

Arabian Gulf

Doha Bay

Port

Doha International Airport

N

CITY LAYOUT

Doha has grown up around an east-facing bay. The city's layout is based on a set of semi-circular ring roads that fan out from that bay beginning with the Corniche. The north end of the Corniche has the omnipresent *Doha Sheraton Hotel*, the West Bay and diplomatic areas. The south-eastern end of the Corniche is where the port and customs facilities are as well as several of the older five-star hotels. The middle of the Corniche and the area immediately inland from it is the oldest and most interesting part of Doha. The **souks** and banks, the **National Museum**, many of the cheaper hotels and fisherman's jetty are located here.

Arrival and Departure. Doha International Airport is small but has an ATM, a bank, a cafeteria, car hire booths and a duty free. Located a short way out of central Doha, it should cost you around QR6 (£1.15/$1.60) for the cab ride into the centre of Doha.

City Transport. Public transport in Doha is limited to the taxi as there is no municipal bus network. The good news is that the fares are significantly cheaper than in other Gulf States. If you need a ride stick out your hand and make sure the driver puts the meter on.

ACCOMMODATION

The majority of the hotels in Doha cater for the business traveller and are quite plush.
Al-Zahra Hotel: tel 4321 503; fax 4439 785. This is the cheapest place in town and is on al-Asmakh Street, very close to the Dhow Roundabout, close to the heart of the city, and charges QR80/120 (£16-24/$22-33). The rooms are very basic but come with an en suite 'bathroom', a television, air-conditioning and a fridge.
The Dana Hotel: This hotel is quite hard to find but is signposted from Ali bin Abdulla Street opposite the mosque and waste ground. It is one of those middle of the road hotels that you find in the Middle East (nothing wrong with it but lacking in soul) offering a basic room for QR120/160 (£24-32/$33-44).
The Doha Palace Hotel: tel 4360 101; fax 4423 955; e-mail dpalace@qatar.net.qa. This hotel is on Wadi Musheireb Street towards the Dhow Roundabout. Although it is pretty ropey and overpriced it is in a conveniently central location and they will sort out visas should you need to be sponsored. It charges QR180 (£35/$49) for a single, QR220 (£43/$60) for a double and rooms come with ensuite bathroom, television, air-conditioning and fridge.
Sheraton Doha Hotel: tel 4854 444; fax 832 323. The rooms in this hotel at the northernmost point of the Corniche are not as opulent as the lobby and architecture may suggest. Prices begin at around QR550 (£108/$151) plus taxes.
Oasis Hotel: tel 4424 424; fax 327 096. At the opposite end of the Corniche to the *Sheraton Doha*. This hotel is quite far from the centre of things but the back rooms have good sea views. Expect to pay around QR250/328 (£49-65/$68-90) plus taxes.
Ramada Hotel: tel 4417 417; fax 4410 941. Up on the C Ring Road this hotel is in a fairly convenient location if fast food joints are your bag. Singles and double rooms start at around QR390 (£77/$107) plus taxes.
Regency Hotel: tel 4363 363; fax 4325 232. This four-star hotel is across from the *al-Zahra*, is very new and charges QR230/300. As with all the hotels in the Gulf – prices are negotiable.
There are also several hotels up on the Museum Road all charging around QR140/200 (£26-38/$38-54) per night the best of which is probably the *al-Safeer Hotel* (4353 999). Others along that road are the *New Mushriq*, the *Tourist Hotel* and the *al-Bustan Hotel*.

Sheraton Doha Hotel

EATING AND DRINKING

The *al-Bandar* group of restaurants and cafés on the fisherman's jetty is very popular with an upmarket crowd of Qatari nationals, expats and business travellers. These restaurants are themed with waiters wearing traditional Qatari garb (which you will find either cool or cringeworthy) and as there are three main restaurants all serving a different type of cuisine there should be something to suit everyone's taste.

Thai Noodles on al-Bareed Street has a good selection of food from that country. Main courses will set you back about QR12 (£2.30/$3.25), rice an extra QR3. The restaurant is good, clean and very popular.

The Red Rose Restaurant on al-Jabr Street in the centre of town is another place of about the same quality as *Thai Noodles* serving an eclectic mix of Indian, Chinese and Western food. Main dishes start from QR10-12.

If you are beginning to pine for European food try the *JG Sandwich Cellar* (tel 4357 559) on Ras Abu Abboud Street near the flyover by the Corniche. A coffee shop and café, it is a cosy place run by a couple of British expats.

Elsewhere, because dining out is one of the main recreations of the Doharian, many of the top hotels have themed nights where a different national cuisine is offered, often at relatively bargain prices.

Fast Food

Fast food is popular with the locals and on the road to Salwa, by the Ramada Junction, there is a glut of fast food restaurants: *Ponderosa Steakhouse, Caravan, al-Tazaj bar-b-q Chicken, Pizza Hut, Taco Bell, TCBY* and *Arby's* among others. All are relatively cheap. *Dairy Queen* (another burger joint) is on the corner by the Ramada junction traffic lights. You will find the standard fare, a tad cheaper than back home admittedly, at *McDonald's* and *Burger King* which are located adjacent to each other on the C Ring Road just north of the fast food restaurants. There is another *McDonald's* on al-Ahmed Street in the souk area of central Doha.

Near *The Centre* hypermarket there is an outlet of *KFC* and the *Colosseum* pizza/pasta restaurant. *Fuddruckers*, a pretty tasty alternative to the usual burger experience is part of the Khalifa International Tennis and Squash Complex behind the Central Post Office.

There are also a lot of cheap eateries and street stalls along Wadi Musheireb Street and Abdul Aziz bin Ahmed Street near the Sofitel Hotel downtown. The *Calicut Cafeteria* on the street running along souk al-Waqif has pretty good fresh fruit juices and serves shawarmas.

Coffee Houses

The *Mahmodiya Café*, next to the mosque on the corner of an empty building lot opposite Souk al-Ahmed is a great place for sitting out in the evening taking a tea and reading the papers. It is a favourite haunt of the local contingent of old men who come here to gossip and lounge about in the assorted falling to pieces armchairs and sofas. The owner serves mainly tea, coffee and fresh juices.

Try the *Batteel Café and Bakery* (tel 4312 313) on Salwa Road for a more upmarket experience. The café is done out like a traditional Qatari house and serves patisseries, sandwiches and fresh fruit juices.

The *Paradise* is a traditional coffee house in a large tent selling tea, coffee and shisha along the eastern end of the Corniche towards the Doha Club by Rafco Marina and the Port buildings. The sign is in Arabic but you should have no trouble spotting the place by the sound of Middle Eastern music and the aromatic waft of shishas being smoked by a mostly local crowd. Another place similar to this lies across from the HSBC building, on the right of the road up to the al-Bandar group of restaurants on the fisherman's jetty near the Oyster and Pearl Monument.

The *Layali* coffee shop on the eastern side of the Corniche is an expensive but architecturally very impressive place with a full complement of wind towers and ample parking space for the luxury vehicles that arrive here driven by a fast crowd.

Water Sports

Doha Mariott Gulf Hotel (tel 4495 527) offers water-skiing at the rather hefty price of QR25 (£4.90/$6.85) for 15 minutes and jet skis can be hired for QR150 (£29/$42) per hour. Scuba diving courses can be had in Doha though there are better places to dive in the Gulf. For information on what is available call *Coral Diving School* on 4675 141 or *Pearl Divers* (tel 4449 553).

SHOPPING

Doha has several main shopping areas: the area around the centre of town is pretty much contained in an area bordered by four roads: Jabar bin Mohammed Street, Ali bin Abdulla Street, Grand Hamad Street and Abdulla bin Jasim Street. Within these boundaries are the old and new souks, small department stores and the cheaper restaurants. There is also a lot of gold around here and at night the place gets crowded with all nationalities barging about on shopping expeditions. Abdulla bin Thani Road has a couple of good and interesting souvenir emporiums on it. The district around al-Marqab al-Jadid is the place for high street shopping with retailers selling electrical goods, hardware, sports goods, CDs and cassettes, and some of the more upmarket restaurants.

Supermarkets and Malls

The Mall is a huge building out on the D Ring Road opposite al-Ahli Sports Club. It is one of the newest shopping centres in Doha, is quite a way from the centre of town but has most of the high street and fashion shops from Britain and America housed within its walls plus a very good cinema. The *Landmark* shopping centre is a pink mock-fortress building on ash-Shimal Road near Immigration Roundabout which houses *Marks and Spencer*, *BHS* and other well-known brands of store. It also has a Multiplex cinema. *Carrefour Hypermarket* is one of the biggest and best places to shop and is out past the Doha Sheraton.

Food Palace supermarkets are a chain open from 7am-midnight every day with stores throughout Doha. A central one is on Wadi Musheireb Street before you come to the flyover heading out from the city centre. *The Centre*, over the flyover, is a hypermarket with a bookshop, a supermarket with an abundance of imported goods from Britain and America, and franchises such as the *Body Shop*, cosmetic brands and clothes manufacturers such as *Benetton*. There is a small cafeteria inside. Close to *The Centre* is the *New Trade Gallery* – home to a number of rather posh boutiques.

Souk al-Ahmed is a two-storey shopping mall full of boutiques in the centre of town on Grand Hamad Street. There are also a lot of international boutiques and designer label shops along as-Sadd Street.

Souks

The *Central Market* is quite a way out of town on Salwa Road. It houses the fruit, vegetable and fish and meat markets and it is best to get there sometime in the early morning to see the vendors in full flow. There is an additional market area close to the *Central Market* also on Salwa Road which takes place only on Thursdays and Fridays. Here you will find stalls selling falcons and falconry equipment, traditional handicrafts and anything else not covered by the main markets. Salwa Road is also where most of the furniture and interior design shops are located should you need to furnish a house.

The best souk, for real Middle Eastern ambience and for what you can buy in it, is *Souk al-Waqif*. It is a maze of corrugated iron-covered alleyways with hoards of people from all walks of life wandering about the lanes. Haggard porters wheel trolleys about or are asleep on them and if you are looking for a bargain this is probably the place to visit. Everything closes up at midday when those shopkeepers without shutters to pull down over the entrance to their shops cover their wares in tarpaulin. As is traditional in the Middle East souks, shops selling similar products are grouped together so if you think the one you're in is charging too much you can wander into the next shop to compare prices.

Exploring

The Qatar National Museum

This award-winning museum (tel 4442 191) is open 9am-noon and 3-6pm Sunday to Thursday and 4-7pm on Friday. It is closed on Saturday. The museum is housed in the grounds of the old palace of Sheikh Abdulla bin Qasim al-Thani and was built in 1901. It was restored in the early 1970s with additional buildings added to house the main museum exhibition hall and aquarium.

Walking in through a large ornately carved door you enter a spacious courtyard with several low square buildings dotted in and around it. These contain various themed rooms that give you a good idea of what life was like not so very long ago in Qatar before the discovery of oil. Re-creations of a kitchen, a bedroom, and a pottery accompany exhibits of stoneware, wooden utensils, weaving, and traditional medicines (with rather gory photographs of the methods used for the bleeding of patients). There are also rooms dedicated to the reigns of several of the previous rulers of Qatar including a selection of Sheikh Ali bin Abdulla's thrones and Sheikh Abdulla bin Jassem al-Thani's wheelchair.

In the middle of the courtyard stands the old palace with the interior a re-creation of the ruler's *majlis*. Within this building are exhibits of gold and silver jewellery, medals from around the world that have been awarded to the Sheikhs, perfumes and a mock-up of the old school house.

At the time of writing the main museum building was closed for refurbishment but the **Maritime Museum** and **Aquarium** were open. The Maritime Museum concentrates on the pearling industry, boat building and fishing past of Qatar and the natural history of the peninsula. The central display cases have a fascinating array of fossils found in Qatar as well as a very tempting exhibit showing different qualities and variety of pearls.

Downstairs is the Aquarium which has a large number of well-lit and labelled tanks exhibiting different types of the indigenous aquatic life. The largest tank is the most interesting with a couple of green turtles, and a *cobia* (a small shark) doing laps, languidly pursued by a lovesick *remora*.

In the grounds of the Museum is also a large man-made lagoon with several types of dhow afloat on it and marooned around it. A separate building houses a collection on antique vehicles including a couple of great old Cadillacs once used by the sheikhs.

al-Koot Fort

The fort (tel 4412 742), also locally known as Doha Fort on Jasim bin Mohammed Street near the Dhow Roundabout, is a beautifully restored and airy two-storey 19th century building with rooms built along the walls of the courtyard. Exhibits covering Qatar's national heritage include reconstructions of the various trades of the 19th and early 20th century such as tailoring and dressmaking, fishing, blacksmithing, boat building, gold and silver-smithing, weaving and rope making. There are exhibits, photographs and one room is packed with ornately carved old doors and bedsteads. The art of gypsum designs is also explained. The upper storey gives good views over toward the souk area.

Weaponry Museum

It is well worth checking with a local tour company about getting a visit to the Weaponry Museum at al-Laqta in the northern suburbs of Doha. Originally Sheikh Hassan bin Muhammed bin Ali al-Thani's private collection of Qatari weapons the museum is now operated by the *Department of Ruins and Museums*. The collection of around 2,315 exhibits includes swords, *khanjars*, canon and rifles, photographs and paintings. Some of the collection dates back to the Amayad and Abbassid eras.

The Ethnographic Museum

This museum (tel 4436 008) gives a glimpse of what life was like in a traditional Qatari family before the coming of oil. The building also features one of the few remaining wind towers that were once an important part of every dwelling in the region. Admission to the museum is free. It is situated off Grand Hamad Street, recognisable by the huge wind tower, and is open 9am-noon and 3-6pm, Sunday to Thursday.

Doha Corniche

The Corniche is one of the most impressive in the Arabian Gulf and stretches for 7km from the Sheraton Doha Hotel in the north of the city to the Ras abu Abboud flyover in the east. The Corniche has a paved walkway separated from the corniche highway by lawns planted with palm trees that are a great place to rest up or have a leisurely picnic. There are parking places all along its length where the sports car driving Qatari youths stand around chatting about the day and discussing different makes of supercharger. The Corniche is marked out every 100m to let the jogger know how far they've gone and is a beautiful and safe place to take a constitutional stroll at any time of the day or night. The Corniche has been built on reclaimed land; the original shoreline was much further inland – next to the lagoon of the National Museum.

The Clock Tower, Doha

The Postal Museum

This small museum has its entrance on al-Bareed Street and is open 4-6pm Saturday to Thursday, closed Friday and has exhibits from the first post office established in Qatar. For those of a philatelic bent there is also a display of local stamps at the Main Post Office on the Corniche.

PARKS AND GARDENS

The **al-Bidda Park** opposite the Corniche is a pleasant enough place for a stroll and an especially good place to take the kids. It consists of lawns, walkways beside a shallow canal, a skateboarding rink, souvenir shops and a shop selling paintings from the *Fine Art Society*.

Aladdin's Kingdom (tel 4831 001) is situated past the Sheraton Doha Hotel in the West Bay area. It has a load of amusement park rides and is open from 3.30-9pm Sunday to Friday.

Palm Tree Island (tel 4869 151) is run by *Qatar National Hotels Company* (the nearest equivalent to a Tourist Board in Qatar) and sits in the middle of the bay. It can only be reached by launches operating from a jetty near the Sheraton Doha Hotel on the Corniche. The cost of the return trip is QR15, which includes entry to the island and it is worth going to the island to take a look at Doha from the sea. There is a swimming pool, kids rides and a private beach together with a pricey restaurant (you are not permitted to take your own food and drink to the island). The rides cost extra. It is open 9am-9.30pm every day, but Monday and Fridays are reserved for families only. Launches run to and from the island and the Corniche every ten minutes.

Doha Zoo is situated about half an hour's drive to the south-west of the city. It has the usual caged animals and kids play areas, a cafeteria and is open from 3-9pm daily except Saturday.

Along the Corniche by the Pizza Hut there are always a few small dhows moored that offer trips around the bay during the late afternoons and evenings. You will need to haggle a bit over the fare but expect to pay around QR10-15 per person for a half hour trip.

Further Afield

Khor al-Adaid

Khor al-Adaid, also called by tour operators the Inland Sea, is probably the highlight of the sites and sights in Qatar. A tidal lake out to the south of the country, it can only be reached by 4WD. It is quite a way into the desert through a large area of sand dunes and trips out there should either be done in a convoy or arranged through local tour operators. The whole area around Khor al-Adaid is extraordinarily beautiful with huge Lawrence of Arabia sand dunes and if you can arrange to spend a night out among them it is definitely worth the effort and expense. The sense of peace and tranquillity is something that you won't forget, and the stars at night out in the desert shine more brightly than you will have ever seen before.

Mesaieed Sealine Beach Resort

This holiday complex is located beside the sea with some of Qatar's beautiful sand dunes behind, about 55km south of Doha. With chalets, rooms and individual villas the place is a bit of a weekend getaway for the rich with the usual toys that a resort has to offer. Day membership is available and is probably the best bet. Some of the surrounding sand dunes have been disfigured by 4WDs skidding around on the pristine slopes and you will need a 4WD to explore the coast past the Resort and the hinterland. There is a **public beach** off the main road to the left before you reach *Sealine* (tel 4770 380) though it isn't signposted. Unfortunately there is no shade here at all so you will need to bring your own.

Shahaniya

The **Oryx farm** near Shahaniya, about 30km west of Doha, has been set up to preserve and breed the threatened **Arabian Oryx**. Although the farm is a private concern trips can be made here in conjunction with one of the local tour companies operating out of Doha.

al-Khor

Al-Khor is a pretty little town, about 60km north of Doha, with a very attractive corniche with shade and umbrellas and an attractive beach. On the way up from Doha, about 20km north of the city, you will pass **Umm Salal Mohammed**, a large village that is home to one of the few forts in Qatar.

Up until the bottom fell out of the market in the 1940s al-Khor was the centre of the pearling industry in Qatar. Next to the corniche is a very busy **fishing harbour**. It is best to get here early in the morning to watch the crews of the assorted dhows loading and unloading cargoes of fish and ice, mending nets and refuelling and making up the *garageer* fish traps. There is a restaurant, *Thai Asea*, opposite the corniche selling reasonable food. Dotted around the town are old **watchtowers**.

Al-Khor Museum (tel 4721 866) is in an old police fort along the corniche. Opening times vary from summer to winter and the museum is closed on Friday and Monday but if you visit between 8am and noon, or 4-6pm you should find it open. However, it is advisable to call to check opening times.

Al-Khor Gardens. are not signposted on the road as you approach al-Khor so you will need to double back on yourself after you sight the fort-like turret of a plantation wall and a small mosque on your left just before the al-Khor roundabout. Do a U-turn after this. The gardens are a very peaceful place and a haven for wildlife stuck out in the middle of the desert landscape. Quite tame birds sing their heads off, there are several species of butterfly and lots of different species of trees and flowers here. The place must cost a small fortune to irrigate as it covers quite a large area. The gardens come alive at the weekend but if you visit during the week you are likely to have the place to yourself. There is a kids' playground with slides and swings, a cafeteria and parking.

Fuwairit

Fuwairit is about 90km north of Doha and is reachable in a saloon car on a tarmac road, though to reach the beach you will have to walk if you don't have a 4WD. The village is practically abandoned and has an air of a ghost town in a 1960s movie complete with broken down, crumbling buildings and pigeons roosting among the ruins. Abandoned and rusting Cadillacs and Landrovers lie along the seashore and in garages whose doors have been left open hanging off their hinges. The sea here is a beautiful colour of aquamarine and there are mangroves. On either side of the village there are a couple of very large inhabited villas, some sporty speedboats anchored among the mangroves and more building work is going on. People do live here and there are several animal pens in use but the deserted feeling of the place makes a great change from the pace of life in Doha. Fuwairit is a good place to go for a camping weekend, especially if you can get hold of a boat to explore the area.

Just up the coast from Fuwairit is the village of **al-Ghariya** where you can drive right up to the beach without a 4WD. The colour of the sea here is also fantastic but on land there isn't much here except sand.

al-Ruwais

On Qatar's northernmost point, al-Ruwais feels a bit like being at the end of the world. There is a causeway leading out to an outlying island and a few restaurants and cold stores in the town. The beach below the town with a huge antenna, fishing boats drawn up and goats pottering about looking for food and shade, has a pretty postcard look. There are some low-lying islands out to sea and it could be worth asking one of the locals to take you out in a boat for a look about.

Zubarah Fort

The road from al-Ruwais to Zubarah passes a great many defence stations and radio masts so taking a detour off the main road in order to head back towards the sea (and you will need a 4WD to get there) may lead to a few questions being asked by suspicious military personnel if you are seen. However, there are a few abandoned villages here which are interesting and definitely worth taking a look at. One of them, **al-Khuwair**, has a deep narrow channel cut into the coral that is thought to have been used by pirates based there in order to escape pursuers.

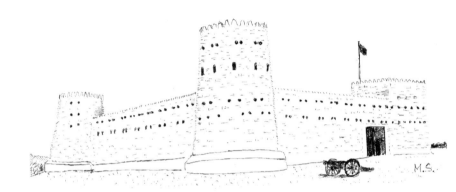

Zubarah Fort and Museum

Zubarah was once the stronghold of the al-Khalifa, the ruling family of Bahrain and a large trading centre. The fort was built in the 18th century and until 1986 was used as the local police post. There remains little evidence of the commercial centre that Zubarah was though the fort has now been restored to its former glory. The fort (tel 4701 252) commands the surrounding countryside and it is practically the only building of any consequence for miles around. It is open officially from 9am-noon and 3-6pm everyday except Saturday and is looked after by a caretaker who lives in a prefab next to it. If it is locked seek him out and he'll open up for you. As with all government employees he is unlikely to be paid a lot so a tip will be appreciated. There is not a lot to see in the fort. Some of the rooms have exhibits of potsherds from the 18th and 19th centuries that were excavated during the reconstruction of the fort in the 1980s, and a few photographs, though unfortunately all explanations are in Arabic. However, you can climb up the turrets and look out across the bleak landscape that surrounds the fort towards the blue sea a few miles away. Nearby are the ruins of other coastal fortifications but you will need a 4WD to get out to them.

United Arab Emirates

The Blue Souk, Sharjah

For anyone who has only ever visited the northern Middle East and traditional Arab holiday destinations of Egypt, Jordan, Lebanon and, to an increasing degree, Syria the United Arab Emirates make for a major change. The truth is that the UAE doesn't feel particularly Middle Eastern. The country is a cosmopolitan mix of nationalities who outnumber the indigenous population and who have built the country up into a bizarre mishmash of styles. You will hear more English and Hindi spoken than Arabic and the classic Middle Eastern sights of the poorer countries to the north such as donkey and carts, crowded buses belching exhaust fumes and beggars are rarely if ever encountered in the UAE. The country is rich and everyone in it either works for a living or has enough money not to need to work. The buildings are elegant, large and spacious, the infrastructure is well planned and the citizens are well provided for. Dubai has become the success story that everyone hears about, a place of rampant consumerism with an annual shopping festival, the world's most valuable prize in the horseracing calendar, some of the world's most well appointed golf courses and great beach hotels. Less than half a century ago there was no United Arab Emirates, the area was desert with small settlements dotted around the coast and in various oases. Today the greening of the desert in the UAE has and is being achieved with incredible success. The cost of a holiday in the emirates isn't particularly cheap, but with warm seas, blue skies, the desert and great shopping opportunities the area is well worth exploring.

GEOGRAPHY

The United Arab Emirates (UAE) are a confederation of seven independent sheikhdoms ruled by seven emirs located on the Arabian Gulf across the water from Iran and bordered by the sea to the north and the east. The country also has borders with the Kingdom of Saudi Arabia (KSA) to the south and southwest and with Oman to the south and east. The Omani territory of Musandam lies to the north of the United Arab Emirates on the Strait of Hormuz. There is also a small Omani enclave surrounded by the Emirates at Madha in the mountains of the east coast.

The UAE has coastline on the Arabian Gulf and the Gulf of Oman and has a total area of about 83,000 square kilometres, most of which (85 per cent) lies along with the majority of the oil reserves, in Abu Dhabi. Dubai is the second largest, and second richest emirate of the confederation, with an area of 3,900 square kilometres, and Ajman is the smallest emirate with 260 square kilometres. Much of the country is barren land, characteristically consisting of *sabkha* (arid salt flats) in the coastal regions and gravel desert plains further inland.

Towards the Saudi Arabian border is the vast area of desert known as the Empty Quarter with rolling waves of sand dunes (some over 300 metres high) and isolated oases. To the east of the country one finds the Hajar mountain range which forms a natural barrier between the rest of the country and the emirate of Fujairah on the east coast. The northern emirate of Ras al-Khaimah is the agricultural centre of the country where the soil is very fertile due to the run-off from the surrounding mountains. The country's coastline stretches for approximately 1,318 kilometres and is characterised by long sandy beaches and warm waters year round.

CLIMATE

The **best time** to visit the United Arab Emirates is during the winter months of November to March when temperatures average around 24°C. From March temperatures soar, occasionally reaching over 50°C, but usually staying in the low 40s. On the coast humidity can often go over 100 per cent and those who can afford it either leave the country during the peak summer months or have holiday homes in the mountains on the east coast or in the oases such as al-Ain inland. When the sea temperature can reach 35°C in the summer a swim in water hotter than the body's normal temperature is more akin to having a bath than a bathe.

Rainfall is low, averaging 42 millimetres a year and mostly falling in December to January. When it does rain, even for a short time, the desert suddenly comes into bloom and a drive into the interior after rains can put the landscape in a completely different light. Occasionally during the winter sandstorms (*shimals*) whipped up from the Saudi Arabian desert and the Empty Quarter may blow through the region.

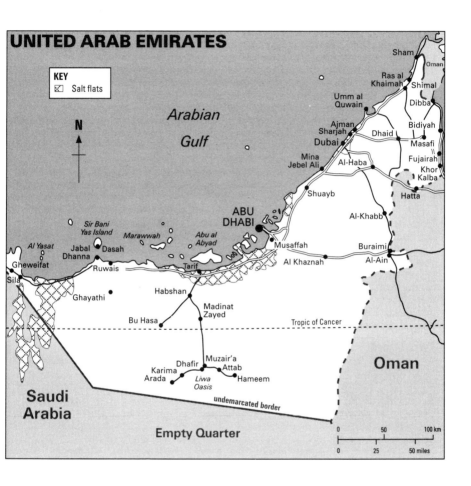

HISTORY

Ancient History

Located as it is on a major trade route between the East and the Mediterranean, the main occupations of the inhabitants of the Gulf coast have always been trade, seafaring and fishing. Inland, evidence has been found of the existence of agriculture and a sedentary as well as a nomadic way of life being pursued way back into the mists of time. Excavations on the island of Umm an-Nar in Abu Dhabi have traced the habitation of the UAE back to around BC3000. The civilisation that lived there at the time, named Umm an-Nar (Mother of Fire) after the island in which its remains were found, is thought to have taken influences from the Indus valley and Mesopotamia and to have extended its range along the coast and into Oman. It is also believed that camels were first domesticated around the time of the Umm an-Nar. The region was also touched by the Magans whose empire was centred on the Batinah coast in Oman near to the copper mines that it exploited so well.

During the 1st Millennium BC Arab tribes from central Arabia arrived in the region and settled. They intermarried with those sedentary farmers who were already living in the area who then took on the tribal affiliations so customary of the Arabs. The Greeks also marched into the area in the 1st Millennium BC attracted by the trading possibilities and stayed to leave their influences. Later the Persians also came and settled in the region. With the coming of Islam from across the sands in the 7th century AD the area quickly converted to the new religion, a final defeat of the unbelievers taking place at the battle of Dibba on the east coast of the present day United Arab Emirates in 635AD.

During the Middle Ages the Gulf region was under the rule of the Kingdom of Hormuz, which had its stronghold on the island of Hormuz north of the Musandam Peninsula with trade largely in the hands of the Arab and Persian merchants of the area. After the discovery of the sea route to India by the Portuguese in 1497 the Gulf was opened up to European influence with the Portuguese, French and British all vying for supremacy. For many years the Portuguese dominated the region, conquering Hormuz, occupying Bahrain and important Gulf ports. The Portuguese were finally ousted from the region by Persian, British, Dutch and Omani forces and during the early 1700s the collapse of both the Safavid dynasty in Persia and the ruling Imamate in Oman led to an increased British influence in the Gulf.

Two Tribes

At around this time, in the 1700s, two strong tribal groups emerged as supreme in the Gulf, the Bani Yas and the Qawasim. The Bani Yas were and are a powerful confederation of tribes who in those days were nomadic herders (Bedouin) wandering in the desert and returning to their oasis base at Liwa in the Empty Quarter. They earned their living by traditional Bedouin means – camel rustling and trading, the cultivation of dates and fodder, acting as guards to caravans and as guides to desert explorers such as Doughty, Thomas, Thesiger et al. In 1793 the Bani Yas moved their base from Liwa to Abu Dhabi, attracted by the abundance of fresh water to be found there, and the riches to be made from the pearling industry that was centred around it. They established their seat of government there and built the fort that stands there today - the oldest building left standing in a modern city of high-rise blocks. Today the rulers of both Abu Dhabi and Dubai are members of the Bani Yas tribe.

The other powerful tribal group that emerged during the late 1700s was the Qawasim. A seafaring people, for a long time they dominated both the Persian and the Arab coasts of the Arabian Gulf from their base at Ras al-Khaimah which had replaced the ancient settlement of Julfar in importance. Conflict arose over territory and influence over trade in the region between the Qawasim and the ruling al-Bu Said dynasty in Oman. The increasing importance of India to Britain meant keeping control over the routes to India and so when Emperor Napoleon Bonaparte marched into and occupied Egypt in 1798, blocking the Red Sea route, the British entered into and signed an alliance with the al-Bu Said dynasty. Although this alliance was to prevent Napoleon from gaining a power base in Oman and disrupting the trade routes to and from India, it turned the British into the enemy of the Qawasim who began attacking British vessels.

By the late 1700s the British East India Company was seeking to get the British government to impose a number of treaties on the Arabs of the Gulf in order to protect its trade routes with India, and to curb what it called 'acts of piracy' against its ships. However, what the East India Company saw as acts of piracy against their vessels was seen as fair game in the rules of power mongering by the Qawasim who continued to hound the British to such an extent that the region became known as the Pirate Coast. In 1809 a British punitive mission was sent to attack the Qawasim ships followed by several other such missions in subsequent years. In 1820 a British fleet was sent to destroy all Qawasim ships along with the coastal bases of the tribe. The British then occupied Ras al-Khaimah and imposed a General Treaty of Peace on the region whereby the sheikhs of the individual emirates agreed to refrain from piracy. Today the descendents of the Qawasim still rule Ras al-Khaimah and Sharjah.

Trucial States

Further treaties were signed between the sheikhs and Britain to end the lucrative slave trade that was also going on in the Gulf at the time. In 1853 the Treaty of Perpetual Maritime Peace was signed by all the sheikhs of the region which led to the formation of what became known as the Trucial Coast (also known as Trucial Oman). Until Indian Independence in 1947 all British/Gulf affairs were looked after by the British Indian government who sought to influence external relations and defence while refusing to interfere in the internal tribal wars that continued in the region.

Towards the end of the 19th century Germany, France and Russia all had designs on the Gulf and in 1892 the political resident Major-General Grant Keir, on behalf of the British government, signed separate but identical treaties with all the rulers of the Trucial States whereby, in return for protection against outside attack, the rulers promised not to cede, mortgage, or otherwise dispose of parts of their territories to anyone but the British government, nor to enter into any relationship with a foreign government other than the British. These treaties were to put an end to European rivalry over the region and from that moment until the withdrawal from the Gulf in 1971, Britain was the dominant player in the region.

With the conclusion of maritime hostilities after the signing of the treaties which had also prevented the building of large ships, the region, especially Abu Dhabi, became renowned for its pearling industry; the shallow and warm waters of the Gulf providing ideal conditions for oyster beds. Then, with the collapse of the old Qawasim emirate of Lingeh on the Persian coast, many traders who had been based there returned to settle in Dubai – now ruled by the al-Maktoum family, a branch of the Bani Yas. When the British began to use Dubai rather than Lingeh as the main port of call in the Gulf between India and Britain in 1903 the area flourished as a centre of cosmopolitan trade, although to the British the importance of the Trucial States was still only as a strategic point on the route to and from India. To this end British involvement was never far reaching in the region and did not involve posting a permanent political agent or getting involved in the land disputes that were a way of life for the various tribes. The first airport in the region was built in Sharjah in 1932 in order to serve passengers on the long distance British Imperial Airways flights to India rather than for any military purpose.

In the 1930s the pearl trade went into a slump due to cheaper cultured pearls being available from Japan. Many of the Gulf Arabs left to find work outside the Trucial States. With oil prospectors combing other regions of the Gulf hoping for strikes (oil was discovered in Bahrain in 1932), rulers of the Emirates were also hoping for the same bonanza as their neighbours and granted oil concessions to the Iraq Petroleum Company. With the granting of these concessions there came a need for territory boundaries to be defined and this finally gave rise to the carve up of the seven emirates of today.

After Indian Independence in 1947 the affairs of the Trucial coast were handled by the British Foreign Office which in 1952 set up the Oman Trucial Scouts to act as a defence force in the region. Local police forces were formed several years later along with the Abu Dhabi Defence Force. Also in 1952 the Trucial Council was established so that all seven rulers would meet twice a year to pursue a common policy of development and administration of the region. With the decline of the British Empire and the rise of Arab Nationalism in the early 1950s, self-government for the Trucial Sheikhs didn't seem too far off.

Oil and Self-rule

Oil production began in Abu Dhabi in 1962, with Dubai coming online in 1966. Although Britain had intended to relocate its main military base in the Gulf from Aden to Sharjah, and started work on building military areas there in 1966, in 1968 the British Labour government announced its rather shock decision to withdraw all its forces from the Gulf by the end of 1971.

A way of replacing Britain's military and political clout in the region was needed. With the large oil reserves in the region security from invasion was uppermost in the minds of all of those involved in finding a solution and it was decided that a federation would be the best way to protect the interests of the seven independent sheikhdoms. Despite the traditional rivalry that existed between Abu Dhabi and Dubai these two sheikhdoms were the first to form a political alliance, inviting Ras al-Khaimah, Sharjah, Ajman, Fujairah, Umm al-Quwain, Qatar and Bahrain to join them. The smaller emirates knew that they would need the richer emirates in order to survive as independent states, while the ruler of now oil-rich Abu Dhabi, Sheikh Zayed bin Sultan al-Nahyan stated that his emirate's oil wealth could be of benefit to all Emirates if they joined him. Discussions ensued but Qatar and Bahrain both felt they would be better off as separate independent states and pulled out of the nascent federation.

In July 1971 all of the emirates with the exception of Ras al-Khaimah merged to become the United Arab Emirates. The new country was declared on 6 December 1971 and joined the United Nations and the Arab League in 1972. Sheikh Zayed of Abu Dhabi became President of the Federation, with Sheikh Rashid bin Saeed al-Maktoum of Dubai becoming Vice-President and Prime Minister. A Provisional Constitution was put in place that was originally to be superseded after five years by a permanent one, however this has never happened and the provisional Constitution remains in force. At the time of the British withdrawal from the area Iran occupied the island of Abu Musa and the Greater and Lesser Tunb islands which belong to the Emirates and to this day the Iranian occupation remains a bone of contention in the region, and continues to jeopardise any full integration of Iran into the Gulf Co-operation Council.

Modern Arabia

The 1970s were a boom time for the United Arab Emirates with construction schemes rampant and the building of a swiftly constructed modern state. Sheikh Zayed was re-appointed President of the Federation (and remains in that position to this day). In the 1950s the 'town' of Abu Dhabi had consisted of a fort surrounded by a few dwellings; by the 1980s it had become a well-ordered capital city.

After the breakout of the Iran-Iraq war in 1980 the Gulf States of Oman, Saudi Arabia, Kuwait, UAE, Bahrain and Qatar formed the Gulf Co-operation Council (GCC) in 1981 in order to bring about economic, cultural and political co-operation between these neighbouring oil-rich countries. Although agreement on many of the objectives that the GCC set out to put in place has been slow to arise, an internal free trade market, common external tariffs and a cautious military integration (the Peninsula Shield) has been achieved. The end of the Iran-Iraq war in 1988 lifted the threat against shipping in the Gulf only to be supplanted by the Iraqi invasion of Kuwait in August 1990. However, as a base for the forces of the allied coalition the UAE did pretty well out of the conflict and along with other GCC countries sent troops into the fray.

Despite the disparity of wealth that exists between the Emirates (the majority of oil and gas is produced by Abu Dhabi, Dubai and Sharjah) the Federation has remained strong and remarkably stable in a region that is not renowned for its political stability. From a poor underdeveloped area the UAE has sprinted to catch up with the West developing infrastructures, communication lines, health and social

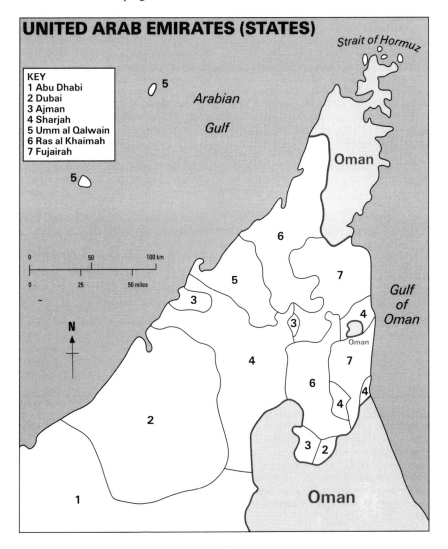

UNITED ARAB EMIRATES (STATES)

Strait of Hormuz

KEY
1 Abu Dhabi
2 Dubai
3 Ajman
4 Sharjah
5 Umm al Qalwain
6 Ras al Khaimah
7 Fujairah

Arabian
Gulf

Oman

0   50   100 km

0   25   50 miles

N

Gulf
of
Oman

services through oil and gas revenues. The side effects of this have been the massive influx of workers; skilled and unskilled into the country. In 1968 the population of the UAE was 180,000 of which 63 per cent were nationals. By 1979 the numbers had increased to 1,015,000 and decreased to 22 per cent. Today the population is estimated at about three million, of which 80 per cent are non-nationals.

Emirati nationals are well educated and skilled and there are approximately 12,000 of them entering a theoretical workforce every year. However, although emiratisation (making it illegal for companies not to employ a certain quota of Emiratis) is being attempted there isn't really a work culture amongst a populace who have been brought up spoilt by a lifestyle subsidised by oil wealth. Occupations such as teaching are looked upon as being lowly paid and of low status because foreigners have always done them. Most Emiratis simply do not need to get their hands dirty when they are given enough by the State to pay others to do whatever they need doing for them.

POLITICS

The independent nature of the rulers and the lack of a common policy throughout the country has led to some duplication of services; of airports, port facilities etc., and wasted revenues. Ill-defined borders have led to internal disputes in the past though in 1974 a border agreement was finally signed between Saudi Arabia and the UAE over the Liwa oases which led to Saudi Arabia recognising the United Arab Emirates and the two countries exchanging ambassadors.

The popular President, Sheikh Zayed is 86 years old and in ill health. He returned home to a rapturous welcome after a kidney transplant operation in America in 2000 and continues to keep a high profile but his eldest son Sheikh Khalifa has since assumed a greater role in government affairs and is likely to succeed his father as President.

As for external threats to stability within the region and to the UAE, there is the continued quarrel with Iran over the sovereignty of the three disputed islands together with the continued isolation of Iraq. Greater freedom on foreigners owning businesses outright in the Gulf is likely to bring more investment into the country and Dubai is fast becoming the business centre of the Middle East and Central Asia – construction there is rampant with offices and leisure centres continually being built.

The Constitution has been in force since its inception in 1971. Although at the time is was declared a provisional constitution it has held good for nearly 30 years.

ECONOMY

The United Arab Emirates are rich – having the highest per capita income in the Arab world, though some are wealthier than others. Abu Dhabi owns most of the country's oil reserves (about 90 per cent of the total) and is the third largest producer of oil in the Gulf after Saudi Arabia and Kuwait. Dubai has built up over the years a reputation of being the commercial centre of the region and today is growing increasingly important as a business hub between the markets of Asia, Africa and Europe. Other emirates produce construction materials, service the oil and gas industries, have tax free zones and seaport facilities which draw in investors from around the world. Diversification has been the watchword in the Emirates for several years now and the tourist industry is being strongly courted by Dubai and increasingly by the sister emirates as well. The Emirates are a powerful economic force in the world.

THE PEOPLE

UAE Nationals

Because of the Emiratis' lack of expertise and experience of building and running a modern state once oil revenues began pouring in, hordes of expats were drafted to help the Emiratis construct their dream. Unfortunately, the upshot of this influx of foreigners is that the Emiratis are now a minority in their own country. However, this hasn't meant that the Emiratis have lost control over their country. Non-nationals are not allowed to own property but must rent from Emirati landlords, and until very recently any business had to have an Emirati partner – silent or not.

Expats

Most of the westerners who work in the Gulf States come from Britain, America and Canada, with a lesser number of continental Europeans. Drawn by the tax-free salaries, very often free housing and a very comfortable lifestyle, these are professionals working in the areas of engineering, marketing, health, education and business. The clichéd image of the expat driving a big new four-wheel drive vehicle (4WD) with his blonde wife in the passenger seat and a couple of kids (at least one being a baby) in the back is alive and well in the Emirates. And you will see this image far more frequently in the UAE than in any of the other Gulf States. For many (something like 80 per cent of the total population of the Emirates – over 2 million people) a job in the Emirates is the pot of gold at the end of the rainbow. A tax-free income, more sun and sea than you can ever need, a practically stress free life living in a nice house on a sunny street with a flash car and a load of money is a dream.

Expats are mostly not entitled to claim nationality and even though in theory this is possible in some cases, it is extremely rare. Because many expats have been living and working in the Gulf for so long, they are now parents of young adults who have been brought up in the Gulf, been to school there and stayed on to work. Yet these young adults are not legally nationals of the country in which they were raised and can get none of the benefits to which their local peer group are entitled. Although these offspring of expats hold a passport from their parents' country of origin, that country is likely to be a foreign land to them. They may have gone there to visit relatives once or twice a year but they will have no great emotional bond with the country and so very often feel rootless, going on to produce another generation of expats.

Guest Workers

The Arabs from non-Gulf states who come to work in the UAE tend to be educated, multilingual and a mix of Muslims and Christians from the poorer countries of Lebanon, Syria, Jordan, Egypt and Palestine/Israel. They will be employed as professionals in education, industry and business - many have their own businesses in the Emirates - but they will be paid less than a westerner for doing the same kind of job. This can cause a certain amount of resentment among the Arabs and the relationship between the rich Gulf Arabs and the poorer neighbours whom they employ is not one of empathy. There are many well-educated Indians working in the UAE who may have been living and working there for generations and have family present and so are able to live a normal life in family units. They are the lucky ones.

The Labourers

At the bottom of the heap are the labourers, employed to clean, sweep and dig. Brought over from the poorer countries of Asia such as Bangladesh, Pakistan and India the cleaners are poorly paid, housed in labour camps and bussed to and from the work place. Some of these labourers are imported by companies for specific contracts while others have arrived illegally and so are paid even less when they can find work. But, like everyone else in the country, they will make more money in the UAE than they could do at home. They may manage to get back to see relatives, wife and family infrequently and send most of their earnings home. They often stay in the UAE until they are old and unemployable then return home to be looked after by their children and grandchildren. Their chances are improved if they can speak Arabic or English in which case they may be able to rise above drudge jobs and work in the service industries. Because these poorer immigrants are a society of men and cannot bring their wives to live with them they are a lonely bunch.

Making Friends

The United Arab Emirates is one of the larger countries of the Gulf and can seem at first a little arid, not only in the landscape but socially as well. The Emiratis tend to keep themselves to themselves, socialising amongst themselves often at home behind the high walls of their well-appointed villas. Among the expat community the different nationalities also seem to socialise separately with like mixing with like; the individual traditions and cultures remaining surprisingly undiluted in what is, or could be, a very cosmopolitan environment. If you are staying in Dubai – the most freethinking and freewheeling of the Emirates – the many bars, restaurants and nightclubs are a good place to find entertainment and to meet people. If you are staying in one of the beachside hotels you are likely to fall into conversation with fellow guests. Joining one of the tours that take visitors out on desert safaris and wadi bashing is also a good way to make connections with people. Sport also brings people together and a good way to get an idea of the lifestyle of some of the expats, although not the Emiratis, is to go on a run with the local Hash House Harriers.

Getting to know Emiratis can be difficult as they seem to be so distanced from the rest of the inhabitants. But many of them have visited Britain, worked in or been to school or university in Britain and if you can get an introduction to an Emirati family your view of the Emirates will be a unique and fulfilling one.

FURTHER READING

The Dubai/Abu Dhabi Explorer, Explorer Publishing, 2000.
From Trucial States to United Arab Emirates, Frauke Heard-Bey, Longmans, 1982.
Off-road in the Emirates, Dariush Zandi, Motivate Publishing, 1993.
Oman and the UAE: Insight Guide, Dorothy Stannard (Ed.), APA Publications, 1999.
Oman and the United Arab Emirates, Lou Callan and Gordon Robison, Lonely Planet Publications, 2000.
Sharjah, The Guide, Vanessa Jackson, Sharjah Commerce and Tourism Development Authority, 2000.
The United Arab Emirates, Peter Vine and Paula Casey, Immel Publishing, 1992.
UAE: A MEED Guide, Jane Matthew, MEED, 1999.

PRACTICAL
INFORMATION

Red Tape

Passports

Except for nationals of the GCC countries (who require only an identity card), all visitors to the United Arab Emirates require a valid passport with at least six months validity left to run. You should also ensure that your passport has enough blank pages left for visas and entry/exit stamps (generally a page is taken up by each). If you have an Israeli stamp in your passport you are very likely to encounter problems moving about the Gulf and may well be refused entry so it is best to apply for a new, clean, passport before travelling.

VISAS

At the time of research visas were required by all visitors except the following: nationals of the UK for a maximum of 60 days, nationals of the GCC countries and transit passengers who hold valid onward or return documentation and do not leave the airport. For routine travel, visas for tourists and travellers (intending to visit family) must be arranged via a sponsor (a hotel or tour operator, or a UAE resident). At the time of writing visa regulations are going through change and the latest information on visas should be sought from the nearest UAE embassy or consulate. The UAE is seeking to attract more tourists to its shores and sponsored visas may soon become a thing of the past.

Visa Extensions

A 60-day visit visa can be renewed for a further 30 days by paying a fee (an extortionate Dh500 – about £100/$136). Contact the *Department of Immigration and Naturalisation* (in Dubai telephone 398 0000). For those nationalities that can get a visa stamped in the passport on arrival, a popular alternative to the visa extension is the visa run. This entails taking a flight to one of the neighbouring countries (Oman, Qatar, Bahrain or Kish Island (Iranian territory) are popular choices) and getting an exit and then an entry stamp which will allow you to stay in the Emirates for a further two months. If you have found work in the Emirates a visa run will be a far cheaper option than returning home while you wait for your residency application to be processed.

Visas to Other Places

It is advisable to get those visas needed for onward travel before you leave home but if you are going to be staying in the Emirates indefinitely the validity on visas got several months earlier may run out. If this is the case a lot of the Embassies and Consulates that you may need to visit in order to obtain visas for other destinations including Oman can be found in Dubai. Across the main highway near the Embassy area are several typing and photocopying offices where the employees will probably know more about what you need to present to the consular staff than you do. A visa to Oman will cost a British citizen Dh200 (£39/$54) if obtained in Dubai.

Onward Travel

Dubai is a good place to pick up cheap tickets for onward travel to the East, Africa and to Europe. Many international flights stop over in Dubai and it is also a charter flight destination. You can travel overland to Oman but will need to fly to Bahrain or Qatar. If you are able to obtain the requisite visas there are ferries across the Gulf to Iran and Saudi Arabia has borders with the Emirates.

Immigration

Immigration procedures for British citizens arriving at either Dubai or Abu Dhabi airport are pretty straightforward and swift. However, the recently refurbished and award winning Dubai Airport is a massive city of a place and getting from the plane to immigration takes quite a while, wandering along walkways and up and down escalators. When leaving from Dubai remember the large size of the airport and leave enough time for getting through departure procedures.

CUSTOMS

The duty free allowance is 2,000 cigarettes, 400 cigars, 2kg of tobacco, two litres of spirits and two litres of wine (alcohol allowance for non-Muslims only) and a 'reasonable amount' of perfume. If you have missed out on buying your duty free before leaving the UK don't fret as there is probably more choice, and cheaper prices at the duty free shops on arrival in the Emirates, especially at Dubai Airport.

As in other Muslim countries if you are carrying books, video cassettes, DVDs or magazines they may be confiscated and checked by the Ministry of Information if it is suspected that they contain material of a salacious or politically seditious nature. If you are bringing prescribed medicines make sure that you have a doctor's prescription for them so that you can order more if you run out and also to show any suspicious customs official. You will need an import licence for guns and ammunition.

EMBASSIES OF THE UAE ABROAD

Australia: 36 Culgoa Circuit, O'Malley, ACT 2606 (tel 2-6286 8802; fax 6286 8804).

Britain: 30 Princes Gate, London SW1 (tel 020-7581 1282; fax 020-7581 9616).

Canada: World Exchange Plaza, 45 O'Connor Street, Suite 1800, Ottawa, Ontario, H1P 1A4 (tel 613 565 7272; fax 613 565 8007).

South Africa: 980 Park Street, Arcadia, Pretoria 0083 (tel 12-342 7736; fax 12-342 7738).

USA: 1255 22nd Street, Suite 700, NW, Washington, DC 20037, USA (tel 202-955 7999; fax 202-337 7029).

The Arab Emirate Dirham (Dh) replaced the Gulf Rupee in 1971 and has been tied to the US Dollar since 1980. The dirham has remained pretty stable ever since. The official rate is £1=Dh5.27 and $1=Dh3.67. There is no restriction on the amount of money you import or export from the country.

Notes and Coins

The dirham is divided into 100 fils (if you ever hear an Arab calling for 'floos' he will be wanting money; floos being the plural of fils). Notes come in denominations of Dh5, 10, 20, 50, 100, 200, 500 and 1000. Coins come in Dh1, 50 fils, 25 fils, 5 fils and 10 fils though you are less likely to receive the lower denominations. You should also be aware that new and smaller versions of all the coins were minted a few years ago and now both versions are legal tender, which can cause a little confusion to begin with. Keep hold of coins and lower denomination notes for taxi and bus rides and for buying cold drinks and snacks.

Exchange

Changing money is easy and straightforward. The network of banks in the Emirates is one of the most efficient you will find in the Middle East and the services the banks offer are very similar to those back home. There are also moneychanger kiosks in the larger towns and hotels will always be able to change whatever you have; cash or travellers' cheques – though the exchange rates they give will be low. You are best avoiding changing money at the airports as the rate will be slightly worse than that offered elsewhere. If you need dirhams on arrival there are ATMs in the airports.

Banks. Banks are open Saturday to Wednesday from 8am-1pm with some of them opening again from 4.30-6.30pm. They also open on Thursdays from 8am-12noon.

Credit and Charge Cards

Credit and charge cards are accepted almost everywhere in the main cities of the UAE and in most of the souks as well. It is a good idea to check with your card issuer before you leave home whether your card is globally accepted. As a rule if you are carrying a MasterCard, Visa, Access, Cirrus, Plus, Diners Club or American Express card you are going to have no problem using the card to shop with and to draw cash with.

ATMs

As elsewhere in the Arabian Gulf automatic teller machines (ATMs) are conveniently located in many areas including airports, shopping malls, supermarkets and in some of the top-end hotels. There are several international banks in Dubai and Abu Dhabi which have cash points and a number of the local UAE banks such as *Emirates Bank International* and *National Bank of Dubai* are also linked into the global access network. To find out where the nearest *HSBC* ATM is when in the Emirates you can call 800-4440 toll free.

COSTS

Like the other Gulf States, the United Arab Emirates are not cheap places to visit but they are not prohibitively expensive either. An average hotel room in Dubai will cost slightly more than a good bed and breakfast does in Britain but a decent meal can often be had for less than in Europe or the USA. However, if you like a drink alcohol is dear – a pint can cost up to £4/$6 and more in some of the bars. Hotels are scarcer outside Dubai and therefore generally more expensive although Fujairah, Sharjah and Dubai all have youth hostels where beds are cheap. Travelling by local shared transport is also cheap and even if you hire a car, fuel won't break the bank.

Dubai has made a name for itself as the duty free shopping centre of the world and although prices of luxury and designer goods are perhaps 10 per cent lower than in Europe the range of goods is far more limited than what you would find back home. Also, you will find that the latest stock from manufacturers often hasn't reached Dubai yet.

Taxes. Different emirates add different percentages on to hotel and restaurant bills but you can expect another 15-20 per cent to be added on to the net total on any bill.

TELEPHONES

The communication system in the United Arab Emirates is run by the monopoly *Emirates Telecommunications Corporation* or *Etisalat* which has offices in all of the Emirates, recognizable by the huge golf ball atop their mini skyscraper buildings.

Mobiles

Mobile phones are big business and very popular in the UAE. Ask your phone operating company before you go if you will be able to receive a signal in the Gulf. If you have a mobile phone that cannot receive while abroad you can buy a temporary SIM card from Etisalat to put in your phone and you can also hire phones from the company. Ask about Etisalat's SpeakEasy Service and take your passport. There are a lot of shops that deal in mobile phones (or GSM phones as they are known locally) and these will be able to sort out any problems you may have getting a roaming service.

Coin Operated Phones

There are a few public telephone booths that take coins remaining in the streets but increasingly these are being replaced by telephones that will only take phone cards. These cards can be bought from supermarkets and most of the small kiosks scattered about the town and countryside that sell snacks and cigarettes; the lowest denomination of card that you can buy being Dh30.

Numbers

Due to the huge demand on telephones in the UAE numbers are often being changed, usually by adding a prefix to the existing number. If you call one of the old numbers a recorded message will remind you of the new prefix. Mobile phone numbers in the UAE are all prefixed with 050 followed by a seven-digit number. If you are dialling a mobile number from outside the UAE dial +971 50...then the area code, then the number. Directory enquiries can be contacted on 180, the operator by dialling 100. Dial a service is big business in the UAE and you will find that most restaurants, video stores etc., operate a home delivery service. To dial direct to the UK from the UAE dial 00 44 followed by the area code leaving out the initial 0 of that code. To dial direct to the USA from the Emirates dial 00 1 followed by the area code.

Fax

There are Etisalat offices throughout the Emirates that are open 24 hours a day where faxes and telegrams can be sent and received. Be prepared to give a local address and telephone number to the operator of the fax machine in these offices. Some of the small stationery shops that have photocopying and typing services can also send faxes and may charge less than the Etisalat offices.

Information

The international country code for the United Arab Emirates is +971. There are local dialling codes of which the most important to be aware of are: Abu Dhabi (02), Ajman, Sharjah and Umm al-Quwain (06), Ras al-Khaimah (07), Fujairah (09), Dubai (04).

Charges

All calls made within the same emirate on a private landline telephone are free of charge. Off-peak rates can be had from 9pm-7am weekdays and all day on Friday and public holidays. Calls made from hotels are, as ever, at least twice the price of a call made locally from a public telephone.

POST

The postal services throughout the UAE are provided by the *General Postal Authority*. Post offices are located throughout the Emirates and stamps can be obtained from post offices, some hotels and supermarkets and aerogrammes are also available. There is no home delivery system in the Emirates – everyone rents post office boxes. This can make trying to find out where a business is actually located a pain as everyone is listed in the telephone directories under their post office box number, even embassies and hospitals. PO Boxes can be rented on a yearly basis for around Dh150 (£29/$40). You should post outgoing mail in post boxes attached to post offices rather than in the red letter boxes dotted around the towns to ensure a swifter passage to its destination. Allow 2-3 days delivery time within the UAE, 7-10 days to the USA, Australia or Europe, and a bit less for Asia.

Parcels

Parcels coming into or leaving the country are likely to be searched. It is advisable to send packages by registered delivery through the post office or by one of the international courier firms such as *DHL*, *Fedex*, *TNT*, or the local express mail service *Mumtaz Express*. Although sending post by this method is expensive it will ensure prompt delivery.

E-mail and the Internet

Arabs love to communicate and have taken the Internet to their collective bosom. Chat rooms are an addiction for many and some very posh Internet cafés are springing up all around the Emirates. Etisalat is the sole Internet Service Provider in the Emirates and because of the conservative nature of the region and the telecommunication company's concern for the moral well-being of the citizens of the UAE some Internet sites are censored. If you find that the perfectly innocent website address that you have tapped into a computer keyboard is censored then you can report it to help@emirates.net.ae.

THE MEDIA

Television

All the Emirates have television broadcasts in Arabic. *Dubai Channel 33* and *Abu Dhabi Channel 2* also broadcast programmes in English. You may also be able to pick up Oman TV and broadcasts from Qatar depending on the weather conditions and reception. Most hotels and homes have satellite links to channels from Asia, Europe and the rest of the Middle East with the usual mix of films, pop, news and sports programmes.

Video

Almost all videos bought or rented in the UAE will have been through the censors' offices in Saudi Arabia. The same applies to DVDs. The operating system for videos in the UAE is the PAL system as used in most of Europe and Australia. There used to be a roaring trade in pirate videos and pirate pretty much anything else but this practice has been stamped out of late.

Radio Frequencies

There are several radio stations transmitting in English in the Emirates, the majority of which are located in Dubai, and pumping out pop tunes, news and the occasional talk show. *Dubai FM* (92Mhz), Ajman's *Channel 4FM* (104.8Mhz), *Emirates FM1* (99.3Mhz), *Emirates FM2* (98.7Mhz) are some of the more popular stations. There are also radio stations in other Emirates catering to the Asian community such as Ras al-Khaimah's *Radio Asia* (1152khz). Look in the local newspapers for frequencies of other radio stations. The *BBC World Service* can also be picked up, details of frequencies and programmes can be found on the BBC website www.bbc.co.uk/worldservice.

Newspapers and Magazines

The English-language newspapers published in the UAE are *Gulf Today* (published in Sharjah), *Gulf News* and the *Khaleej Times* (published in Dubai). They all cost Dh2; Dh3 on Friday (when they are accompanied by supplements). All three dailies carry pretty much the same stories; a mix of national and international with large sections devoted to news in the Philippines and the Indian Subcontinent. They are all broadsheets and widely available. There are several magazines produced locally such as *Aquarius, Connector, What's On* and *Living in the Gulf* that cover local events and issues and have large and useful listings sections. All are available from supermarkets along with most of the more popular lifestyle magazines and newspapers from abroad (which will cost a lot more than they do at home). You will often see hawkers with a selection of newspapers and magazines beside traffic lights on the streets of Dubai and Abu Dhabi.

Maps

Geoprojects publish a countrywide map of the Emirates but it is expensive and somewhat out of date (the building of roads continues, like all else in the emirates, at a frantic pace). The bookshops in Dubai have a range of locally produced maps, the most comprehensive of which is called *Road Maps United Arab Emirates* and covers the entire country with city maps of the larger emirates. It cost Dh15 and is worth getting. The most detailed map of Dubai is the *Dubai Tourist Map* published by Dubai Municipality which costs Dh35 (£6.85/$9.53).

Place Names

People in the Emirates navigate more by landmarks and an insider knowledge of places than by the official names and numbers of streets and buildings. You may also find that though a street is called x on your local city map it is called z by the people that live there. You will also find that almost everyone on the street will be disinclined to give a frank 'I don't know' answer when asked the direction to somewhere. This polite but annoying habit will mean that you will often be sent off on a wild goose chase as each successive person that you approach for information points you in the first direction that comes into their head. It is therefore best to telephone ahead and get accurate directions to your desired destination before stepping onto an unknown street.

ARRIVAL AND DEPARTURE

Most people visiting the Emirates will fly into either Abu Dhabi Airport or, more likely, Dubai Airport. If you are coming overland from Oman you will hit the border of Dubai near Hatta or, if you are travelling up on the eastern Batinah coast, at Khor Kalba which is part of Sharjah Emirate. Between the individual emirates there are no passport controls or checkpoints to go through and access is unrestricted.

Airports

The two main airports for arrivals to and departures from the United Arab Emirates are Abu Dhabi and Dubai, though increasingly there are international arrivals at Sharjah airport. Abu Dhabi and Dubai International Airports, located as they are at the crossroads for flights between Europe, Asia and Africa are very modern, very plush, with very good duty free shops and restaurants. Dubai airport is the home to the UAE's national carrier *Emirates Airline*.

Reservations

It is very advisable to reconfirm any flight out of the Gulf as overbooking is common practice. If you are flying with *Gulf Air* it is absolutely essential that you reconfirm 72 hours before your flight is scheduled to leave otherwise your place will be given to someone else.

CITY TRANSPORT

Apart from the very useful municipal bus services in Dubai you will be moving around the cities of the Emirates either on foot (which can be a bit of a slog as the Emirates are of their time and are built with the convenience of the internal combustion engine firmly in mind) or by taxi. Walking about is feasible during the winter months but it is unlikely that you'll want to stroll about in the heat of the summer. There are service taxis plying the routes between the individual Emirates and if your starting point is Dubai there are inter-emirate buses that run to destinations throughout the country. In Dubai you can cross the Creek in *abras* – small water taxis.

Bus

Only Abu Dhabi, Dubai and al-Ain have local bus services and because of the small size of the main cities of the other Emirates a public transport system is not felt to be necessary. The most useful buses are operated by Dubai Municipality. Although Abu Dhabi and al-Ain also have municipal bus services these run along routes carting workers to and from labour camps and are unlikely to be of benefit to the visitor. *Dubai Transport Corporation* also runs an efficient and cheap minibus service to many places in the Emirates.

Taxi

Taxis are not difficult to find in the UAE. Depending on the emirate some taxis are metered and others are not. Taxis are metered in Dubai and Abu Dhabi. You will need to get a feel for what is an appropriate fee when taking a ride in a taxi or stick to radio cabs which are nearly always metered. It is illegal for a taxi that is registered in one emirate to pick up a fare from another for the trip back home though they are allowed to make a drop taking a passenger from their own emirate to another. As a general rule the flag fall in metered taxis is Dh3 (£0.58/$0.81) which increases by one dirham per kilometre. Some drivers will have an imperfect knowledge of the area where you want to go and street names are not generally as well known as conspicuous landmarks. It's a good idea to keep hold of the telephone number of the place you are going to in order to call for directions if you and the taxi driver get lost. Women should always sit in the back seat of taxis.

Shared Transport

Shared service taxis are the cheapest and often the only way to get around the Emirates if you do not have your own vehicle. Unfortunately inter-emirate bus services are extremely limited. Usually big Peugeot station wagons, the taxis wait at ranks, the drivers calling out their destination, and leave when they are full. It is always a good idea to check the fare before you get in the car. Depending on where you are and where you want to go you might be in for a ten-minute wait or an age. If your stated destination isn't a popular one the driver is likely to tell you that you will have to hire a taxi on your own (which will cost a lot more than a shared one). A trip in a shared taxi is usually a pretty speedy one as the drivers ply the same route several times a day and know the roads well. Also, the more trips they make the more money they make so they tend to drive fast. Women travelling in a shared taxi are usually invited to sit in the front passenger seat away from the cramped conditions in the back.

Cycling
With the talent of most of the drivers on the roads of the UAE you would be foolish to cycle anywhere near a main road even if you could find a place to hire a bicycle - which you will not. However, there are a number of Asians who potter about on bikes, mostly going down the streets on the wrong side of the road, very slowly and without lights should it be after nightfall, providing yet another potential road hazard.

Hitchhiking
Hitching isn't as common in the Emirates as it is in other parts of the Arabian Gulf and with the crazy antics of many of the motorists probably not the safest way to travel. Having said that, hitchhiking is one of the best ways to see a country and to get to meet locals. You will always meet interesting characters and it may be the best way to 'get under the skin' of the country. The Middle Eastern method of hitchhiking is to stick an arm out and point a forefinger down towards the ground. Sticking a thumb out at passing motorists causes offence. Remember to take lots of water.

JOINING A TOUR
There are a number of tour companies, the majority being based in Dubai, offering all sorts of tours including desert safaris, city tours, dhow cruises etc. and the local listings magazines and newspapers have full lists of names and telephone numbers. There are also companies in at home who can organise a full tour for you, and details of some of these can be found in the opening chapter.
Arabian Adventures: 04-303 4888.
Desert Rangers: 04-346 0808.
Lama Desert Safari Tours: 04-273 1007.
Orient Tours: 06-554 9333.
Sahara Tours: 06-552 1153.

BOAT HOPPING AND OTHER OPTIONS
At the time of research the only option of travelling about the region by boat was taking a hydrofoil between Dubai or Sharjah to the port of Bander Abbas in Iran across the Strait of Hormuz. For more information contact the *Oasis Freight Company* in Sharjah (tel 06-559 6325). There are also several yacht clubs in Dubai and Abu Dhabi which may see the occasion globetrotting vessel tied to the pontoons, however, the Gulf is a long way from the usual cruising areas. There are many commercial ships and dhows plying the waters between the UAE and all points east and it may be possible to hitch a ride on one of these. The dhow wharfs in Dubai and Sharjah are the busiest with cargo being loaded daily for destinations such as Pakistan, India and Iran. There are no inter-emirate flights at present but check with Gulf Air or Emirates offices for the latest information on this. There are also several small airfields throughout the Emirates which provide flying lessons and short excursions. There are no railways in the UAE.

DRIVING

Most visitors to the Emirates and those people who live and work out there have tales to tell about the often reckless, arrogant and bullying tactics of other road users in the country. Because of the lack of public transport you will almost definitely need to hire a car while in the country and if you keep your wits about you at all times you will come home safely. Street signs can be confusing at times and because of traffic islands you may spend a fair amount of time doing u-turns in order to get to your destination but once you have got the hang of driving on the right hand side of the road driving in the Gulf can be fun.

Travel times between the Emirates:

Abu Dhabi – Dubai:	1½ hours.
Dubai – Fujairah:	2 hours.
Dubai – Sharjah/Ajman:	1 hour.
Dubai – Ras al-Khaimah:	2½ hours.

Motorcycling

Taking to the roads on a motorbike in the Emirates is an occupation for the strong of heart. There are few motorcycles on the roads although there are several motorcycle clubs - a number of expats run classic motorbikes and go for the occasional outing. Because of the great desert terrain all around the country a lot of expats have trail bikes and bomb about the desert whenever they get the chance. Every November there is a Desert Challenge race where motorbikes, cars and trucks compete in an endurance race over four stages on courses through the desert. *Wolf Motorbikes* (tel 04-345 5770; www.saharabiketours.com) in Dubai rent out Honda XR400R trial bikes as well as quad bikes for those wanting to get into a bit of dirt biking.

CAR HIRE

Hiring a car is by far the easiest option for getting around the Emirates and there are international as well as local firms with offices in all the main cities, hotels and airports. You will need to be 21 years old or over to hire a car and for certain vehicle insurance groups over 25 years old. Even if you intend to pay the hire charge in cash you will need to supply a credit card for deposit purposes and have a full driving licence or an international driving licence. Prices vary depending on the season and company and it is worth shopping around to get the best deal. A typical hire charge for a small saloon car will be around Dh90 (£18/$25) per 24-hour period including insurance, and around Dh600 (£117/$163) for a 4WD vehicle. If you are intending to drive between the UAE and Oman you will need to make sure that you are adequately covered by the car hire firm's insurance policy. Some firms will deliver and collect the vehicle and if you hire from one of the larger firms it is often possible to return vehicles to their office in a different emirate.

The Law

Driving is on the **right**. The wearing of seat belts in the front seat of a car is compulsory and children under ten years old are not allowed to sit in the front seat of a moving vehicle. Penalties for drinking and driving are severe. If tested for alcohol you must show no alcohol present in the blood at all. It is also illegal throughout the Emirates to drive while speaking into a hand held mobile phone. If you are fined for a traffic offence payment must be made in cash. You should always carry driving documentation with you because there are occasional police checks and if you can't produce the car registration documents and your driving licence on the spot fines can be imposed.

Speed Limits

Speed limits vary depending on the Emirate. For example Abu Dhabi's speed restrictions are severer than in neighbouring Dubai where vehicles can travel slightly faster. Speed limits within cities and towns are generally between 60-80km/h and 100-120km/h on other roads. Speeding is a big problem in the UAE and now many stretches of road are monitored by radar.

Penalties. On the spot penalties for breaking the speed limits are common. Speeding fines are on average Dh200 (about £40) but can vary depending on how serious the transgression.

Road Systems

Anyone who can afford to drives in the Emirates and it becomes something of a necessity during the baking summer months. The majority of roads are at least two lane and often three or four lane highways and signposting, though still not great, has improved considerably in recent years. Because of the density of traffic, getting through the centre of the larger cities of Sharjah, Abu Dhabi and especially Dubai can be a slow and frustrating business. There are daily traffic jams on the highway between Dubai and neighbouring Sharjah from where, because of cheaper rents, people commute. If at all possible try to avoid travelling between these two cities between 6.30-10am and from 7-9pm when the traffic is at its worst.

Parking

Apart from the busiest downtown areas you will be able to park almost anywhere free of charge. This is a boon when the temperature is soaring and you don't want to walk too far away from an air-conditioned atmosphere. Increasingly, parking meters are being installed in more central city areas. Meters take coins and restrictions apply during business hours from Saturday to Thursday.

Fuel

Fuel is far cheaper in the Emirates than in Europe and petrol stations are numerous. A gallon of Regular petrol will set you back about Dh3.65 (£0.70/$0.99); so that a full tank of petrol for a small saloon car will cost the beautifully cheap price of Dh40 (£8/$11). Petrol stations often have small shops selling confectionery and drinks. You will not need to get out of your car at a service station because they all have petrol pump attendants who will fill up the car with petrol, take the payment and clean the windscreen while you wait.

Breakdowns and Accidents

If you are involved in an accident it is very important that you do not move your car until the police have arrived to make out an accident report. You will need this report in order to have any chance of making an insurance claim. If the vehicle is a hire car and you do not have a police report you will be liable to pay for all damages. Even if the damaged car is blocking a road or a roundabout you must not move it until the police have arrived. The only exception to this rule is in Dubai where you are allowed to move the car if it is blocking a thoroughfare. There are plenty of garages and repair shops throughout the UAE.

HAZARDS

Desert and Mountain Driving

Desert driving is great fun in the right vehicle. It can also be dangerous and without the right preparations a trip into the desert for a picnic can turn into nightmare. Over preparing is never a bad idea. Treat the desert with as much respect as you would the sea and unless very impractical you should try to travel in convoys of at least two 4WD vehicles (so that is one gets stuck in the sand the other can tow it out). See the *Desert Driving* section in *Oman* for desert driving techniques.

Highway Hazards

Apart from other drivers and your own common sense and driving ability, beware of jay walking pedestrians and men on bicycles pedalling down the wrong side of the road. Camels wandering along the roads are also a potentially deadly hazard.

You will see and drive over a number of speed bumps in the Emirates. These are much higher off the ground than the British 'sleeping policemen' and although warning signs are common sometimes the humps are difficult to see due to layers of sand and if hit at too high a speed they can damage the car bodywork and perhaps your head. Swirling sand looking like smoke drifting across the highway (known locally as *jinns*) is an interesting phenomenon but is not dangerous. You will also see mirages on the roads which can be disconcerting but again are not dangerous.

A point of interest: the lower the number on a vehicle's licence plate the higher up in the pecking order of an Emirate the owner. For example, anyone driving a car with a licence plate number in the low teens is a very important person indeed and if they happen to be driving extremely fast and flashing their lights at you to get out of their way, you would do well to let them past.

Apart from the youth hostels in Dubai, Fujairah and Sharjah, accommodation will be one of your biggest expenses while staying in the Emirates and is not particularly a bargain. Single women may have problems getting a bed in the hostels or in hotels where the clientele at the time is mainly men. Booking a hotel room in advance is also a good idea, especially in those emirates that have less accommodation available. Prices in all hotels are negotiable and there are often special deals giving large discounts running at various times of the year. On the whole expect to pay a minimum of Dh100 (£20/$27) for a single room and Dh130 (£25/$35) for a double in the cheaper hotels, and on average about Dh300/350 (£59/$82).

Youth Hostels

The three youth hostels in Dubai, Fujairah and Sharjah are part of the *International Youth Hostels Federation* and you must have a youth hostel card (available at the hostels) to stay in them. The youth hostels are the cheapest option for accommodation that you will find in the Emirates other than camping or staying with friends, or friends of friends who live out there.

Camping

There are no official campsites in the Emirates but outside the main cities the country is wide open and it is possible to camp on beaches and in the mountains or the desert. The best time to camp is in the winter when a tent won't become too much of an oven. Be aware if camping on the coast or in the desert that temperatures can drop to freezing during the night.

Hotels

The majority of hotels cater for the middle to top-end of the tourist market, and are more used to visitors on business and wealthy free-spending GCC nationals than backpackers. However, package tourism is booming in the region and especially in Dubai. Almost all hotel rooms come with a fridge, air-conditioning and a television as standard but outside the four and five star range of hotels you generally get what you pay for.

Booking Accommodation

It is always a good idea when visiting a place for the first time to book the first night's accommodation before arriving. This saves the hassle of having to find somewhere while lugging baggage around. Part of Dubai's *Department of Tourism and Commerce Marketing* website (www.dubaitourism.co.ae/dtcm/tour) is devoted to hotels in the emirate with the ability to book online.

Other Staying Options

An alternative to hotel accommodation is renting a furnished apartment. These are often slightly cheaper than hotels and are especially good if on a holiday with family. Apartments can be rented by the day, week or month, and give you the option of self-catering but are restricted mainly to Dubai, Abu Dhabi and Sharjah. Letting agents can be found in the business telephone directories.

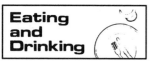

Eating and Drinking

Due to the mix of nationalities living in the Emirates and their differing cuisines the choice of places to eat is really quite incredible. From the top restaurants to hotel bistros to fast food joints to cubby-hole sized street side Asian eateries, the variety of food and prices is considerable.

RESTAURANTS

As a rule, pertinent the world over, the plusher the restaurant the more it'll cost to eat in it. Additionally, restaurants in the Emirates usually have sections reserved for families which are separated from the rest of the dining area, maybe in a separate room or in some other way closed off. They are designed to allow women more privacy, and men are not allowed to eat there.

Opening Hours. Most of the restaurants open from around 11am until 3pm for lunch and again at around 6pm until late. However, because of the nature of the working day restaurants often don't get busy until later in the evening around 9pm.

Service. Dining out is both big business and very popular and the service encountered everywhere is generally excellent with attentive staff drawn from all over the world.

Restaurant Behaviour

Most of the places where you will be dining will no doubt be modern establishments and even if you eat in the smaller workers' cafés you will be provided with cutlery. Should you however have to eat with your hands, remember that you must eat with the right hand only. If by chance you are eating in the vicinity of a veiled Emirati women who continues wearing her veil while eating – delicately placing food into her mouth behind it – do not stare.

Payment

Apart from street stalls and the smaller restaurants, most restaurants will add a 10 per cent municipality tax and a 15 per cent service charge onto your bill. Sometimes it can be unclear whether these additional taxes had been added to your bill and even if it has, it is unlikely that it will be passed on to your waiter or waitress. Tip appropriately.

Fast Food

Most of the franchises imported from America are big business in the Emirates and very popular. McDonald's, a Jewish company, was not allowed into the country until 1995 but now has franchises in all of the emirates. There will often be at least one of the big fast food companies catering to shoppers in a mall.

Street Stalls and Cheap Eats

Street-side stalls are perfectly hygienic and serve some of the most authentic Middle Eastern food such as *shawarma* and *falafel* sandwiches, though you will find that the majority sell Asian, especially Indian and Pakistani dishes. You will also see roasteries selling whole chickens on the spit which, if there are a few of you, make a good ready made meal to take away. The Indian coffee shops that you will see around the country sell coffee, tea and fruit juices, and varieties of sandwich. The supermarkets are well stocked with western food if you are feeling homesick for a certain sweet or savoury experience. They also have very good patisseries with ready cooked pizzas, pies and pastries to take away.

Mealtimes

Because of the early start to the working day in the Gulf breakfast is eaten between 6.30-7.30am with lunch and a siesta between 1-4pm. Depending on the working hours that people keep, dinner may not be eaten until around 10-11pm. Traditionally short snacks, akin to elevenses and afternoon tea, are taken at mid-morning and mid-afternoon. These meals, known as *fualah*, consist of fruit, nuts or sweets and coffee.

Vegetarians

Because of the number of Indians working in the country, many of whom are vegetarian themselves, it is not difficult to find suitably meat-free food in the Emirates. If in doubt as to what is on offer, ask.

Pork

Pork, though forbidden to Muslims, is available in the Emirates. You can buy bacon and sausages etc., in supermarkets such as *Spinneys* where it has to be kept in a separate area to the rest of the food, but it is quite expensive. In restaurants pork will also be prepared and stored in a separate area away from the rest of the ingredients.

Hygiene

Even the smallest shawarma stall has to comply with the strict standards of hygiene imposed by the authorities in the UAE. Eating places are regularly checked and are closed down if found not to be up to scratch.

Foreign Cuisine

Because of the number of expats in the country the variety of foods available is huge - especially in the big cities. Elsewhere you will be dining out in Indo/Asian restaurants. Persian cuisine, due to the long relationship between the Emirates and Iran, is also popular.

REGIONAL SPECIALITIES

Traditional Gulf cuisine is hard to come by and if you do experience it is likely to be served in someone's house rather than in a restaurant. Because of the lack of natural resources and the nomadic way of life that was followed by the majority of Emiratis before the coming of the oil bonanza, choice of food was limited to a staple diet of fish, rice, mutton, goat or camel meat, milk and dates. What regional cuisine exists today is often a version of the cooking that was brought to the area by traders of the surrounding countries.

The traditional dishes you are most likely to come across are *Bilaleet*, cold sweetened vermicelli noodles, served with an omelette; *Harees*, a boiled paste of mutton and wheat slow cooked; and kebabs of mutton or chicken served with rice and flavoured with a variety of spices such as saffron, turmeric, cardamom, coriander, cumin and ginger.

Lebanese Food

Because of the lack of traditional Gulf cuisine restaurants that specialise in Middle Eastern food will almost always be offering the famed dishes from Lebanon. When eating Lebanese, start with the delicious *mezze*, which are small amounts of appetisers such as *humous*, *tabouleh*, *kibbe* and flat bread.

DRINKING

Apart from the dry emirate of Sharjah, you shouldn't have too much trouble finding a drink while visiting the UAE and though it isn't cheap there are a surprising number of bars and pubs for a Muslim country.

Beer, Wine and Spirits

A pint will cost you at least Dh15 (£2.90/$4) and often more. Although all alcohol is imported (thus the expense) you will be able to find familiar draught and bottled beers as most bars. As with the choice of beers, so with wines. A bottle of wine will be a lot more expensive compared to the cost in Europe or the USA, especially in restaurants where the mark-up on a glass of claret can be downright criminal. You will also be able to find pretty much any spirit you wish to imbibe in the Emirates, though you may be hard pressed to find Absinthe just yet.

The Law

Alcohol is only available in licensed bars and restaurants that are attached to hotels but you will also find alcohol served in some privately and government-owned clubs. Outside of the bars, you can't buy alcohol wholesale without a liquor licence and to get one of those you need to be a resident (and a non-Muslim). If you do have a liquor licence you are only allowed to buy so much a month, depending on how much you earn, and no more. So stock up with booze at the duty free and exercise some self-control should an expat invite you home for a drink.

There are allegedly places up in the northern emirates where you can get hold of alcohol without the need for a licence but these are generally found through word of mouth and are technically illegal. Alcohol is forbidden in Sharjah and transporting alcohol between emirates is an offence.

Bars

Bars vary from the seedy drinking hole cum brothel (no frills, though it might run to canned music) to designer dens full of bright young things drinking away the hours before making the next deal. As you would expect, Dubai has the biggest selection of places to drink, followed by Abu Dhabi. Elsewhere you will be limited to the number of hotels that there are in the main cities.

New bars are opening up all the time and the most popular at any one time seem to be those that have just opened. Everyone runs to check out a new face on the map, gets used to it and then wants to see a new one. A number of the less sophisticated bars employ Philippino tribute bands to add character.

Happy Hours and Free Drinks

Many bars and pubs have happy hours with varying degrees of discount offered to the early drinker. Many also run special ladies nights, where members of the fairer sex get free or heavily discounted drink just by stepping through the door. This cynical marketing ploy employed to fill out a drinking establishment with a laughing drunken flirting clientele is pretty successful though it always attracts more single men looking for women than women looking for men.

Soft Drinks

Aside from the usual fizzy soft drinks, cartons of fruit juice (much sweeter than in Britain) and flavoured milk, there are also plenty of juice stalls that for about Dh5 (£0.98/$1.36) will produce for you a refreshing and incredibly healthy fresh orange or mango juice or fruit cocktail, setting you up for the day. Canned soft drinks, such as *Mountain Dew* cost about a dirham. There are a number of drink machines and water coolers around the place, which can be lifesavers during the summer months.

Coffee and Tea

The traditional Arab cafés (*qahwas*) that you find in other parts of the Middle East where men sit about sipping Turkish coffee or black tea, playing a game of cards or backgammon and sucking on shishas are not really a part of the UAE experience. Most cafés are the Indian coffee shops where you will be served a small glass of instant coffee (predictably Nescafé) or ready milked and sugared Lipton's teabag tea. In the smaller emirates there are cafés run by Arabs where you can enjoy the powerful pick me up that is Turkish coffee but elsewhere it'll be an Indian coffee shop or a western coffee bar serving frapuccinos and croissants.

SHISHA

The smoking of water pipes (known in various guises as *shisha*, *nargileh* or *hookahs*) with flavoured tobacco is a traditional part of the culture of the Emirates though it has now been banned in Sharjah. The smoke is cooled on its journey from the stem through the water and along a length of pipe and is gives a mildly light-headed sensation due to the intake of so much cool smoke at once. Flavours include honey, apple and strawberry.

Museums and Galleries

Every emirate has it's own national museum which gives the visitor an idea of how the emirate evolved, and what the ruler sees as the most important aspects of his emirate. Exploring such museums will give you an insight into how the country sees itself – a glimpse of its character. There are a number of art galleries in Dubai and Abu Dhabi, and especially in Sharjah, the culture capital of the Emirates.

Architecture. There is little of the traditional architecture left in the Emirates. The best places to see what the settlements of the region would once have looked like are the restored heritage area in Sharjah and the *Bastakiya* area beside the Creek in Dubai.

Desert

Like Ozymandias' city in the poem by Shelley, the majority of the towns in the Emirates are built on sand. They border one of the largest expanses of sand desert in the world – the **Empty Quarter** (the famed Rub' al-Khali) and this you must see. If you only get to see one thing other than the inside of a shopping mall, your hotel and the seashore during your stay in the Emirates make it **Liwa Oases** in Abu Dhabi Emirate. The area is absolutely stunning and the size of the dunes astounding. However, treks out into the desert shouldn't be undertaken lightly and go well prepared and in company.

Desert safaris and, though to a lesser extent than in Oman, wadi bashing are offered by all tour companies in the region. After going all the way to a place surrounded by sand it would be a shame to miss out on the opportunity to experience, in tourist brochure parlance, 'the majesty of the desert'.

Beaches

There are approximately 1,320 kilometres of coastline in the Emirates all of it sandy beach, though the colour of the sand differs depending where you are; from the yellows of Dubai to the deep orangey red of the beaches in the northern emirate of Ras al-Khaimah. Wide stretches of sand lead down to the sea with little natural vegetation or cover from the sun, which is why many beachfronts have put up sunshades. There are plenty of public beaches and a number of private hotel beachfronts and beach clubs which offer seclusion and good facilities. Single women out on a beach are likely to get stared at. If this is uncomfortable it is better to head to the beach clubs where there is a degree of privacy and nonchalance about semi-nakedness among the clientele.

Mountains

The Hajar mountain range runs through the northeast of the country, especially in the northern emirate of Ras al-Khaimah. Across on the eastern seaboard of the country there are spectacular rock formations, wadis and gorges to explore.

Oases

Oases occur due to the presence of water just below the surface of the ground which can be tapped to produce fertile groves, even in the middle of arid desert. The largest oases in the country are at **Hatta**, **Liwa** and **al-Ain**. The emirate of Ras al-Khaimah is extremely fertile and is the centre of most of the agricultural industry in the UAE.

National Parks

There are several conservation areas in the UAE such as the mangrove forests at **Khor Kalba** on the east coast which are the oldest on the Arabian Peninsula and home to many rare species of bird. Other conservation areas include the **Desert Park** in Sharjah and **Sir Bani Yas Island** off Abu Dhabi as well as marine parks off the east coast where fishing has been prohibited and artificial reefs created to attract marine wildlife. The rulers of the Emirates are very conservation minded and are worried about the increasing threat to the indigenous flora and fauna that modernisation is causing. As this book was going to print an ecological disaster was occurring after the sinking of an oil tanker off the coast of Dubai.

Useful Organisations

Emirates Bird Records Committee (tel 04-347 2277; colinr@emirates.net.ae) is the Emirates Ornithological Society which is worth contacting if you are interesting in bird watching expeditions while in the UAE.

Emirates Environmental Group (tel 04-331 8100; www.eeg-uae.com) is a voluntary non-profit making organisation whose aim is to increase public awareness of the fragile state of the environment.

Emirates Natural History Group (tel 02-627 4049) is based in Abu Dhabi and should be able to give you some valuable local knowledge about what there is to be seen in the way of flora and fauna in the UAE and where you can see it.

Theatre

Theatre isn't a big industry in the Emirates and local playwrights are few and far between although the government is now trying to encourage a cultural revival which includes the development of traditional folklore and theatre.

Most rulers in the Middle East often view plays and novels written by nationals with a certain amount of suspicion as they have been seen to criticise governments and rulers in the past. Censorship plays a big part in any art in Muslim society and artists and writers do not have the same freedom of expression as exists in the west. There are a couple of amateur dramatic societies in the UAE but most theatregoers rely on touring theatrical groups coming to play in the big hotels.

Cinema

Going to the cinema is a common leisure activity among all nationalities in the UAE. Each large town will have a cinema though the majority of them outside the big cities only show films in Hindi. Dubai has an increasing number of all-singing all-dancing cinema multiplexes with more being built all the time, which show big movies from America and Britain. Whether they are the latest releases or not seems to depend on how long it takes the censors to get around to viewing them.

Music and Dance

Unfortunately, due to the rather closed nature of Emirati society, any music and dance that you might experience is likely to be western or modern Middle Eastern pop in a nightclub or bar. Traditional music and dance performances are a rarity though you will see such things if you are invited into the family celebrations of nationals or during Islamic festivals. You are most likely to see traditional dancing taking place at the Eid al-Fitra feast which marks the end of Ramadan. The top hotels in the UAE often host performances from international theatre troupes and pop stars and these will be advertised in the newspapers and on the local radio stations.

Amusement Parks

There are a number of amusement parks in the Emirates with waterslides etc., as well as many health, beach and sports clubs. Details of some of these can be found in the sections dealing with individual emirates. The local guidebooks to the Emirates, published by *Explorer Publishing* (tel 04-282 2661; www.the-explorer.com) have details of many more.

NIGHTLIFE

The nightlife scene is pretty much restricted to the large cities of Dubai and Abu Dhabi which offer cinemas, restaurants, bars, nightclubs and coffee shops. Elsewhere people go to bed, and places close their doors, early.

Nightclubs

Like the bars, the nightclubs range from the sleazy pick-up joint frequented by imported toms looking to turn a trick, to swing-your-pants jive clubs with an imported rock DJ playing the latest sounds to an appreciative co-ed audience. Most clubs are part of hotels but there are a few, especially in Dubai, that are not. You will always find more men than women in any of these places which is a shame for both sexes but a way of life in the Arab world. Drinks will be pricey but there is normally no admission fee.

Because dinner is a late meal in the Gulf nightclubs tend to get going only after around 11pm, staying open till 2-3am. Wednesday, Thursday and Friday nights (equivalent to Thursday, Friday and Saturday in the West) are the most crowded nights.

SPORT

Many of the expats and nationals are sports mad and you should find that any sport you want to partake in – on sea, land or air – can be found in the Emirates and there are many sports clubs and societies that cater to the sports fan. Check out listings in the English-language listings magazines available locally. Dubai and Abu Dhabi also host several important international sporting events throughout the year such as the Dubai Desert Classic, the Dubai World Cup (a horserace offering the world's largest prize money), the Dubai Tennis Open, the UAE Desert Challenge and Powerboat races.

Water Sports

The fabulous weather and sea temperature is ideal for water sports and they are not surprisingly very popular in the Emirates. Sailing, sport fishing, scuba diving, powerboat and dhow racing are all popular and practised. The local guides and magazines have listings which include pretty much any water sport you might want to have a go at.

Hash House Harriers

Wherever expats congregate in the world you will find a Hash club. There are several in the UAE. The Hash House Harriers were started in the 1930s in Kuala Lumpa, Malaysia by British servicemen as a not particularly competitive way to go for a run in company around a set course. It is a good way to meet the local expats, as after the run there is usually a fair amount of drinking done (you may have to pay an admission fee that includes beverages). Locations differ for every meet and runs start just before sunset and finish before dark. There are at least four 'chapters' in the UAE including the *Desert Hash House Harriers* (tel 04-203 2720; www.deserthash.net) and probably more. Check the local guides and the newspapers for contact details.

Horseracing

Horseracing, especially in Dubai and Abu Dhabi, is big business and a passion of several of the ruling sheikhs. The al-Maktoums of Dubai are unquestionably the most important figures in horseracing worldwide with Dubai home to the Godolphin Empire, set up in the 1980s at the cost of many millions of dollars, which flies horses from the Godolphin stables to all the major races all over the world. The driving force behind the family's initial involvement and then domination of the sport is Sheikh Mohammed bin Rashid al-Maktoum. Sheikh Zayed bin Sultan al-Nahyan, the ruler of Abu Dhabi and President of the United Arab Emirates is also a prominent racehorse owner and breeder with the largest stock of Arabian horses in the world.

There are regular meetings during the racing season which runs from November to April. Admission to the races is free, and there is a mix of night and day races held under floodlights and run on dirt. The world's richest horserace, the Dubai World Cup, inaugurated in 1996 and held every March, attracts the top breeders and trainers from around the world due to the phenomenal amount of prize money (US$12 million in the year 2000).

There are five racecourses in the Emirates, two in Dubai, two in Abu Dhabi and one in Sharjah. Meetings attract large crowds of spectators and are thoroughly good fun. Although betting is strictly forbidden in Islamic law all spectators to the races receive a competition card where, if they guess the first six winners correctly they win a cash prize. There are also desert endurance races, show jumping and gymkhanas held during the winter months.

Camel Racing

Camel racing is also a very popular sport in the Emirates with good racetracks in Abu Dhabi and Dubai and a very dramatic setting at the track in Ras al-Khaimah. Training runs take place in the cold early mornings shortly after sunrise with races held most Fridays during the winter with additional races on some Wednesdays, Thursdays and on public holidays. The size of the prize money to be won in these races is far lower than the price of some of the prize camels, an asking price in excess of US$100,000 for a good racing camel is not uncommon.

Great attention is accorded to the feeding and training of camels (still mostly bred by the Bedouin) with huge training camps similar in feel to Chantilly, Newmarket or Newbury close to the racecourses. Camel jockeys are very short and very young, often no more than six years old, and rumour has it that they are stuck on to the saddle by the seat of their trousers using Velcro. Camel races are very long endurance tests. The camels, which can reach speeds of around 60km/h, are accompanied around these tracks by their owners, who bomb along beside them in 4WDs. Details of races are carried in the newspapers or ask tour companies.

Falconry

Falconry is still practised in the Emirates and there are several falconry hospitals in the region owned by the sheikhs, including one out near the Nad al-Sheba racecourse in Dubai. Unfortunately it is very difficult to get an invitation to a hunting party because the sport is practised mainly by the very rich and has become very exclusive.

Golf

Golf was imported into the country with the expats who would play on sand courses (called browns) until the first grass course, the *Emirates Golf Club*, was opened in 1988. There are now a number of world-class grass courses in Abu Dhabi and Dubai and although the green fees are pricey (reflecting the high cost of running a large expanse of green lawn in the middle of a desert) the facilities and the courses are excellent. There are also a number of brown courses where green fees are far more realistic.

Ball Games

Rugby, football, cricket and tennis are all well catered for in the Emirates. Many of the top hotels have tennis courts and keep international coaches on call for any guest who may need their services. The US$1million Dubai Duty Free Tennis Open is a major international event that takes place every February. Rugby is popular among the expat crowd with regular games being played and the annual Dubai Rugby Sevens that takes place every December attracts top international teams. Cricket is on a par with football as the country's most played sport amongst the Western as well as Indian, Pakistani and Sri Lankan expats. The cricket ground in Sharjah often plays host to local as well as international matches. Football remains the biggest and favourite spectator sport in the Emirates with the UAE Football Association comprising of 26 football clubs and two league divisions. Check the local press for fixtures.

Clubs

Beach clubs, sports clubs and health clubs; there are plenty of clubs to join if you are planning to spend time in the Emirates and the facilities offered are excellent. Being a member of a club holds a certain cachet in the Emirates. The local guidebooks and magazines have complete listings of the club scene. Some places may allow day membership but all are expensive.

 Shopping is one of the biggest hobbies in the Emirates, especially in Dubai where an annual international shopping festival is held in March/April. If you find yourself haunting the shopping malls in Dubai after only a week or so of exploring the country don't be surprised. The desire to consume becomes unquenchable. Of all the Emirates, Dubai has the best souks and the most choice, though you may find some bargains and curios in the souks and markets of the smaller emirates such as Umm al-Quwain and Ras al-Khaimah. The Blue Souk in Sharjah is also a very good place to hunt for bargains.

Haggling

Bargaining or haggling is part of the fun of travelling in the Middle East, though if you don't enjoy it it won't be. Apart from the supermarkets where all items are priced, you can just about haggle anywhere else. Ask the salesman for their final price and then haggle a bit more. In the souks it's worth offering half the price that is originally asked by the shopkeeper. Be polite but firm and don't be browbeaten into paying more than you think something is worth. If you really want something it is worth being persistent, leaving the shop and then going back later to discuss the matter of price some more is always a good ploy. Don't be surprised if you are invited to sit and drink a tea or coffee during discussions.

Shopping Hours

Shops are open from about 8.30am-1pm and again from 4-8.30pm Saturday to Thursday. Shopping malls and the large supermarkets such as *Choithram's* and *Spinneys* are often open 9am-9pm daily. Most shops are closed on Friday mornings but may well open during Friday evenings.

Complaints. Complaints concerning anything retail can be directed to the *Emirates Society for Consumer Protection* (tel 06-551 4000; www.escp.com).

Shopping Centres

Well-stocked supermarkets with groceries from all over the world, shopping centres and shopping malls are plentiful in Dubai. There are less of them in Abu Dhabi and Sharjah, and far less in the rest of the emirates. Shopping centres are open all day and have the very latest boutiques etc., from the West and visiting them can become addictive.

Souks

Although the old souks with their alleyways and open-fronted stalls have all but been demolished to make way for the new, there are still areas that are called souks and consist of small shops selling goods from around the region as well as from around the world. These can still be extremely colourful and exotic places to wander in and prices will be less than what you would pay at home.

Books. Dubai has the best bookshops of all the Emirates by far. There are a couple of decent bookstores to be found in Abu Dhabi, and a bookshop/café for literary types in Sharjah.

Carpets

Oriental carpets are beautiful, the patterns fascinating and the prices large. Carpets and *kilims* arrive in the souks from Iran, Kashmir, Pakistan, Afghanistan, Turkey, China and Central Asia and are both machine and hand-made. It is difficult to tell the difference between the two but as a rule a hand-made carpet will have slight imperfections in the design (and will be more expensive than a machine-made carpet). If you are serious about buying a carpet try and find someone who knows about them to accompany you on a buying trip. Salesmen will be very helpful but at the end of the day their profits come from sales to customers.

Clothes

If you are after designer-wear you'll find it in the shopping malls in droves. There is also a profusion of tailors in the Emirates and they will be able to make up garments to patterns of your choosing, or even from photographs or advertisements from magazines or catalogues. You pay for the material separately and then negotiate a fee for the tailoring – which will be a great deal less than you would pay at home.

Electrical Goods

There are a plethora of shops selling electrical goods at relatively bargain prices in the Emirates. You should always make sure before handing over the cash that any system bought will work back home. It is also important to be aware that not all warranties are valid internationally.

Gifts

Presents that reflect the region could be *dishdashas* (the long full-length dress shirt worn by Emirati men), prayer beads, brass coffee pots and ornate trays, *khanjars* (the curved daggers traditionally worn by the Bedouin), *shishas* or ornately carved wooden chests. Verses from the Quran and designs of Arabic calligraphy are very beautiful and often incredibly intricate. Spices are a cheap present and it can be fun spending some time in the souks discovering the different spices that are available.

Gold

Dubai is famed for its gold souk and is one of the most important importers and exporters of gold in the world. Priced according to the worldwide daily gold rate (published in the local newspapers) the majority of gold is available in 22 and 24 carats, which is much more of a yellow gold than normally seen at home. There isn't a great deal available below 18 carats. For an additional charge the goldsmiths will make up any design that you wish; from necklaces, bracelets and earrings to watchstraps and can even hand the gold over to you in ingots if you wish – though you should check with your embassy about import/export restrictions on gold.

Jewellery

Chunky Bedouin jewellery is becoming a rarity with the loss of traditional craftsmen in the region though you may find jewellery from Oman and Yemen where such stuff continues to be fashioned. More widespread – though not appreciatively cheaper – is silver jewellery from India. If you have a design that you would like to have made up, this is easily possible in the souk jewellery shops. The wearing of flash watches is one of the penchants of people in the Emirates and the choice in the shops is larger than what you would find on the high street back home.

Incense and Perfumes

The Middle East is a fragrant place. Perfumes from all over the world are available, reasonably priced and a good buy. In the souks you will find small perfumeries where you can have any fragrance under the sun made up while you wait.

Music

CDs and cassettes can be found at much cheaper prices than in Europe. The range available is pretty good and up to date though you will have to allow for the musical taste in the Emirates. It's much more 'poppy' than in Europe or the USA – far less miserable in tone – and Enigma are still perennial favourites there. Videos and DVDs are also a good buy but remember that they will have been censored before being put on the shelves.

Textiles

Textiles come into the country from all over the world and you can pick up reams of your favourite cloth for making into garments back home. Cloth is also quite a good gift to take home. Pashmina shawls are widely available in a variety of colours – ideal and stylish for the little lady back home or, if you are the little lady, for you. You will also find plenty of tie-dye, appliqué and mirror-work wall hangings from India in the souks.

Health and Hygiene

Hospitals, clinics and health services throughout the Emirates are on the whole modern and efficient places and the practitioners very competent. All GCC nationals and resident expats are entitled to free medical health care but as a visitor you will have to pay should you fall ill or need treatment. Details of the major medical centres/hospitals to be found in each emirate are below.

Abu Dhabi: Corniche Hospital (tel 03-724 900).
Ajman: Ajman Medical Centre (tel 06-422 866).
Dubai: Al-Maktoum Hospital, Deira (tel 04-221 211).
Fujairah: Fujairah Medical Centre (tel 09-232 555).
Ras al-Khaimah: Ras al-Khaimah Medical Centre (tel 07-333 780).
Sharjah: New Medical Centre (tel 06-536 936).
Umm al-Quwain: Umm al-Quwain Hospital (tel 06-656 888).

Medical certificates and particular immunisations are not required before being allowed into the country but check with your local GP before you go as to what immunisations are advised. The heat and aridity of the Emirates makes malaria a rarity in the region but again check with your GP as to the current situation. The main illnesses that may affect you are to do with the heat; heat stroke, sunburn etc., so be vigilant. Wear a hat and drink a lot of water (five litres a day is recommended during the summer months) and generally follow the advice in the main *Practical Information* chapter.

Medical Treatment

If you are unlucky enough to fall seriously ill you will receive emergency treatment in one of the government hospitals. If you have holiday insurance you should contact the insurance company immediately. They often have agreements set up with individual establishments. Out in the villages among some of the older generations of Emiratis traditional medicine practises such as fire healing, bloodletting and the use of herbs still continues but you are unlikely to encounter any of these.

Emergency Procedures

The telephone number for the emergency ambulance service is 998/999 wherever you happen to be in the UAE. The operator will also be able to give you the address and location of the nearest hospital but this number should only be called in an emergency. The locations of hospitals are also printed in the newspapers.

Doctors and Dentists

Embassies will be able to provide a list of recommended doctors and dentists. There are also a number of private clinics throughout the country and you will be able to find one by checking in the newspapers, asking at your hotel or a pharmacy or in the telephone directories. Addresses can also be found in the listings sections of the English-language magazines such as *Connector* and *Aquarius*.

Pharmacies

Pharmacies are common, stock pretty much everything you can get back home and are very useful places if you have a minor illness that needs diagnosing without having the hassle and expense of finding a doctor. Each Emirate has at least one 24-hour pharmacy and the address and telephone numbers of these will be listed in the newspapers. Otherwise pharmacies are often open late into the night even on Fridays.

Gastric Problems

You should stick to drinking bottled water during your stay in the Emirates. Tap water is safe to drink but because much of it comes from desalination plants it doesn't taste great and may take some getting used to. Tap water is fine for washing and cleaning your teeth with. If you eat out a great deal while abroad your stomach may take some time getting used to the 'foreign' bacteria in the food. This shouldn't cause any major concerns but may take a day or so to level out.

Toilets

Depending on where you are, public toilets can vary from the unwholesome, rarely-if-ever-cleaned squat hole-in-the-ground bogs to pristine thrones. Toilet paper is generally provided in the western style versions of the lavatory but you will need to bring your own should you find your bowels dying for release in a service station or roadside café. The mini watering can that you see in most toilets is filled with water and used for cleaning oneself, accompanied by the left hand – which is why the left hand is seen as an unclean appendage in most of the Eastern countries of the world. The hose that is fast replacing the little watering cans is used for the same purpose.

Creatures to Avoid

Camels can be grumpy but if you leave then alone they'll not bother you. The same goes for goats, sheep and the odd cow that you may come across. **Snakes** are shy creatures and you may spot the occasional one if you spend a long time in the mountains. Make sure not to annoy it. The seas are relatively free of fierce man-attacking creatures, the main malignant beast being **jellyfish**, which are common. Though rarely deadly, a sting from a jellyfish can be pretty painful. Try and douse the infected area with vinegar (if you happen to have some at hand) and seek assistance. If you are staying in a beachside hotel there will be attendants near enough to warn swimmers of any dangers. In some areas **riptides** can be quite powerful at certain times of the year but often there will be signs warning visitors about this.

Insects

Should you come across a camel-eating spider then the best thing to do is to move away from it. If you are camping out in the desert you should be cautious when moving any rocks away from your camping site as **scorpions** like to lurk under them. In the mornings shake out your footwear if camping, as again scorpions find dark cool places a good place for a snooze.

SECURITY

The United Arab Emirates are a long way from the tempestuous regions of the northern Middle East both in terms of standard of living and political machinations. Although Gulf Arabs support the Palestinians, the troubles in Palestine/Israel are not going to upset the continued peace of the Gulf Region.

Pickpockets, bag snatchers and hotel theft are very uncommon in the Emirates. The laws on crime are relatively harsh and a prison sentence or worse isn't something that anyone would particularly want to risk. Prison is looked upon as a place of punishment not of rehabilitation and expats, wherever they may originate from, are glad to have the chance to earn a better salary than they could at home and don't want to jeopardise their residency. Any non-GCC resident in the Emirates is going to have a job (you cannot remain in the country for long without one) and therefore will be earning enough to live on and send a little of what they earn home.

There isn't a culture of unemployment and petty thievery in the UAE. The only acts of violence that you may come across are road-rage and perhaps the beating of donkeys – camels are treated with a deep respect. In business conmen may be prevalent as they are in all countries of the world and you may find that you have paid too much for this souvenir or that taxi ride but if you don't worry too much about it and put it down to experience you'll feel happier.

Bribery, though not really viewed by many in the region in the same way as we think of it, is a way of life, though becoming less so. Competition in the big cities of the Emirates is fierce, especially in the continually booming construction industry, and people need to get ahead of their rivals. In the Arab world a token payment for a service rendered is not seen as a bribe but as a gift. *Baksheesh* works on the same principle.

Police

Police are all Emirati nationals and, as anywhere, are to be avoided if possible. You will often see a police 4WD parked up on a roundabout looking for traffic offenders and should you at any time be stopped by them be very polite and courteous. Do not attempt to bribe a policeman.

Arrest and Summons. Avoid it. The police will allow you to phone your Embassy eventually but if you are in the wrong the embassy staff won't be too sympathetic, though they will find you a lawyer.

Drugs

Islam is a very anti-drug religion. Coffee was seen as sinful for a long time when it was first introduced into the region and the qat-chewing Yemenis across the way in the southwest corner of the peninsula are looked upon with scorn. The newspapers often carry stories of guest workers (usually from the poorer end of the scale) being imprisoned or deported for possession of even small amounts of cannabis. Should you be in the vicinity of a friend who is caught in possession of drugs you may be found guilty by association and subject to the same penalties.

Ethnic/Religious Rivalry

In the unlikely event that such a thing should blow up in a country that is far more concerned with making money than religious or ethnic rivalry, you are unlikely to be affected. The system of control in the Emirates is that at the top of the heap sit the nationals who have all the power and who own all the property and a share of businesses. Below them are the whites who have built the infrastructure and continue to supply the improvements and know-how that help to keep the country abreast of the West. Below them are the Arabs from the poorer Arab states and below them are the Asians who work in the service industries, labouring etc. Everybody is looking to make money, and each stratum mixes and socialises with its own kind. When it comes to business these strata happily deal with each other, when it comes to home time they split. The people at the apex of this pyramid control all the other levels (it is their country after all) and they hold the strings to how things are done. The Emiratis are Muslims and though they tolerate the antics of the guest workers, the country is still a Muslim country and Islam is the state religion upon which the state law is based.

Photography

As with anywhere in the conservative Gulf you should ask a person's permission if you wish to take their photograph. Apart from the courtesy of asking permission locals, especially Gulf Arabs, are sensitive to any intrusion in their lives by outsiders. You should avoid taking photographs of any building or area that may be construed by the authorities to be of military or political importance. There are plenty of photography shops selling the latest equipment and getting high quality film isn't a problem.

TOURIST INFORMATION

The only emirate with a tourist board is Dubai, the *Dubai Department of Tourism and Commerce* has offices in several countries and a website www.dubaitourism.co.ae.

Tourist Offices Abroad:

Australia: Dubai Department of Tourism and Commerce, Level 7, 210 Clarence Street, Sydney 2000, (tel 02-92677871).

Britain: First Floor, 125 Pall Mall, London, SW1Y 5EP (24-hour brochure line tel 020-7839 0580).

South Africa: 5th Floor, Sandton City Office Towers, Sandton City, Johannesburg (tel 11-784 6708).

USA: 8 Penn Centre, Philadelphia, PA 19103, (tel 310-7524488).

There are several good websites with information and links to further sites devoted to the Emirates: www.arab.net, www.arabia.com, www.uaeinteract.com, www.planetarabia.com, www.desertship.com and www.arabnet.

The supermarkets in the Emirates have good notice boards, especially the bigger ones such as *Spinneys* and *Choithrams* and are a good place to look if you are seeking work or a new car or a place to live.

EMBASSIES & CONSULATES

Embassies are open 8.30am-1.30pm Sunday to Thursday. Many countries have embassies or consulates in both Abu Dhabi and Dubai.

Bahrain: tel 02-631 2200 fax 02-311 202.

Kuwait: tel 02-446 888; fax 02-444 990.

Oman: tel 04-397 1000; fax 04-397 0666.

Saudi Arabia: tel 04-266 3383; fax 04-266 2524.

United Kingdom: tel 02-326 600; fax 02-342 676.

United States of America: tel 04-331 3115; fax 04-331 4043.

Yemen: tel 02-448 457; fax 02-447 978.

USEFUL INFORMATION

Business Hours

Government offices are open from 7.30am-2.30pm while private businesses generally work from 8am-1pm and 4-8.30pm, Saturday to Wednesday. However, many businesses will work a 9am-5pm day. The official weekend is taken from Thursday afternoon until Saturday but again this may vary from business to business and some employees will have Friday and Saturday as their weekend. It is a good idea to telephone ahead before visiting any non-governmental establishment.

Time. United Arab Emirates local time is GMT + 4 hours.

Electricity. The electric voltage in the Emirates is 220V AC. The British style three pin plugs and wall sockets are used. Adaptors are available in the shops all over the Emirates.

Places of Worship. Islam is a very tolerant religion and respects other creeds and the different needs of the faithful. You can find churches representing all Christian creeds, Hindu and Buddhist temples in the United Arab Emirates.

Emergency Services Numbers

All toll free: Police, Ambulance, Fire 999.

PUBLIC HOLIDAYS AND CELEBRATIONS

Islamic holidays are dependent on the Islamic calendar rather than the Gregorian and so fall on different days each year. The United Arab Emirates observe the five feasts and festivals common all over the Muslim world. Details of these can be found in the main *Practical Information* chapter. The United Arab Emirates' **National Day** is celebrated on 2 December every year and Emiratis also take a holiday on 1 January. Individual Emirates also have their own National Days to mark the accession of their ruler. Ramadan, the month of fasting during daylight hours, will fall in the cooler months of October, November and December for the next five years.

EXPLORING THE EMIRATES

DUBAI

Dubai is a small emirate of about 3,900 square kilometres but it is the most vibrant emirate of the country. From the early years of the 20th century Dubai city has been a cosmopolitan trading port with large populations of Persians, Baluchis and Indians doing business and prospering. Originally a port settlement based around the Creek, Dubai has spread far out along the coast and into the desert hinterland. Looked back at from the outskirts, the city appears like some wannabe Manhattan with its skyscrapers reaching up from the desert into a smoggy sky.

Dubai Skyline

Dubai's oil reserves are expected to run out within the next ten years and the rulers of the Emirate are putting plans into motion that will keep Dubai on track as the commercial heartland of the UAE. Dubai Airport is one of the busiest in the Gulf region and the Emirate hosts many international festivals, internationally renowned sporting events and is increasingly attracting tourists to take advantage of the weather, the tax free shopping, restaurants, beaches and luxury hotels. Its free-zone **Jebel Ali** – which allows full ownership of businesses by foreigners, tax exemption and business freedoms – was opened in 1985 and has been a great success, drawing many companies with interests in the Gulf, Africa and Asia to base themselves in Dubai. It is very likely that you will be based in Dubai during your stay in the United Arab Emirates.

Sheikh Maktoum bin Rashid al-Maktoum is the ruler of Dubai and belongs to the Bani Yas tribe. He is also the Vice President of the United Arab Emirates.

Getting Around

Arrival and Departure

If you fly into Dubai Airport, you will find that although you have a long way to travel between the plane and the immigration desks, once out of the airport door you are relatively near to the city centre. Expect to pay around Dh15 (£2.90/$4) for the 20-minute ride from the airport to the Gold Souk area in downtown Deira.

If you are looking for flights out of the Emirates the Airline Centre (tel 04-295 0000) in the *Dubai National Airline Travel Agency* (DNATA) building over the Clock Tower Roundabout at the top of al-Maktoum Road is the place to head for. Under one roof there are about 100 airline offices.

If you are heading to Oman, coaches to Muscat operated by *Oman National Transport Company* leave at 7.30am and at 5.30pm from the Ponderosa parking lot by the Airline Centre at the top of al-Maktoum Road. You can either buy a ticket on the coach or to be sure of a seat buy it from the Airline Centre. At the time of research the tickets were being sold from the Philippines Airline desk but ask at the information desk. A one-way ticket to Muscat costs Dh57 (£11/$15) and the journey takes about six hours.

City layout

Dubai Creek divides the city in two. The northeast side (Deira) is joined to the southwest side (Bur Dubai) in three places: by the Shindagha tunnel close to the mouth of the Creek and by the al-Maktoum and al-Garhoud bridges inland. The other way to cross the Creek is to take the *abra* water taxis that motor back and forth all day and late into the night. From the two centres of Deira and Bur Dubai the city spreads out. The southwest area of the city is home to the main business district and the newer suburbs where many expats live and work. The northeast residential areas extend towards the neighbouring emirate of Sharjah. Most of the main sites are on either side of the mouth of the Creek. These areas are the oldest and are where the souks, museums and many of the cheaper hotels are located. Dubai is a large city and many of the better restaurants and bars, shopping malls and cinemas are spread out in the newer parts of the city.

City Transport

Because of its large size you are likely to do a fair amount of travelling by taxi, bus or a hire car. The municipal bus service in Dubai is the best of all the Emirates; the two main bus stations being al-Ghubaiba in Bur Dubai serving all points south and the Deira or Gold Souk bus station serving all points north. Buses are cheap – fares costing between Dh3.50 (£0.68/$0.95) and Dh1 depending on the length of the journey. Timetables and routes are posted at the bus stations and on the front of the buses in English and Arabic. Bus No. 8 is a useful bus, travelling through the centre of town from the Deira Gold Souk Station – al-Ghubaiba Station – Dubai Zoo – Beach Resort – Jumeira Beach Park. Another is Bus No. 28 which serves al-Karama – Dubai Zoo – al-Satwa Bus Station – Trade Centre.

Taxis are numerous in Dubai and come in various hues. Not all are metered but you can order the camel-coloured taxis, which are metered, by calling 04-208 0808. These taxis are managed by *Dubai Transport*, all the drivers are uniformed and because they are metered it saves the hassle of having to haggle over the fare.

Down on the Creek the only way to travel is by *abra*. These small wooden boats wait until they have a full contingent of 20 passengers before the driver collects the 50 fils fee from everyone and then reverses the *abra* out onto the creek for the five-minute crossing. Descendants of the old rowing boats that would have done the trip in the past, an *abra* crossing is a must, especially towards sunset.

For longer inter-emirate journeys, *Dubai Transport* minibuses run from the taxi station on Omar ibn al-Khattab Road and wait until they are full before motoring to their destination. Strangely, the buses have to return to Dubai empty and so although it may be cheap to get to some of the more out-of-the-way destinations, getting back to Dubai is likely to be something of an adventure, involving a possible hitchhike to the nearest town and then a taxi ride back to the hotel.

One-way fares from the Dubai minibus station are:

Dubai to:	*Abu Dhabi:*	Dh33 (£6.45/$8.95)
	Al-Ain:	Dh30 (£5.87/$8.16)
	Sharjah:	Dh5 (£0.98/$1.36)
	Masafi:	Dh20 (£3.92/$5.45)
	Khor Fakkan:	Dh30 (£5.87/$8.16)
	Ajman:	Dh7 (£1.37/$1.90)
	Umm al-Quwain:	Dh10 (£1.96/$2.72)
	Ras al-Khaimah:	Dh20 (£3.92/$5.45)
	Fujairah:	Dh25 (£4.89/$6.80)

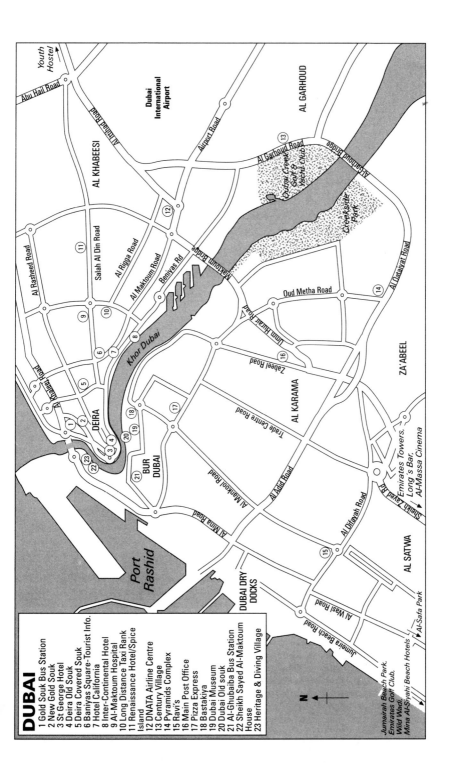

DUBAI

1 Gold Souk Bus Station
2 New Gold Souk
3 St George Hotel
4 Deira Old Souk
5 Deira Covered Souk
6 Baniyas Square-Tourist Info.
7 Hotel California
8 Inter-Continental Hotel
9 Al-Maktoum Hospital
10 Long Distance Taxi Rank
11 Renaissance Hotel/Spice Island
12 DNATA Airline Centre
13 Century Village
14 Pyramids Complex
15 Ravi's
16 Main Post Office
17 Pizza Express
18 Bastakiya
19 Dubai Museum
20 Dubai Old souk
21 Al-Ghubaiba Bus Station
22 Sheikh Sayed Al-Maktoum House
23 Heritage & Diving Vilage

N

Youth Hostel

Abu Hail Road

AL KHABEESI

Dubai International Airport

Al Ittihad Road

Airport Road

AL GARHOUD

Al Garhoud Road

Al Garhoud Bridge

(Dubai Creek Golf & Yacht Club)

Creekside Park

Al Rasheed Road

Salah Al Din Road

Al Rigga Road

Al Maktoum Road

Beniyas Rd

Maktoum Bridge

AL KHABEESI

Khor Dubai

DEIRA

Al Khaleej Road

Al Khaleej Road

Port Rashid

DUBAI DRY DOCKS

BUR DUBAI

Al Mina Road

Al Mankool Road

Al Adni Road

Al Seef Road

Trade Centre Road

Oud Metha Road

Umm Hurair Road

Zabeel Road

AL KARAMA

Al Diyafah Road

Al Safa Park

ZA'ABEEL

Al Wasl Road

Jumeirah Beach Road

AL SATWA

Emirates Towers, Long's Bar, Al-Massa Cinema

Sheikh Zayed Rd

Al Qataiyat Road

Jumairah Beach Park,
Emirates Golf Club,
Wild Wadi,
Mina Al-Siyahi Beach Hotels

ACCOMMODATION

A lot of the cheapest hotels (though none are particularly cheap) are located down around the Deira Souk area and listed below are several staying options. Dubai is overrun with hotels suitable to all budgets and the *Dubai Department of Tourism and Commerce Marketing* runs a website which has details of more staying options (www.dubaitourism.co.ae/dtmc/tour).

Dubai Youth Hostel: tel 04-298 8161. The hostel is quite a way out from the centre of things on the Qusais Road – on the wrong side of the airport – but is the cheapest place going at Dh35 (£6.85/$9.53) per night.

Hotels

Al-Khaleej Hotel: tel 04-221 1144; fax 04-223 7140; khotel@emirates.net.ae. A good hotel centrally located on Baniyas Square in Deira near the Creek. Rooms start from around Dh600 (£117/$163) for a single room.

Arbella Hotel: tel 04-222 6688; fax 04-227 2645. This hotel is on Naif Road by the Naif Roundabout and charges from Dh120 (£24/$33) per night.

Also on Naif Road you could try the *Karnak Hotel* (tel 04-226 8799; fax 04-2252793) which charges about the same as the *Arbella Hotel* but is closer to the centre of town.

Hotel California: tel 04-224 2429. Down past Baniyas Square on al-Maktoum Hospital Road is a hotel where hopefully you will be able to check out and leave at your leisure. It charges Dh150/200 (£29-39/$41-55) and lays on live music and dancing from India and the Middle East.

St George Hotel: tel 04-225 1122; fax 04-226 8383. Offers rooms with a view and has a good location near the spice souk with views over the Creek. Prices for a single room start from about Dh600.

A number of five-star international hotels are located on the Creek edge in Deira. The *Inter-Continental Hotel* (tel 04-222 7171; fax 228 4777; intercon@emirates.net.ae) offers the business traveller treatment with views for Dh 1,400 (£274/$381) per night for a single.

Along the seafront in Jumairah, out by Mina al-Siyahi on the southern outskirts of Dubai, there is a string of four and five-star hotels the best of which is the *Ritz-Carlton* (tel 04-399 4000; fax 04-399 4001; rcdubai@wmirates.net.ae) which looks beautiful and understated but does charge a wopping Dh2000 (£392/$545) a night.

The cheapest of the hotels along this stretch of beach is probably the *Sheraton Jumairah Beach Hotel* (tel 04-399 553; fax 04-399 5577) which charges from Dh800 (£156/$218) per night.

EATING AND DRINKING

Dubai has more restaurants and bars than anywhere else in the Emirates and the choice is phenomenal. The local guides *What's On* and *Dubai Explorer* have listings of all restaurants and bars in Dubai. Here are a few more options:

Century Village: tel 04-282 4122. The *Aviation Club* by the Tennis Stadium in al-Garhoud has a lot of international restaurants: *The Plaice* (fish and chips), *Café Costa, Majaz* (traditional coffee and shisha bar), *Chinawhite* (Chinese), *Da Gama* (Portuguese), *St.Tropez Bistro, Sushi Sushi,* and *La Vigna* (Italian) and the themed *Irish Village* pub.

Fuddruckers: tel 04-342 9639. In the *Town Centre* on the Jumairah Beach Road is this burger joint that serves burgers freshly made while you wait and is very good value for money.

Pizza Express: There are a couple of branches of this British chain of pizza/pasta restaurants (tel 04-394 5616) in the Atrium Building on Khalid bin al-Walid Road in Bur Dubai just past the *Four Points Sheraton Hotel.* There is another in the al-Safa Centre on al-Wasal Road in Jumairah. Prices are comparable with what you would pay in Britain.

The Pyramids Complex: tel 04-324 9603. This complex in Oud al-Mehtha has four restaurants under its apex: *Sphinx, Tour de France, Ruan Thai* and *Carters'.* They all have special deal evenings at least once a week, for example *Sphinx* has an eat and drink as much as you want night for Dh140 (£28/$38) + tax. *Carters'* bar is large, loud and is a great place to start off an evening with food and a few beers before clubbing it.

Ravi's: tel 04-331 5353. This famed eatery on the Satwa Roundabout is open 22 hours a day and offers cheap Pakistani fare.

Seville's: tel 04-324 4777. This is a new Spanish tapas bar and restaurant in the al-Wafi Centre in Oud al-Mehtha. Your meal will be accompanied by live Spanish guitar music and if you are lucky flamenco dancing later – once the sangria has begun to (over)flow.

Spice Island: This restaurant in the *Renaissance Hotel* in Deira has an all you can eat and drink night with a choice of Italian, Mexican, Chinese, Japanese and Middle Eastern cuisines and house beverages including beers, wines and spirits. You choose the ingredients and everything is cooked at live cooking stations. Drinks are included until 11.30pm and it costs Dh125 (£24/$34) per head; about half that for kids under 12 years old. It's a huge restaurant and a good place to go out to make a night of it.

For **cheap eats** the area around Baniyas Square has quite a few eateries. Check out the *Hatan al-Tai* restaurant behind the square on the creekside. For some of the best **pastries and bread** in the Gulf take a trip down Sheikh Zayed Road to the *French Connection Patisserie.* There are also plenty of **coffee houses** in Dubai from American coffee bars to more individual places. Try *Tavalino Café* in Baniyas Square or the stylish *Café Mozart* on Baniyas Road down a side alley next to *Hotel Riviera.*

ENTERTAINMENT

Cinema

Cinemas has been springing up all over Dubai in the last year which attests to the popularity of the medium. Several of the larger cinemas are located in the big shopping complexes. Details of timings and titles can be found in the entertainment sections of the daily newspapers. The biggest choice of films can be found at the *al-Massa Cinema* (04-343 8383) which is attached to the Metropolitan Hotel on Sheikh Zayed Road, and the *Cinestar* (04-294 9000) in the Deira *City Centre* complex.

Pubs and Bars

Long's Bar in the *Tower Rotana Hotel* on Sheikh Zayed Road is a new place with colonial décor (polo mallets and palm paddle fans) and a fast crowd. *The Red Lion Pub* in the *Metropolitan Hotel* on Sheikh Zayed Road is like a typical 'ye olde English pub' with horse brasses, draught ales, pub meals and dartboard. *The Boston Bar* is a Cheers-like pub in the Jumairah Rotana Hotel (04-345 5888) which serves draught beers and also has big screens with satellite sports coverage. The *Jumairah Rotana Hotel* also has three restaurants offering Italian, German and pub food.

Harry's Place (04-262 5555) in the *Renaissance Hotel* is also a bit of a giggle with live music and theme nights. If you are desperate for a fine wine the *Agency Wine Bar* in the *Emirates Towers* on Sheikh Zayed Road serves wines from all over the world accompanied by tapas. An upmarket and high up drinking venue is on the

51st Floor – at the very top – of the smaller of the two Emirates Towers. The *Vu Bar* has stunning views 305 metres above Dubai, similar to those you get from the inside of an aeroplane. There is a sister restaurant on the next floor down.

Nightclubs

Nightclubs can be a hit and miss affair and all get busiest between midnight and 3am. Downtown many of the clubs which are part of the hotels, such as *Arif Castle*, are pretty rough and ready but interesting nonetheless while elsewhere venues such as *Cyclone* at *Leisureland* in al-Karama (04-336 9991) and the *Kasbar* at the *Royal Mirage* (04-399 9999) remain firm favourites. On the Shiekh Zayed Road *Scarlett's Bar and Nightclub* (04-330 0000) in the Emirates Towers is a good *craic* if slightly pricey. It also has a restaurant on the premises. Also on the Sheikh Zayed Road is *Atlantis* (04-399 2222), located next to the *Hard Rock Café*. The place is far more western than eastern in tone and is a massive place with a 1,000 people capacity.

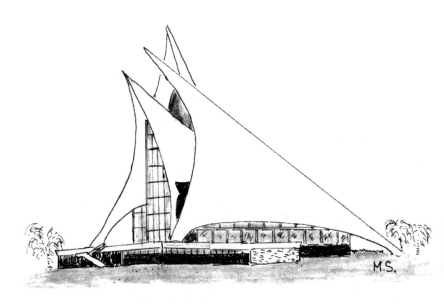

Dubai Creek Golf & Yacht Club

SPORT

Dubai offers pretty much any sport you may like to have a go at. *The Dubai Explorer*, available in the Emirates, has comprehensive listings of sports and much else.

Water Sports

Water sports are very popular throughout the Emirates and along the beaches you will often find **jet skis** for rent, especially along the beachfronts of the more upmarket hotels. Most hotels located on the sea will have water sport facilities for hire, though if you are not staying in the hotel you will have to pay a day membership of between Dh100-200 (£19-39/$27-54).

If you fancy a go at **wake boarding** (snowboarding on water) you can get in touch with the *Dubai Water Sports Association* on 04-324 1031. Hiring windsurfing equipment from the hotels is likely to set you back about Dh100 per hour. There are several **Scuba diving** schools, many of which take their divers out to the east coast where the waters are clearer. *Al-Boom Diving* (04-394 1267), based on Jumairah Beach Road offers PADI open-water courses from Dh1,500 (£294/$409); you could also contact *Scuba International* (04-393 7557) who have an office in the Heritage and Diving Centre in al-Shindagha in Deira.

Deep Sea Fishing

If you fancy yourself as a bit of a Hemingway you can charter a boat to take you out into the Arabian Gulf, however, it doesn't come cheap. *Bounty Charters* (04-348 3042) offers tailor made itineraries while *Creek Cruises* (04-393 9860) can take up to seven people out on its 42 ft yacht. Prices for a four-hour trip start at Dh1,200 (£235/$327) for the boat and equipment.

Camel and Horseracing

Both these sports take place in the Nad al-Sheba district. Timings can be found in the local newspapers or from your hotel but both sports only take place during the winter season of September-April. Camel races take place very early in the mornings on Thursdays and Fridays; horseracing in the evenings from 7pm.

Golf

Golf is big in Dubai and some of the finest courses in the world have been laid out on turf planted on top of the desert. The *Nad al-Sheba Club* (04-336 3666; www.nadalshebaclub.com) is situated next to the racecourse and is an 18-hole fully floodlit course (6,248 yards, Par 71). It has a golf academy, a shop, a restaurant and bar. Tee times are available from 7.30am-10pm and green fees start from Dh180 (£35/$49). The famed *Emirates Golf Club* (04-347 3222) – the venue of the Dubai Desert Classic – is on the road to Jebel Ali to the south of Dubai and has two Par 72 courses: the Wadi course and the Majlis course both of approximately 7,100 yards. Its sister club, the *Dubai Creek Golf Club* (04-295 6000) is an 18-hole, Par 72 championship course of 6,839 yards and is in a beautiful location beside the Dubai Creek Marina. Both golf courses are immaculately laid out and provide excellent facilities but aren't cheap to play on. Green fees start at Dh330 (£65/$98) for an 18-hole round.

SHOPPING

The Souks

The souks of Dubai are the biggest in the Arabian Gulf and offer some of the best shopping to be had. You'll be able to find the **Spice Souk** by following your nose as you climb up to the street from the *abra* water taxi station in Deira. Shops line the narrow alleyways on the other side of Baniyas Road, packed with sacks of cloves, cinnamon and cardamon – and that's only the spices beginning with the letter *C* – carried to Dubai from all over the world. The **Gold Souk**, running along Sikkat al-Khail street in Deira and covered by a mahogany-coloured roof, is one of the largest gold markets in the world, and one of the cheapest. The souk has been refurbished to give it a real feeling of old Arabia and the glint of yellow from every shop window will draw in even the shyest visitor to take a look at what is on offer. The goldsmiths can make up any design that you'd like. **Deira Covered Souk**, off al-Sabkha Road in Deira behind the al-Sabkha bus station sells pretty much everything: clothes, watches, luggage, kitchen utensils, crockery, electrical equipment etc. **Dubai Old Souk** is by the waterfront of Bur Dubai just inland from the *abra* water taxi station. This covered souk has been restored and traders here sell souvenirs, textiles and clothing. It is a great place to wander about in towards sunset when the nearby creek shows its most romantic side.

The Malls
Jumairah Beach Road is the place to look for those western goods at cheaper prices than you'd find back home. There are a glut of shopping malls along this long road where you'll find boutiques and all kinds of lifestyle shops. *Magrudy's, Jumeira Plaza, Town Centre, Spinneys* supermarket and *Jumeira Centre* are all within easy walking distance of each other (though few people in Dubai really walk anywhere) and will just about cover all your needs. There is also an ATM at *Spinneys* and if you have a liquor licence a branch of *Maritime & Mercantile International* (liquor importers).

Books
Book Corner next to the Golden Fork restaurant on al-Maktoum Road opposite the Emirates Bank International has a good selection. *Magrudy's Bookshop* on Jumairah Beach Road also has a great selection of books while *Jumeira Plaza* next door has the second hand bookshop *House of Prose* (tel 3449 021) and another branch of *Book Corner*. *Bookzone* (tel 3515 702) is another second hand bookshop, in *al-Rais Shopping Centre* in Mankhool.

If you are interested in acquiring local artwork the *Dubai International Art Centre* (04-3444 398) opposite the *Jumeira Plaza* on Jumairah Beach Road holds exhibitions and craft fairs throughout the year.

HELP AND INFORMATION
Tourist Offices
The main tourist information centre is on Baniyas Square but it is pretty useless and you may be offered an out of date tourist map but that's about all. It is open daily from 9am-3pm and again from 8pm-midnight but don't be surprised if the place shuts at odd hours. You can telephone them on 04-228 5000. The official tourism marketing board address is *Department of Tourism and Commerce Marketing*, PO Box 594, Dubai, United Arab Emirates; tel +971 4 2230000; fax +971 4 2230022; e-mail info@dubaitourism.co.ae; website www.dubaitourism.com.

Car Hire Firms
Avis: tel 04-282 121.   *Hertz:* tel 04-282 4422.
Budget: tel 04-282 3030.   *Thrifty:* tel 04-337 0743.

Telephone Office
The main Etisalat office is on Omar ibn al-Khattab Road towards Baniyas Road in Deira. It is recognisable by the large white golf ball perched on the top of the building. It is open 24 hours a day and you can send faxes and telephone from there.

Post Office. The main post office is on Zabeel Road, al-Karama, Bur Dubai. There is another on al-Sabkha Road in Deira.

Internet Cafés

The *2002 Computer Café* in the Jumeira Plaza is on the Jumairah Beach Road and charges Dh15 (£2.90/$4) for an hour's surfing. *Meraj Typing Centre* opposite the *Swiss Plaza Hotel* in Bur Dubai is centrally located and charges Dh10 per hour. The *Internet Café* in the Dune Centre in al-Satwa charges Dh15 per hour.

Medical Services

al-Maktoum Hospital, Deira: tel 04-222 1211.
Rashid Hospital, Bur Dubai: tel 04-337 4000.
General Medical Centre, Jumairah: 04-349 5959.

Useful Addresses and Organisations

British Consulate: al-Seef Road, Bur Dubai; tel 04-397 1070.
American Consulate: 21st Flr., World Trade Centre, Sh. Zayed Road; tel 04-331 3115.
British Council: 04-337 0109.
The Welsh Society: 04-394 7825.
Dubai Irish Society: 04-348 9853.
Dubai Caledonian Society: 04-394 9110
St Mary's Roman Catholic Church: 04-370 087.
Holy Trinity: 04-370 247.

Exploring

Dubai is a city that has thrown open its portals to commerce and replaced the old with the new a long time ago. What this has meant is that Dubai is short on sights.

Dubai Museum

This state of the art museum (04-353 1862) is open 8.30am-8.30pm Saturday to Thursday and 3-9pm on Fridays and well worth a look. Admission costs Dh3. The museum is housed in the **al-Fahaidi fort** which was originally built in 1800 and acted as the residence of the ruler of Dubai. The courtyard has displays of bronze cannon, an abra and a fishing dhow but the best thing is a replica of a *barasti* house. Built of palm tree branches these houses were warm in winter and cool in summer. Off the courtyard there are rooms displaying weaponry with traditional sharkskin shields, spears and martini rifles. Another room has displays of local musical instruments and a large video screen showing demonstrations of war dances. A ramp leads from the courtyard down into the new galleries. After a multimedia trip through Dubai's past the visitor walks through a series of mock-up souk stalls with recorded sounds and life-size models. The museum is a great place to wander around in and get a lesson on the Emirate's past.

Heritage and Diving Villages

These villages (tel 04-393 7151) are purpose built tourist attractions attempting to recreate the traditional village life of the region and focusing on the Bedouin way of life and the pearl diving industry that was once the lifeblood of Dubai. There is a restaurant and shops that sell locally made handicrafts. The village is located next to Sheikh Sayed al-Maktoum House in the Shindagha area near the mouth of the Creek and is worth a look to get an idea of pre-oil life in Dubai.

Sheikh Sayed al-Maktoum House

Previously home to the present ruler's grandfather and now a museum housing a collection of photographs and documents from Dubai's history, the restored palace dates from the late 1800s. The house stands near the mouth of the Creek in Shindagha and is one of the few remaining examples of traditional architecture in the city. The Museum is open daily from 8am-9pm, 3-9.30pm on Friday. There is an admission fee of Dh2.

Dhow Cruises

Opposite the Inter-Continental Hotel is the *al-Mansoor Dhow* which offers a daily lunchtime cruise at 1.30pm; a sunset cruise at 6.30pm and a dinner cruise at 8.30pm. The boat is run by the Inter-Continental Hotel and reservations can be made on 04-205 7333. *Coastline Leisure* (tel 04-336 8407) also offers hour-long guided cruises in a beautifully restored dhow around the creek from its berth on the quayside opposite the Dubai Municipality building. The cost for adults is Dh35 (£6.85/$9.53) and Dh20 (£3.92/$5.45) for kids.

The Creek and Bastakiya

Another place to walk around while exploring the Creek is the Bastakiya area. This small area of buildings is pretty much all that survives of old Dubai with its narrow streets and mud brick housing. It is being renovated as an ongoing process and is very peaceful compared to the rush of cars just three minutes walk away. At number 69, the **Majlis Gallery** has displays of and sells pottery, silver, needlework and paintings.

Wild Wadi

This is a 12-acre water park with 24 interconnected water rides situated next to the Jumairah Beach Hotel at the end of the Jumairah Beach Road. The water park has some of the biggest and best rides in the world (yes really!) and admission costs Dh95 (£19/$26) for adults, Dh75 for kids. Wild Wadi is open from 11am-7pm daily.

Beaches

By the string of five star hotels near Mina al-Siyahi there are public beaches between the hotel beachfronts. It's easy to walk along the whole stretch and you can probably use the hotel easy chairs. However, if you order anything from the waiters you may be asked for a room number to charge it to.

PARKS

Dubai has a number of public parks, most of which charge admission – presumably to help with the cost of irrigating such large expanses of turf. One of the largest is **Creekside Park** which extends for 2.6km along the Creek between the two bridges of al-Maktoum and al-Gharhoud. A new cable car offers rides along the length of the park beside the Creek at a height of 80 metres. The park is open 8am-11pm Saturday to Wednesday (Wednesdays for women and children only), and 8am-11.30pm on Thursday and Friday. Admission costs Dh5 (£0.98/$1.36), cable car rides are extra.

Jumairah Beach Park is a great place to chill out for a day and is located on Jumairah Beach Road next to the *Hilton Beach Club*. The 12 hectares of park include that all-important beachfront. It is open from 8am-10.30pm daily, Saturday for women and children only. Admission costs Dh5.

Al-Safa Park on al-Wasl Road is open 8am-11pm daily, though Tuesday is for women and children only. The place is packed on Fridays with families out barbecuing and enjoying the funfair. There are stalls selling herbs, patchwork quilts, Kashmiri shawls and Pulkari clothes. There is also a boating lake, large areas of lawns, ponds and gardens and this is a great place to take a picnic and watch the other inhabitants of the emirate.

Dubai Zoo

If you are interested in animals then Dubai Zoo on Jumairah Beach Road is worth a visit. It houses over 1000 animals including some of the endangered species of the Arabian Peninsula such as the Arabian Wolf and the Lappet-faced Vulture. It is open daily from 10am-6.30pm, closed Tuesday.

Further Afield

HATTA

Hatta, nestling in the Hajar mountains and part of the Dubai emirate, is about 100km southeast of Dubai city and definitely worth a trip out. The main reason for going there is to see **Hatta Pools**, **Hatta dam**, the **fort** and the **heritage village**. The road to Hatta passes through Omani territory but you do not need a visa to visit. However, if you are using a hire car you should make sure that the insurance covers you for driving on Omani soil. On the way out to Hatta you will pass some of the most dramatic desert scenery in Dubai, a large area of sand dunes and home to a 100 metre high dune known as **Big Red** -- just right for a spot of sand skiing, dune driving or just striking suitable desert explorer poses. As the road climbs above sea level the landscape changes into mountain and wadi scenery before arriving at Hatta.

Hatta Pools

South of the main town and officially over the border in Oman (though you don't need a visa to visit them) are canyons scoured out of the wadi bed and there is usually water in them year round. Unless there has been heavy rainfall getting to the pools presents no problem in a saloon car but exploring the surrounding area calls for a 4WD. The other main sights of Hatta are the **heritage village**, which recreates a traditional pre-oil boom mountain village and **Hatta Fort**, which dates back to 1790 and is the oldest fort in Dubai.

The only hotel in the area is the rather luxurious *Hatta Fort Hotel* (04-852 3211; fax 04-852 3561). The hotel is a very popular weekend retreat for many Dubai residents and offers many sports facilities including archery, tennis, a very good golf course, horse riding and a swimming pool. Rooms are in individual chalet style accommodation and mountain and desert safaris can be arranged. Obviously all this luxury comes with a hefty price tag. Rooms start at Dh450 (£88/$120) plus taxes.

Al-Maha Desert Resort

This rather tasteful resort lies 55km from Dubai and is set in its own 27 square kilometre nature reserve. Guests stay in one of the 30 'Bedouin tent' suites with views out over the desert. The inspiration for the layout of the 'camp' came from an old Thesiger photograph of Liwa oases in Abu Dhabi. On-site activities such as falconry, and horse rides are offered and the surrounding area is sand desert so you will get the full feel of the desert experience but with the added bonus of being able to appreciate it from an air-conditioned room. Rates start from Dh1290 and al-Maha can be contacted on 04-303 4222; www.al-maha.com.

ABU DHABI

Abu Dhabi is the largest of all the Emirates and the richest, with one of the highest per capita incomes in the world. About 85 per cent of the UAE lies in Abu Dhabi and the Emirate holds much of the oil and gas reserves of the country. Its oil reserves are almost on a par with Saudi Arabia and Kuwait and are expected to last for around 200 years at the present rate of consumption. Much of the territory is desert; on the coast salt flats stretch for hundreds of kilometres westwards towards the border with Saudi Arabia. Inland the desert is scrub and rock before giving away to the fantastic 200 metre high dunes around the Liwa Oases. The eastern region is bordered by Oman and the Hajar mountain range. The oasis town of al-Ain, 120km away from the capital is a garden city where many residents of the Emirate own second homes and can return to a more traditional way and pace of life after the hectic thrum of the cities.

Its ruler Sheikh Zayed bin Sultan al-Nahyan, a remarkable man, is also the President of the United Arab Emirates and belongs to the Bani Yas tribe. He has ruled Abu Dhabi since 1966 when he took over the reins of power from his brother Sheikh Shakhbut. Sheikh Zayed is a keen conservationist and sees the greening of the desert as paramount and Abu Dhabi is the greenest of the emirates.

Arrival and Departure

Before the building of the causeway in 1953 anyone wishing to cross over to Abu Dhabi Island from the mainland had to wait for low tide before wading across the channel that separates the two. Now the island is connected to the mainland by the al-Ain and al-Maqta bridges. The airport is about 30km and 30 minutes away from the city centre by car. Bus number 901 runs between the airport and the main bus station on East Road. However, the bus station is quite a way out from the city centre.

City Layout

The capital city of the Emirates lies on an island, with a conglomeration of high rise offices, skyscrapers and wide boulevards making up the grid-lined city centre. Although Abu Dhabi City is very spread out and is impossible to explore on foot, the main commercial area and home of most of the sights runs just inland from the corniche. Most of your ambling in Abu Dhabi can be confined to this area where the fort and the main shops and souks are located.

City Transport

All taxis in Abu Dhabi are metered. The main bus and service taxi station is located south of the city centre on East Street. Buses and taxis run fairly regularly to towns inside the Emirate, especially al-Ain, and to a lesser degree to Liwa. You should have no difficulty getting a shared taxi up to Dubai and from there you can catch minibuses run by Dubai Transport to many other destinations around the UAE.

Accommodation

There are a number of hotels in Abu Dhabi, mostly catering to business travellers rather than backpackers. There is no youth hostel.

The Federal Hotel (tel 02-789 0000; fax 02-794 728) and the *Majestic Hotel* (tel 02-710 000; fax 02-710 011) are next to each other on Sheikh Khalifa bin Zayed Street across from the much more expensive *Forte Grand Hotel*. Both hotels offer decent rooms in a central location from Dh200 (£39/$54).

The *Hotel Inter-Continental* (tel 02-666 888; fax 02-669 153) has good sea views from its position on the western end of the corniche.

A couple of good hotels with sea views are the *Mina Hotel* (tel 02-781 000; fax 02-

791 000) and the *Hotel Regency* (tel 02-765 000; fax 02-777 446), both on the eastern end of the corniche near to the *Sheraton Hotel* (tel 02-773 333; fax 02-725 149).

The cheapest place in town is still the *Zakher Hotel* (tel 02-275 300; fax 02-272 270) on Umm an-Nar Street near Capital Gardens in the centre of town.

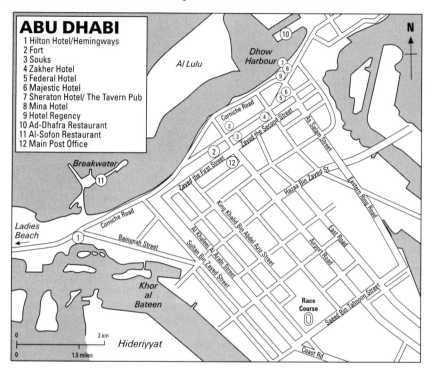

ABU DHABI

1 Hilton Hotel/Hemingways
2 Fort
3 Souks
4 Zakher Hotel
5 Federal Hotel
6 Majestic Hotel
7 Sheraton Hotel/ The Tavern Pub
8 Mina Hotel
9 Hotel Regency
10 Ad-Dhafra Restaurant
11 Al-Sofon Restaurant
12 Main Post Office

Eating and Drinking

Many of the hotels have themed cuisine nights and are the only places where you will be served alcohol with a meal. There are plenty of restaurants in Abu Dhabi and a full listing can be found in the locally published *Abu Dhabi Explorer* and *What's On* magazine.

The most famous eatery in Abu Dhabi is the *al-Sofon* fish restaurant out on the breakwater which has beautiful views back towards the city. At the other, eastern end of the corniche is the *ad-Dhafra* restaurant in the dhow harbour which offers evening cruises accompanied by dinner. *Hemingways*, at the Hilton Hotel on the western end of the corniche offers jazz with your South American meal.

Shopping

Abu Dhabi's ambience is more that of an office than a bazaar and it has far less souks, malls and supermarkets than Dubai or Sharjah. If you are looking for a bargain or choice then you really would do better to shop in Dubai.

What little remains of the old souk is in a pedestrianised area on either side of Sheikh Khalifa bin Zayed Street near Ittihad Square. The shops here aren't selling anything you can't find elsewhere in the Emirates but it's interesting to watch other foreigners looking around for bargains.

Books. Though not as well served as Dubai, Abu Dhabi has several good bookshops – the best of which is *All Prints Bookstore* on al-Nasr Street.

ENTERTAINMENT

Nightlife

Abu Dhabi's nightlife is less hectic than in neighbouring Dubai but there are still many hotel bars and nightclubs to cater for those that want to rock. *The Tavern* is an English pub in the Sheraton Hotel and for that Oirish night out check out *Finnegans* in the Grande Forte. Again, for a complete run down of what's on offer check out the *Abu Dhabi Explorer* and *What's On* magazine.

Horseracing

Racing takes place at the *Equestrian Club* (tel 02-445 5500) in the Embassy district of the city close to Mushrif Palace, and at *Ghantoot Racing and Polo Club* (tel 02-562 9050) 45 minutes' drive from Abu Dhabi on the highway to Dubai. Racing starts at 7pm on Thursdays, four times a month during the racing season

Camel Racing. The camel racetrack is at al-Wathba, 40 km east of the city on the road to al-Ain. Races take place during the winter season.

Golf. Abu Dhabi has several golf clubs, the best is the *Abu Dhabi Golf and Equestrian Club* (tel 02-445 9600) next to the racecourse on Sayed bin Tahnoon Street near the Mushrif Palace.

Running. If you fancy a run during your stay in the Emirate the *Abu Dhabi Island Hash House Harriers* can be contacted on 02-650 163.

EXPLORING

Abu Dhabi, though in many ways more traditional than Dubai, lacks 'sights'. The oldest building in the city is the **Fort**, the former palace of Sheikh Zayed who lived here until moving to the opulent Presidential Palace on Ras al-Akhdar in 1972. The fort was originally built in 1763 to guard the freshwater well – water being a very precious commodity in the arid Gulf. The fort stands on Khalid bin al-Waleed Street and is now a centre for documentation and research. It is open to the visitors from 7.30am-1.30pm Saturday to Wednesday, and 7.30am-noon on Thursdays.

Sheikh Zayed Heritage Village

The Heritage Village is located on the outskirts of the city near the sports centre between the coast and the airport roads, and has been created as a living heritage museum. A souk is held there on Fridays and there are often celebrations staged here during public holidays of folk songs, poetry and dancing.

The Breakwater

The Breakwater is a pleasant place to wander along and look back at the high-rise skyline of Abu Dhabi. It is reached by turning right at the Hilton Hotel roundabout on the western end of the corniche. It has a few parks and promenades and a large Landmark shopping mall is in the process of being built there.

Petroleum Exhibition

For those who are interested in the history of oil discovery in the region the Petroleum exhibition (tel 02-269 715) located on the eastern end of the corniche near the Admo-Opco complex may be of interest. The exhibition houses aerial photographs of the region and explores the discovery of oil.

Beaches

The best beaches in Abu Dhabi are located in front of the five-star hotels on the coast and all charge for day membership. However, for women there is the **Ladies Beach** located on Ras al-Akhdar near the Presidential Palace which is enclosed by a wall and is the domain of ladies and children under ten only. It is open 1-6pm, Saturday to Wednesday; noon-6pm on Thursday and 10am-6pm on Fridays.

Further Afield

LIWA

It takes between two and three hours to reach Liwa from Abu Dhabi and though much of the trip is through monotonous flat desert the oases at the end of it are worth all the trouble in the world to get to. Liwa is a semicircular strip of villages spread over 150km amid the dunes on the edge of the Empty Quarter. The area's secret is the abundance of fresh water that lies only a metre or so below the surface of some of the highest dunes in the world.

Travelling from Abu Dhabi, fill up with petrol before heading out on the drive to Tarif that takes you through miles of flat *sabkha* desert. If you are coming from Dubai on the highway make for **al-Mafraq** at the first roundabout you come to, then at the next head for **Tarif** otherwise you will end up going all the way to Abu Dhabi. There are no petrol stations until Tarif – 130km west of Abu Dhabi – where there are also several tea shop/restaurants, grocery shops and recovery garages. At Tarif take the turning signposted for **Madinat Zayed** and **Habsham**. Once you have passed Madinat Zayed you will be nearing Liwa. The road between the villages of **Muzair'a** and **Hameem** at either end of the Liwa crescent is a fast four-lane highway with steep descents and inclines past farms and dramatic dunescapes. A tarmac road runs past Hameem in the east far out into the desert and you can drive on until you run out of petrol or you lose your nerve. There is nothing out there for miles except rolling dunes and loneliness.

The place to stay is the *Liwa Hotel and Restaurant* (tel 02-8822075), which is run by the *Abu Dhabi National Hotels Company* (the closest thing that the Emirate has to a Tourist Board) and is located off a roundabout on the road to the village of **Arad** on the western edge of the oases. The rooms are large with en suite bathrooms, television and fridge and cost Dh165 (£32/$45) for a double room including breakfast. The hotel is often full at weekends so book ahead. The restaurant serves the usual mix of Indian and international dishes and is cheap.

There is also a new hotel reaching completion high up on a dune near the Liwa Hotel. Confusingly also named the *Liwa Hotel*, there are signs up to it but at the time of research the hotel was still not in operation. When it is, it will be a five-star luxurious establishment in a breath-taking location. On the road to Arad there is a graded track on the right which runs far into the dunes and would be a good place to camp.

Buses and shared taxis run to Liwa from Abu Dhabi, though it is likely that you will need to take a bus to Medinat Zayed and take a bus or taxi on to the oases from there. Because the area is so spread out it is definitely worth hiring a car to explore this region rather than relying on public transport.

AL-AIN

Al-Ain is about a 90 minute drive from Abu Dhabi along a fast highway. It is the birthplace of Sheikh Zayed who, until he became ruler of the Emirate was Governor of this eastern region. Al-Ain is the second city of the Emirate and has had a lot of money spent on it. It is a place of parks, tree-lined streets and date palms lying in the shadow of the 1,340 metre high **Jebal Hafit**. It is also on the border with Oman and the Omani town of **Buraimi** practically joins with al-Ain City. You do not need a visa to travel between the two towns and the juxtaposition between the richer al-Ain and the more traditional Buraimi makes a trip out to this oasis well worth it. Omani riyals and Emirati dirhams are interchangeable in the area.

Al-Ain Museum is open 8am-1pm and 3.30-5.30pm Sunday to Wednesday; 8am-noon and 4.30-6.30pm on Thursday; 9-11.30am and 4.30-6.30pm on Friday. There is a purpose built museum housing exhibits next to **Eastern Fort** – the birthplace of Sheikh Zayed. The museum features exhibits of local natural history and of the archaeological excavations that have taken place in the vicinity. The museum is located on the Zayed bin Sultan Road just past the Coffeepot roundabout.

There is also a **camel souk** that takes place in neighbouring Buraimi just off al-Masoudi Street to the north of the town that is worth a look to get a closer view of the beasts. The souk is open daily in the early mornings and then again in the late afternoons.

The area around al-Ain has a number of important archaeological associations – the region having been inhabited since the 3rd millennium BC. An important site can be seen about 8km to the north of al-Ain at the **Hili Archaeological Gardens** which are open daily from 4-11pm. Inside the gardens is a very beautifully reconstructed tomb dating from between BC3200-3000. Discovered by Danish archaeologists in 1963, it was restored by an Iraqi team in 1973.

There are several hotels in al-Ain, all of them five-star establishments. A cheaper place to stay is at the *Rest House* (tel 03-838 333; fax 03-838 900) about 10km south of the town. It is in **Ain al-Faydah** which is a resort complex based around mineral springs. Rooms cost from Dh110 (£22/$30).

SHARJAH

If Abu Dhabi is the seat of government and Dubai the commercial hub of the UAE, then Sharjah is indisputably the capital of culture within the Emirates. In fact, in 1998 UNESCO declared Sharjah the cultural capital of the Arab world due to its commitment to traditional culture, the arts and learning.

Sharjah is the third largest of the Emirates with a population of around 500,000 and acts as something of a dormitory town to its neighbour Dubai. It has territory on both the west and east coasts including the important port of Khor Fakkan, and it was the location of the first international airport of all the Emirates. Sharjah (it should really be called *Sharqah* if you transliterate from the Arabic) has a free zone and a busy port as well as two thirds of the Emirates' industry. It is a success in every way. However, because of Sharjah's total ban on both the consumption of alcohol and the smoking of shishas many visitors go to Sharjah on a day trip for the shopping and heritage sites while staying in the hotels of Dubai. Sharjah has a dedicated website at www.sharjah-welcome.com.

The ruler of Sharjah is Dr Sheikh Sultan bin Mohammed al-Qassimi. He came to power after the death of his brother in 1972. He is a member of the Huwalah tribe.

City Layout

Sharjah City is rather sprawling and finding the right road in and out of it can take some time due to the paucity of road signage. The main areas that visitors will want to see are along the **corniche** road where there is the **dhow wharfage**, the various **souks** and the views over the busy port. Many of the hotels are located on a spit of land that juts out into the Gulf, connected to the rest of the city by Sharjah Bridge. In the centre of town, **Rolla Square** is a large area of lawns, trees and a couple of fountains where the locals come to meet and lie about in the shade of the trees playing cards or calling meetings. It's a great place to people watch. Another interesting place for a stroll if it's not too hot is the area by the port and the dhow wharfs which is always full of activity, more so than in Dubai, and also more accessible.

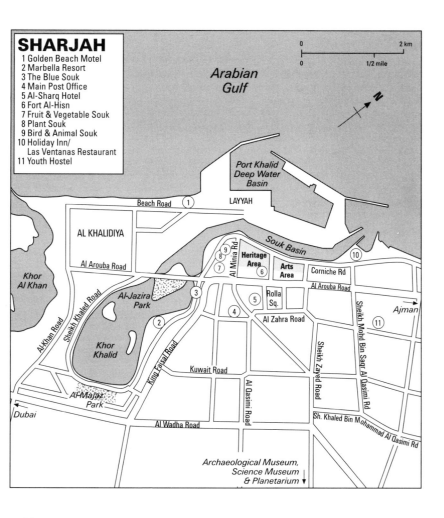

SHARJAH

1 Golden Beach Motel
2 Marbella Resort
3 The Blue Souk
4 Main Post Office
5 Al-Sharq Hotel
6 Fort Al-Hisn
7 Fruit & Vegetable Souk
8 Plant Souk
9 Bird & Animal Souk
10 Holiday Inn/
   Las Ventanas Restaurant
11 Youth Hostel

Arabian Gulf

Port Khalid Deep Water Basin

Beach Road

LAYYAH

AL KHALIDIYA

Al Arouba Road

Khor Al Khan

Souk Basin

Heritage Area

Arts Area

Corniche Rd

Al Arouba Road

Al-Khan Road

Sheikh Khaled Road

Al-Jazira Park

Khor Khalid

Al Minia Rd

Rolla Sq.

Al Zahra Road

Ajman

King Faisal Road

Kuwait Road

Sheikh Zayed Road

Al Qasimi Road

Sheikh Mohd Bin Saqr Al Qasimi Rd

Al-Majaz Park

Dubai

Al Wadha Road

Sh. Khaled Bin Mohammad Al Qasimi Rd

Archaeological Museum, Science Museum & Planetarium ▼

There is no municipal bus service in Sharjah and therefore you will have to rely on taxis to get around the city or walk. Luckily the sites of most interest to the visitor are in a relatively compact area, and apart from in the heat of mid summer exploring on foot is entirely feasible. Taxis and minibuses arriving from Dubai drop off near Rolla Square opposite al-Hisn Fort. Shared taxis back to Dubai leave from the Clock Tower side of Rolla Square.

ACCOMMODATION

There are a large number of hotels but most of these are out of the budget traveller's league. Unless you are after a quiet nightlife, you are better off staying where the action is in Dubai (and the cheapest hotels in the Emirates) and day tripping it to Sharjah.

Youth Hostel. The Youth Hostel (tel 06-522 5070) is located in a two-storey villa on al-Zahra Road just down from Sheikh Abdullah bin Ali al-Mahmoud Square. A bed costs Dh35 (£6.80/$9.50) per night in segregated dorms.

Hotels

The *al-Sharq Hotel* (tel 06-562 0000; fax 06-562 0011) on Rolla Square is in the heart of things and charges Dh120/180 (£23-35/$33-49) per night. Its central location makes it a convenient place to base oneself. Front rooms have views over the square and there is a restaurant.

There are a lot of large beach resort hotels along al-Mina (Beach) Road away from the centre of town charging between Dh350-Dh600 for a double room. *The Golden Beach Motel* (tel 06-528 1331; fax 06-528 1151) is at the end of this road and is smaller than the rest of the complexes with a private beach and self-catering chalets.

If you want to push the boat out a bit and mix it with the Sharjah in-crowd then try the *Marbella Resort* (tel 06-574 111; fax 06-572 6050) which is a large Spanish-style complex located on the edge of Khalid Lagoon. It has several restaurants serving international food and is very popular.

Other Options

If you are planning to stay for a week or so, there are several places that offer short-term furnished accommodation which tend to work out cheaper than hotels. Try *al-Buhairah Residence*, situated close to Khalid Lagoon (tel 06-556 2818; fax 06-556 2633; www.basmaa.com) or *al-Khalidiya Residence* (tel 06-528 6057; fax 06-528 4898), opposite al-Khan Lagoon. Both these places charge around Dh250 (£68/$95) per night but prices fall depending on how long you intend to stay.

EATING AND DRINKING

Although alcohol, shisha smoking and pork are banned in Sharjah there are still quite a number of very good restaurants to serve those residents and visitors who don't need a drink with their hallal meal. Apart from the hotel restaurants there are also places serving Italian, Continental, Mexican, Far Eastern, Middle Eastern and seafood. A couple worth trying are:

Las Ventanas (tel 06-537 1111) at the *Holiday Inn* in al-Seef is the only Mexican restaurant in Sharjah and worth exploring for its hot fajitas.

The Sanobar Restaurant (06-528 3501) on al-Khan Road is a privately run seafood restaurant that pulls in a mixed crowd of locals and tourists from the hotels that line the beach road.

There are also a number of bakeries, coffeehouses and street stalls to choose from. Explore.

Sharjah has a great many souks scattered throughout the city centre, from the huge barn-like *Blue Souk* to the small, beautifully restored *al-Arsah Souk* as well as the fish, plant, fruit and vegetable souks. These souks are among the best places to hunt for souvenirs in the Emirates.

The Blue Souk

The Blue Souk (also known as the Central Souk) is beside Khalid Lagoon near al-Ittihad Square and is difficult to miss because of the vastness of the place. With over 600 shops on two floors the Blue Souk is probably the best place to go souvenir hunting in the Gulf. It consists of two long buildings running parallel that are connected by walkways. The architecture is really quite breathtaking with a series of wind towers running along the structure to keep the shops well aired, and a façade of blue mosaic and arabesque. The souk is so big and the shops so many that the interior is a bit like some Aladdin's cave with carpets and 'antiques' a speciality – especially on the upper floors. The ground floor shops tend to stock electrical goods and the usual oddments seen in markets all round the Gulf. The souk is open daily from 9am-1pm and 4-11pm. On Fridays the shops are closed in the morning but open in the late afternoon till late in the evening.

Souk al-Arsah

Souk al-Arsah, across from the dhow wharves on Corniche Road, is perhaps the most evocative of all the souks in the Gulf with the exception of Muscat souk. Recently restored using traditional building materials of palm, coral and gypsum, the narrow alleyway of the souk is home to a number of antique shops, the last of the Gulf pearl traders, and a coffee house where you can rest and contemplate that next purchase. Opening times are as the Blue Souk.

Bird and Animal Souk

Though it is unlikely that you will be wanting to buy any livestock while on holiday, the bird and animal souk is definitely worth a visit if only to take a look at the falcons that sit hunched on perches waiting to be carried away. Located behind the *Eppco* garage on al-Mina Street, the market is divided into two areas: livestock and pets. You won't see any dogs or cats here (considered unclean animals to the Muslim) but the large variety of birds on sale from ducklings dyed a shocking pink to large falcons and macaws make it an interesting trip. The livestock available range from goats to sheep to camels and the place can get quite chaotic when the farmers are bringing in their beasts for sale.

The Plant Souk

The Plant Souk, just up from the Bird and Animal Souk on Corniche Road beside the Creek, has shrubbery, plants and pots of all sizes and types for sale – just the thing if you are planning to stay a while or looking for a suitable souvenir of your trip out East.

The fish and fruit and vegetable markets are also in this area and wandering about them makes you understand why Sharjah is considered to be the most heritage conscious of all the Emirates. This is Gulf life as it has been lived for hundreds of years.

Souk al-Majarra

This souk is easy to spot by its distinctive gold dome on the Corniche Road. With over 50 shops, if you can't find what you are looking for in the Blue Souk then this is the place to go.

Books

Sharjah's best bookshop is the *Book Mall* on al-Khan Road. This spacious bookshop cum coffeeshop is designed as a literary hang-out with books available in Arabic, French and English and a good selection of titles on the Gulf and the rest of the Middle East.

GALLERIES AND MUSEUMS

The Arts Area

Art is very important in Sharjah and a draw for artists from all over the UAE. The Arts Area is in al-Shuwaiheyen where five old town houses have been restored and now house the art centres and galleries that Sharjah has become renowned for.

Sharjah Art Museum

Sharjah Art Museum (tel 06-551 1222) is open daily from 9am-1pm and again from 5-8pm, 5-9pm on Fridays. Located within the Arts Area and opened in 1997 at a cost of Dh20 million, this is the largest art museum in the Gulf, three storeys high and home to the personal collection of the ruler, Dr Sheikh Sultan al-Qassimi. There are a number of paintings, lithographs and watercolours by 18th century Orientalist painters such as the great **David Roberts** depicting life in the Middle East, as well as prints of 19th century battles between the British and the local resistance forces led by the al-Qassimis. Local and international artists also frequently exhibit here. Sculpture is also shown at the museum and there is a bookshop, cafeteria and an international reference library for the use of scholars.

Sharjah Art Institute

Across the road from the Art Museum the Sharjah Art Institute has had a colourful history, being at one time or another an American Missionary hospital, the home to the present ruler's father, and before that the home of the British Commissioner's agent for the coast of Oman. Today the building serves as a centre to promote and to teach art, sculpture, pottery etc., in the Emirates.

Nearby there are several art galleries and studios including **Bait Obaid al-Shamsi** where artists from all over the world come to stay and work. Several other restored houses in this area are used by artists as places to work and to exhibit, creating a supportive environment for a part of the Arab culture that is often under-funded and underexposed. **The Very Special Arts House** is dedicated to disabled artists where there is a gallery exhibiting the works created there. An **Arts Café** (open daily 5-7pm) in the other half of this house opposite the Art Institute, is a traditional coffee house and the nearby square is often used by local artists who come out to paint in the cool of the evenings.

On the opposite side of Hisn Avenue to the Arts Area is **Arts Square**, which focuses on the performing arts. This area has also been renovated and the buildings here house the **Sharjah Institute of Theatrical Arts** (call 06-552 1333 to find out the latest productions), the **House of Poetry** (which has a library of over 6000 books and is open to the public), and the **Emirates' Writers' Union**.

Sharjah Archaeological Museum

The museum (tel 06-536 6466) is open daily 9am-1pm and 5-8pm; Friday 5-8pm; Monday ladies only; closed Sunday. It is a fair distance away from the other central sights – near Cultural Square and the Science Museum. The Archaeological Museum is housed in a modern building with hi-tech educational facilities for the schoolchildren who are regularly brought here from all over the country. The museum has displays and exhibits of the archaeological finds from over the years and explains the development of this part of the world from BC5000-600AD. There are exhibits from sites from all over the Arabian Peninsula as well as from the personal collection of the present ruler, Dr Sheikh Sultan al-Qassimi.

The Sharjah Science Museum and Planetarium

This museum (tel 06-551 4777) is near the Archaeological Museum and Cultural Square and is a great place to go either alone or with kids. It also makes a change from visiting heritage museums while in the region. With over 40 exhibits the Science Museum is a hands-on interactive place where you can learn about such things as cryogenics, light, electricity and all things extraterrestrial. All exhibits are in English and Arabic and there are special learning sections for kids under 5 years old. Admission to the Science Museum costs Dh5 (£0.98/$1.36) and it is open Saturday to Tuesday 9am-2pm; Wednesday to Friday 3.30-8.30pm.

Sharjah Fort

The al-Hisn Fort (tel 06-537 5500) was originally built in 1820 as a residence for the ruler of Sharjah. The fort fell into grave disrepair before being saved by the present ruler Sheikh Sultan, who set about its restoration in 1996 with the help of old photographs and the reminiscences of local people to recreate the design accurately. The immaculately reconstructed two-storeyed fort is now home to a museum that chronicles both the history of the fort and of Sharjah through themed rooms, videos and, should you wish to hire them, guides. The fort is located on Hisn Avenue, which separates the Arts Area from the Heritage Area and is clearly visible from Rolla Square. It is open Tuesday to Sunday 9am-1pm and 5-8pm, Friday 5-8pm, closed Monday.

The Heritage Museum

The Heritage Museum (tel 06-551 2999) is open Sunday to Thursday 9am-1pm and 5-8pm; Friday 5-8pm; closed Monday, and is situated in the Heritage Area. Once the two-storey home of the al-Naboudah family, this building recreates the living conditions of how that family would have lived 150 years ago. A guide accompanies you through the various themed rooms.

PARKS

Sharjah City has several parks of various sizes most of which are free to enter. The largest is **al-Majaz Park** located between Khalid Lagoon and Gamal Abdul Nasser Street at the southern end of the Lagoon. It is open daily from 4-11pm and 10am-midnight on Fridays. Another, **al-Jazira Park** is on an island opposite the Blue Souk over which Sharjah Bridge runs. It is the only park that charges admission and is open daily from 3.30-10.30pm and practically all day on Fridays. The park has a mini-train that takes you around the park and there are funfairs, a swimming pool and several fairground rides. Entry costs Dh5 for adults and Dh2 for kids.

Sharjah Natural History Museum and Desert Park

The Museum and Park (tel 06-531 1411) are located on the highway heading north out of Sharjah towards the town of al-Dhaid past Sharjah Airport – about 28km from Sharjah City. Open Saturday to Wednesday 9am-7pm, Thursday noon-7pm, Friday 2-8pm, the Museum has five exhibit halls which take you through the miracles of the natural world. Completed in 1995, the Museum covers *The Natural History of the Emirate, Man and His Environment, A Journey Through Time, The Story of Oil* and *The Living Sea*. Exhibits are mechanical and interactive. There is also a **botanical garden** and the Desert Park is the home of the famous *Arabian Leopard Trust* and a breeding centre for endangered Arabian wildlife.

Sharjah also has an important **National Park** of 630,000 square metres with well-maintained lawns and trees; an oasis of green in an arid stretch of the Emirates. The park is open 4-10pm daily and 10am-10pm on Thursday, Friday and public holidays. The National Park is signposted at intersection number 5 on the Sharjah to al-Dhaid highway and is well worth a visit.

Beaches

Sharjah City has several strips of beach, the best of which runs along the front of the beachside hotels from al-Khan to the Golden Beach Motel near Port Khalid. The second strip of beach runs along the corniche near the Coral Beach Hotel. Elsewhere, due to the shelter they provide from the wind, the lagoons are often used for water skiing and jet skiing.

AJMAN

Ajman, with a total area of 260 square kilometres, is the smallest of the seven Emirates and at only 10km from Sharjah the buildings of the two Emirates practically merge into each other along the coast. There are also two Ajmani enclaves in the interior, both of which are southeast of the main territory: Masfut, 100km away in the foothills of the Hajar mountain range near Hatta and the Omani border, and Manama, a fertile date growing region 60km away from Ajman City.

With the exception of pearling, the traditional industries of fishing and dhow building continue in Ajman and the waterfront and port is one of the busiest in the world – repairing ships and supplying offshore oilrigs. Unlike many of the other emirates, oil production was found to be uneconomical on Ajman's territory. The Ajman free zone was set up in 1995 allowing 100 per cent foreign ownership of businesses within its confines, tax exemption and no import or export duties among other benefits. It has proved very successful in attracting international companies in spite of the emirate's small size. Ajman has good white sandy beaches and one of the most luxurious hotel/resort complexes in the country. It also has a very good shopping mall.

The ruler of Ajman is Sheikh Humaid bin Rashid al-Nuaimi who came to power after the death of his father in September 1981. Ajman's ruler is a member of the Naim tribe who also inhabit al-Ain, the oasis town some 150 kilometres away in Abu Dhabi emirate.

City Layout

Ajman centre is small and due to the relative paucity of 'sights' you probably won't spend much time looking around. The **museum** and the **dhow yards** are interesting and you can get a drink in the hotels and some of the restaurants. The activities on the wharves are also worth a look.

Because Ajman is so close to Sharjah and Dubai (Dubai is an hour away by road), it is becoming a dormitory town with people commuting daily to the larger cities. There is no municipal bus service within Ajman and although you can pick up a minibus to Ajman from Dubai you will be restricted to taxis to get you around the town and away again.

Accommodation

There are several plush hotels on the beach road (Arabian Gulf Street) such as the *Ajman Beach Hotel* (06-742 3333; fax 06-742 3363) which play host to package holiday makers and unless you need to stay in Ajman you will find much cheaper rooms in Dubai. However, the sea views are pleasant and the town beach is one of the best in the Emirates.

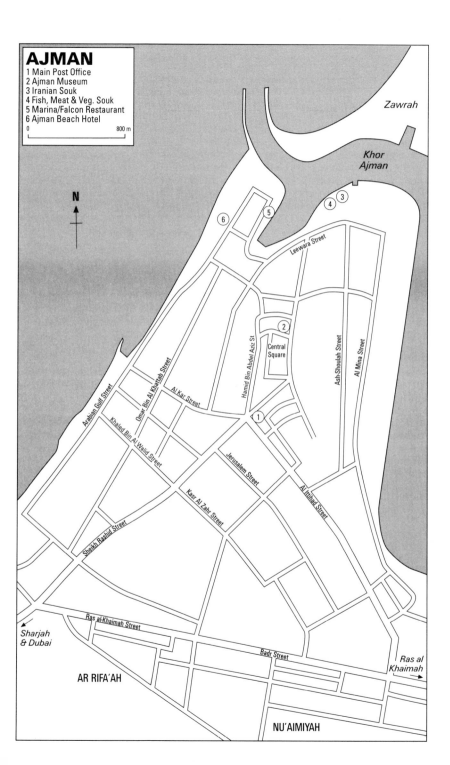

AJMAN

1 Main Post Office
2 Ajman Museum
3 Iranian Souk
4 Fish, Meat & Veg. Souk
5 Marina/Falcon Restaurant
6 Ajman Beach Hotel

0   800 m

N

Zawrah

Khor
Ajman

Leewara Street

Central
Square

Ash-Shoulah Street

Al Mina Street

Arabian Gulf Street

Omar Bin Al Khattab Street

Al Kar Street

Khaled Bin Al Walid Street

Hamid Bin Abdel Aziz St

Jerusalem Street

Kasr Al Zahr Street

Al Ittihad Street

Sheikh Rashid Street

Ras al-Khaimah Street

Badr Street

Sharjah
& Dubai

Ras al
Khaimah

AR RIFA'AH

NU'AIMIYAH

The relatively new five-star *Ajman Kempinski Hotel and Resort* (06-745 1555; fax 06-745 1222; www.ajman.kempinski.com) is located on Arabian Gulf Road, has four restaurants serving food from around the world, a bar and a beach club.

Eating and Drinking

Aside from the usual small Indian eateries around town there is the *Falcon Restaurant and Bar* in the Marina which serves decent food with a view over the small harbour. On Leewara Street, across the road from the fishing boats, is a traditional café serving Turkish coffee and *shisha*. It's a hang-out for the local fishermen and the owner is an Arab – which makes a change. There are a number of fast food restaurants in the Ajman *City Centre Shopping Mall* on the main Emirates Highway just outside Ajman and quite close to the Dhow yards.

EXPLORING

Ajman Museum

Ajman Museum, located by the Clock Tower Roundabout and Central Square, is open 9am-1pm and 4-7pm Saturday to Wednesday, 4-7pm on Friday, closed Thursday. Housed in a beautiful fort that until the 1970s served as the residence of the present Emir's father, the museum is one of the best of its kind in the region covering life and traditions in the Emirate and an interesting exhibit of passports that were once issued by the Ajmani government.

Dhow Yards

Ajman is well known for its dhow yards where traditional methods are still used in their construction. To get a good look at the yards follow the coast road round from Leewara Street towards the Emirates Highway and look for a sign to *al-Boom Marine* on Tariq bin Zayed Street. Ask if you can go in to take a look around.

There are 5km of **wharfage** in Ajman and although much of it is out of bounds to the casual visitor there is an open area up from the Marina off Leewara Street where there are tug boats tied up, an **Iranian Souk** and the **fish, meat and vegetable souks**. Definitely worth a look. The beaches, tourist resorts, and most of the hotels can be found on Arabian Gulf Street.

UMM AL-QUWAIN

Umm al-Quwain (UAQ) is the second smallest of the Emirates with an estimated population of around 40,000. Umm al-Quwain City lies on a spit of land that curves round a large lagoon off the main Emirates Highway between Ajman and Ras al-Khaimah. The Emirate extends east from here and includes a region of fertile land around Falaj al-Mualla used for agriculture and raising poultry, and several important archaeological sites. Off the coast of UAQ is the island of **as-Siniyyah** which was home to the original settlers until the water supply dried up. It is now a **wildlife sanctuary** home to waders, turtles and dugongs (sea cows), and the private retreat of the ruling family.

Like Ajman, UAQ hasn't benefited from its own natural resources but has received help from the richer emirates. Umm al-Quwain in a quiet place, without the construction boom of other emirates and it can seem a very sleepy place in the afternoons when there are more cows than inhabitants wandering about the land between the harbour and the sea. Fishing is the main industry of UAQ though there is a small port and free trade zone and some light industry.

The main attractions in and around UAQ are the Museum, the long stretch of

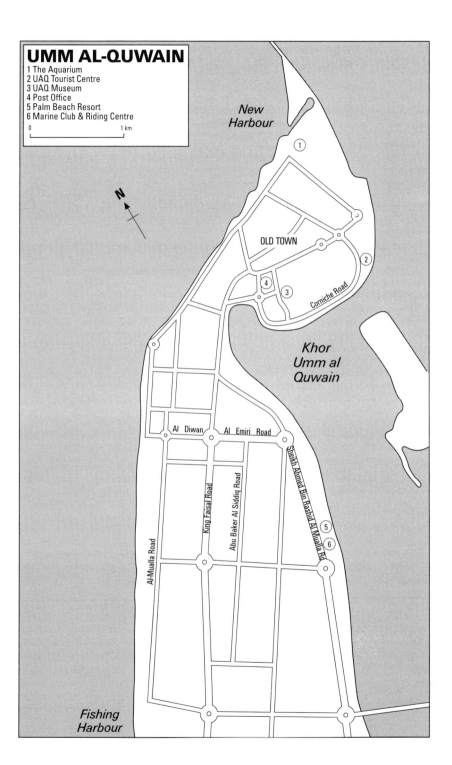

UMM AL-QUWAIN

1 The Aquarium
2 UAQ Tourist Centre
3 UAQ Museum
4 Post Office
5 Palm Beach Resort
6 Marine Club & Riding Centre

0   1 km

N

New
Harbour

①

OLD TOWN

②

④
③

Corniche Road

Khor
Umm al
Quwain

Al Diwan   Al Emiri Road

Sheikh Ahmed Bin Rashid Al Mualla Rd

King Faisal Road

Abu Baker Al Siddiq Road

Al-Mualla Road

⑤
⑥

Fishing
Harbour

dune-backed beach and the surrounding mangrove swamps which attract winter migrants and are a favoured spot with local ornithologists.

The ruler of Umm al-Quwain is Sheikh Rashid bin Ahmed al-Mualla who became ruler upon the death of his father in 1981. He is one of the al-Ali tribe.

City Layout

Umm al-Quwain is situated on a spit of land. To reach the old town and the sea you need to turn off the Emirates Highway and drive over a fair number of roundabouts and past the modern shopping area. The centre of town is very quiet and today feels very much like a little India with all the trappings of an Indian town. The west coast of the spit is an area of low sea dunes and marram grass, of seawall fortified by huge boulders. There are also several watchtowers along Mualla Road towards the Aquarium. The eastern, corniche side of the spit is an old-fashioned fishing village.

Umm al-Quwain does not have a bus service. You can get to UAQ from Dubai by minibus but you will have to take a taxi to get around and away from the town. The taxi rank is some way out from the more interesting older part of town.

Accommodation

The Umm al-Quwain Tourist Centre (06-765 0000; fax 06-765 0001) is located on the edge of the old part of town beside the fishing village. It is by the sea, close to the lagoon, and is a pretty much self-contained place offering **water sports**, **fishing** (day and night) **dhow cruises** and it has a licensed bar and restaurant. There is also a swimming pool. Rooms cost from Dh350 (£68/$95) for a double with the usual television, fridge and en suite bathroom.

The Palm Beach Resort (06-766 7090) is on the edge of the lagoon next to the Marine Club and Riding Centre on Rashid al-Mualla Road. Rooms are in self-contained portacabins.

Eating and Drinking. Umm al-Quwain isn't known as a gastronome's destination and you are limited in terms of choice. There are plenty of small Asian eateries and the big hotels have restaurants.

EXPLORING

Umm al-Quwain Museum

The recently opened museum is housed in an old fort by the lagoon that until recently was the police post. It is situated by the roundabout and is open from 9am-1pm and 5-8pm and on Friday from 5-9pm. It is closed on Monday and on Tuesdays is open for women only. Next to the museum are several ruins of the **old town** originally constructed from blocks cut from coral. The nearby **lagoon**, due to its sheltered position, is a popular place from water-skiing.

The Marine Club

You can hire equipment for water sports, or hire a horse, at the *Marine Club and Riding Centre* on Rashid al-Mualla Road (06-665 446) which is run by the ruling family of UAQ. It is best to call and book ahead as the place can get very busy at weekends.

Dreamland Aqua Park

Dreamland Aqua Park (06-768 1888) is on the seafront of UAQ on the Ras al-Khaimah Road. Open daily from 10am-7pm (Fridays are reserved for families only) admission costs Dh40 (£8/$11). Dreamland is one of the largest aqua parks in the world covering an area of over 250,000 square metres and offers rides with frightening names such as *Black Hole* and *Kamikaze*. There are restaurants, cafés, a Jacuzzi bar and plenty of lawns to lie about on. There is also a go-kart track.

The Aquarium. The Aquarium at the *Agriculture and Fisheries Ministry's Marine Research Centre* (06-655881) is located right at the end of the spit and well worth a look if marine creatures are your bag.

Bird watching is best at **Khor al-Baydah** – the area of mangrove between the spit and the mainland – and on **as-Siniyyah island**, permits may be arranged by contacting *al-Diwan al-Amiri* (tel 06-656 125) or the *Emirates Bird Records Committee* in Dubai (04-347 2277).

UAQ Shooting Club (06-768 1900) offers paintballing and the chance to fire a selection of firearms big and small in indoor and outdoor ranges.

UAQ Flying Club (06-768 1737) is about 15 kilometres north of UAQ City on the Emirates Highway towards Ras al-Khaimah near Dreamland Aqua Park. It offers flying lessons, skydiving, and every other thing to do with flying in light aircraft, gliders etc. You can jump out of a plane attached to an instructor for about Dh720 (£141/$196).

RAS AL-KHAIMAH

Ras al-Khaimah emirate is located at the fertile foot of the eastern Hajar Mountains, stretching to the Omani border to the north, and inland towards Fujairah eastwards. Approaching Ras al-Khaimah (RAK) from the south you will see the Hajar mountain range in the distance ahead of you, and then a big area of red sand dunes on either side of the road. This emirate, unlike some of those to the south, has elevations and is quite pretty. Driving through it you will often come across the surprising phenomena of turf farms.

The present ruler is Sheikh Saqr bin Mohammed al-Qassimi who is of the Huwalah tribe. Sheikh Saqr has ruled Ras al-Khaimah since 1948.

City Layout

The town has two separate districts to it: the **old town** with the museum, the souks and many of the ministry buildings, and **al-Nakheel** – the newer commercial district across the Creek. Arriving from the southern emirates on the main highway, if you continue straight on at the Clock Roundabout you will get to the old town; take a right and you will drive down into al-Nakheel. There is a rather bumpy track running alongside the corniche road that makes for a pleasant stroll and the beaches here have very red sand and few people on them. The corniche stretches for several miles and there are some good stretches but it gets increasingly grubby as you get closer to town.

Because of the lack of a bus service in RAK if you haven't arrived in your own vehicle you will need to rely on the unmetered taxis that cruise around looking for a fare. The service taxi rank is a short way out of town on King Faisal Street before the Clock Roundabout and near to the Bin Majid Beach Hotel. You will be able to pick up a ride from here to most other places in the UAE but if you want to share a taxi your waiting time will depend on where you are heading. All destinations southwards should present no problem but less people make trips over to the east coast and you may have to wait some time before your taxi fills up. If you are heading on up to the

Musandam Peninsula in Oman some of the drivers will have the necessary paperwork to be able to drive all the way to the main town of Khasab but others will only be able to take you as far as the border post at ash-Sham. You will need to pay the land departure tax of Dh20 (£3.90/$5.45) when leaving the UAE. If you are travelling to Musandam in a hire vehicle make sure that the insurance covers you for driving in Oman.

Accommodation

If you are feeling particularly flush and fancy a night's stay in a themed 1001 Arabian Nights style hotel/beach resort then the newly opened *al-Hamra Fort Hotel* (07-446 666) may be for you. For around Dh550 (£108/$150) a night you get three restaurants, six kilometres of private beach, a fitness centre and tennis courts among other things. You can't miss the coffee coloured building or signs to the hotel on the way to RAK from Dubai.

The *al-Nakheel Hotel* (07-222 822) on al-Muntasar Street in al-Nakheel is pretty much the cheapest option in town charging from Dh150 (£29/$41) per person per night. It has a pub, the *Churchill*, to recommend it.

The *Bin Majid Beach Hotel* is better placed than the *Bin Majid Beach Resort* but both are expensive costing the equivalent of £50 ($68) per night. If you are staying in RAK you can probably get day membership to use the pool in the Beach Hotel.

The other place to stay is the five-star *Ras al-Khaimah Hotel* (07-352 999) which has a fantastic location on top of a hill overlooking the town.

Eating and Drinking. Apart from the hotel restaurants there are the usual Asian restaurants and a KFC. Ras al-Khaimah is getting more developed and it is very likely that more fine restaurants will be established in the near future.

EXPLORING

National Museum

The National Museum of Ras al-Khaimah is housed in a fort that was the residence of the rulers of RAK from the 19th century until the 1960s. It is open 8am-noon and 4-7pm Wednesday to Monday. Thursday is for women only. The museum is located next to the police station on al-Hosn Road near the clock tower and has displays relating to the natural history, ruling family and archaeology of the Emirate. It also has a working wind tower so you can cool down during your trip through RAK's history. The area around the fort is what remains of the **old town** and the buildings and alleyways are interesting to walk around to get a feel of what it must have once looked like.

Camel Racing

Digdagga is the home of Ras al-Khaimah's camel racetrack. Races occur in the early mornings throughout the winter but check for timings with locals or tour operators. Remember to keep out of the way of the camels and their speeding owners, and trainers.

FURTHER AFIELD

Khatt Springs

Khatt is a very pretty village just on the edge of the mountains with hot springs and places to explore nearby. The surrounding area is very beautiful (especially after the flatlands of the southern emirates) and is a great place to go camping for a few days.

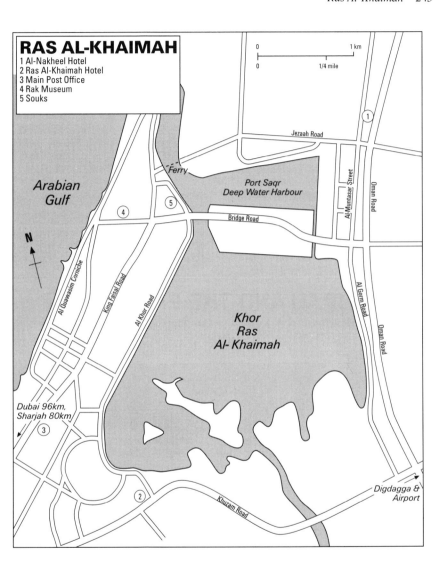

RAS AL-KHAIMAH
1 Al-Nakheel Hotel
2 Ras Al-Khaimah Hotel
3 Main Post Office
4 Rak Museum
5 Souks

The village is on the road that runs from al-Nakheel towards Ras al-Khaimah Airport and onwards through Digdagga to Manama. Driving along this road you will pass the **Saqr Public Park** on you left and shortly afterwards the left turn-off for Khatt. Unfortunately it is not very clearly signposted. Once in Khatt village, turn left at the roundabout – the road then swings round to the hot springs. If you carry on along the road to Manama, where you turn left to head towards the east coast, you will pass some absolutely stunning scenery with high orange **dune fields and mountains** stretching away on either side of the road.

Near the springs are several places to stay. *Ain Khatt Touristic Resort* (07-448 414) has rooms and its own private hot pools. *The Family Resthouse* (07-448 181/2), a few yards away, offers the same. There is also a new, very plush resort next door with bedrooms, restaurant and its own plunge pool that was about to open at the time of research. The official *Khatt Springs Touristic Site* charges Dh3 (£0.59/$0.81) and there are separate pools for men and women. If you are really strapped for cash you could join the locals in other pools around the area.

The Mountains

The road north from Ras al-Khaimah passes under the lee of the Hajar Mountains and is a scenic drive, even when passing the huge cement works that dominate part of this area. **Rams** is a pretty fishing village which was once, back in the times when this part of the world was known as the Pirate Coast, a fairly big harbour. The British fleets attacked it several times in the early 1800s.

Ras al-Khaimah is also the starting (or finishing) point for a **wadi-bash** over the mountains between the east and west coasts, passing through Omani territory and the dramatic scenery of **Wadi Bih**. You will need a reliable 4WD vehicle and an Omani visa to travel this route and should travel in a convoy of at least two vehicles. The route can get washed out and blocked with boulders after rain (it does actually rain up in the mountains here) so be prepared and take the usual precautions with regards to carrying enough fuel, food and water.

FUJAIRAH AND THE EAST COAST

Fujairah established itself as an emirate in 1952 and was the last of the seven to do so, after gaining independence from Sharjah. It is one of the most beautiful of all the Emirates and is a popular place for locals and expats to get away to at weekends with its warm seas, long stretches of empty beaches and mountain/wadi scenery. The main industries of Fujairah are fishing and farming due to the richness of the sea and the soil, which is fed by runoff waters from the Hajar Mountains in the hinterland. Due to its unique location in the UAE (it is the only emirate with no territory on the Arabian Gulf) it has a thriving port and free zone and its international airport is becoming increasingly popular with carriers bringing over package holidaymakers from Europe. It is also the only place outside of Oman where you can watch the spectacle of **bull-butting**. Fujairah is definitely worth a visit and is a pleasant place to relax after the sometimes rather hectic pace of Dubai and Abu Dhabi.

The ruler of Fujairah is Sheikh Hamad bin Mohammed al-Sharqi who took office in 1974 aged 26 upon the death of his father. He is the youngest ruler in the UAE and one of the al-Sharqiyyeen tribe. Sheikh Hamad is a keen environmentalist and has constructed artificial reefs along the coast, which have attracted marine wildlife and with them scuba divers from all over the world.

City Layout

Fujairah City is about 160km from Dubai by road (the scenic drive through the Hajar mountains takes about 90 minutes), and sits on the edge of the Gulf of Oman. Like all the cities in the UAE, the town is a mix of the old and the modern, though Fujairah city retains more of its charm than the steel and concrete charisma of its west coast cousins. The city is rather spread out but unless you are staying for a while, or you are visiting during summer, you are best off parking along the corniche and exploring the surrounding seafront, fort and museum on foot. The other attractions of Fujairah lie in the surrounding countryside.

There is no local bus service in Fujairah emirate so you will have to rely on taxis. There are fixed charges for shared taxis to the main destinations of Dubai, Sharjah, Khor Fakkan and Dibba but you will be in for a spot of bargaining to get to the other sites mentioned below. Bear in mind that you are unlikely to pick up a shared taxi to less in-demand destinations such as Ras al-Khaimah or Umm al-Quwain and will need to negotiate a fee for a taxi ride there.

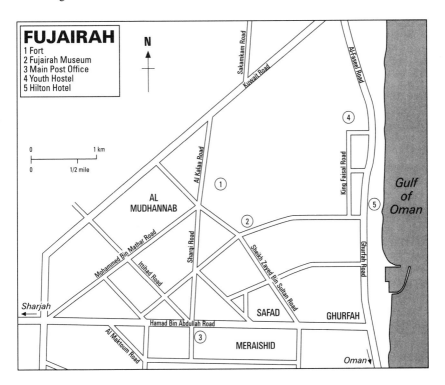

ACCOMODATION

Fujairah is one of the few emirates that has a *Youth Hostel* (09-222 2347). It is located off the al-Faseel Corniche Road past the Hilton. It will cost you Dh15 (£2.93/$4) with an International Youth Hostelling card. As with other hostels, and some of the smaller hotels in the country, if you are a lone woman traveller the management may not give you a bed unless it is possible to give you privacy i.e. to segregate you from male guests).

The *Fujairah Hilton* (09-222 2411; fax 09-222 6541) is small and charges Dh630/700 (£123-137/$172-205) + taxes. The Hilton is a good place to escape to if you are based in Dubai and it has water sport facilities for hire including windsurfing (Dh40 (£8/$11) per hour), banana boat rides (Dh25 (£4.90/$6.80) per person), kayaks (Dh25 per hour), pedal boats (Dh30 per hour) and water skiing and wake boarding. The hotel can also organise two-hour sunrise and sunset fishing trips and there is a good beachside restaurant and bistro.

The *Holiday Beach Motel* (09-244 5540; fax 09-244 5580) is on the east coast between Dibba and Khor Fakkan and is a convenient place to stop to explore this lesser known region of the Emirates. Located right on the Indian Ocean, two hours drive from Dubai, the Motel has upmarket studios and chalets from Dh385 (£73/$105) per night. There is also a dive centre should you want to get a PADI diving qualification and they can organise boat and diving trips up to the Musandam Peninsula.

Sandy Beach Motel (09-244 5555; www.sandybm.com) is at al-Aqqa on the road between Bidiyah and Dibba and is actually part of Dubai Emirate. The motel sits on a beautiful open stretch of beach between two cliffs and is easily spotted as it is opposite an outcrop of offshore rock known locally as *Snoopy Rock*. This rock, it has to be said, does look a little like its namesake though from another angle it resembles a sun-worshipping rabbit. The motel is very popular with weekenders due to its good location and excellent facilities. There is also a diving centre next to it, which hires out equipment and offers PADI diving lessons.

The *Breeze Hotel* (09-277 8877), just outside Kalba in the south is one of the cheaper hotels along the east coast and is near the wonderful beaches and mangrove forests of Khor Kalba. Rooms are available in rather shabby cabins.

EXPLORING

Most, but not all of the east coast of the UAE is in Fujairah emirate. Some of the places described below are part of Dubai and Sharjah emirates.

Fujairah Museum

The museum (09-229 085) is open Sunday to Thursday 9am-1pm and again from 4-6pm, on Friday from 2-6pm, and closed on Saturday. It houses exhibits of local archaeological finds and traditional Fujairan life. The museum is located near the 300 year-old **Fujairah Fort** off the al-Kalaa Road. This area is the oldest part of town and you can get an idea of what the area was like and the conditions in which the townsfolk lived before the coming of oil.

Khor Kalba

South of Fujairah City lie the Sharjah enclaves of **Kalba** and **Khor Kalba**. Kalba has a fine corniche leading to the fishing village of Khor Khalba with its long stretch of red sandy beach renowned for the shells that are thrown up there, and mangroves stretching towards the border with Oman. The **mangrove forests** here are the oldest in the Arabian Peninsula and over 2000 years old. Khor Kalba is a **nature reserve** and conservation area and is home to many indigenous species of birds as well as migratory visitors. The forest, caused by tidal salt water and fresh water runoff from the land, is home to the rare **white collared kingfisher** which breeds here and nowhere else in the world. Boats can be hired from locals if you fancy exploring the creeks.

Bull Butting

This sport takes place in Fujairah and nowhere else in the Emirates. The only other place you will see it is down on the Batinah Coast in Oman. The sport is thought to have been introduced by the Portuguese during their occupation of the area in the 16th century. Big Brahmin bulls are brought together from the surrounding countryside to a meet, and pairs are pitted against each other. The bulls snort and paw away at the ground before being led into the centre of a ring where they commence to butt and push each other about. Eventually the weaker bull loses its nerve and is either brought to the ground (rarely) or runs away. In this way farmers can show off their best beasts – the stronger the beast the higher the price it will fetch at market. These trials of strength take place during the winter on Friday afternoons before sunset on the road to Oman south of Kalba. Ask locals for exact details of time and place.

Bithnah Fort

On the road through the Hajar Mountains that separate Fujairah from the western emirates you will drive through the village of Bithnah (pronounced Bitna) which has a fort that is definitely worth taking a detour to look at. The fort was built to defend the Ham Pass that divides the two emirates of Sharjah and Fujairah. You will see the fort from the main road and will need to drive down into the village and cross a wadi to get to it. The fort's custodian is a wizened old man who sleeps in the courtyard in a large iron bed. The fort is pretty run-down although the towers still stand intact and the view from the top is dramatic. Bithnah is also the site of a large T-shaped communal burial tomb dating back to before the coming of Islam.

Bidiyah Mosque, Fujairah

Bidiyah

Bidiyah is one of the oldest settlements in the UAE. It is believed to have been inhabited since about BC3000 and it is where the oldest mosque in the UAE is located. **Bidiyah Mosque** (or the Othman Mosque as it is known locally) was built around 640AD only eight years after the death of the Prophet Muhammed. The mosque is a small low white building, standing on a hillside below two watchtowers, and has no minaret and is still in use today. Non-Muslims are forbidden from entering but are permitted to wander about the area and take photographs.

Dibba
Dibba is the last town before the Omani Musandam border to the north. The town itself is divided between the territory of Sharjah, Fujairah and Oman but it is possible to wander all over this fishing community and its pretty bay and beaches. Dibba is still a traditional and conservative place set in a remote spot surrounded by high mountains. The town remains relatively untouched by the weekend tourist traffic from the rest of the UAE. Dibba is also the starting/finishing point for a 4WD excursion through the Hajar Mountains and Omani territory across to **Wadi Bih** and Ras al-Khaimah on the west coast.

Khor Fakkan
Khor Fakkan (which translates as Creek of the Two Jaws) is part of Sharjah emirate on the east coast and about two hour's drive from Sharjah City. The town has been developed as a beach resort and is home to a very important port which allows ships to unload cargo much quicker than if they were to sail round the Strait of Hormuz to unload on the west coast. The ruler's palace sits atop a massive hill overlooking the bay and the town. The best place to stay in Khor Fakkan is the *Oceanic Hotel* (09-238 5111) where a room will cost around Dh460/590 (£90-115/$125-160) per night. Situated at the end of the corniche, the hotel has good restaurants, a private beach and water sport gear for hire.

Index

Glossary

4WD: Four-wheel drive vehicle.

Abbaya: All enveloping black robe worn by women.

The Arab League: Organisation of Arab States formed in Cairo in 1945 in order to strengthen and co-ordinate political, cultural, economic and social programs of its members, and to mediate in disputes.

Baksheesh: Token payment given for services rendered.

Barasti: Traditional building made from woven palm leaves.

Bedouin: Nomadic peoples of Arabia

Blacktop Road: Tarmac road.

Caliph: Chief civil and religious leader; successor to Muhammed the Prophet.

Cold Store: Small grocery shop.

Dishdasha/Thobe: Ankle-length garment (often white in colour) worn by men.

Diwan: Ruler's office; cabinet office.

Dhow: Traditional sea-going vessel.

'Eid al-Adha: Festival celebrating the end of the Hajj season.

'Eid al-Fitr: Festival celebrating the end of Ramadan.

Falaj: Traditional system of irrigation found in Oman.

Frankincense: Incense made from the dried resin of the *Boswellia* tree.

Fualah: Mid-morning/mid-afternoon snacks eaten in the United Arab Emirates.

Garageer Fish Trap: Large wire mesh trap in the shape of a lobster pot.

GCC: Gulf Co-operation Council (Alliance of Gulf oil producing countries: Bahrain, Kuwait, Oman, Qatar, Saudi Arabia, the United Arab Emirates).

GPS: Global Positioning System; a portable device allowing the user to navigate in areas that have no distinguishing landmarks, features etc.

Hajj: The pilgrimage to Mecca.

Hallal: Meat that has been slaughtered according to Islamic tradition.

Imam: Spiritual leader in Islamic society.

Jebal: Mountain (Arabic).

Jebali: Inhabitants of the mountains in Dhofar, Southern Oman.

Jinn/Djinn: Name given to the phenomenon of sand swirling ethereally across highways.

Khanjar: Short curved dagger in an ornate scabbard traditionally worn by men in Oman.

Khareef: The monsoon that affects Dhofar, Southern Oman.

Khor: Creek (Arabic).

Kilim: Small woven rug.

Kumma Cap: Embroidered cap worn by men in Oman.

Majlis: Reception room; Parliament.

Maria Theresa Dollar: Silver dollars, all dated 1780 – even those minted in the 20th century. Originally put into circulation during the reign of the Austrian Empress Maria Theresa (1740-1780) and circulated all over the Middle East, and North and East Africa. Used as currency during those times that these regions had no currency of their own in circulation.

Minaret: Tall slender tower of a mosque from which the Muezzin calls the faithful to prayer.

Mirage: Optical illusion seen in desert countries where the refraction of light causes distant objects to appear near at hand, as though reflected in a sheet of water.

Muezzin: Man who calls faithful to prayer.

Nejd: A region of Saudi Arabia.

ONTC: Oman National Transport Company.

OPEC: Organisation of Petroleum Exporting Countries.
Potsherd: Broken piece of earthenware.
Qahwa: Traditional café in the Middle East serving Turkish coffee, tea and shisha.
Qat: A plant grown in Yemen. Chewing of the leaves produces a state of mild intoxication.
Ramadan: The 9th month of the Islamic calendar marked by fasting during daylight hours.
Rub' al-Khali: The Empty Quarter; a vast tract of sand desert.
Sabkha: Salt plains
Semitic: Relating to the languages and peoples of South West Asia.
Sheikh: Head of Arab tribe, family or village.
Shisha: Water-pipe used in the Middle East for smoking flavoured tobacco.
Sultan: Sovereign of an Islamic state.
Sweetwater: Drinking water.
Wadi: Watercourse; riverbed.
Wali: Governor of a *Wilayat.*
Wasta: Knowing someone who knows the right people or the right way to get things done.
Wilayat: District; Region administered by a *Wali.*

Vacation Work publish:

	Paperback	Hardback
The Directory of Summer Jobs Abroad	£9.99	£15.95
The Directory of Summer Jobs in Britain	£9.99	£15.95
Supplement to Summer Jobs in Britain and Abroad *published in May*	£6.00	–
Work Your Way Around the World	£12.95	–
The Good Cook's Guide to Working Worldwide	£11.95	–
Taking a Gap Year	£11.95	–
Taking a Career Break	£11.95	–
Working in Tourism – The UK, Europe & Beyond	£11.95	–
Kibbutz Volunteer	£10.99	–
Working on Cruise Ships	£10.99	–
Teaching English Abroad	£12.95	–
The Au Pair & Nanny's Guide to Working Abroad	£10.99	–
Working in Ski Resorts – Europe & North America	£10.99	–
Working with Animals – The UK, Europe & Worldwide	£11.95	–
Live & Work Abroad - a Guide for Modern Nomads	£11.95	–
Working with the Environment	£11.95	–
Health Professionals Abroad	£11.95	–
The Directory of Jobs & Careers Abroad	£11.95	£16.95
The International Directory of Voluntary Work	£10.99	£15.95
The Directory of Work & Study in Developing Countries	£9.99	£14.99
Live & Work in Australia & New Zealand	£10.99	–
Live & Work in Belgium, The Netherlands & Luxembourg	£10.99	–
Live & Work in France	£10.99	–
Live & Work in Germany	£10.99	–
Live & Work in Italy	£10.99	–
Live & Work in Japan	£10.99	–
Live & Work in Russia & Eastern Europe	£10.99	–
Live & Work in Saudi & the Gulf	£10.99	–
Live & Work in Scandinavia	£10.99	–
Live & Work in Scotland	£10.99	–
Live & Work in Spain & Portugal	£10.99	–
Live & Work in the USA & Canada	£10.99	–
Hand Made in Britain - The Visitors Guide	£10.99	–
Scottish Islands Book 1: The Western Isles	£11.95	–
Scottish Islands Book 2: Orkney & Shetland	£11.95	–
The Panamericana: On the Road through Mexico and Central America	£12.95	–
Travellers Survival Kit: Australia & New Zealand	£11.95	–
Travellers Survival Kit: Cuba	£10.99	–
Travellers Survival Kit: India	£10.99	–
Travellers Survival Kit: Lebanon	£10.99	–
Travellers Survival Kit: Madagascar, Mayotte & Comoros	£10.99	–
Travellers Survival Kit: Mauritius, Seychelles & Réunion	£10.99	–
Travellers Survival Kit: Mozambique	£10.99	–
Travellers Survival Kit: Oman & the Arabian Gulf	£11.95	–
Travellers Survival Kit: South Africa	£10.99	–
Travellers Survival Kit: South America	£15.95	–
Travellers Survival Kit: Sri Lanka	£10.99	–
Travellers Survival Kit: USA & Canada	£10.99	–

Distributors of:

Summer Jobs USA	£12.95	–
Internships (On-the-Job Training Opportunities in the USA)	£18.95	–
Green Volunteers	£10.99	–

 Plus 27 titles from Peterson's, the leading American academic publisher, on college education and careers in the USA. Separate catalogue available on request. ★

Vacation Work Publications, 9 Park End Street, Oxford OX1 1HJ
Tel 01865 – 241978   Fax 01865 – 790885

Visit us online for more information on our unrivalled range of titles for work, travel and gap years, readers' feedback and regular updates:

www.vacationwork.co.uk